The Christian Connexion Library
Volume 9

MEMOIRS

of

DECEASED CHRISTIAN MINISTERS

(Corrected and Annotated)

E.W. HUMPHREYS

with corrections and annotations by
Bradley S. Cobb

Charleston, AR
COBB PUBLISHING
2022

The Christian Connexion Library Consists of:

Vol. 1: Memoirs of Abner Jones—New Expanded Edition
Vol. 2: Elias Smith Autobiography—New Critical Edition
Vol. 3: Complete Works of James O'Kelly
Vol. 4: Autobiography of Mark Fernald
Vol. 5: Memoirs of David Millard
Vol. 6: Sketch of Elder Daniel Hix
Vol. 7: Memoirs of Elijah Shaw
Vol. 8: Autobiography of Joseph Thomas
Vol. 9: Memoirs of Deceased Christian Ministers
Vol. 10: History of the Christian Denomination in America
Vol. 11: Autobiography of Matthew Gardner

Published in the United States of America by:
Cobb Publishing
Charleston, AR
www.CobbPublishing.com
Editor@CobbPublishing.com
479-747-8372
ISBN: 979-8-3303-2320-3

PUBLISHER'S PREFACE AND INTRODUCTION

In the study of Restoration Movement history (falsely called the "Stone-Campbell Movement" by so-called "scholars"), the Christian Connexion is a part most ignore—as though it is a part of our movement that we would like to forget. (Much like how we ignore that a Restoration Movement preacher helped start the Mormon Church, or how another one founded the Christadelphians). The Christian Connexion, like almost every religious group, had good and bad, conservative and liberal within its ranks.

In 1879, E.W. Humphreys sent out a request via the *Herald of Gospel Liberty* for information about any preacher associated with the Christian Connexion (by that point, going by the name "Christian Church"), who had passed away from 1793 to the then-present day. He included a list of names that he had, but requested additional names that others might have. He ended up with 973 names. And it was certainly not a complete list.

By the time this book was originally compiled, the Christian Church/Connexion had fully embraced denominationalism, and had more or less coalesced around some specific doctrines: Unitarianism (Jesus is not God, but is the Son of God), baptism is immersion, but *not* a requirement for salvation, recognition of all denominations as containing Christians, and Christian character being the only evidence required for church membership.

But just because these were the views of the 1880 version of the Christian Church/Connexion, it doesn't mean it was the views of many of their early preachers.

Mark Fernald, for example, flat-out condemned instrumental music in worship, as well as women preachers (you'll notice a handful of women preachers are listed in this book). Abner Jones and James O'Kelly both asked people to leave denominationalism behind and just follow the Bible. Barton W. Stone insisted that baptism was in order to receive the forgiveness of sins.

All that to say, just because someone is described in this book, doesn't mean they were right, because some of them certainly weren't. But it also doesn't mean someone's inclusion in this book means they were wrong either, because some of them were truly teaching and following the Gospel of Jesus Christ.

We present this book to you in a corrected edition (several dates in the book were wrong, and when possible, corrected). An appendix from the original edition, giving names and information about several preachers, has been integrated into the main book, alphabetically. And we have annotated where we felt more information could be supplied from other sources.

Enjoy Volume 9 of *The Christian Connexion Library*.

Bradley S. Cobb, Editor
February 25, 2022

<u>PREFACE</u>

In introducing this work to the notice of the brethren, I do not intend to offer any apology, though there are doubtless many imperfections in the work, and some that might have been avoided had I time and means to correct them. When I undertook this work, more than twelve years ago, I had no clear conception of the extent of the labor it would require. The first plan was to write the biographies of a few of our leading ministers; but, in examining the list, it was found very hard to decide where to stop. Then extending the plan, so as to include more names, the same difficulty was met, as before. It was then decided to insert the names of all the ministers that could be heard from, who died in the church work, although, by this plan, the notices of each would have to be short, to avoid having the work larger than was desirable.

Having decided on the latter plan, such names as were ascertained were twice published in the *Herald of Gospel Liberty,* accompanied with a request to the brethren for further information. By this, and diligent search through all the periodicals, letters, and biographical works on hand, or that could be borrowed, nearly 1,000 names of deceased ministers have been found. There are doubtless hundreds more whose names and histories never came to hand.

The plan first proposed was to insert no names except those who remained in the denomination until death, but on further consideration, it was found that some among the leaders and founders of the church had united with other denominations, and some others had their labors partly identified with the Freewill Baptists, Adventists, Disciples, and other denominations so that it was impossible, in every case, to decide where they stood; it was thought best to insert the names of all who had been prominent workers, as ministers, in the church, without a strict regard as to what church the most of their labors were bestowed during lite.

I desire to express my sincere thanks to those who have done so much to assist in this work. Many persons that I never knew before sent me letters, manuscripts, pamphlets, and periodicals, which have been of great value to me in gathering items, without any fee or reward. Some of the most active in the beginning of this work have since died, and their names are entered here, in the list of the deceased.

I desire to say to those who sent long, and often well-prepared, biographies of their friends, that it would have been a pleasure to have inserted the whole, without alteration; but, in keeping with the number of names and the size of the volume, it was impossible; so, I had to abbreviate.

It was my intention, until lately, to insert in the beginning of the volume, a short history of the church, from its rise in 1793 to the present time, and items to that effect were gathered; but on account of pressure of other business, and the advice of friends not to make the volume too large, I decided to publish the biographies alone. That, together with the abbreviating of the notices of the ministers, makes the work somewhat smaller than was at first intended.

This small volume is now sent forth, and hoping that it will stimulate our brethren to more diligence in their labor, and that it will be a forerunner of much that will follow of the noble deeds of our brethren who are gone, I close a labor that has given me much pleasure for many a spare hour, in the last few years of my life. I am sure that I have been made better and stronger for the future, in fighting over again the noble battles of life with these worthy dead. May the same influence be exerted on the mind of those that may read these pages.

E.W. Humphreys.

June 1, 1880.

INTRODUCTION.

As a distinct body, the Christian Church has had an existence of only eighty-seven years, the issue that gave it a being having begun in Baltimore, Md., in 1793, the leaders of the two parties being, James O'Kelly and Francis Asbury. From the days of the Apostles, however, there have been people, in all countries, holding views similar, if not identical, to those held by the Christian Connection of today. Minorites always advocate the right of private judgment in the interpretation of the Bible. The Waldenses, in the mountains of Italy, Wickliff, in England, Luther, in Germany, together with all reformers, claim this right. Luther said to his opponents, "Convince me by the Bible that I am wrong, and I will recant;" also, "The Bible is the creed of Protestants."

The rise of the Christian Church seems to have been accidental or Providential. Neither O'Kelly, in Virginia, Jones, in New England, nor Stone and his co-laborers, in Kentucky, intended to organize a distinct denomination. O'Kelly opposed the appointment of bishops, only; Jones and Smith sought to modify the rigid Calvinism and the exclusive close communion of the Baptist Church; and Stone and his co-laborers desired to organize a reformed system of Presbyterianism, only in self-defense—as they were disowned by the old body for no other fault than their Christian liberality.

In tracing the lives of these ministers, we see them imperceptibly drifting, little by little, farther and farther, away from the bodies with which they had been connected, and finding in each other congenial spirits seeking the same end—liberty to worship God, untrammeled by man-made creeds,—and the Christian Church took its existence. As is seen in the lives of James O'Kelly, William Guirey, Francis Williamson, in the South, the controversy on the subject of baptism became bitter. While O'Kelly demanded liberty of worship, without a bishop, he was not willing to grant the same liberty as to the mode of baptism. But, finally, this troublesome controversy was settled, and peace ensued. From that day to this, many of the Southern ministers practice sprinkling and pouring, for baptism, and others immersion only; but there is no dissension.

In New England, where the body emanated from a Baptist connection, immersion is the rule, and it is seldom, if ever, that we find members of churches in that section that have not been immersed—and the rite is generally performed before admission into the church; so that, in New England, there is not now, nor ever has been, much disagreement on that subject. In tracing the lives of these ministers, however, it will be seen that other issues are more strife in that section of the church than in others. The New England mind is much given to speculation—inherited, doubtless, from the Pilgrim Fathers,— and our denomination is no exception. It is possible, indeed, that, on account of our great liberality, we have had more than our share. Not to mention the "Farnum," the "Cochran," the "Niles," and other fanaticisms, it was in this section that the "Come-out-ism," the "Millerism," and other speculations originated, and some of our ministers led in these movements. It will be observed, in tracing these memoirs, that many of our ministers were carried away from their moorings with the expectation that the world would end in 1843.

In the West, while the brethren in that section are more uniform on the subject of immersion for baptism than those in the South, yet many continue in the church for life who have never been immersed, and some who come from Quaker connection, who have had no water applied in any way, yet it is very seldom that any mode but immersion is practiced by any of our ministers in that part of the country. It will be observed, also, that the educational standard in the ministry has been lower in the 'West, than in the South, and certainly lower than in the East. The early ministers in the church, in all sections where it originated, were men, if not of the highest attainment in knowledge, yet respectable; but with-the zeal awakened in the Cane Ridge revival, the great liberality of the reformers, and the great need of self-sacrificing workers in the cause, the motto was, "Let him that can, teach." From this grew up a system, at first, of lay preachers; but finally, the more successful ones were ordained as pastors in certain localities, and sometimes persons with very limited knowledge, as well as limited opportunities, were ordained in the same way. When conferences were more generally organized, the right of ordaining ministers was vested in them by general consent, and to some extent, a check was put upon the principle of ordaining persons disqualified for the work. Yet these, also, leaned to the principle of charity, and set apart many who were poorly qualified for public teachers. It is astonishing, however, how many of those, with very limited knowledge at the commencement of their ministry, became giants in intellect in a few years, and many of them filled some of the widest spheres in the church.

As is often stated in these sketches, the Christian Church had to fight for every inch of ground it gained. It was thought by the older sects that this new body, if successful, would undermine the very foundation of religion; thus, anything to oppose their progress was considered promotive of the glory of God, and of the good of society. This opposition brought out the combative element in our speakers, so that, for many years, every Christian preacher was a champion in debate; still, with all his tendency to controversy, he never lost sight of the main duty—the conversion of sinners. It looks strange to us, in these peaceful times, when we see that, in the midst of the most bitter debates, frequently, hundreds were soundly converted to a holy life. This opposition also led our ministers to examine the Scriptures with peculiar zeal; thus, oftentimes, men who not only never attended colleges or theological seminaries, but not even a common school, would quote fluently such authors as Mosheim, Clark, McNight, and other theologians and historians, and even repeated Greek and Hebrew passages— and that correctly—with readiness. Their traveling companion, the Bible, was marked on the margin with all these passages, so that they were ready at a moment's warning. Necessity was to them the mother of invention. For this purpose, the *Herald of Gospel Liberty* was published by the versatile Elias Smith, as early as 1808, the first religious periodical in the world; *for* the older denominations never thought, as yet, of the necessity of such an instrumentality. The "Christian Palladium," "Gospel Luminary," *Christian Messenger,* and *Gospel Herald* followed soon after, all brimful of matter conducive to the growth of the church.

Denominational institutions of learning were suggested very early in New England, New York, Ohio, Iowa, Indiana, Virginia, and North Carolina, and were established at different times. In 1844, some of the leading ministers united with the Unitarians to establish a theological school at Meadville, Penn. Scores of our ministers were educated in that institution. But finally, our own Biblical School was established at Stanfordville, N.Y., and, at the present time, is doing an excellent work. The ministry of the church is becoming more and more educated; yet it is doubtful whether our present preachers, or the ministers of any other denomination, can show more efficient speakers, in point of talent, learning, eloquence, and devotion, than those of our early ministers who were deprived of the advantages of college and seminary education.

Most of the ministers, whose lives are recorded in this volume, were peculiar for self-sacrifice. In the older churches, in many places, about the beginning of the present century, the ministry was a profession oi ease. Salaries were fixed, and the labor, with many, was made light for the want of zeal in the work. The early Christian ministers seeing this, went to the other extreme, and, partaking of Quaker views, cried out against a regular salary. Some of them would receive nothing at all, not even as a gift. This made the work of preaching, whether as a pastor or as an evangelist, exceedingly difficult to men in limited circumstances, as it was impossible for a poor man to devote much time either to study or travel, without a serious loss to his family. Yet hundreds of them, regardless of any compensation, went forth and labored as few men did, with a view to no other reward than to advocate the principle of liberty, and to see sinners converted. Elias Smith, Abner Jones, and the early ministers of New England traveled far and near, from Maine to Connecticut, and farther on to New York, New Jersey, Pennsylvania, and sometimes to Virginia and Ohio. The North Carolina and Virginia ministers traveled through Tennessee, Kentucky, and sometimes returned the visits of their northern brethren by visiting New England and the Middle States. The Kentucky brethren extended their travels through the entire West, and when the cause was started in Ohio, we see our Walter, Long, Ladley, and others visiting our brethren in the South and East. The "White Pilgrim," a poor, sickly boy, starting out from his Virginia home, in the midst of poverty and obscurity, became a flame of fire in the church., rousing the multitude to repentance, south, west, and east, and finally died, triumphantly, of the smallpox, in the midst of strangers. In an early day, this was a characteristic of Christian ministers generally. The homes of many of them were in any place where they could do good. As we read these biographies of ministers, in the city as well as in the country, in all sections of the land, we find all to have been a devoted, zealous, and self-sacrificing class of men.

<u>Levi Abbot (1822—1851)</u>

This brother was born in Preble County, O., September, 1822, and died in Wabash County, Ind., March 15, 1851, in his twenty-ninth year. He was a man of good, native talents; but on account of his location in the far West, his early education was quite limited. He was converted, and was baptized by Elder Peter Banta, and soon after commenced exercising in public. These exercises soon led him to a more thorough study of the Bible and other good books. Such was his thirst for knowledge, that he worked hard during the day and studied equally hard at night; and whenever he had a dollar to spare, he laid it out in books; thus, through perseverance and industry, he soon acquired considerable knowledge, especially of the Bible.

About 1845, he married Miss Susan Roberts, daughter of Elder Joseph Roberts. Soon after this, the work of the ministry presented itself to his mind with a great responsibility. After a short struggle he gave himself entirely to the cause, and was ordained January 24, 1849. In the ministry, he was zealous and successful, and was counted a good scripturalist. His manner was mild and gentle, and he was much beloved both by professors and non-professors. He died young, with the armor on, leaving a sorrowing wife, and children.

<u>John Adams (1770—1858)</u>

The substance of the two following sketches is from the pen of the late Elder Levi Purviance.

Elder John Adams was born and raised in North Carolina. His father was a Ruling Elder in the Presbyterian Church, and undertook to educate his son John for the Presbyterian ministry; but before his education was completed his health failed, and he gave up the idea of the ministry. He married Nancy Ireland, and engaged in farming, and teaching school. Not long after his marriage, he moved with his wife into Bourbon County, Ky., and settled on Cane Ridge. He bought land, and commenced opening a farm in the dense forests and canebrakes of Kentucky. He worked on his farm in summer, taught school in winter, and sometimes taught singing. He was very frugal and economical, and with his little means he managed to raise his family comfortably.

He and his wife were members of the Presbyterian Church. When the great revival took place on Cane Ridge in 1801, under the labors of Barton W. Stone and others, he and his wife became subjects of the revival, and he became a very active worker in the church, and was quite useful in carrying on meetings. He was gifted in singing, prayer, and exhortation.

In the year 1802, he sold his possessions in Kentucky, and settled on a farm in Wilson County, Tenn. He still continued to exercise his gifts in the churches in Tennessee. It is likely that he had a license from the Presbytery to exhort. In the year 1803, a difficulty took place in the Presbyterian Church on account of some of the preachers advancing doctrines contrary to the teachings of the Westminster Confession of Faith. Charges were preferred against some, and Barton W. Stone and others seceded, and took their stand on the word of God alone. Elder Adams was among the number, and became a member among those who acknowledged no name but that of "Christian." He became deeply impressed with the importance of the Christian ministry, and felt as Paul, "Woe is me if I preach not the gospel." He did not long "confer with flesh and blood," but soon became "a workman that needeth not be ashamed." He labored as an evangelist, traveled considerably, and was instrumental in doing much good. He believed that God heard and answered prayer, and that he actually gave his Holy Spirit to them that asked him; so that he had no sympathy with mere ceremonial worship.

When he was first married, his father gave him a negro boy for a slave. While in Tennessee, his mind became much exercised on the subject of slavery; and by reading and searching the Scriptures, and praying to know the truth, he became fully convinced that negro slavery, as practiced in parts of the United States, was a great sin. He had his negro recorded free at the age of twenty-one. The colored boy afterwards became a respectable preacher in the African Episcopal Methodist Church, Elder Adams having given him a good education. Elder Adams was conscientiously opposed to slavery, and having been surrounded with it all his life, he saw its contaminating influence on the young and rising generation. So, seeing the difficulty of raising a young family in the midst of such degradation, and being determined to seek a purer atmosphere, he sold his possessions in Tennessee, and in the year 1816, moved into Preble County, O. Here, again, he bought land in a dense forest, and commenced operations Upon the beech, ash, poplar, and maple timber of Ohio,—this being the third farm he had opened. Soon after he came to Ohio two of his daughters—both young ladies—died; but he was destined to meet with other trials. In a few years, his wife died of consumption. He afterward married Sarah Purviance, a sister of Elder David Purviance. He was fortunate in having two of the very best of wives.

He preached considerably in Ohio and Indiana. He was a good practical preacher, his language chaste and appropriate, his. voice clear and sonorous, and his discourses connected, well adapted, and never tedious. He could not be called a Reformation preacher. He seldom dwelt in controversy. He was a good business man, useful in conference but not troublesome. He took no pride in long speeches. All denominations loved to hear him preach, and spoke well of him. He was a man of deep research and of humble but dignified deportment. He was a good English scholar, and had some knowledge of the dead languages. For several years before he died, he was very deaf; during this period, he read a great deal. His judgment was good, but he complained of failing memory. He was an obliging neighbor, an affectionate husband, and a kind father. He died in 1858, being eighty-eight years of age. For several weeks before he died, his sufferings were great, but his confidence in his God never failed. He was always through life considered to be a man of a weakly physical constitution. His long life may, in part, be attributed to his temperate habits. He rose early, went to bed regularly when at home, and drank no spirituous liquors.

<u>Thomas Adams (1798—1831)</u>

The subject of this sketch was the son of Major George Adams, who served with distinction in the American Revolution. Thomas was born in Montgomery County, O., in 1798. At the age of sixteen, he embraced religion, and not long after, began to speak in public. His manner, at first, was so unattractive to his hearers that many discouraged him from preaching; but Elder George Shidler and others held him up, till, by practice and a liberal education, which he acquired after his first labors in the ministry, he became a good orator and an attractive speaker. In 1821, he had a severe attack of fever together with a hemorrhage of the lungs, from which he never fully recovered.

In May, 1822, he was married to Miss Ann Carnahan, who died a few months afterwards—a great shock to the young husband. She was buried in the Burlington church-yard, where, in a few years, the body of her husband was laid by her side. His health failed rapidly after this period. When his wife was dying, he could hardly leave his bed to bid her farewell. For a while, however, he recovered, and accomplished much as minister and school teacher. He was a hard student, doing nothing by halves, but probing every subject to the bottom. The name of Thomas Adams stands high with the people of Hamilton County, O., where he spent much of his time, not only as an able preacher and a thorough scholar, but as a devoted, humble, and faithful Christian man.

He died in Lexington, Ky., of consumption, May 8, 1831, aged thirty-four years.

<u>Isam Adkinson (1787—1857)</u>

At the time of his death, Mr. Adkinson belonged to the Tippecanoe (Ind) Conference. Before the organization of the above conference, it is probable that he was a member of the Cole Creek (Indiana) Conference, as he was a co-laborer with Elders Scott, McKinney, Lowe, Dudley, and other old ministers in that conference. His home for many years had been in the western part of Indiana. When I saw him in 1848, he was a fine-appearing, venerable old man, and was highly respected by his brethren. He died the confer-ence-year preceding the session of 1857, being not far from seventy years of age.

A.S. ALDERMAN (1826—1876)

Of this brother's early life, I have been able to find no account. When he died, in 1876, he was a man not far from fifty years of age. His home, for many years, was on Sunday Creek, Perry County, O., He was a member of the Monroe Christian Church, and a leading minister of the Eastern Ohio Christian Conference. He was both a convert and a co-laborer of Elder John McDonald, and their farms were in the same neighborhood. As a minister, he stood high with his brethren. He was a good speaker, and a zealous worker. Being a farmer, and having a family, and living in a country where ministers' salaries were small, he could not devote the time for acquiring such knowledge as he felt was necessary to a minister of the Gospel. Nevertheless, he filled a wide place in the church, and his death, before the period of old age had weakened his physical and mental powers, was a great loss to the church, the conference, and the denomination.

ABRAM ALDRIDGE (1796—1874)

Elder Aldridge was born in the State of Vermont, November 29, 1796. He came to Ohio with his parents in 1806, and the family settled on the Ohio river where Cincinnati now stands. In 1812, he moved into Clark County, where he remained till death.

In 1814, he united with the Christian Church, and in 1817, he began his labors as a minister. He joined the Deer Creek Christian Conference, and was ordained to the full work of the ministry. He was zealous in the work, and was possessed of considerable talent as a thinker and speaker. Living in a country where ministers received but a scant support, he studied medicine, and became a practicing physician—which profession he pursued through life. Yet he never abandoned the ministry, but labored whenever he could in the Master's service.

He died at his home in Clark County, in his seventy-eighth year, mourned by all his acquaintances. He left a widow, and children. The entire family were zealous workers in the Christian Church.

AMOS ALEXANDER (1781— 1846)

This Elder was a native of Georgia. In early life, he joined the Methodist Episcopal Church, and became a local preacher in that connexion. He moved to Ohio, and soon after joined the Christian Church on Ludlow Creek, in Miami t County. He became a pastor of the church, and continued in that relation for fifteen years. He became a member of the Miami Conference. His labors were chiefly local, confined to the church of his charge and surrounding churches. He died, July 3, 1846, in triumph, greatly lamented by his acquaintances and friends.

ARCHIBALD ALEXANDER (?—1829)

This brother was born and raised in Virginia, and occupied an important position in the Christian Church for some twenty or twenty- five years before his death; yet, so few were the facilities for printing in those days, and so few of the books and periodicals of that time are preserved that all I can find are a few lines in Elder David Millard's journal of his trip to Kentucky and Ohio in 1834, and part of an obituary in the *Christian Messenger,* published by Barton W. Stone, March, 1830.

Mr. Millard, speaking of his visit to Georgetown, O, says: "The church of that place was organized about 1810, by Elder Archibald Alexander, who was among the early Christian preachers in the West. He seceded from the Presbyterian Church. He was a learned man, and an able, minister. He resided on Licking River, in Kentucky, and died, suddenly, about three years ago (1830)."

The biography in the "Messenger" reads: "Died, recently, in Bracken County, Ky., Archibald Alexander. Brother Alexander had been a preacher for twenty-five years in the Christian Church. He died suddenly and triumphantly."

It would be a great satisfaction to us of the present day to follow these worthies through their wearisome labors; but, when this is denied us, it is a consolation to know that their record is on high, and that "their works do follow them."

<u>Thomas Alexander (1815—1838)</u>

This young man was only twenty-three years old when he died. From a retired, timid youth of few words but much thought, he became, before his death, a person of great prominence. In person, he was heavy set, of fresh countenance, and sandy complexion. He had a clear, ringing voice, and positive, emphatic utterance. His writings, of which he has left quite an amount, are not only clear and terse, but there is a grasp of thought in his ideas uncommon at that early age. He was born in Hartwell, Me., converted in Portland under the labors of Elder Shaw, and was baptized by him. He also became a member of the church in that city in 1830. At the suggestion of his pastor, (Elder Shaw,) he visited Amesbury, Mass., and there preached his first sermon, in 1835. He was invited to labor for the church. He consented, and continued Us work there and at Salisbury for two years. He was ordained at the latter church, December 7, 1836. He accepted a call from the Second Christian Church in Lynn, Mass., and commenced his labor there on the first Sunday in February, 1837. The church prospered greatly under his labors, and many souls were converted, and added to the church during his short administration. All were united on him, and the future looked unusually prosperous. In the midst of his career, he was cut down, greatly lamented by his brethren. He was a young man of uncommon talents. His mind was quick, his memory retentive, and his delivery earnest and easy; and, better than all, he was a man of unsullied character. All the New England churches mourned over the death of Elder Alexander.

<u>John Alkire (?—1830)</u>

The subject of the following sketch was one of the first Christian ministers that preached in Pickaway, Madison, and adjoining counties in Ohio. He was converted at Cane Ridge, by hearing the young converts in that great revival speak of the goodness of God. Before that, he was an unbeliever, holding to Deistical views. He commenced preaching soon after his conversion.

Elder Long, one of his converts, says: "He was a tall, heavy man with sandy complexion. He had a loud, strong voice with somewhat of a slow delivery, but was very pathetic and powerful in exhortation, and great reformations followed his preaching, wherever he went. His preaching was never systematic, but his appeals were directed to the hearts of sinners."

He lived not far from Mt. Sterling, Madison County, O., where he acquired considerable wealth, for those times. He and a co-laborer, Forgus Graham, both farmers and ministers, were in the habit, in early times,—about 1812,—of holding camp-meetings near their own homes, killing their own beeves, and feeding the great multitudes that came to hear them preach. Hundreds of these were converted under their administrations. When they received any pay for their labors, it was hardly ever more than a dollar for a three days' meeting, or twelve dollars a year for "Once a month preaching." Such was the self-sacrificing labor of this man of God. With all his activity and prominence, however, I cannot find the precise date or place of his birth or death.

Brother Joseph Bonner, of Jewell, Kans., states that Elder Alkire moved from his home in Ohio about 1824, to Indiana or Illinois, and died about 1830, at his home in the West.

GEORGE ALKIRE (1782—1868)

I find in the older periodicals of the church, that the name of George Alkire stands high in the record of all traveling preachers, as one of the main men in the central part of Ohio. I also find many able articles written by him in the "Luminary" as early as 1830. In an article of his, published in April, 1832, he states that almost fifty years had passed over his head, that he had been engaged in the ministry for twenty-five years, and that he was ordained twenty years ago. From the above we are able to state that George Alkire was born near 1782, commenced preaching in 1807, and was ordained in 1812.

He was tall and slim in person; his peculiar fort, as a preacher, was his earnestness as a reasoner. He was plain and somewhat old-fashioned in his appearance. While he was anxious for revival and spirituality, he was still more anxious to connect with these, order and system in the government of the church. In the article referred to in the *Christian Luminary,* he says: "The Christian Church has advanced, but its government has been but little improved; consequently, the church has been in a state of confusion, and many individual churches have wasted away; all, I am confident, for want of the proper administration of government. In this state of affairs, the greater part of the labor of the traveling minister is lost." From this Elder Alkire proceeds to show the remedy; that is, the appointment of Ruling Elders in each church to take the spiritual oversight of the same, and the Deacons to confine their labors to the temporal wants of the church, leaving the preachers free from all pastoral work. He brings forth a great many passages to prove that this was the ancient order, and the article all through is quite ingenious in its construction and strong in its proofs.

From some of his letters in the *Gospel Herald,* I find him, in 1844, in Pike County, Ill., laboring with his usual energy. Two of his co-laborers from Ohio, Elders Burbridge and Roberts, were with him. The two had been quite sick, doubtless from the effects of the malaria so common to a new country, and the burden of the work fell upon Elder Alkire in his advanced years.

He had an independent mind, a good heart, and a self-sacrificing disposition. He was quite partial to the Presbyterian system of church government; but he, as a Bible man, could not unite with that body, it being, in his mind, a sectarian one. From this, and from his liberal and loving spirit, and from his friendly intercourse with the followers of Alexander Campbell, he was accused by some of his brethren of leaning towards the latter body; but he always claimed that he stood upon the old ground. It is also stated, that, in his last days, he partially embraced the Advent Doctrine of the coming of Christ, etc.

The truth is, Elder Alkire was an honest man, somewhat inclined to speculation, and when an idea struck him favorably he embraced it. He was so free from sectarianism, that it might properly be said of him, that he was partially a member of all churches, and of none, as to entire union of faith.

I am able to find but a meager account of his labors in distant Illinois during his old age. Brother Joseph Bonner writes that he died in Illinois in 1868, in his eighty-sixth year.

C. ALLEMONG (?—1872)

The home of this brother was in the Shenandoah Valley, Va. He was a zealous and good man, and was a member of the Valley Virginia Christian Conference. He died at an advanced age, in the year 1872.

ASA ALLEN (1797—1828)

Elder Allen was born in Cambridge, Washington County, N.Y., February 16, 1797. His parents moved to Charleston, Montgomery County, N.Y., in 1800 or 1801. Asa was a good, quiet boy, raised to the occupation of a farmer. In 1813, he -was converted under the preaching of Mrs. Nancy G. Cram, baptized by Elder James Wilson, and united with the church at Charleston. Soon after his conversion, he began to preach, and, in September, 1818, united with the Eastern New York Christian Conference. He was ordained soon after, in the Northern New York Conference.

On September 29, 1824, he married Miss Maria Spoor, sister of Elder John Spoor, and in 1826 he moved to Cranberry Creek and became the pastor of the church. In 1828, he moved to Clarkson, Monroe County, N.Y., where, in a few weeks, the entire family was taken with a fever. From this, all but the Elder recovered. Dropsy followed the fever in his case, and the best medical treatment was of no avail. H? suffered with patience, and asked his friends if he was dying: when answered in the affirmative, he responded with an emphatic "amen."

He was a young minister of great zeal and energy, and his talent as a speaker was counted of a high class. As a man he was beloved by all his acquaintances, for his mild and loving disposition.

He died September 22, 1828, aged thirty-one years.

<u>Ira Allen (1790—1866)</u>

The following quotation is from Professor Ira W. Allen, a son of the deceased. Ira W. Allen's ancestors on his father's side were of Welsh descent. His grandfather lived in Weston, fifteen miles from Boston; here Ira's father, John Allen, was born in 1749. He moved from Massachusetts, with his wife and two children, to Vermont. Ira was born in Reading, Windsor County, Vt., on the 20th of. May, 1790. On the twenty-second of April, 1810, one month before he was twenty years of age, Ira solemnly resolved to give himself to God, to be his alone.

He entered the ministry in 1816, when about twenty-six years old. He was married in Westerfield, Vt., December 15, 1822, and in January, 1823, removed to Potsdam, N.Y. Here he remained until the day of his death, in 1866. Here he preached for over fifty years, and many will be the stars in the crown of his rejoicing."

The above gives us the outline of an active, stirring, and useful life of more than fifty years. Few of our ministers did more to advance the cause of the Redeemer than Elder Allen. Many of his cc-laborers traveled more than he did, for his labors were confined to one part of the country—the Northern New York Conference. There he stood as a central figure for more than half a century. His work was not altogether confined to his own conference nor to the State of New York, however, but, through his writings, so highly appreciated by the church in his day, he exercised a lasting influence on the denomination. His writings, in the periodicals of his day, are the mediums by which we judge, mostly, of the man. As a leading officer in his own conference, he issued many circulars clearly setting forth the duties of church members, both as to local and general measures. All his articles are short but clear, terse, and directly to the point. He had the faculty of entering at once into the heart of his subject, the reader, becoming interested, was often sorry that the writer did not continue longer. Some of his articles were continued from one number of a periodical to another; as, "Addresses to the young," etc.

As a writer, Elder Allen excelled most of his co-workers by choosing subjects that were practical, and had a direct bearing on the issues of the time. His faith in God, in the Scriptures, and in the triumph of Christianity was always apparent. His tone was cheerful, hopeful, and as one satisfied with his labors, however arduous. Doubtless, he had his misgivings, his discouragements, and his gloomy periods, but he never mentioned these to his readers. His wife, Betsy Allen, as a writer, possessed much of the same spirit of trust and hope as her husband, showing us that he was blessed with a congenial companion.

Our limits will not allow us to insert any of Elder Allen's writings in this sketch; but we are glad to announce that two of his sons (Professor Ira W. Allen, of Chicago, Ill., and Elder Alden Allen, of Rockland, R.I.,) expect to publish a biography of their father. It is to be hoped that they will do so soon.

ROBERT ALLEN (?—?)

This Elder was a Vermont preacher, a co-worker with Stevens, Knight, and Rollins some forty years ago. We have no dates of any of the leading events of his life. Elder Josiah Knight, of Enon, O., says, that his power of rousing people to religious activity was so great, that Amos Stevens and himself organized eight churches, consisting of persons converted under the labors of Elder Allen previous to his ordination. Still, he continued local in his labors. Toward the close of life, he embraced the doctrine held by the Adventists as to the personal coming of Christ.

<u>Samuel P. Allen (1775—1846)</u>

We have but a short account of this servant of God. The first that we gather from the periodicals, is that he was converted in Otsego County, N.Y., in early life, and is supposed to have been ordained as a minister of the Christian Church about the year 1806, the first Christian minister ordained in the State of New York. Under whose labors he was converted, and what his previous life had been, must remain a mystery for the present. The fact of his becoming a pioneer minister in a new church which was opposed by the older denominations, no less than his own language, which was always plain, independent, and bold, shows him to have been a man of courage and originality, as were all his comrades in the Reformation of that early day.

His career as an active worker in the ministry was short, though efficient. He was subject to asthma, of which he finally died. This disease prevented him from active traveling and speaking, so we find that after twelve years of devoted ministerial work he had to desist. In 1822, he moved to Fairview, Erie County, Penn., where he raised a family of twelve children, acquired some wealth, had a meeting house erected on his own farm, and, as Elder Hance, his biographer, says, "served his generation with dignity as a citizen and neighbor, respected by all who knew him." He was a true friend to the cause of religion and humanity.

Elder Allen wrote but little for any of our periodicals; consequently, it is difficult to tell much about his habits and manner of address. I find one able letter from him to the "Christian Palladium," Vol. I, 1833, in which he says: "Though unaccustomed to writing, superannuated, and troubled with my old complaint, the asthma,—my infirmities are such that I have been unable to preach for many years,—yet I love God, his cause, and his people, and often think of former days, of health, of friends, and of privileges with a melting heart. My work is done. I can not be young again. Many of my old associates are gone before me; and while I linger on these mortal shores, my old friends may be assured that my soul doth wish Zion well, and for her prosperity and peace I will still pray."

He loved the "Palladium," but had his doubts about the phrase "Liberal Christianity." Of it, he says: "For we know not, by these terms, what is meant; whether Unitarianism, Mormonism, Campbell ism, or any other ism, or all of them together; or whether it means the pure spirit of the gospel. I can not fellowship every thing; for the apostle says, 'If any come unto you and bring not the doctrine of Christ, receive him not.'" After quoting several similar passages, he closes his letter by saying: "Some such passages, in connexion with the whole, form my creed."

Commenting on the above, Elder Badger, the editor of the "Palladium," says: "The above — from a father in the ministry — deserves double interest, as it comes from one who is now worn out in the service of his Divine Master. We had the pleasure of a personal acquaintance with Mr. Allen in his better days; he is now but a shadow of what he once was. We had not heard from him for a long time, and this letter is like a voice from the grave. We look back to the first formation of a Christian Conference in this state (New York,) in which the writer of this note nominated Mr. Allen to preside; and he did so, with honor to himself, and satisfaction to his brethren."

From this, we see much of the spirit of the man—bold, daring, and independent in what he considered truth. In person, he was tall and thin—a pioneer no less by nature than by habit and education.

SETH ALLEN (?—1830)

All we can find concerning the present subject are the accounts gathered from his fellow laborers in Vermont. Before he moved to Stowe, Vt., he had attended school for some time in Wilbraham, Mass. He was ordained soon after 1824. By trade, he was a shoemaker, which business he followed all his life. In person, he was slenderly built, and had a dark complexion. He was a far better pastor and instructor than a revivalist. He died, very happy, about

1830, in the same house that Elder Reuben Doges had died in, two years previous.

<u>Reuben Allerton (1788—1832)</u>

This brother was an earnest worker in the vineyard. It does not seem, from an examination of our old periodicals, that he wrote much, as I find no letters from him. Many speak of him in high terms, and mourn his early departure. At the time of his death, he had a large field of labor in Putnam and Dutchess counties, N.Y., and in the adjoining counties in the State of Connecticut. As to what his gifts and habits were before conversion, we are unable to say.

In the "Gospel Luminary," (N.Y.,) of February 1, 1832, Amos Pease says: "Died, at my residence in Putnam County, N.Y., on the 28th ult., Elder Reuben Allerton, aged forty-four years, pastor of the First Christian Church in South East Patterson and Danbury, Connecticut. In the death of Elder Allerton, a wife and six small children have been deprived of a kind husband and an affectionate father, an important church of its pastor, and the community of one of its most useful citizens." On a visit to Green County, N.Y., he took a cold which turned into typhus fever, which, in twenty- five days, terminated fatally. He died triumphantly, his last words being, "I long to depart and be with Christ," The writer adds "The large field in which he labored is now left destitute of the ministration of a free gospel."

Six years before Mr. Allerton's death, Elder Badger, speaking of this field of labor in Putnam and West Chester counties, said: "The people are very destitute of preaching, though the assemblies are large and respectable. Elder Reuben Allerton, who resides in Putnam County, is the only Christian preacher in that region. I had an agreeable intercourse with him, and found him to be a man of good report among his neighbors. He has recently been much engaged, and has done much good."

Elder David Millard, in 1850, in his "Rise of the Christian Connexion in the State of New York," says, speaking of Mr. Allerton,

"One of the number raised in the Freehold church now sleeps in death; viz., Elder Reuben Allerton. He was a good, efficient laborer in the cause. He died in Duchess County a few years ago. His grave, with a neat monument set to it, may be found in the burial ground near the Christian chapel in Milan."

ELISHA, JOHNATHON AND SAMUEL ALLEY

From some letters received from Indiana, I learn of three Christian ministers of the above name who labored in the southern part of the state about 1825. It is said, they were co-laborers of David Douglas, Joseph Cooper, David McGahy, and others.

WILLIAM T. ANDERSON (1825—1855)

The subject of this sketch was a young man, who was cut down in the very beginning of his usefulness. He was a member of the Rhode Island and Massachusetts Conference. His career, though brilliant, was short.

Elder Albert G. Morton gave the following account of him at the time of his death: "William T. Anderson died at Killingly, Conn., January 13, 1855, aged twenty-seven years. He experienced religion when quite a youth, and consecrated himself to his Master's service for life—a life that was terminated at an early date. He commenced preaching about 1851, was ordained in May, 1853, but in consequence of failing health he was obliged to suspend his ministerial labors in August, 1854, to resume them no more. Elder Anderson was a brother whose intellectual and moral excellence gave unusual promise of future usefulness and success, and we can not but regard his death as a loss to the church. His labors in the ministry were principally bestowed on the Christian Churches in South Dartmouth, Mass., and vicinity. In his field of labor, he won the esteem and secured the affections of such as became acquainted with him."

He died of consumption, and was buried by the side of his wife, who had died four years before, in the Fiskeville cemetery.

HUGH ANDREWS (?—?)

Hugh Andrews was a minister in the western part of Ohio at an early day, and assisted at the ordination of Elder John Hardy in 1810.

JAMES ANDREWS (1771—1845)

There are but few men in any age whose lives have been so devoted to one purpose as has that of this veteran. Could the materials be collected, his life's history would be a curiosity and an entertainment to thousands of readers. His carelessness in dress, his unyielding faith in prayer, and his self-sacrifice and devotion were wonderful. The best we can gather concerning his life is a sketch written by Elder John Ross, and published in the "Christian Palladium," April 1, 1846, five or six months after Andrews' death. In it he says: "Of the early history of Elder Andrews, or of his family connections we have no knowledge. We believe his native place was North Carolina. It was about the year 1827 that he first visited the eastern part of the State of New York in the character of an evangelist—an itinerant Christian minister. He was about fifty-five years old, and had spent twelve or fourteen years in the ministry. During this period of ministerial service, he had traveled extensively in the Western and South-western States. He was a contemporary laborer in the Gospel field with Elders Barton W. Stone and William Kinkaid, and had formed an acquaintance with most of the Christian ministers then in the West. In 1827 or 1828, he offered himself for membership in the New York Eastern Christian Conference, and on the satisfactory testimonials of Christian, ministerial character, which he presented from brethren at the West, he was received as a minister of that body— in which communion and fellowship he lived and died.

It was about the year 1828 that he was married to the widow, Phebe Wood, daughter of Elder Steven Whitaker, of Herkimer County, N.Y., and soon after took up his residence with the church at Union Mills. Here, and at Cranberry Creek he resided for several years. And though he traveled much abroad, doing the work of an evangelist, yet he was very particular to preach one half of the Sabbaths of the year to the church where he resided. Some years ago, he moved to Livingston County, in Western New York, where he finished his mortal career. The only daughter and child of Mrs. Andrews by her former husband having married, she was provided with a comfortable home with her daughter, while her husband— our brother—was permitted, with but few worldly cares upon his mind, to pursue the one great object of his life —the work of an itinerant minister.

Of the particular character of the deceased, we hardly know how to speak. He was no ordinary or common man. Like Kinkaid, he was so little studious of etiquette, that, to the stranger, he appeared somewhat eccentric, and not so easy of access, or as sociable as most men. But after a mature acquaintance, Elder Andrews was found to be companionable, and often highly interesting in social converse. But if we would know the man, we must see him at home. His home was in the Bible or in the pulpit. He was always himself, never at a loss and never embarrassed. He possessed several distinguishing characteristics.

1st. He was a man of very fervent piety. If we had among us a man of prayer, that man was Elder James Andrews. To this testimony, many of the readers of this article will bear witness, when they recall the numerous times, while visiting at their dwellings, they have called him from his knees, in the closet, the bed-chamber, the barn, or the grove, to partake of his usual meals with the family.

2nd. He was favored with a very active and retentive memory. This manifested itself both on particular and general subjects.

3rd. He was emphatically a Bible student. He read much, and his Bible was his constant companion. Hence, few men possessed so general a knowledge of the Scriptures as he did. Where little known, and his name not familiar, he was inquired after or referred to as 'that Bible man, that living concordance? And, indeed, the epithet, 'Bible man,' was no misnomer "when applied to him. For the Bible, through grace, had made him what he was, and this was his theme to preach, and song to sing.

4th. His assiduity and faithfulness in the work of the minis-' try is one of the finest examples delineated among us. He was no drone in the hive, no idler in the Lord's vineyard.

We believe that while in New York he never entered into the pastoral relation. To the particular duties of that office he seemed not to have turned his attention. His whole mind seemed absorbed in the one work of preaching the gospel to men. For this alone he appeared to Eve. While in health, he was anxious and sought opportunity to preach daily; and two or three sermons a day did not discommode him, a few years ago. Though apparently of a slender frame, yet he spoke with ease, and could endure abundant ministerial labor. He traveled on horseback and often, when calling on a friend, he would inquire, before alighting, whether it was convenient to have meeting or not; if not, he would choose to seek another place where he could labor in the gospel field. We believe he was never considered a great revivalist, though warm and pathetic in his addresses. But his labors were better calculated to enlighten the understanding than to affect the passion. Wholly absorbed with his subject, he preached with about the same earnestness to the few or the many. His great strength lay in his capability of concentrating and pouring the whole fight of the Scriptures upon the subject he was discussing. In the prosecution of this work, he continued until his last sickness to perform long journeys on horseback, to face storms and winds, and preach almost daily."

On his way home from Charleston Four Corners, N.Y., he was taken sick, but reached his home on the Erie Canal on the 26th day of September, 1845, meeting his wife at the landing. He was taken home next day on a bed in a carriage. His disease was typhoid fever, and no medical remedy was of any avail. He died in triumph. While dying, he said, "My mind is as calm as a summer morning; I have no doubts or fears." And he manifested a perfect willingness to die in the faith that he had preached to others. He died October 5, 1845, aged seventy-four years.

<u>WILLIAM P. ANDREWS (1794—1854)</u>

The first account we have of this brother is that he lived in Clark County, O., and attended church at Knob Prairie, about 1813. In that year he was married to Catherine Lee, with whom he lived happily for many years. After the death of his first wife, he married Dorcas Moore, whom he left a widow with six children at the time of his death.

From Ohio, Elder Andrews moved to Indiana, about 1848, and soon began to exercise in public by way of exhortation— in which he succeeded well. In 1849, he was ordained. For five years before his death, he was a pastor of a Christian Church in Jasper County, Ill. On the second Sabbath in December, 1853, while at prayers, after kneeling about five minutes he made an effort to rise to his feet but found he could not. Afterwards he spoke but few words, and on Monday evening following he breathed his last. He died in the triumph of that religion which he had preached so earnestly to others.

<u>JOSEPH ANSHOTS (?—1874)</u>

The death of this minister is recorded in the *Herald,* February 21, 1874. He was a faithful preacher till disabled by sickness. He died near the beginning of 1874.

<u>BOLTON ASHLEY (1826—1864)</u>

This brother, at the time of his death, lived in Darke County, O., where he labored for the Delisle Christian Church. He lived on a farm which brought him his principal means of support. He never traveled much as a minister, nor did he devote his whole time to the work; yet his influence was felt for good where he lived. He was a member of the Bluffton Indiana Conference (now Eastern). As a member of the Ohio National Guard, he went to the service, and on returning from the field, died at Camp Dennison, near Cincinnati, O., in 1864, aged thirty-eight years. He was a young minister of good report and studious habits, and it is probable that, had he lived longer, he would have filled a wider sphere in the church.

20

JAMES AND JOSEPH ASHLEY

These two ministers, perhaps brothers, lived and labored in Bartholomew and Johnson counties, Ind. They were among the early ones that came to the country, likely from the South, and are highly spoken of by the old settlers.

LOAMI ASHLEY (1784—1855)

We find from an obituary written by Elder William Nealigh, and published in the *Gospel Herald* of October 13, 1855, that Elder Loami Ashley was born in the State of Vermont, August 9, 1784, moved to Ohio in 1817, and in 1819 joined the Christian Church at Liberty, Montgomery County, O., under the labors of Elder Nathan Worley. He was a deacon of the church for many years, but in 1843 he began to preach, and joined the Tippecanoe (Indiana) Christian Conference. He died in Montgomery County, O., after an illness of four days, September 25, 1855, aged seventy-one years.

WILLIAM H. ASHLEY (1786—1875)

Captain William Ashley, father of Elder William Ashley, was an officer in the Revolutionary War, and left the service about three years before his son William was born. Captain Ashley and family moved to Chenango County, N.Y., when William was quite young. While in the State of New York, William was married to Miss Betsy Thompson. During this time, he was engaged in rafting lumber on the Susquehanna River. Not long after his marriage, he moved with his small family to Pittsburg, Pa., and in 1816, moved from that place to Licking County, O. In 1817, he moved again—this time to South Bloomfield, Morrow County, O., (then Knox County,) where he continued till death.

Hitherto he had never made a profession of religion. About this time, Mr. Carr., a Methodist preacher, came to the neighborhood, and organized a Methodist class. By the request of Mr. Ashley and others, James Smith, a Christian minister of Mt. Vernon, came to labor in the community. During these meetings, Mr. Ashley joined the Christian Church. Meetings of both denominations were held at his house.

In 1818, Mr. Ashley began to preach, and soon became pastor of the Christian Church in Bloomfield Township, (now Sparta,) and continued in this relation until old age disqualified him for the work. His wife, who died in 1854, was a zealous and efficient helpmate to her husband. They had five children.

Elder Ashley's power consisted mainly in deep piety, strong faith, and great earnestness as a speaker. He was a Reformer in every sense of the term, was opposed to slavery, whisky, and secret societies, and was a strong believer in the Christian power of healing the sick—yet he was no fanatic. Without agreeing with our deceased brother as to the continuance of the healing art in the churches of today, yet there were many instances of healing—more than five hundred—recorded by Elder Ashley, that are difficult to account for on any other principle.

Whatever his peculiarities in matters of this kind, Elder Ashley was acknowledged, by all who knew him, to be a man above the average in natural ability as a preacher and pastor, with an honest heart and deep devotion.

ELISHA ASHLEY (1796—1865)

The substance of the following is from Elder Ashley himself. It was published in the "Christian Banner", Indianapolis, Ind., June 12, 1861. "As I am getting up in years, and do not expect to stay here much longer, perhaps it would be interesting to some to have a short history of my travels. I was born in Herkimer County, N.Y., February 25, 1796. When I was quite small, my father moved to Chenango County, in the same state. When five years old, I was taken back to Herkimer County, to live with one of my uncles. I lived there six years and then returned to Chenango. We remained in the latter County till 1813, when we moved to McKane County, Pa. While here, I was married to Sally Baker. In 1817, we moved to Montgomery County, O. Here I commenced my Christian warfare under the labors of Elder Nathan Worley, and was baptized by

Samuel Rogers. In 1820, I moved to Darke County, O., where I commenced my ministerial labors, and, in June, 1823, was set apart to the work of the ministry by fasting and prayer, David Purviance and George Shidler officiating.

The first thing I came in contact with was Campbellism, and I had several debates on that subject. The next was the Second Advent doctrine and then Mormonism. I have fought through them all and am still bending my course onward and upward.

In the year 1841 and '42, I traveled the bounds of the Indiana Bluffton Conference, and broke down at it. I would be gone from five to six weeks on every round, preaching from fifty to seventy-five times. I moved to Indiana, settled near Hagerstown, and had the care of several churches till my lungs gave out so that I was unable to preach any more. I then moved to Farmland, Randolph County, where I am yet (1861). Pray for me that my faith fail not."

Elder John B. Robertson, an intimate friend and former fellow-laborer, speaks in the highest terms of Elder Ashley, of his soundness of faith, of his ability as a defender of the Christian doctrine, etc. He proceeds to state his success as a pastor, and his self-sacrificing spirit as an itinerant minister in the new regions of Ohio and Indiana. He concludes by saying: "Thus he spent thirty-five or forty years of the prime of his life and the strength of his days in the gospel field. He had a clean record. He lived to a noble purpose, and died in faith and triumph. His rest is glorious."

In the latter years of his life, Elder Ashley moved from Farmland to Merom, Ind., where he buried the wife of his youth. He died in Merom, Ind., June 17, 1865, aged sixty- nine years.

HARRY ASHLEY (1798—1841)

The youngest of the four brothers, whose lives are here recorded, was Harry Ashley. He was a man of great earnestness. For many years after his death, he was remembered, in Licking and surrounding-counties, with more than ordinary regard as one of the most efficient ministers in his neighborhood—not in education and eloquence, but in deep piety and earnestness as a faithful, self-sacrificing man of God.

Elder James Hayes, his biographer, says: "Elder Harry Ashley departed this life at his residence in Appleton, Licking County, O., after an illness of twenty-one days. Elder Ashley was in his forty-third year. He was ordained in 1819, since which time he has been traveling to preach the Gospel to his fellow men. To the cause of his Master, he devoted his life."

Though somewhat local in his labors, and in limited circumstances as to worldly possessions, his field of labor was one of the most important. In his later years, he lived near Appleton, Licking County, O., and was an honored member of the Ohio Central Christian Conference. He was a man of great energy, and there was no sacrifice too great for him to make that he might win souls to Christ. This devotedness to the work, doubtless, was one cause of his great success. His name is embalmed in the affections of thousands, and his works have followed him.

These four brothers, sons of Captain William Ashley, originally from the State of Vermont, were, in many respects, peculiar. The education of each, as to books, was limited; yet they occupied prominent positions in their different fields of labor. William and Harry in the central part of Ohio; Elisha in Western Ohio and Eastern Indiana; and Loami, the oldest, who entered the ministry late in life, hence not so conspicuous as the other three, in Central Indiana.

None of them were deficient in natural talent, and, while limited in learning, their holy lives, earnest zeal, and self-sacrificing spirit gave them high positions as ministers. William, probably the most prominent of the four brothers, had a great influence in leading young men into the ministry. But few surpassed him in that trait.

ALFORD ATWOOD (1823—1865)

The parents of Elder Atwood were residents of Preble County, O. Elder Atwood was born there, December 12, 1823. Six years later, he moved with his parents to Vermillion County, Ill., where

he was married to Miss Diadama Bloomfield, in 1847. His education was limited. He joined the Christian Church, and was baptized
in 1850. He soon became so active a worker in the church, that, in
1852, he was ordained by Elders Emely, Wilkins, and Welch.
From this till the war of the Rebellion, while sustaining himself
mostly by his trade as a blacksmith, he labored extensively as a
minister, in Vermilion and adjoining counties. When the war broke
out, he joined the 125th Ill. V. Regiment. Brother Masters, a comrade of his in the regiment, speaks highly of Elder Atwood's religious zeal during his army life; how he preached to his comrades
as often as he could; and how he was loved by all for his probity.
In 1864, his health failed, and in March, 1865, he was discharged,
and returned to his home, wife, and children. June 21, 1865, he
died in the triumph of that faith that he had preached to others. He
left a sorrowing wife, three sons, and one daughter.

CHARLES AYERS (1798—1852)

In the obituary of this brother, Elder Joseph Kingsley states that
he died of consumption, aged fifty-two years; that he died triumphantly, having made all necessary arrangements for his funeral, as well as his temporal affairs; and that he said, "My hope is
firm and unshaken; I have no fear of death,—no, not the least." '

Elder Ayers, speaking of himself, says: "I was born May 29,
1798. At the age of fifteen; I was left without a father. At the age
of nineteen, I embraced the Gospel. After much anxiety, I made up
my mind to unite with the Christians, believing their foundation to
be right; and I have never been shaken, but now stand firm, in view
of death."

He united with the Christian Church in 1817, became a member
of the Northern New York Christian Conference, June 26, 1834,
and was ordained to the work of the Gospel ministry, May 1, 1842.
His labors were mostly confined to his own vicinity, and especially
to the church in Houndsfield, of which he was a member.

Joseph Badger (1792—1852)

Joseph Badger, the son of Peaslee and Lydia (Kelly) Badger, was born at Gilman- ton, N.H., August 16, 1792. He was. the fourth son in a family of nine children—five sons and four daughters. He was named after his grandfather, General Joseph Badger. When about five years old, he was taken to his grandfather's residence, a short distance from his father's, where he first heard prayer; and being ignorant of the object, the operation was a great mystery to him; but it was not long till he learned to repeat prayers of his own. Though he forgot, in a measure, the solemnity awakened by the prayers at his grandfather's, yet it returned, and finally resulted in conversion. In accordance with the custom of the times, it was a long while, many years indeed, before he received a clear evidence of his acceptance with God.

In 1801, his father, with his large family, moved from Gilman ton to Compton, Lower Canada, at that time, a howling wilderness. In this wild country, with but few settlers, the Badgers opened the forest for cultivation; and here young Joseph learned to battle with the difficulties of life, preparatory to the great work before him. The few Christian people in that part of Canada were the Freewill Baptists and Methodists. For years, young Badger was company for no one, having left the society of fun-lovers, and being unprepared to enter the society of the religious. During this time, his principal religious teacher was Elder Avery Moulton, of whom Mr. Badger always spoke in the highest terms. Having finally ' given his heart to God, he was baptized by Elder Moulton, September 29, 1812, in the presence of a large number of people. Among these was Mr. Badger's own father, who, though he did not oppose his son in this step, yet had but little interest in the performance.

Having given his heart to the Lord by conversion, and having put on Christ by baptism, it was but a short step for him to enter fully into the thorough work of the ministry. He was not a man to be deterred by difficulties, or he would never have embraced religion under the circumstances.

From 1812 to 1815, the time of his ordination, Badger was very active. One thing in particular gave him a boldness that many years of ordinary labor would hardly have given him. In the beginning of his ministry, the war of 1812, between England and the United States, was raging, and things were in a very confused state in the province of Canada where his family lived. The young preacher was taken up, and tried before three drunken 'Squires on the charge of disloyalty to the British Crown. He and his companion, a Mr. Bishop, also a minister, by a peculiar boldness, came out victorious, having secured the sympathy of the people.

At this time, one of his colleagues in the ministry was a young man by the name of Adams, who joined the Methodist Church. Badger stood aloof from all organization, and continued, as he considered it, a freeman of Christ. He and his friend parted in love and tears. The places where he labored during his stay in the Province, were Compton, Ascott, Westbury, Oxford, Brompton, Ringsey, Shipton, etc.

In June, 1814, he started on a journey to Gilmanton, N.H., preaching every day, wherever he could find an opening; sometimes with one denomination, and sometimes with another, but always independent. He had great success in preaching among his friends in New Hampshire.

January 19, 1815, he was ordained to the full work of the ministry at the residence of Elder Wilson, of Barnstead, N.H. The ordination sermon was preached by Elder William Blaisdell, and Elders Young, Boody, Shepherd, Wilson, Knowles, and Piper assisted in the ordination. On account of his success in the ministry, and his disconnection with any denomination, there were several efforts made to have him ordained in other connections. The condition required by all others, however, was, as Badger states it, that "he should walk on two legs—one the Christian and the other the denominational leg." He considered his ordination by those brethren to be, entirely free.

During his labors in New Hampshire, he was in the habit of visiting the house of Captain Anthony Peavy, in Farmington. Captain

Peavy had two sons, John and Edward, who became active ministers in the Christian Church. In this family, also, Elder Badger found a congenial spirit in the person of Mary Jane, the daughter of Captain Peavy, to whom he was married, July 17, 1816, In October, 1816, he left his young wife at her father's, to start on a long tour of the State of New York. His labors, during this trip of several months, were immense. It was a constant preaching through a new country, a new form of worship—for, in that day, the Christians were few in the State of New York. Yet such was the success of this bold, earnest, and indefatigable man, that we find him, in the June following, (1817,) moving his family to Pittsford, N.Y., a central place around which a few churches and many preaching places were already established. This part of New York was to be Elder Badger's home the rest of his life.

It is not the purpose of this sketch to dwell at length on the multifarious labors of Elder Badger in this, his new field of labor. He had already commenced holding public discussions with ministers of different denominations; this he continued through life, both in speaking and writing. In his early ministry, he commenced writing to the different periodicals. This work increased on his hands, till his strong constitution was broken down by paralysis. It is the opinion of many besides the writer, that Elder Badger's writing talent was his greatest talent. His labors in public speaking, at funerals, in public debates, at general meetings, and as a pastor and missionary were immense. Beside the above, he was also engaged extensively, as a committee man, in drawing up constitutions and by-laws, remonstrances and petitions, and many such things as were needed in those times for the new church.

The following are some of the external changes in the life of Elder Badger. January 30, 1820, he lost a little son. April following, his wife, Mary Jane, died of consumption, leaving one child, a little daughter. To a man of the strong affections of Elder Badger, this must have been a heavy stroke. Soon after the death of his wife, he closed his house at Mendon, and went forth to the field to travel as a missionary. March 21, 1821, Elder Badger was again married,—this time to Miss Eliza Maria Sterling, of Lima, N.Y.,

In 1822, he attended the general conference of the Christian Church, at Greenville, N.Y., and extended his labors to Saybrook and Lynne, Conn. In 1823, he made a tour of Pennsylvania as far as Lewisburg. In 1824, he spent considerable time in the service of the state as spiritual counsellor of D.D. House, the murderer of Mr. Church. In 1825, he made an extensive tour through the West and South, and was the means of doing much good in uniting the Eastern and Western wings of the church, In 1826 and '27, he labored with the church in Boston, Mass. In 1830, he attended a debate in Milford, N.J., between Elder McCalla, of the Presbyterian, and Elder Lane, of the Christian Church; and in May, 1832, he became editor of the "Christian Palladium." He continued his connection with the "Palladium" for seven years —until 1839.

In May, 1839, he buried his second son, Joseph, which proved a shock so severe to the father that it is doubtful whether he ever was the same man again. In 1843, he passed through two events that bore heavy on his constitution. The death of Elder Seth Marvin, his son-in-law and an intimate companion, and the Millerite excitement that was so high during this year. On July 2, 1845, he received a stroke of paralysis, which, to a great extent, ended his public career; not that he was inactive after this, far from it; he traveled extensively, and had the charge of many churches—Conneaut, on Lake Erie, Fall River, Mass., and many others. He also preached some very able sermons, delivered able lectures on various subjects, and wrote much for the papers; yet it was done with a borrowed capital. Seven of the last years of his life were years of labor, but they were also years of suffering. He died May 12, 1852, aged fifty-seven years.

Much has been written of the life of Elder Badger. All agree in giving him the following characteristics.

1st. Great presence of mind under embarrassments.

2nd. Concentration of thought upon the subject in hand.

All his letters, lectures, sermons, and debates show this trait at first sight. Everything that bears on the subject is in readiness, and is applied at the proper time and place.

3d. Interest in the topic. Few men seem to feel the interest in the subject on hand as did Elder Badger.

4th. Great cheerfulness, and hope of success in connection with his theme. I do not now remember any single instance in which Elder Badger expressed any doubt of the triumph of his plans. He wrote much upon all subjects—of death and disaster, such as the Miller excitement of 1843—but he was always hopeful.

I never saw Elder Badger till after his paralytic stroke, in 1845. Disease was written on his face, his utterance was much affected, and he had the appearance of a broken-down old man; yet, of all the visitors that came to our school at Meadville from 1845 to 1848, none carried the hearts of the students of Theology in that Institution as did Elder Badger. His presence of mind was perfect, his concentration was complete, his interest in the subject was inexhaustible, and his cheerfulness arid hope were without a cloud. One of Badger's short addresses was talked of and commented upon weeks after its delivery, to the great enjoyment of the poor students; and each desired, doubtless, that, when fully developed as a speaker and writer, he might become a second Badger.

SIMON BAGLEY (1798—1873)

Simon B. Bagley, father of Elder Simon Bagley, was born in Providence, R.I., in 1739. His son, Simon, was born in Grafton, N.H., April 26, 1798, and was brought up, mainly, in Sharon, Vt. He was married in Sharon, in 1819, and, in 1825, moved from that place, with his family, to Athens County, O. He moved from there to Knox County, the same state, in 1829. In 1838, he moved to West Liberty, Iowa, and in 1844, to Cedar County, where he lived on a farm for five years. In 1849, he moved to Tipton, the county seat of Cedar County, where he remained till death. He died of apoplexy, December 3, 1873.

He went to Iowa full of zeal for the cause of the Master. But few ministers of the Christian Church were in the territory in 1838, and Brother Bagley became a strong supporter of the work. Soon after his arrival in Iowa, he commenced holding meetings, and, about 1840, was ordained by Elders Martin Baker and Elisha Beardsly. He assisted in the organization of the first Christian Conference in the territory. From this time, Elder Bagley became one of the leading workers in the denomination in Iowa.

Elder Bagley joined the Christian Church in Sharon, Vt.; in 1816, under the preaching of Abel Burk, and was baptized soon after by Elder Jeremiah Gates. During his entire Christian life, since his conversion in Vermont, he was active in the cause. Meetings were held in his house in Knox County, O. For two years, in Iowa, as a lay brother, he was as zealous as during the thirty-three years of his ministry. It was natural that, with such zeal in the cause, he should enter the ministry, for his heart was in the work.

Brother and Sister Bagley raised eight children—six sons and two daughters. Two of his sons, William and James, entered the ministry. William is now an efficient worker in the church in Iowa, after serving three years, part of the time as Chaplain, in the war of the Rebellion. James, who had also studied law, died in Davenport, Iowa, the day before he was to have been mustered out of service.

Elder Bagley, though a man of ordinary talent, and though forty-two years old before entering upon the full work of the ministry,—and he likely entered into the work then on account of the great need of ministerial labor in the field where he was placed,—yet, by his prudent course, his peace-loving disposition, and his earnestness in the work, eternity alone will reveal to us the amount of good he accomplished in this life.

JOSEPH BAILEY (1786—1866)

Joseph Bailey was born in the town of Partridgefield, Berkshire County, Mass., September 1, 1786. His parents were Calvinistic in their Theology. Joseph was converted in his seventeenth year, in Vernon, N.Y., at a prayer meeting, by the exhortations and prayers of a pious Methodist sister. About a year after this, he moved to New Haven, Oswego County, N.Y., and, for a season, neglected his religious duties, and lived in a backslidden state.

On the fifth of April, 1807, he was married to Miss Patty Tullar, of Mexico, Oswego County, N.Y., with whom he lived thirty-nine years, and raised a family of seven children—four sons and three daughters. In 1808, the sudden death of an intimate friend, who died in an unprepared state, made such an impression on the minds of Mr. Bailey and his companion that it awakened them to a sense of duty. For a year they lived a religious life out of any church. They finally joined the Methodist Church, that being the nearest of all others to their views of Christian duty. In 1817, he became acquainted with the Christian Church at New Haven, and feeling that this came the nearest to carrying out his views of gospel order of any other, he joined the church, and was baptized by Elder Jonathan S. Thompson. From this time, he labored in public, and in 1818 joined the New York Western Christian Conference.

In February, 1820, he moved to North East, Erie County, Penn., and was ordained to the work of an evangelist in the town of Mill Creek, in the fall of that year. Soon after this, he moved to Pomfret, Chautauqua County, N.Y., where he organized the first Christian Church in that county. He lived in Chautauqua County fourteen years, and during that time, organized six or seven churches, and assisted in planting many others in the adjoining counties.

In 1834, he moved to Marion, Wayne County, N.Y., where he labored for years with great success. From Marion, he moved to Arcadia, where he finished his course.

In 1841, he buried his second son, and, in 1843, his youngest daughter. These bereavements he bore with Christian fortitude, but by several shocks of paralysis his physical and mental energies were prostrated; after lingering for some time, a mere wreck of his former self, he closed his earthly career, July 15, 1846, in the sixtieth year of his age.

From an account of the labors of Brother Bailey, given in the periodicals of his day, I find that he was considered entirely reliable, energetic, self-sacrificing, and consecrated to the Work of saving souls. His manner of writing was plain and pointed. He was not a great writer, but his articles are always full of good sense, his subjects are of the practical kind, and his articles are short and pithy.

But few Christian ministers of that time are so frequently referred to as is Elder Joseph Bailey. One reason of this is, doubtless, that he was a pioneer, and that his work was of a lasting kind. To this day, Elder Bailey's name is a household word in all the Christian families of Chautauqua County, N.Y., and Erie County, Pa.

GEORGE C. BAILEY (1790—1868)

This was a brother of the preceding, and, like him, was raised in the Baptist Church. In a letter of his in the "Christian Palladium/' from Shumla, N.Y., April, 1834, speaking of the prospect of the Christians in that part, he says: "Brother Barr spends his whole time in publishing the glad tidings. Brother Joseph Baily has several churches under his care, but he is about to leave this place and move to the County of Wayne, N.Y. I am not idle in the vineyard. It is about twenty years since I left the Baptist Church, and united with a Christian society. My soul is engaged in the cause of liberty, and could I see the church free, I think I could depart in peace."

Like his brother, Joseph, he moved early to Western New York and Western Pennsylvania, and had charge, as a pastor, of various churches in Chautauqua County, N.Y.,—such as Gerry, Stockton, Miria, and others.

In the *Herald* of March 6, 1869, I find the following items: Elder Bailey was born in Massachusetts in 1790, was converted in 1805, commenced preaching in 1828, and was ordained by Elders Whitehead, Fairly, and Chase, June 23, 1828. He moved to the neighborhood of Arkwright Church, Chautauqua County, N. Y,, in 1831. He died of paralysis, December 26, 1868.

JOHN F. BAILEY (1789—1854)

In the "Christian Palladium," September 23, 1854, I find a notice, written by Elder William Griffith, of the above Brother. It says that he was born in the State of New York, about 1789, and died in Jefferson County, Wis., July 7, 1854. He was converted in 1819, and soon after commenced preaching. In 1825, he moved to Canada in company with Thomas McIntire. He baptized many, among the rest, the late Elder Thomas Henry. He continued in Canada about eleven years, when he moved to Illinois. Thence, in 1839, he moved to Watertown, Wis., where he died, as stated above, full of years and labor.

<u>Joseph Baker (?—1854)</u>

There were but few ministers in his day who exerted more influence over a large territory, in a local way, than Joseph Baker. He wrote with considerable ability, mostly on doctrinal subjects; but little can be gleaned from these to form a biography.

Elder Daniel Long says of him: "He was a man of medium size, firmly built, dark complexioned, and one of the best sermonizers in the country. His sermons, like his writings, were of a doctrinal character. He was an earnest speaker, and a successful revivalist. He was active in conferences, and was a leader of men." His home, in his latter days, was near Chillicothe, O. He was once a member of the Deer Creek Christian Conference; but, at the time of his death, he was a member of the Salt Creek Conference, which was organized mostly by himself.

In the "Christian Palladium," September 1, 1834, he writes; I commenced laboring here about fifteen years ago, when the people were altogether unacquainted with the doctrines and practices of the Christian Church. In that time, about one thousand have united with the people called Christians in this region. About seven hundred are united in a few churches near this place. Where I live, one year ago the church numbered about thirty members; now it has over one hundred. We erected two meeting-houses this summer; one is a mile and a half east, the other two miles and a half west of my residence. Both are free for all societies to worship in.

We are uniform in faith and practice in the conference to which I belong. We have ten ordained, and a number of un-ordained preachers, and more than twenty churches."

Commenting on the above, Elder Badger, the editor, says: "The individual that heads this article has been a bold, invincible, and able advocate of Christian liberty in the West for many years. Many have been the privations and hardships he has been called to encounter while proclaiming the word of life through different sections of Ohio, when the country was new, and society, in many places, very much uncultivated. He has been involved in many controversies; but his critical knowledge of the Bible, his original, ingenious manner of treating his opponent, and his unquestionable piety has, in all cases, we believe, given him a decided victory. He is a strong, original man, endowed with the grace of God, and few, in our age, have endured more, or been [more successful in advancing truth."

The editor, however, excuses himself from publishing Elder Baker's "Forty-three different kinds of Trinitarians," though he considered it ingenious and diverting. This "Forty-three different kinds of Trinitarians" shows us the peculiarity of the man. He was independent, honest, original, and ingenious in his investigations of truth. The Bible, to him, was all in all. Take that away, and there is no telling how far his inquisitive mind would have led him.

In the latter part of life, he differed slightly from the generality of his brethren of the Christian Church, as to the relation of baptism to the remission of sin, he leaning, somewhat, in views toward the followers of Alexander Campbell. Such was the influence of Joseph Baker on the Salt Creek Conference that the members still (1880) continue to hold the very tenants of their successful leader. Outsiders, speaking derisively, say that these brethren swear in the name of Joseph Baker

From a short obituary in the *Gospel Herald,* February 1, 1855, by James Baker, I find that he died triumphantly, in Vinton County, O., November 7, 1854. His age is not given.

Martin Baker (1779—1849)

Martin was a brother of Joseph Baker, though, as a minister, he was far from equal to Joseph in his influence on the public. Elder Simon Bagley says of him: "He was an able defender of the Christian-doctrine. He labored principally in Ohio, Indiana, and Iowa. He died in 1849, aged about seventy years."

James Baker (?—?)

Elder Long says that James Baker, a relation of Joseph and Martin, lived near Clarksburg, O. He was a good man, of ordinary talent as a minister, but he never traveled much as a preacher. He died at his residence, but I am unable to give the precise time. He must have been past the middle age. He left a large family of children, most of whom became prominent members of his own church.

James A. Baker (1807—1877)

Brother James A. Baker was born in Greenville, Greene County, (N.Y.,) July 26, 1807; died in Northern Iowa, July 30, 1877. He was converted in 1826, under the labors of Elder John Hollister and soon after moved to the West. While living in the State of Illinois, he improved his ministerial gifts among the churches and was ordained by Elders John Walworth and John Towner. In 1850 he moved to the State of Iowa, and settled at Strawberry Point.

From this time till death, his labors were constant. Hundreds, and perhaps thousands, were converted through his earnest appeals. He was known and loved through all the Christian Churches in Iowa. He was a man of limited education, but his zeal knew no bounds. He was known as the "Weeping John." His faithful wife died in 1875. He married again, but his life was drawing to its close, and his labors ending. He was kicked by a horse, and the injury was so severe that he died in four hours. He spoke but few words after the accident.

Like many of our self-made men, Elder Baker made good use of what talent he had, consecration and zeal making up, in a great measure, for a liberal education. He died, lamented by the many churches -where he had labored.

MELYN D. BAKER (1800—1852)

This brother, for the short period of eleven years, occupied one of the most useful positions in the ministry of the Christian Church. He was a descendent of an old Presbyterian stock. His father and mother, Jonathan and Sarah (Mulford) Baker, were members of that church, at their home in Essex County, N.J. They moved to Ohio in 1802, and after staying a year or two near Cincinnati, they moved, in 1805, to Enon, Clark County, O., where, the next year, 1806, they joined the Christian Church at Knob Prairie, in that County.

Melyn was but two years old when his parents left New Jersey, and five years old when they settled in Clark County, O. The boy's educational facilities were poor, but were improved as much as could be expected. In 1817, he had a severe attack of rheumatism that made him lame for life; during this period, also, he was converted, and three years later, he made a public confession of religion and joined the church at Knob Prairie. The mode of procedure in joining church in those days was, the candidate was to read a portion of Scripture, the Creed, and make such remarks as were prompted by the state of his mind. Brother Baker, in his remarks, among other things, said: "I've listed in the holy war," whereupon old Judge Layton cried out "Amen to that," "Thank God for that." From this time on, for twenty-one years, Brother Baker continued an active, zealous, and efficient lay brother in the church. In 1822, Brother Baker married Miss Margaret McClure, with whom he lived happily till February 1825, when she died; and August of the same year he buried a little daughter, the only child of this union, which made the world dark and dreary to the grief-stricken father and husband.

In May, 1826, he was married to Miss Mariah Lane, half-sister of Elder William Lane, of Burlington, Ohio, with whom he lived happily to the end of his mortal career, and who had mourned the loss of an affectionate husband for more than twenty years before she joined him above.

During the twenty-one years, mentioned above, Brother Baker felt many times, as if the Lord had a more extensive field for him to occupy than a member in a local church. His zeal prompted him to a wider sphere, but a lack of education, bashfulness, and timidity kept him back. In September, 1841, however, he was received a member of the Miami Conference, and from that time to the close of his life, he was constantly at work, an active Watchman on the walls of Zion. In April, 1842, he was ordained to the full work of the ministry, at the Knob Prairie Church, the following ministers being present: Elders I.N. Walters, D.F. Ladley, L. Purviance, and Amos Stevens

The following tabular summary of his labors for ten years, found in his biography written by Elder John Ellis, shows the precision and system of the man.

1st year, traveled 2300 miles, preached 170 times, recd. $ 70.00			
2nd year	3125	211	$150.00
3rd year	2885	185	$171.00
4th year	2050	130	$191.00
5th year	2225	120	$142.00
6th year	2310	120	$131.00
7th year	2125	112	$127.00
8th year	1975	135	$171.00
9th year	3725	157	$205.96
10th year	3805	130	$147.37

The preceding table does not speak of the ministry as a very re-munerative employment; and yet it is doubtful whether any other persons of that day enjoyed life more than Elder Baker. Those of us who met him in our public gatherings, and saw with what promptness he responded to every call of the denomination, and knowing that, as one of our leading men, he was preaching to some of our most popular churches, little thought that his average in-come for all his traveling and labor was but a trifle over one hundred and fifty dollars per year.

Elder Baker's position in a central part of the Miami Conference in the neighborhood of our publishing department in the West, his intimacy with the active men of the church—as Walters, Ladly, Williamson, etc.,—together with his entire reliability and zeal in the cause called out all the energy of the man at once. He was one of the most active men in the publishing department of the church, and a leader in our missionary operations; and whatever position he occupied he filled to the satisfaction of all his brethren.

Elder Baker lived in one place during all his ministerial life, and traveled to distant places. As we see in his journal, he preached regularly for some time in Southern Ohio, especially in Ripley, where he was the principal ministerial agent in building that fine house of worship—one of the best in the State of Ohio at the time it was built. These churches in Southern Ohio must have been nearly one hundred miles from his home. He preached, also, for several years for the West Liberty and Glady Creek churches, in Logan County, O., thirty or forty miles from his home.

In regard to the peculiarities of Elder Baker, he had as few as almost any of his brethren. He was cheerful, a peace-lover and a peace-maker. Naturally, he had a strong mind, not as a genius to grasp a problem at one glance, but rather he possessed a vein of strong common sense that enabled him to grasp the pith of his subject. His sermons, therefore, were instructive, and those who heard him once were desirous of hearing him again. This gave him a strong hold on his hearers. This affection for the preacher increased ten-fold when they formed, the acquaintance of the man. They felt not only that the doctrine he preached was true, sound, and useful, but, furthermore, that the man himself was an embodiment of what he preached.

Elder Baker died at the age of fifty-two, in the very midst of his usefulness. Lamentation and mourning were felt through all the churches in Ohio when the news of his death reached them through the "Gospel Herald." It was a shock to all the brotherhood, for his value had but lately been found out, and we had looked for him to grow in influence for more than twenty years in the future. His death was very triumphant. His last expression, "this is the happiest hour of life," was repeated everywhere, and all felt that such a triumphant death was some compensation for our great loss.

<u>Luther Baker (1770—1857)</u>

This veteran was very noted in his day as an able, zealous, and reliable man, with a vein of mirth and eccentricity running through all his actions.

Elder Moses Howe says of him: "In person, he was over six feet in stature, rather slim, gentlemanly looking, sociable in his intercourse, and a good preacher of the old school type. He was an efficient revivalist and a great Scripturalist. He came over from the Baptists, and was a pastor of the Second Christian Church in New Bedford from 1832 to 1835."

An obituary in the *Herald of Gospel Liberty,* April 30, 1857, says: "He was pastor of a Baptist Church in Warren, R.I., for some years, and afterwards became a pastor of a church of the same denomination, in Providence, R.I., with which he continued until 1822, when, through a controversy going on at that time in New England, he became convinced that the doctrine of the Trinity, as held by his church, was erroneous. He left the Baptist and joined the Christian Church, and took charge of the Christian Church in New Bedford."

In 1836, at his own request, he gave up the charge of the Second Christian Church in New Bedford. From that time till 1857, the year he died, though not connected with any church as a regular pastor, yet he was considered by all a very useful man, filling many important places, wherever his labor was needed, and he was always considered a safe counselor. Between 1836 and 1857, he was a representative to the Massachusetts Legislature for several sessions.

Few men were more known and respected than Elder Baker, and his witty sayings were repeated very generally among the ministers. Elder Baker had a clear head and a quick perception; hence his striking remarks were treasured up and respected by his friends.

Elder Baker was a great friend of education, and an advocate for the support of the ministry. A person who cared for neither said to him, "I preach for nothing." "It is just worth it," said Elder Baker. Another said, "I can prepare a sermon in half a day." "And make nothing of it," said the Elder. Hundreds of such sayings are quoted among his friends to this day.

Elder Baker was a man of great originality as well as independence of mind—one of the Daniel Hix type of men. As we. see from his age, his early character was formed in the rough days of the Revolutionary War. When his religious nature was developed, he naturally drifted to the Baptists—the most Democratic church in New England, in that day. But when the Baptists began to urge such doctrines as, "Unconditional Election" and "Trinity" on its members, then such men as Hix and Baker were displeased. It was natural that they should seek a more congenial people—a people as full of zeal as the Baptists but who granted to all the right of private judgment. These they found among the early Christians of New England.

<u>Isaac Banister (1794—1852)</u>

From a sister, a daughter, and a co-worker (the late Elder Starkey) of Elder Banister I have the following: Elder Banister was born in Royalton, Vt., March 10, 1794. When he was eleven years old, his father sold his farm in Royalton, and moved to Bethel. When he was twenty years old, his father gave him his time, and, with a view of making money speedily, he worked very hard, by which he lost his health. His disease was inflammation of the lungs, from which he never fully recovered.

In the winter of 1815, he taught school in Turnbridge, Vt., and, June 5, 1816, he commenced the study of medicine with Dr. John Edson. He made rapid progress in his studies, and his earthly prospects were brightening. In the midst of all, however, his mind became troubled on the subject of religion. In 1818, a great revival was in progress in Bethel and Randolph, Vt., and among many others, Isaac was converted, and was once more happy. As usual in

New England, the light of truth came slowly, so in the case of Isaac. After struggling for three years with his conscience and God, in November, 1818, he went to meeting. The pressure was so great that he had to speak or die. He spoke and the burden of sin was removed.

In June, 1819, he was ordained, and, in the same year, was married to Mrs. Aldrich, a widow lady. She was a woman of considerable talent as a writer, and one of deep and fervent piety. After his marriage, he lived three years in Plymouth, Vt., traveling and preaching in the northern part of the state.

He finally settled in Randolph, where he buried his two oldest children, a son and daughter. In 1827, he moved to South Edmunds, St. Lawrence County, N.Y. In 1837, he lost his first wife, he and four children being left in great sorrow. He married again, a lady by the name of Melinda Ford, of whom he had two children, and with whom he lived happily to the end of his days. He died peacefully, January 15, 1852.

Elder Banister was a faithful worker in the church. His education was quite good but his health was often poor. That he was a conscientious man the fact of his leaving the lucrative profession of medicine for the self-sacrificing and laborious work of the ministry is a sufficient proof.

ISAAC BANTA (1810—1847)

Elder Isaac N. Walter, in a short biography of this brother, published in the *Herald* Vol. IV, page 367, states that he lived, since 1810, in Preble County, O., that he was converted in 1840, that he was ordained February 20, 1843, that he buried his wife October 1, 1845, and that he died, after a short illness, December 16, 1847.

He was a zealous and very energetic man, efficient in revivals. He labored, mostly, in Preble and adjoining counties, •during his short ministerial career. He was highly spoken of as an useful, good man.

<u>Hallet Barber (1798—1849)</u>

When the news of the death of this veteran reached the Christian Churches through Ohio and Indiana there was a shock such as is seldom felt, even at the death of a good minister. One reason of this, beside the attachment to the man, was that his field of labor, for the fifteen or twenty years previous, had been so extensive as to reach from the central counties of Ohio to the Wabash River, in Indiana. In hundreds of log cabins through that newly settled country, the name of Barber had a charm to the inmates that few others possessed.

Hallet Barber was born in the State of New York in 1798, was married in Delaware County, O., in 1818, entered the ministry in 1829, and died of the cholera in 1849.

The substance of the following is from the pen of one of his intimate friends, a fellow-laborer during sixteen years through the wilds of Indiana and Ohio, Elder J.B. Robertson: "I first met Elder Barber at the brick church on the Derby Plains, Union County, O., in 1833. The meeting was conducted by Elders Jeremiah Fuson, the pastor, Hallet Barber, Edward Lewis, and Joseph Thomas, the White Pilgrim. The latter two soon went East only to find graves in the land of strangers —Lewis in Pennsylvania, Thomas in New Jersey. During this meeting, Elder Barber, as was his custom with young men inclined to the ministry, urged me to the work. His home at this time was in the central part of Ohio. He moved from there to Darke County, O., where he cleared the third piece of land that he had cleared since he began to preach. From his home in Ohio, Elder Barber made several trips to Indiana, and organized a number of churches in Ohio and Indiana, and .among them the church at Marion, the county seat of Grant County, Ind. From these sprang the organization of the Bluffton Christian Conference.

We became traveling companions in the wilderness. We traveled together constantly for eight or ten years. We were often out three months at a time, without resting, having meetings every day or night, or both, during the whole time. We had many soul-stirring revivals and communions where we never spent one Sunday with the people. The Elder was the most thorough-going and persevering man I ever knew. He never stopped for anything that could be encountered by any human being. I have known him to swim his horse across a river in cold weather, and, with his clothes frozen stiff upon his person, he would preach and attend to all the duties of the occasion before having his clothes dried. It was never too hot or too cold, nor was the water ever too high, or the snow too deep, or the season too sickly for him to reach his appointments.

At one time, which I well remember, we traveled from his home in Darke County, O., to Marion, Grant County, Ind., in a zigzag course of some sixty miles. The ponds were filled with water and frozen on top, so that a great part of the way we had to carry a club to break the ice before the horses, the water being quite deep. At one place; where there was an island, we found a foot bridge to the mainland, but no way for the horses. We carried our saddles and drove, our horses in. The poor beasts made their way through mud, ice, and water, and stood trembling and bleeding on the bank, on the other side. When we came up to them, the Elder observed, 'This would be a sin for anything else but to save perishing sinners.'

Another time, on a long ride, he became so exhausted that I helped him from his horse, and laid him in the shade of a tree, as I expected, to die. He spoke very pathetically of his having spent so much of the prime of his life from home, preaching and laboring for thousands of families who lived in affluence. Then, referring to the destitute condition of his own family (which I knew full well) in such terms that now, after the lapse of more than twenty-five years, I can hardly refrain from shedding tears upon the paper before me, as I remember his words. He spoke of his wife, laboring and economizing to- save herself and children from want—which impressed my mind that ministers' wives will share with their devoted husbands the crown of unfading glory.

Opposition always brought out his greatest strength. The doctrine of the Trinity and baptism for the remission of sins, as preached in his field, brought out his giant mind to combat them. In one place, the infidels boasted that they would hold the ground against him; but, to their consternation, reformation broke out, through his preaching, so that the infidels were left almost alone."

Elder Barber was a believer in organization and the support of the ministry, and system throughout the work; but, as Elder Robertson observes, he would never stop traveling because he received no pay. Elder Robertson relates one instance of poverty and relief, looking like a miracle. After traveling for two months and a half in the northern part of Indiana, in a thinly settled country, they stopped all night at a stranger's, who charged them so much for lodgings that it took all the two ministers had to pay, the bill. They congratulated each other that they had enough, and that their Bibles and hymn books were not taken. In a short time, however, Elder Barber found a piece of money in the road about the amount he had paid, and observed to his companion that a little distance ahead they would find the amount of Elder Robertson's bill; and, sure enough, in a short distance another sum was found.

There are many instances of Elder Barber's success, like most pioneers, in turning the rough people with whom he had to deal. While baptizing in the Salamony River, a lady, sitting on a horse, was observed, weeping through the whole ceremony. When the audience was dismissed, the Elder asked of a neighbor the cause. The answer was, that the woman wanted to be baptized, but Tier husband, a very rough man, opposed it. The Elder, proposing to go to the house and reason with the husband, they tried to dissuade him, saying the man was a desperado; but he went, and by the time Elder Robertson and others reached the house the ruffian was overcome, and, with tears, he promised to do better, to seek the Lord, and never again to oppose his wife in her religious duties.

Elder Barber left a widow and several children. A son and a grandson, Elders Emerson Barber, of Missouri, and Myron Tyler, of Rhode Island, are taking the place of their faithful predecessor. Though dead he yet speaketh.

<u>NICHOLAS BARHAM (?—?)</u>

Nicholas Barham was a minister of prominence for many years in Chatham, Wake, Franklin, and Warren counties, N.C. Many were added to the church through his preaching. He labored as an itinerant minister for some time, and was highly respected by outsiders as well as members of the church. He died many years ago.

<u>DOLENA BARNS (?—?)</u>

This brother was a member of the Erie Conference, Pennsylvania, and a student at the Meadville Theological School from 1844 to 1846. He was an earnest, fluent speaker. His ministerial career was short, mostly confined to his own conference. Though a fellow-student of Elder Barns, I have not been able to find the precise date or particulars of his death.

<u>OLIVER BARR (?—1853)</u>

The public life of this brother covered a space of some twenty-seven years—from 1826 to 1853. His fields of labor may be classified as follows: The first seven years of his ministry, from 1826 to 1833, he labored in Chautauqua and adjoining counties in New York and Pennsylvania; from 1833 to 1841, in Conneaut, O.; from 1841 to 1843, in Honeoye Falls; and from 1843 till 1847, in Aurora, Ill. Such is the classification given in the "Palladium," May 21, 1853. The six years from 1847 till 1853, the time of his death, were years of fruitful labor.

All the knowledge I have of the Elder is, a slight acquaintance with the man during life, and what I gather from his and others' writings in our periodicals during a period of some twenty years.

When Elder Barr was converted, the probability is that his family lived in Western New York, and that none of them were members of the Christian Church. In July, 1832, he wrote to the "Palladium" of the baptism, by himself, of his brother and his wife, in Salem, (Conneaut,) O. He says: "To me, this was a good day, as from the time I united with the Christian Church I became a stranger to all my mother's children. When we got to the water, my brother turned to the pa altitude and confessed, that when I united with this people, who are everywhere spoken against, he considered me lost, that my presence was ever painful to him, and when I moved from the town where we had formerly lived, he was rejoiced, for he had considered me a disgrace, etc."

From this we gather that whatever religious connexion his family sustained they were bitterly opposed to the Christians. In 1837, the Elder joined the New York Western Conference. His progress in the ministry, at first, must have been slow, for it. is generally reported in his early field of labor that he was told repeatedly by the advocates of respectability in the ministry, that if he could earn his living by manual labor he had better try, for it was clear to all that he would never make a preacher.

During his seven years' life in Chautauqua County, N.Y., his labors must have been arduous, but his support was meager; and yet his disposition was such that he was never satisfied with half-way measures. Elder E.G. Holland says, in a sermon delivered on the occasion of Elder Barr's death: "Zeal was a property of his temperament, an attribute of his whole career in life. I once heard him say, 'I expect to meet a sudden death, when I die. The rush of blood to my head and other liabilities of my constitution lead me to think this.' At another time, he said, 'I have regarded myself these many years as a minute man, not knowing at what moment I may be called from duty.'" Speaking on the same subject, Elder E. Fay says: "For twenty years he had breasted such surges of affliction as would have intimidated and subdued a less courageous spirit. Three times he had been nearly killed by accidents, twice completely disabled by epileptic fits, which nearly •cost him his life, and once or twice entirely lost his voice and was driven in silence from the gospel field. For almost a year, in Conneaut, O., he was unable to ascend the pulpit except on his hands and knees,—which he did regularly,—in consequence of a paralysis in his limbs; and many times he has been carried from his sick bed to the sanctuary of God that he might pour out the pent up feelings of a burdened and holy heart."

In connection with the preceding, as illustrative of the same subject, I here introduce an extract of a letter written by himself to the "Palladium, March, 1841, when he had lost his voice. He says: "My health is good but my organs of speech have failed. I feel that I am a broken reed, yet I would desire to submit all to the direction of him in whose hand is the breath of life. I cannot describe my feelings when I look back upon the imperfection of my past labors in the cause of Christ, and see before me but little prospect for the future. I have prayed a thousand times that I might die in the gospel field. I have a desire with my last breath to proclaim the Lamb of God. Yet it may not be so. If I do not recover my voice I can preach but little. Well, let the storm rage and let the billows roll, let my voice be lost and all my mental powers fail, yet my Redeemer lives, and because he lives I shall live also—yes, though I die I shall live again; and though I sink in silence, Jesus will be preached, his gospel will triumph, and the church shall be redeemed."

The preceding noble sentiment, expressed by a true Christian spirit, man-ward is dark and gloomy, God-ward it is light and triumphant. However, for the Elder there were other and brighter days. Soon after this, we find, through his letters, that his voice is restored, and the same untiring zeal and ambition is. expressed. In all his letters, there is a constant appeal made for more laborers in his field. In 1837, he writes that Elders Nutt and McKee had been with him, but as they were leaving to enter other fields there was a territory in Western Pennsylvania and Eastern Ohio that had no preacher that he knew of within thirty miles east, fifty miles south, and one hundred and fifty miles west. In this territory, six churches are left destitute of ministerial labor. In the fall of 1835, with all the ministerial calls for scores of miles around, he yet had to work with his hands, preparatory for winter, for self and family. After working hard for a few weeks, he was struck down with paralysis.

In 1837, he went on a preaching tour to Michigan; from there he planned a missionary operation to assist in that new country. During this year, he attended the dedication of the Christian Church in

Conneaut, O. Whenever he wrote to our periodicals, he took in a wide field of operation, not only the church or churches where he himself labored, but all the churches and ministers for many miles around; this shows a large heart and cosmopolitan spirit.

In 1838, he attended a Union meeting with a Mr. Day, a Presbyterian minister, a man of large heart and catholic spirit. In this operation, Elder Barr's whole soul was enlisted. In 1839, we find him making a long trip to Maryland and Virginia for the recovery of his voice. Wherever he goes, however, the same anxiety for the prosperity of Zion is manifested in all his letters. He received much benefit from this trip.

His faith in God never failed. His frequent afflictions served to increase his faith in Providence. He was a warm advocate of the general measures of his own church, and a zealous reformer. The temperance, the anti-slavery, and other such movements found in him a warm advocate.

Such is a brief outline of the life and character of Brother Barr. His sudden death, by the shocking catastrophe at Norwalk, Conn., connected with the noble mission in which he was engaged was a fit sequel for such a man. Feeling the- great need of a Theological School among the Christians, he consented to act as an agent to raise an endowment for the purpose. From the character of the man, and the worthiness of the enterprise, all felt that it would prove a success. After laboring with considerable success in the West, he started on his mission to New England. Having spent a few Sundays in New York city, his former field of labor, he started to Boston on the 8 a. m. train, on May 6, 1853. He parted with his friends in New York in his usual cheerful manner. On the way to Boston, at Norwalk, Conn., a drawbridge having been left open for the passage of a vessel, and the signals not being understood by the engineer, the whole train, with its valuable cargo, was plunged into the surging waves; and Oliver Barr, the faithful servant of God, with many others, was ushered to eternity, without a moment's warning. "He died with his armor on," as he had "prayed a thousand times" that it might be so.

<u>Burwell Barrett (1769—1836)</u>

The subject of this sketch was the son of Edmond and Jannett Barrett, and was born April 3, 1769. In 1788, he married Lucy Tharp, after whose death he married Mrs. Nancy Davis, who survived him. He died of cancer in the face, September 5, 1836. In 1789, he joined the Methodist Church, and commenced preaching in that body; but, in 1794, he joined what was then called "O'Kelly's band" of radical Methodists. They soon adopted the name of Christians, and Mr. Barrett continued an active member of that body till the time of his death.

He was an energetic, zealous, and talented man, of strong, conscientious determination to discharge his entire duty, whether with the few or many. For many years before his death, he was looked upon as authority in church matters by those of his own denomination. His preaching was of the practical kind. His field of labor was mostly in South Hampton, Va.

<u>Mills Barrett (1788—1865)</u>

This, a son of the preceding, was born in South Hampton, Va., December 25, 1788. April 30, 1811, he was married to Sarah J. Smith, of whom he had six children, two of whom are now ministers—S.S. Barrett, of Norfolk, Va., and M.B. .Barrett, of Ivor, Va. One of his daughters married a minister, William R. Stowe, of Henry, Ill. His first wife died, September 22, 1844, and in 1845, he married Mrs. Nancy Boykin. He died at his residence in Isle of Wight County, Va., April 2, 1865, in his. seventy-seventh year.

Mills Barrett was converted about 1810, under the labors of his own father and Elder Joseph Thomas, the White Pilgrim. He commenced preaching soon after, and traveled for some time in company with Joseph Thomas. He at once took a positive stand as an advocate of Christian liberty. We can easily see how a young man of ardent disposition, trained under such leaders as Burwell Barrett, Joseph Thomas, and their contemporaries, should be filled with zeal in such a worthy cause. Such, we find our subject. He not only preached with fervency, but he took the pen, also, as his father had done and was doing, and in every way helped on the great work of reformation.

He traveled constantly in those early days, and soon became a powerful revivalist. After the organization of the Eastern Virginia Conference, he became its clerk—an office he held till compelled by old age to resign. During his ministry, he had charge of Wells Chapel, Barrett, Providence, Antioch, Cypress Chapel, and Spring Hill. As a writer, he was clear, terse, and comprehensive, full of matter, with enough of earnestness to impress the thought on the mind of the reader. For many years of his useful life, he was a representative man in his region of country.

His second wife died about one year before him. His son, Elder M.B. Barrett, says: "Father often spoke of death in his last years, but his sky was always clear." And why should it not be? Such a life could lead to nothing but a happy and triumphant death.

JOSEPH BARTLETT (1781—1861)

Joseph Bartlett was born in Brookfield, Mass., December 17, 1781. He moved to Vermont, with his parents, in 1783. He was converted in Kingston, Vermont, in 1792, and was baptized by Robinson Smith at Barnston, Lower Canada, in 1801. Soon after, he joined the Freewill Baptist Church. In 1809, he moved to Western New York, and for some time lost his interest in religion. In 1819, he began to preach, and in 1822, he joined the Christian Church in Collins, Erie County, N.Y. He labored for many years with that church; in the meantime, he traveled considerably in other states and Canada, and was ordained by Elders William True, Joseph Bailey, and Simon Bishop. Later, he moved to Southern Michigan.

He was a man of advanced ideas in regard to a better organization of churches and conferences. His health was often poor but his labors were quite extensive.

Z.S. Vail says, in the "Palladium," Vol. XVII, page 57: "The last years of his life were sad years. In August, 1846, he gathered his little all together, and took his family to White Pigeon, Mich., where, in a little over a year, he buried within a month of each other a wife and a daughter. It was a sickly season, in a new country, and the Elder himself was down with the ague and all his worldly means exhausted. Being assisted by brethren, he started on his way back to New York. At Maumee, O., his horse was maimed. After waiting eighteen days for the horse to become better, it was finally given up, and another animal was given him by his friends. Sick, tired, and discouraged, lonely and sad, with the companion of his youth and a lovely daughter buried in a strange country, he made his way, on April 12, 1848, to my home in York, Sandusky County, O."

He visited New York in 1860, where he had a warm welcome from the churches. He died in Alton, Kent County, Mich., about eighty years old.

THOMAS FRANCIS BARRY (?—1846)

Elder Barry was a young minister of great zeal and pure life. From his writings, it seems that he was a man of considerable knowledge, and a smooth fluent writer. He wrote frequently, but, like many others of our ministers, he was carried away with the current of Adventism; during several years of this period, he devoted most of his time to lecturing on the speedy coming of Christ. In this he was very successful, and great revivals followed his labors.

Elder Barry died, I believe, in some part of Western New York, while on a preaching tour. He had, in a measure, given up his Advent ideas, and if he had lived would, doubtless, have been a strong man in the church of his first choice. His widow has been for many years an efficient matron in the Tremont Street Orphan Asylum, in Boston.

All agree that whatever erroneous ideas he embraced in regard to the coming of Christ in 1843, he was honest and conscientious in what he considered to be the truth of revelation upon that subject. He was a man of small stature, conscientious in his advocacy of truth, and a plain, forcible, and clear speaker.

Miles Bascom (1801—1829)

This Brother was born in Milton, Vt., of poor parents, in 1801, and was converted in 1819. His field of labor, as a minister, was in Genesee and Monroe counties, N.Y. He was married to Miss Lydia Foster, of Byron, Genesee County, N.Y., in 1824. He had three children—one son and two daughters. He died of consumption, at Bergen, N.Y., August 28, 1829, aged twenty-eight years. He stood high in his profession, for so young a man.

Caleb Bates (1796—?)

Mr. Bates was a minister in Ohio. He was born in 1796, began to preach in 1817, joined the Shakers, left them in 1821, married a Shaker lady, and moved to one of the Eastern States where he labored faithfully in the Christian Church. He was a member of the Legislature for several terms. He was considered a good grammarian, and somewhat of a scholar and preacher.

Reuben Bates (?—1872)

Reuben Bates was a member of the South Wabash Christian Conference, in the State of Illinois. He baptized Elder Austin Hutson in 1848. He died the conference year preceding October, 1872. He was a faithful workman.

Anne Baton (?—?)

Anne Baton was a female laborer in the church, in Tuscarawas County, O.

John Batterall (1793—1845)

This Elder was born in Montgomery County, Va., in 1793. His father moved from Virginia to Miami County, O., when John was small. In 1806, John became deeply convicted of sin, but, like many others, he fought his convictions, and tried in every way to drown the voice of God in his heart. His burden of sin increased, however, till he was compelled to call for mercy. In 1812, he joined the army of his country, and served six months in the war.

In 1815, he was married, and soon after the old impression that he should preach, stifled for a time, came back with double power.

He finally yielded, and commenced preaching with the Freewill Baptists in Miami County. In 1831, he moved to Delaware County, Ind., joined the Christian Church, and in April, 1833, was ordained by Elders C. Vanausdall and H. Mossburg. From this time till death, he labored in this part of Indiana. The Elder was considered a good, zealous, and useful minister. He died in his prime, fifty-eight years of age, of erysipelas or black tongue, after a sickness of four and a half •days. We have no knowledge of his family. He had one son who has been an acceptable minister in the Christian Church for many years.

W.B. H. BEACH (1832—1875)

This was a young minister even when he died, yet, when we think of the many changes in that comparatively short life, we are impressed with the peculiar activity and energy of the man. He was born, near Rochester, N.Y., June 10, 1832, died at Cheshire, N.Y., January 13, 1875. His father died in 1842, when the son was ten years old. The family was in limited circumstances. The mother was left with four small children, William being the oldest. After struggling hard for two years, the mother followed the father to the spirit land, in 1844. At that time the family lived in Medina County, Ohio. The four small orphans were separated.

About this time, the subject of our sketch joined the Baptist Church, and in 1848, with a stout heart and four dollars, the boy of sixteen years left Ohio for the great city of New York, and arrived at his destination with ten cents. As usual in such cases, there was no work for the strange boy in the great city. He was nearly starving when brother Stratton, a member of the Christian Church, found him and took him to his own house and gave him employment. Here he first became acquainted with the Christians, through his kind guardian. He joined the church under the preaching of Elder William Lane.

In 1853, he entered the college at Oberlin, O., for the purpose of teaching, and, at the opening of Antioch College, in Yellow Springs, O., he entered there as a student and continued so for eighteen months. His object at this time was to acquire an education, he having no particular object in view. Soon, however, the work of the ministry presented itself to his mind, and he preached his first sermon in Stanfordville, N.Y. His first charge was in Columbia County, N.Y., where he was ordained in 1858. From this time till the close of life, his labors in the ministry were constant. He labored, as a pastor, with the churches of Warrenville, Day, Hartwick, South Westerloo, Starkey, Rock Stream, Naples, and Cheshire.

Beside his pastoral work, in which he was quite successful, he labored extensively in the general work of the church. He was the prime mover in the organization of the New York State Christian Association, and acted as president and agent of the same. He did much, also, in raising an endowment for Union Christian College, Merom, Ind., and for Starkey Seminary, Starkey, N.Y. It mattered not to him in what part of the country the cause required help, he was ready.

He was a conscientious man when it cost something to carry out his principles. When fourteen years of age, and very poor, he gave up a remunerative employment in a drug store rather than sell whisky to his fellow-men, contrary to his convictions.

At his death, he left a mourning wife and four small children. His death was a great shock to his fellow-laborers in the State of New York.

ASA BEAN (?—1838)

All I have found concerning this minister is a statement of Sister E.D. Allen, of Charlotteville, N.Y., that he died in Bangor, Me., May 13, 1838.

EDWARD BEAN (1795—1839)

We have no history of this Brother except the following dates. He was born in 1795, and died in Mercer, Me., aged forty-four years.

JEREMIAH BEAN (1783—1835)

The subject of this memoir was born in Gilman ton, N.H., in 1783. When he was a child, his parents moved to Redfield, Me. As he grew up he acquired great muscular power; his mind, also, was very strong. In 1801, he embraced religion, and soon after became a public speaker among the Freewill Baptists. He labored as a minister for some years with that people, but finally joined the Christians, with whom he continued as a faithful minister until death. He was a member of the Kennebeck Christian Conference, and was considered by all a man of talent and great integrity. His usefulness as a minister, however, was, to a great extent, diminished on account of the asthma—a disease that affected him seriously for a long time.

The death of this good man was very singular. On the sixth of January, 1835, he rose from his bed as usual and prayed with his family; but about 10 A.M. he told his friends that "nature must yield." He then lay down, closed his eyes, and expired, aged fifty-two years. His funeral was attended by a large concourse of people, when a discourse was delivered by Elder Josiah Bradley.

MOSES BEAN (?—?)

In the "Christian Journal," Vol. IV, page 55, I find this short notice of Elder Bean: "Died in St. Joseph, Mich., Elder Moses Bean, formerly of Candia, this state."

WILLIAM BECK (?—?)

William Beck was a young minister of great moral worth and considerable talent. His labors were mostly confined to Boon and Montgomery counties, Ind. He was raised in Union County, Ind. He married young, and soon after commenced laboring as a public gift in the above mentioned counties. He was ordained in 1858. His home was in Boon County, oh a farm, not far from Thornton. He joined the Western Indiana Conference, and, I believe, was ordained in that body. He was very zealous, and though his education was limited, yet his upright life, his zeal, and his self-sacrificing nature made him an useful man. He died early—perhaps 1860—leaving a family and large number of friends to mourn his departure.

JOHN BELDING (?—?)

John Belding was a minister that labored in New Bedford, Mass., and vicinity, and died there some years ago.

NEWMAN BENSON (1808—1848)

This is one of the many ministers who found resting places in the old grave-yard at Conneaut, O. He was for some time of a skeptical turn of mind; but when convinced of the truth of Christianity, he became a strong advocate of the same. I think he was a spiritual child of Oliver Barr. He was ordained May 2, 1844, at Conneaut, O. Sermon by E.G. Holland; other parts by Professor Huidekoper, and Elders Fish and Church.

Elder Badger, in a letter to the "Palladium," Vol. XVI, page 37, speaks of Elder Benson as a man of good talent and upright life, and that he had labored with the church at Conneaut in 1847 with great success. He died about 1848, in the prime of life, not far from forty years of age.

JOSEPH BERRY (?—1834)

This brother was a Southern man. He lived, labored, and died in the State of Louisiana. His death took place September 29, 1834.

HENRY BIGLOW (?—1869)

This brother was a licentiate in the Eel River Indiana Christian Conference. He died in 1869.

? BIGLOW (?-1876)

This brother was a member of the North-western Ohio Christian Conference, and died the conference year preceding September, 1876.

ROGER BINGHAM (?—?)

In the early days of the Christians in Rhode Island and Connecticut, the name of this Elder was frequently mentioned. Elder James Burlingame, of Coventry, R.I., writes: "Elder Bingham was a man of talent, respectability, and wealth; but during his long life he never traveled- far from home."

THOMAS BIRD (?—?)

In an early day, there was a minister of the above name who labored in Kentucky.

DAVID BIRELY (1823—1858)

This minister was a member of the Miami Christian Conference, and lived in Miami County, O. When quite young, he lost his father. He sought the Savior under the preaching of Elder John Williams, of whose family he was a member. In his ministerial career he first joined the Tippecanoe Indiana Christian Conference but was transferred to the Miami Christian Conference.

He died January 10, 1858, of typhoid fever, about thirty- five years old. At the time of his death, he was pastor of the church on Ludlow creek, where he was buried. His death was deeply felt by the churches of Hopewell, Ludlow Creek, and Granville Creek, where he labored.

? BISHOP (?—1850)

Bishop was the name of a minister of the Central Conference, O., who lived near Sunbury, and died not far from 1850.

Joseph Blackmar (1800—1878)

This minister was born in Dudley, Mass., March 13, 1800. In 1801, his parents moved to Greene County, N.Y. In 1817 and '18, Joseph attended the Greeneville Academy, and in 1818, he attended Hamilton College. In September of the same year, he buried his mother. In 1821, he joined the Methodists, and in 1822, was baptized by pouring; this same year he was licensed to preach. Soon, however, he became dissatisfied with his baptism, and other doctrines and usages of the Methodists, and traveled several miles to consult with Richard Davis, a Christian preacher, who baptized him by immersion. At once, he commenced laboring with the Christians in and around Scipio, N.Y. Hitherto, he had supported himself by teaching.

In 1834, he concluded to devote his whole time to the ministry. At this time, he was near Conneaut, O. In company with Elder Jesse E. Church, he went to Canada, where he remained thirty-two months. In 1833, he was married to Eliza Jane Philbrick, of Andover, N.H. At this time, in summing up the labor of nine years, he found that he had traveled 23,717 miles, that he had preached 1,730 sermons, that he had attended 1,350. additional meetings, that he had baptized seventy-six persons, and married seven couples. For all this time his compensation was next to nothing, as he peremptorily refused any donation from non-professors, and asked nothing of church members. After this, he felt that, others were dependent upon him for support, and that he should be compensated for his labors.

As the support from ministerial labor was insufficient he turned his attention to business. The time from 1835 to 1844 —nine-and-a-half years—he spent in Philadelphia engaged in various pursuits —teaching, publishing books, peddling, and raising silk worms and mulberry trees. In these transactions, he made thousands of dollars and lost them again. In 1849, he moved to Boston, Mass., where he continued the balance of his life.

Few men have passed through more changes than this Elder. In early life, he had the advantages of property. For nine or ten years he endured the greatest self-sacrifice for the sake of doing good; part of this time was spent in Ohio, Canada, New York, and New England. After his marriage he was sometimes in affluence and at other times in poverty; for some years before he died he was in good circumstances. His views, also, underwent many changes. In early life, his views on religion were of an impracticable kind, as to revivals and finances; but he worked faithfully to his convictions and never murmured. Later in life his religious views were liberal and very practicable. An article of his, published in the *Herald* of 1866, on revivals, is full of good sense. He was always cheerful, active, and ingenious. Both he and his companion worked through life for the benefit of the young—training them for life's work, in Sunday Schools and in the temperance cause. They were useful in life and happy in death.

<u>WILLIAM BLAISDELL (1783—1854)</u>

William Blaisdell was born in Southampton, N.H., January 7, 1783. He was taken by his parents to Gilmanton, N.H., when about five years old. He was converted in 1805, and soon commenced his labors in the ministry, among the Freewill Baptists. He soon heard of the Christians, met and joined them, and continued an active member of that church through life. He was married to Betsy Martin, daughter of Elder Richard Martin and sister of Elder C.W. Martin. When he commenced preaching, he was teaching school in Gilmanton, and preached his first sermon in the school house where he taught.

October 9, 1809, he was ordained to the full work of the ministry by Elders Elias Smith, Richard Martin, and others. He continued to preach in Gilmanton and the surrounding churches for about thirty years—with occasional visits to the churches of Sandwich, Barnstead, Meredith, Sanbornton, Canterbury, Candia, London, Stafford, Allentown, etc., in New Hampshire with occasional preaching tours through Vermont.

In 1839, he moved to Tufftonborough and took charge of that church. He continued his labors with this church until 1841, and preached there and with the surrounding churches until August 7, 1853, when he preached his last sermon at Wolfsborough, from Rev. 20:4th and 5th verses. He died October 23, 1853, of inflammation of the stomach, aged seventy- one years. He left a widow, ten children, and a host of friends- to mourn his departure.

From letters in my possession, from Elder Simeon Swett, and others of Elder Blaisdell's acquaintance, I understand that he was a well-proportioned man, tall and of commanding appearance. His voice was feeble, smooth, and musical. He was free and easy in conversation, modest and deferential, yet graceful in his manners. He was a companionable associate and an impressible speaker, convincing all of sincerity of purpose and goodness of heart. His library, though not large, was choice. He seldom attempted to present a subject without previous examination. His preaching was extemporaneous though studied. He stood high in the estimation of his neighbors, both as a minister and as a civilian. Beside receiving from him the message of grace as from a messenger of Christ, they elected him to several offices of trust and honor as a civilian. He served as a town clerk for twenty-one years, and represented them in the Legislature for some time.

It is probable that Elder Blaisdell had some weaknesses, as he was a man; but, from all the accounts I have been able to gather concerning his history, he must have possessed a good heart and a well-balanced mind.

LEWIS BLAKE (?—1877)

This brother was a member of the Ohio Christian Conference. He died preceding the conference session of August, 1877.

WILLIAM BLANCHARD (?—1868)

This minister was a pioneer of the church in Illinois, and was one of the organizers of the Spoon River Illinois Christian Conference. Elder Isaac Goff says of him: "He was one of our first ministers, and best of men. He died in 1868." He himself writes to the "Palladium," Vol. X, page 239, (July 24, 1841,) that a few years before he knew of no members of the Christian Church in all the country. Now he had organized a Christian Church of nineteen members (near Princeville, Peoria County, Ill) of which four of his own children were members. He may be called the father of the Spoon River Conference.

JOSEPH H. BLAND (?—?)

Brother Bland was one of the ministers of the North Carolina Conference from 1800 to 1820. He used to visit Elder John Hayes.

HENRY BLISS (1790—1872)

This Brother was born in the eastern part of the State of New York, October 5, 1790. In early life, he embraced religion, and joined the Baptist Church. In 1831, he became acquainted with the Christian Church, and under the preaching of Elder Oliver Barr he was convinced that its people held a correct view of the Bible. He joined the church, in which he continued faithful to the end of his long life.

In 1838, he left the State of New York and moved to Pec- ria County, Ill., then a thinly settled country. Soon he found brethren of his own faith, and with them he joined in worship. He joined the church where Elder John Scott was preaching, and was soon set apart to the work of the ministry, being ordained by Elder Scott and others. July 6, 1839, he wrote back through the "Palladium" to his friends in [Chautauqua County, N.Y.: "I left Chautauqua County a year ago last March for Illinois, and arrived at Peoria the fourth day of May. I set up a meeting in my own house immediately on arriving here. I have preached to good effect, I trust, in private houses of Presbyterians, Baptists, and Methodists. Five weeks ago, I went west twenty-seven miles to Knox County where I had a meeting. The next day, we had a meeting at Maquon; we had two divisions—one by myself, and one by Elder John Scott. It was the happiest day I ever saw."

What the labors of this Elder were from 1839 to 1872, the time of his death, we do not know.

Elder Blanchard, who wrote his biography, which was published in the *Herald of Gospel Liberty,* September, 1872, says that for some time the old father was kept much at home by the sickness of his wife, who was subject to fits. He died At the house of his son, in Peoria County, Ill., September 14, 1872, eighty-two years old.

JOHN BLODGET (?—1826)

Few men in the Christian Church have been more sincerely and universally respected than the subject of this sketch. Most of the writers to our periodicals mention the names of Blodget and Lawrence as two of our most prominent men, who died in the same place (Conneaut) and were buried side by side. From the information I could gather, Elder Blodget came from some of the New England States, probably New Hampshire, to New York and Ohio. In the "Memoirs of Elder Joseph Badger," page 185, we find that Elder Blodget accompanied Mr. Badger from New Hampshire to New York, in 1817. On page 187 we find that Mr. Blodget was ordained at Pittsford, N.Y., August 30, 1817, at a general meeting.

He moved to Conneaut, O., and became the pastor of the church there. He was very successful, and was highly esteemed by the people. September- 25, 1826, he died at his post, leaving a wife and three children to mourn his early departure.

IRA BONNER (1800—1851)

This Elder was born in 1800. He commenced his ministerial labors in the bounds of the Michigan Western Christian Conference, of which he was a member. He was ordained while on a visit to New York as an evangelist. He labored faithfully as a minister for a few years, and died in Kinderhook, Branch County, Mich., January 12, 1851, in his fifty-first year.

JOSEPH BOODY (1773—1860)

From a statement made by Elder Moses Howe, of New Bedford, Mass., who was well acquainted with this brother, I find that Joseph was born in 1773. He embraced religion and was ordained to the ministry among the Baptists. He joined the Christian Church at an early day, and was a co-laborer in New England with Abner Jones, Elias Smith and others. He was one of the ministers who assisted in the ordination of John Band, in 1806— the first minister ordained among the Christians as a distinct people.

Elder Boody's home was in Durham, N.H., where he officiated as pastor of the church. He died there in 1860, eighty-seven years of age. In person, he was full six feet tall, and quite heavy. His education was good, for those times. His social powers were great. He was full of anecdotes, lively and cheerful, and a great friend of children, who were drawn to him on account of his mild and loving disposition.

JOHN BOOTHBY (1781—1878)

This brother was born October 1, 1781, and died in Saco, Me., April 4, 1878. About 1800, he was converted, and was baptized by Elder John Buzzell. October 12, 1812, he was ordained by Elders Henry Frost and Moses Rollins.

This was one of our oldest ministers in New England. At his funeral, in Saco, there were some twelve ministers present. They all spoke feelingly of the labors of the old patriarch, and how faithful he had been in a ministry of more than sixty-eight years. All of them had looked upon him as a pillar, and his death at the advanced age of ninety-six years was considered a great loss.

JOHN BOREN (?—1871)

John Boren was a minister who labored in the south-western part of Indiana, and died in 1871.

ISAAC BOUSER (?—1878)

Isaac Bouser was a member of the Ohio Eastern Conference, and died about 1878.

JACOB BOWEN (?—?)

June 1, 1817, this Brother was ordained at Coventry, R.I., in company with Caleb Morse and Archibald Bates, the board of Elders consisting of Douglass, Farnum, Nathaniel Burlingame, Joshua Perkins, and Henry Brown. Archibald Bates says that Bowen was a single man at the time of his ordination, and that he died soon after.

WILLIAM BOWMAN (?—1861)

This brother was a member of the Bluffton Indiana Christian Conference. He lived and labored in Delaware, Wells, and Bluffton counties, Ind. He was a good and useful man, but his labors were chiefly local.

JOHN BOWMAN (?—1829)

Barton W. Stone speaks of this minister, in the *Christian Messenger,* Vol. HI, page 96, as follows: "Died at his residence, near Murfreesborough, Tenn., the 7th of January, 1829, Elder John Bowman. He died the third day of his illness, perfectly composed and resigned to the will of God. With him, the editor (Elder Stone) has enjoyed an acquaintance of thirty-five years. He was educated and ordained a Presbyterian minister in North Carolina a short time before my acquaintance with him. Some years after, he moved his family to Tennessee, and united with the church of Christ, to which he was truly a father and guides His piety and good sense were never disputed."

SAMUEL BOYD (?—?)

This minister lived and died in Wayne County, Ind. He died at the age of eighty-one years.

DANIEL BOYER (1825—1853)

This Elder was of German descent, his father being the pastor of a German church in Crawford County,. Pa. In his youth, he joined the Methodist Chu.ch, and continued a member of that body till after his entrance into the Meadville Theological School. He was a printer by trade, which made him a correct and fluent writer. At the opening of the school in 1844, he entered it as a Methodist. He soon changed his views on the use of creeds and confession, and during his three years stay in Meadville he was quite liberal.

After his graduation, in 1847, it was his intention to visit New England as a candidate; but on his way, he settled in Rock Stream, and took the charge of the church in that place, and of another church at Sellonton, in the same county— Yates. In this, his first field of labor, he had considerable success. There were several additions at Rock Stream, and over twenty at Sellonton. During this time, also, he was married to a daughter of Elder Ezra Marvin, of Rock Stream, and became a member of the New York Central Christian Conference. After continuing in his first field of labor three years, he spent one year at Jefferson, N.Y., when he received a call to visit a Unitarian congregation, at Cannelton, on the Ohio River, in Indiana. During his labor of two years in this place, a church was organized, and the prospect before him was quite flattering; but, in the midst of his usefulness, he was cut down by the fell destroyer. He died February 24, 1853, aged twenty-eight years.

DANIEL BRACKETT (?—1865)

This brother was a member of the New York Western Christian Conference, and lived at Clarendon, in the same state. Farming was his occupation. His education was limited, but he was an efficient exhorter. He died in 1865.

J.L. BRADBURY (?—1867)

J.L. Bradbury was a member of the Bluffton Conference, Ind., and died in 1867.

HENRY S. BRADFORD (1806—1845)

In the *Gospel Herald*, Vol. HI, page 366, is given an account of this brother. In 1809, he was born, near Seneca Lake, N.Y. His father died when he was young. In his nineteenth year, he made a profession of religion, and soon after began to preach, being quite successful in the conversion of sinners. About 1832, he moved to Ohio, and in 1839, took charge of the churches of Williamsport and Mt. Sterling. Of these churches he continued pastor for three or four years. From 1837 to 1841, he wrote to the "Palladium," from Williamsport, O.,. In most of his letters he gave accounts of large additions to the church. In one letter, he writes of great excitement in the place about a discussion on the doctrine of the Trinity; the champions in this discussion were Elder Perkins, of the Christian Church, and the Presiding Elder of the M.E. Church. In the last years of his stay in Williamsport, he devoted the most of his time to teaching school. He held the office of a clerk to the Deer Creek Ohio Conference for several years, and was very active in improving the organization of the conference and churches.

July 29, 1845, he left Williamsport with his family to take a tour through Indiana and Illinois, with the intention of leaving the latter in the neighborhood of Knob Prairie church, in Clark County, O. At the house of Elder M.D. Baker, he was taken sick, and continued growing worse till the 22nd or 23rd of August when he died, aged thirty-nine years.

JOSIAH BRADLEY (?—?)

Josiah and Jonathan Bradley are always spoken of together. They lived in the same part of the State of Maine; they were both at the ordination of Prescott and Clough; they were probably brothers. Elder W.H. Nason, of West Springfield, N.H., says of the Bradleys, 1873, "They were elderly men forty years ago.'

JOHNATHAN BRADLEY (1770—1839)

Elder J.B. Prescott writes: "Elder Bradley was born in 1770, and died in Vienna, Me., October 21, 1839. His disease was dumb palsy. He was one of the first in Kennebeck who came out and took the grounds of the Christians, disowning all other names." Elder Prescott speaks of him as a talented and useful minister, and a worthy citizen.

In the "Life of Elder Prescott," page 84, I find that Elder Bradley baptized Elder Simon Clough in Monmouth, Me., in 1817, and that he was one of the committee in the ordination of Prescott and Clough, November 2, 1817.

W.N. BRAGG (?—?)

This was an active, zealous minister of the North Carolina Christian Conference. He died in North Carolina about the close of the War of the Rebellion.

MARTIN P. BRALEY (1802—1872)

From a statement of Elder A.G. Morton we find the following. This brother was born in 1802, was converted in 1822, and began to preach a few years after. His health failed, and it was his lot to suffer for many years. November, 17, 1872, he died, in Dighton, Mass.

A. BRANSON (?—?)

This was a Christian minister in Kentucky, in 1804 and '5. He stood firm against the Shaker influence in the church about that time.

ABRAM BRAYSHAW (?—1855)

Joshua L. Johnson, of Merom, Ind., states that this brother had died in 1855. He was a faithful minister in the Southern Wabash Conference, Ill.

ALEXANDER BRIGGS (?—1851)

This brother was a member of the Tippecanoe Christian Conference, Ind., and lived in White County, the same state. He was a devoted man. He died about the year 1851, in middle age.

MARK D. BRINEY (1810—1876)

This Elder was born in Warren County, O., October 8, 1810. Soon he was left an orphan. Withal, however, the boy managed to care for himself, and to acquire a reasonable education. While young, he embraced religion, and in 1833, he began to preach. Soon he became an efficient preacher, and had charge of several churches, beside laboring extensively as a missionary, as was the custom with most ministers of Ohio in that day. October 29, 1840, he married Miss Amanda Ebersole, who was well qualified for the position of a pastor's wife.

The latter years of his life were devoted mainly to farming, in Champaign County, O. He was forced to this in order to support his large family; yet his interest in his conference— the Central Ohio—never failed. Every year he attended many meetings, and often had charge of congregations. May 10, 1876, he died, at Woodstock, O., leaving a wife and nine children to mourn their loss.

Elder Briney was a man of great earnestness; whatever he found to do he did with all his might. He was a plain spoken man—so much so that sometimes he made enemies; but he had a kind heart, and was a zealous advocate of his church.

BENJAMIN BRITTON (1779—1860)

This was one of our oldest ministers in Ohio. He was born in Frederick County, Virginia, September, 13, 1779. Married Eliza-beth Grace, December 23, 1799, a lady of great piety and zeal. She walked seven miles to invite Noah Fiddler, a Methodist preacher, to preach in the neighborhood, under whose preaching her husband was converted. Mr. Britton moved to Ohio in 1807, and settled in Franklin County. He was a local preacher in the Methodist Church. When he met the Christians, and heard them state their views, he preferred them and he and his wife joined the latter church in an early day. He labored extensively through Ohio, Indiana, Illinois and Kentucky. He preached fifty-nine years and died September 26, 1860.

As was customary in his day, he was strong in the advocacy of the doctrines of his church, and very useful in building up churches and adding strength to the denomination in the days of its weakness.

DANIEL BROMLEY (1775—1858)

Elder Bromley was a member of the New York Western Conference. He died February 4, 1858, eighty-three years old.

JOHN W. BROWN (?—1875)

Elder Brown was born not far from 1808, yet when sixty-six years old he did not look older than a man of fifty. It is probable he was born and brought up in Virginia. As early as 1845 he was an active member in the Central Ohio Christian Conference, where he continued to labor for many years longer. His last labor in Ohio was in the bounds of the Eastern and Ohio Conferences, where he was very successful as a worker. Indeed, he was a leading man in that region of the state.

About 1872 or '73, he moved his family to the Shenandoah Valley, Va., where he labored most faithfully among the scattered churches in that region. He died there in 1875. Elder Brown, in many respects, was a peculiar man. Early in life he devoted his entire self to the ministry of the Christian Church. As such, he improved his natural talent by labor. He became well acquainted with all the doings of the denomination. In the general measures of the church he was always thoroughly enlisted, and was prompt to commend them to the churches where he labored. As a man, Elder Brown was genial and pleasant in his companionship. He was thoroughly denominational. His education was quite respectable, acquired, likely, in his work. As a speaker, he was easy and fluent in delivery, and always manifested great anxiety in the welfare of his people. As a missionary he excelled. He was married twice and brought up a large family of children. As stated before, he looked much younger than his real age would indicate. In a word, Elder Brown was a good man. His loss was greatly felt by the churches.

HENRY BROWN (?—?)

This brother assisted in the ordination of Caleb Morse, Archibald Bates, and Jacob Bowen, at Coventry, R.I., June 1, 1817. He lived and died in Coventry.

JOHN BROWN (?—?)

In the "Christian Palladium," Vol. XIV, page 157, it is stated that Elder Brown was raised in New Hampshire, was converted in 1842, and commenced preaching- soon after. As he was a young man of much information, with a good heart, and a fluent speaker, he took a high position at once. In 1845, he was at Naples, N.Y. In 1849, he took charge of a church in New Bedford. Soon after, he died. He was a good preacher and an excellent man.

JOHN BROWN (?—?)

This was a Kentucky preacher in an early day, a fellow-laborer of David Douglass and others.

ASBURY K. BROWNING (1843—1865)

Elder B.A. Cooper, of Clearville, Pa., furnishes the following. "Asbury was born in Maryland, in 1813, embraced religion in 1854 or '55, and gave great promise for one so young. In 1861, he was licensed to preach, in 1861, he was ordained, and in 1863, he took charge of the churches west of the mountain, in Pennsylvania, where for a year he did great good. As he was a strong Union man in those days of war and treason, he offended some of his congregations. In consequence of this, he went home, sold his horse and started to Antioch College, Yellow Springs, O. There he continued his studies until the summer vacation of 1864, when he hired out in harvest to bind after a reaper. The exertion was too much for him, as it produced rupture of the lungs, which terminated his life in April, 1865."

<u>RUFUS BRUCE (1775—1849)</u>

Christian "Palladium," Vol. XVIII, page 162, gives the following: "Elder Bruce was born in 1775, and died May 6, 1849, at Chester Vt. He buried his wife a short time before. He was a faithful, good man.

<u>JESSE BRUMFIELD (1798—1855)</u>

Jesse was born in Rockingham County, Va., brought up near the Natural Bridge, was converted under the labors of Elder Joseph Thomas, the "White Pilgrim," was baptized by him in 1820, and soon after began to exhort. May 14, 1822, he was married to Miss Sarah Davis, of the Shenandoah Valley, who was a faithful helpmate to him. The same month, he moved to Fairfield County, O., where he at once organized a Christian Church in connection with Elders Palmer, Britton, Patterson, and others. In this county and Ross, he labored extensively, and with great success, until 1830, when he moved to Randolph County, Ind., and settled on a piece of land he had purchased in the forest. Here, also, in connection with his labor of clearing the forest for a home, he preached to his neighbors, soon organizing the churches of Green's Fork, White River, Fairview, Bethel, and others; his co-laborers at this time being Elders Barber and Harland. In 1838, he was ordained by Elders Barber, Ashley, and others. At one time during these revivals, Brother Pleasant Bales came to Elder Brumfield's house at midnight, requesting the Elder to baptize himself and wife. The ceremony was performed at once. In 1853, our subject moved, with a part of his family, to Dallas County, Iowa. His health was failing fast and he returned the next year to his home in Indiana, and August 11, 1855, he died in the triumph of the faith he had preached so earnestly to others.

<u>CHARLES BRYANT (1822—1861)</u>

Charles Bryant was born in South Reading, Mass., February 2, 1822, and was the youngest of eleven children. When four years old his parents moved to Charleston, Mass., where Charles attended school. After studying for some time in the Grammar school in Charleston, he learnt the business of shoemaking. He had strong impressions to preach when twelve years old, but after leaving school he fell into bad company, and this impression left him for a time. In 1839, he clerked in a shoe store, and through the influence of some of the members of Elder Himes' church in Boston, and his sister, Julia Bryant, who was converted under the preaching of Elder Himes, he was led to attend meetings in that church. Before this time he had been very wild, so far even as to using profane language, but Elder Himes' conversation had a great influence in his reformation. February, 1840, he was converted under the labors of Elder Himes, and the July following he preached his first sermon in Portland, Me. After this, he spent six months in traveling through Kittery, Saco, Portland, Wells and Kennebunk, Me.

January, 1841, his means having been exhausted, he went back to South Reading, to work at his trade, and earn money. During this time he attended the Baptist Church, but about 1841 he became cold. Soon after this the great Advent excitement swept through the land and Elder Bryant was reconverted, and at once began preaching with the Adventists with great ardor and continued in this connection until the close of 1843; when the predicted time for the personal coming of Christ had passed he gave up Adventism. In 1844, he was ordained by Elder Lincoln, Edmund, Russel, and Haley and soon after he lost his voice in a measure and quit preaching. In March, 1845, he settled as pastor in Portsmouth, R.I. July 1, 1845, he was married to Miss J. Frances Wright, daughter of N.C. Wright, in whose house he had become a boarder in his Advent preaching of 1843. From this time his life work begins in earnest. He left Portsmouth, R.I., October 13, 1849, and moved to Somerset, Mass., where he continued three years. He was very minute in his accounts. At the close of the year 1847, he had preached 183 sermons; seven funerals, married two couple, baptized six, gave the hand of fellowship to six, sat in one ecclesiastical council, assisted .in the organization of a church, and held two protracted meetings. He 1 ad several revivals in Somerset. October

1, 1849, leaving Somerset, he moved to Eastport, Me., where he continued until October 1853. Daring this time he had it spell of bleeding at the lungs. From Eastport he went to South Reading to resuscitate, but he was called to Portsmouth, N.H. He continued in Portsmouth until May, 1854, when at the New England Convention of that year, he engaged in the Home Missionary Society of that body, leaving his family at South Reading, Mass.

November 12, 1854, he moved to Saundersville, Mass., where he continued to labor for more than four years, and during this time he also became a corresponding editor of the *Herald of Gospel Liberty.* During these four years he enjoyed good health, and had good success in his ministry. January 28, 1859, he went to Skowhegan, Me., on trial, and March 1, he moved his family where he continued to labor until the close of his mortal career. Sunday, December 22, 1861, he complained of sore throat, but preached twice, as usual, and married a couple the same day. His disease proved to be the diphtheria, which grew worse and worse, until the 26th,'when it terminated fatally. He bore his sufferings with great patience, and when he became sensible that his time on earth was short, he requested his companion to trust in God,, and it would be well. *f* O.E. Bryant labored in New Jersey and Pennsylvania about 1832 to '36. He moved to Vernon, N.Y., about 1839.

WILLIAM M. BRYANT (1879—1874)

Mr. Bryant was born July 9, 1793, and died in Kennebunk Port, Me., January 9, 1874. He commenced preaching in 1834, and preached fifty years. He was a school teacher for thirty-five years. He held all the offices in the town where he died, and was a citizen in the same for forty-five years. He was a zealous worker in the cause of temperance, education, morality and religion. He died suddenly of heart disease in his eighty-first year.

CHARLES BUGBY (1831—1865)

This brother died in Ashley, Me., July 7, 1865, aged thirty-four years.

? BULLARD (?—?)

Brother Bullard was a minister that labored, for a while, in one of the New England States. He afterward moved to one of the Southern States, and died there.

ISAAC N. BULLINGTON (?—?)

Brother Bullington was a member of the Central Illinois Christian Conference, and was present at its organization.

LEWIS BULLOCK (1814—1852)

From the "Christian Palladium," Vol. XX, page 768, we learn that this brother was born in 1814, embraced religion in Chautauqua County, N.Y., and there commenced Ins labors in the ministry. In 1840, he was ordained in Ellington, Chautauqua County, N.Y. Soon after, he moved with his family to the northern part of Illinois. Here he suffered much with disease, and from the constant illness of his family. Hoping to improve the health of his wife, in the Fall of 1851, he went back on a visit to his old friends in New York, and died at New Albion, Cattaragus County, N.Y., of typhoid fever, February 10, 1852, aged thirty-eight years. Elder Barr speaks of him as a modest, timid and very devoted man of God. During his stay in Illinois, he was clerk for several years of the Northern Illinois, and Wisconsin Christian Conference. He wrote frequently for the "Christian Palladium" and other periodicals. His letters are marked with ability, clearness and great zeal in the cause. Though far from home, he died calmly in the triumph of faith.

JAMES BURBRIDGE (?—?)

This brother was a companion of George Alkire and others in the Deer Creek Conference, Ohio, until the fall of 1837, when he moved to Highland, Pike County, 111. For a while belabored with great earnestness in organizing churches, having but one young preacher by the name of Gale, twelve miles away, as a co-worker. But like Alkire, and some others, he partially embraced the Disciple doctrine of "Baptism for the remission of sins," and his labors were in a measure lost to the Christian Church. He was a man of much ability as a preacher, and had been very useful in building up the cause in Ohio. He was a good writer, also, and in early days he wrote much for our periodicals.

<u>ASA BURDICK (1773—1868)</u>

From a sermon and a letter of D.E. Milliard, of Jackson, Mich., we gather the following particulars of this aged veteran. The sermon was preached by Elder Millard on the death of Father Burdick. Elder Burdick was born in Rhode Island, November 26, 1773. Was married to Miss Patty Cheeseboroug, in the town of Brooklyn, N.Y., November 26, 1806. His wife died May 26, 1862, and the Elder died January, 1868, in his eighty-fifth year. In 1806, he joined the Methodist Church, and eight months afterward, on becoming acquainted with the Christians he joined them and continued in that connection until death; with the exception of a few years, he labored with the Seventh-Day Baptists. He was ordained in Brooklyn, Madison County, N.Y., October 10, 1817.

In 1834, he moved to Michigan, and for nearly thirty years lived in the vicinity of Jackson.

As a minister, he never made preaching his exclusive business, seldom had charge of a church, never received much remuneration for his labors, and never kept a record of his work; yet he had a place. He was very spiritual, devoted and cheerful, a great help in protracted meetings, and prompt in his attendance at the sessions of conference. Though old and in poor health, he was always welcomed by his brethren, and was missed by them when he went to his final home.

<u>P. BURDICK (?—1877)</u>

Elder Burdick was a member of the Tioga Christian Conference, Pa. Sermon before the Conference by Elder Cheseman.

HENRY BURGER (?—?)

Henry Burger was one of those who withdrew with Elder O'Kelly from the Methodist Church in 1793.

H.B. BURGES (?—1876)

This brother died at Bement, Ill., in 1876. He was then, and had been for several years a prominent member of the Illinois Central Christian Conference. In 1849, he lived in Henry, Ill. He had commenced preaching a short time before this. Soon after, he attended the Theological School at Meadville. From this time till his death, he was a prominent worker in the church. He was a man of more than ordinary talent, and was highly esteemed by his brethren in the conference. He left a| widow and children.

ABEL BURK (1793—1817)

This brother had a short race from the time of his conversion to his death. He was born in Windsor, Vt., in 1793, was converted in Woodstock under the preaching of Elder Frederick Plummer, and, to the surprise of many, he commenced preaching soon after. Soon, he became an efficient preacher, especially in revivals. Many date their conversion under God to the labors of this earnest man. While visiting his spiritual father, Elder Plummer, in the city of Philadelphia, Pa., he took the smallpox, and died there in a few days. He was buried in the grave-yard of the old Mt. Zion chapel. Scores of his fellow ministers, since 1817, have read with solemnity the writing on that humble *stone* in the corner of the yard with the quaint expression of "his faith in God anti the Christian connexion." His age,, when he died, was twenty-four years.

DAVID BURK (1779—1866)

This brother was born in 1779, and died in Darlington, Canada West, August 9, 1866r near which place he had lived about seventy years. He had been preaching since 1800. First for the Baptist, next for the- Disciples. In 1825, he joined the Christians, under the preaching of J.T. Bailey, and J. Blackmar. He assisted in the ordination of Elder Seth Marvin. Was acquainted with Elder Thomas Henry for fifty-six years. Was in good circumstances,, and never took a dollar for his preaching.

ABRAM BURKET (?—1878)

This was an elderly minister, and a member of the Eel River Christian Conference. He died in 1878 or '79.

AMBROSE BURLINGAME (1804—1864)

This minister was born in Sterling, Conn., in 1804. When a boy, his father moved to Smithfield, Bradford County, Penn. In this place, in youth, he experienced religion and soon after, while on a visit to his native state, he was baptized by his cousin, Elder James Burlingame, of Rhode Island. In 1827, we find him full of fire, at a general meeting at Caroline, N.Y. His preaching was powerful in the conversion of sinners. About this time, after preaching, on a rainy night, he lost his way in the woods, where he remained all night and took a severe cold.

He married Miss Sally Chamberlaine, of Smithfield, Pa., where he labored about three years. In 1830, he moved back to Virgil, N.Y., and, some years later, to Parma, Monroe County, and preached in that and the surrounding counties, to good acceptance for some time. Afterwards, he moved to Lyndonville, where he remained four or five years, and buried his beloved companion and two children. He was left with two small children, the remnant of his family, to fight the battles of life alone, but he trusted in his Heavenly Father. At this time, he traveled extensively in Pennsylvania and New York. In August, 1848, he was married to Mrs. Margaret Howard, in Virgil, where he remained about four years, when he moved to Parma again, and from there to Chemung; he traveled six months through the New England States. After this, he labored in Stafford, Parma, Virgil, and Hafford's Mills, where he died October 7, 1864, leaving a widow and the two children of his first wife.

From the above sketch, we see that the Elder was a worker full of zeal and self-sacrifice. The forty years he spent in the ministry were years of constant labor and suffering; yet we are told that he was always cheerful and happy in his lot, feeling, doubtless that he was in the Master's service.

P.M. BURLINGAME (?—?)

This minister was a member of the Southern New York Christian Conference, and died the year preceding the session of 1875.

NATHAN BURLINGAME (?—1868)

From James Burlingame, a relation of our subject, I learn that Nathan was born in Sterling, Conn., was converted and baptized about 1812, and moved to the Darby Plains, O., in June, 1817, with the Farnum company; that he and Farnum baptized over one hundred converts on the Plains and near Columbus in that summer, and among them two or three ordained ministers. Nathan returned to the East in October following, and died in Summerville, Conn., in 1868. Archibald Bates describes him as tall and slim in his early days, and a slow and pointed speaker. Elder Long says of him, "He was a man of good talent, great mind, and a powerful orator."

T.A. BURLINGAME (1812—1867)

The *Herald* states that this brother was born in Windham, Conn., in 1812, moved to Bradford County, Pa., when quite young, was ordained at Smithfield, Pa., July 10, 1859, by E. Tyler, E. Curry, B. Palmer, and P. Sweet. He united with the Tioga River Christian Conference in 1855, and died in Smithfield, Pa., February 20, 1867, aged fifty-five years.

HEZEKIAH BURNHAM (1814—1870)

This minister was born in Massachusetts in 1814, and died in New York City, on his way home from New Hampshire, July 19, 1870, aged fifty-six years. Elder Clark, who sent an account of his death to the *Herald,* says that he had been in the ministry about forty years. He wrote to our periodicals frequently, but his letters were always short and mainly treat- ng of one subject—the conversion of sinners. The first letter I can find from him is from Amesbury, Mass., February 27, 1840. In that letter, he urges men, with a great deal of ability, to be more thoughtful of their future welfare. Another letter is from New Hampshire, December of the same year, adding to the previous subject the propriety of solemnly examining the probability of the speedy coming of Christ. Two or three letters after this were written in the summer and fall of 1841, from Mason Corner, N.H. Great revivals are reported all around, and thirty or more had embraced religion in one meeting. In the summer and fall of 1842, from the same place, we have more earnest exhortations and more revivals with much of the Advent thoughts mixed in—showing that the Elder's mind was much impressed with the idea of the speedy coming of the Savior. When the time specified by the Adventists had passed and the prediction of the coming of Christ was not fulfilled, the Elder, like many others, gave up the Advent views, but lost nothing in zeal for the salvation of sinners.

I believe it was in 1848 that he took charge of the church in Conneaut, O., and he continued this connection with that church for several years. After leaving Conneaut, he never stayed very long with any church, but traveled as few others have traveled. It was a common saying with him that he was not made for a pastor but for an evangelist. As a public speaker, when things were moving to please him, his eloquence was wonderful. He was not noisy but powerful. The sermons I heard him deliver on such occasions were well prepared, and the language he used, though strong, was chaste, and the words were well selected. The gestures were nearly faultless, and his whole manner was that of a man in deep earnest for the conversion of sinners. His whole soul seemed to reach out after his congregation. At such times, great solemnity pervaded the whole assembly, and many were so entranced with the subject that for the time being they seemed to be unconscious of everything around. After such exertions, however, he seemed to be thrown off his balance; and these were the times when he gave offense.

His constant travel, exposure, and powerful and continued exertions in the pulpit wore on his nerves. The wonder is that he continued vigorous so long, for he was often ailing. It is probable that his sudden death on that hot day, in New York, was partly owing to his previous labors. It is a pity that we have no record of the result of his ministry. The number of his converts must be thousands, and the number of miles he traveled and the number of sermons that he preached must have been immense. He was a wonderful man, and when he died he left none like him.

JAMES BURNHAM (1760—1836)

James was born in 1760. He professed religion when young, and commenced preaching early in life. About 1826, under the labors of Elder Levi Hathaway, he and his family became members of the Christian Church, and from that time, he was a strong supporter of the Christian doctrine. His son Alfred had already, become an active minister in the same body. He died in. Hampton, Conn., May 5, 1836, aged seventy-six years.

G.W. BUSARD (?—1869)

This brother was a young minister, a member of the Tippecanoe Conference, Ind., and a son-in-law of Elder Elijah Tillman, of Logansport. He was born in Bedford County, Pa., moved to Indiana in 1840, was ordained in 1858, and died November 30, 1869. He was a young minister of great promise, and stood high with his brethren.

D. BUTLER (?—?)

This minister was an active member of the North-western Ohio Conference. He died not far from 1860.

<u>James Buxton (?—?)</u>

James Buxton labored in Virginia and North Carolina in an early day. He died many years ago.

<u>James Buys (?—?)</u>

This brother labored in Georgia in 1838.

<u>Peter Buzzard (1808—1849)</u>

Elder Buzzard was born in Virginia in 1808. When young, his parents moved to Licking County, O. He embraced religion in 1838, and commenced preaching soon after. In 1839, he joined the Ohio Central Conference, and was ordained in 1843. He died in Sylvania, O., August 20, 1849, aged forty-one years.

The Elder, while not a great preacher, was a good man, and devoted his entire energy to the cause of Christ. He was a true friend to the poor and unfortunate. As he had no children, he willed all his property, after the death of his wife, to the Christian Home Missionary Society.

<u>Steven D. Buzzell (1796—1871)</u>

Steven was born in N.H., in 1796, and commenced preaching about 1818. His fields of labor were mostly in Chemung, Cortland, Tomkins, Steuben, Wayne, and Chautauqua counties, N.Y., and in Benton and adjoining counties in Iowa. On October 15, 1871, he died, in Palo, Iowa, in his seventy- sixth year. He was in the ministry fifty years, forty of which he devoted exclusively to preaching. About 1860, he moved to Iowa, where he continued to the dose of life, laboring faith- fully as far as age and infirmity would permit.

<u>William Buzzell (?—1841)</u>

William labored in New Durham, N.H., in 1815. He was buried in Middleton, June 16, 1841.

LEWIS BYRAM (1770—1834)

This brother bad been an active worker for forty years before he died. In 1834, he died in Paoli, Ind.

ALEXANDER CARRAGE (1787—1863)

Alexander was born in East Tennessee, in 1787, and died near Brazil, Ind., in 1863. He moved to Indiana about 1832, was converted in the same year, and was ordained about 1834. He labored mostly in Clay and surrounding counties in Indiana. He was local in his labors and limited in knowledge; but he was a faithful minister and a good man.

ISAAC CADE (1790—1844)

Isaac was born about 1790. In person, he was heavy set. He was esteemed a very good Christian of moderate talents. In his views, he was very positive. He died in Union County, O., about 1844.

WILLIAM CALDWELL

This minister commenced preaching in Kentucky when quite young, and traveled through that state and Ohio visiting many churches. Finally, he traveled as far as Bedford County, Pa., where he was married. He was the first to organize churches in that part of Pennsylvania. From Pennsylvania, he moved West. He was one of the four ministers ordained in the starting out of the denomination in Kentucky. He was a good preacher and a fine man.

DANIEL CALL (?—1867)

The brother whose name heads this article is one in a thousand in the ministerial ranks. The Methodists had their Dow, other denominations have had their Boanerges, and we have had our Burnham, McIntire, Doubleday, Andrews, Call, and others; but of all our traveling evangelists, Call, in many respects, stands entirely at the head.

Of his birth and early education, we have no dates. But, from a letter in the "Palladium," in 1858, page 303, he gives a short account of his life and labors, from which we gather the following. He commenced preaching in the spring of 1814; had held 10,000 meetings; had seen 10,000 persons converted; and for all this labor had received twenty-four hundred dollars, or something less than fifty-five dollars a year. Since 1841, in seventeen years, he had held 3,200 meetings, had seen 2,500 converted, and had received but $707. The letter referred to was sent to the editor of the "Palladium," .and through him to the brotherhood in general, appealing for money to secure him a home He was then in one of those •dark periods that occasionally came over him. He had been taken sick after a severe labor in New England, and was apprehensive that his labors on earth were drawing to a close.

Instead of a small sketch, such' as our limits will allow, a large volume could be filled with interesting reminiscences of the labors of this wonderful man. In April, 1836, we find him in Cornville, Milburn, and other places in the State of Maine, laboring under a full headway of reformation. December, the same year, he was at Hannibal, Mentz, Sennet, Camillus, and other places in New York; reformation follows everywhere, and the Elder is in his glory. In May, 1837, and January, 1838, we find that he had been in various places in the State of New York, and through Canada West; reformation following. December, the same year, he was in Philadelphia with Elder Frederick Plummer. He had been through Pennsylvania, New Jersey, New York, Ohio, and farther west. Thus he continued through his ministerial life of about fifty-six years; and yet in his old age he was very poor.

As a specimen of the man I will insert here an extract of a letter published in a "Palladium" of 1845, page 255, to Elder Richards, of Michigan, concerning the money of some missionary society, of which Call was an agent. The letter reads: "Brother Richards wants to know what to tell those who ask him about me. I send these few lines to inform him what I have done for them. It is now fourteen months since I left Michigan. I have traveled 2,000 miles, visited fifty-two churches, traveled in eight states, attended 416 meetings, 105 were converted, received $121.63, paid fifty-five dollars in traveling expenses—thirty of which I paid in visiting churches that I should not have visited had it not been for your cause. For visiting twenty-one of these churches, and holding seventy- four meetings I received twenty-five cents. 1 have received but five dollars missionary money. By this you may see what I have got by being your agent—twenty-five dollars out of jacket and only twenty-five cents for holding seventy-four meetings. I leave it for you and your preaching brethren to say how much I ought to have for my labor; then add that with the $121.63 and then see if any preacher in Michigan has made more sacrifice than I have for the missionary cause. In addition to the $121.63, I have received a very large salary of abuse, mostly from wicked men and priests."

In summing up the life of this peculiar man I wish to say that of his goodness, zeal, and ability there is no doubt. Why, then, had he so many enemies? And why, with such talent, did he lay up nothing for sickness and old age? Elder Call was a man of one idea, and while that idea was in his mind he lost sight of all others. He started out, doubtless, fully convinced that he was right, and that in some way God would take care of him. He was not alone in this way of thinking, especially in his day. It is probable, also, that he had no tact in financiering, and had no desire for money till it was needed. His manner was peculiar—the manner of revivalists generally. He had but little suavity. All he saw in sinners was the need of a Savior, and he addressed and approached them in such a way as to often give offense.

But his long, weary, and laborious life is ended. He rests- from his labors, and the God in whose service he labored will overlook the peculiarities that men could not tolerate; and though very poor in his last years on earth, we believe be is high in glory. Elder B.F. Summerbell states in the *Herald* of February 8, 1868, that Elder Call died of strangulation, in the Dutchess County poor-house, in the State of New York, November 20, 1867. It is stated, however, that he might have had a home with his brethren. In the county house he had every attendance, and a room suited to his diseased condition.

BENJAMIN CALLEY

Benjamin Calley lived and died at Sanbornton, N.H., and labored as a minister in that part of the state.

THOMAS CAMPBELL

Members of churches in Union and adjoining counties in Ohio speak of this brother laboring through that region about 1830. He came from Athens County, was a man of ability and good education for the times, but was in limited circumstances.

JACOB CAPRON (1784—1826)

Jacob was born in 1784, likely in Fulton County, N.Y., was ordained in Broadalbin, and died in Henrietta, at the residence of Amos Ross, August 25, 1826, leaving a wife and seven children. The writers of that day speak highly of his talents and usefulness. In 1831, the New York Central Conference contributed means to build a monument over his grave, on which was engraved in large letters his name and some of the prominent motoes of the gospel he preached, all on the union of Christians as a fundamental doctrine of Elder Capron's church.

JOHN CAPRON (1772—1858)

John was born in Groton, Mass., March 2, 1772, moved to Danville, Vt., in 1797, embraced religion in 1802, under the labors of Elder E. Palmer, and soon after began to preach. At first, his labors were confined mostly to Danville and Peachain; but in 1817, he moved to Mansfield, and labored there and at Calais and Cabot. In 1851, he moved to Stowe to live with his son, and continued there until 1854, when he moved to Morristown, where he remained till death. November 23, 1858, he died, aged eighty-seven years.

It is said of him that he was deep, accurate, and very earnest in all his statements, and a strong advocate of the doctrines of his own church.

THOMAS CARR (1798—1876)

Thomas was born August 31, 1798, in Virginia, and moved to Ohio with his parents in. 1816. He professed religion, and was baptized during a meeting held by Elders Nathan Worley and John Dudley in 1823, in Southern Ohio. In 1843, he was ordained by Elders Worley and Plummer. In an early day, he moved from Ohio and settled in Liberty, Ind., where he continued many years, carrying on a blacksmith shop and preaching to the church at Silver Creek, near his home. He preached for this church more than twenty years, and for the church at Hannah's Creek many years. In 1854, he moved to Crawfordsville, where he continued till his death, which took place April 1, 1876, of heart disease. During his stay here of twenty-two years, he was useful as a prominent member of the Western Indiana Conference. He was a leading man in that part of the country.

Elder Carr was a large, heavy man in his latter years. He was a great reader, had a retentive memory, and was very interesting in conversation. His house was the natural home of traveling ministers, first in Liberty, the county seat of Union, then in Crawfordsville, the county seat of Montgomery. He and his wife were in good circumstances in their latter years, and were liberal with their means in the advancement of the cause of Christ.

HENRY CASE (?—1860)

This minister was formerly from Steuben County, N.Y., and was for several years a member of the Northern Illinois and Wisconsin Conference. He died, after a short illness, at Leroy, Ill., June 7, 1860, leaving a wife and three children. He is termed one of the "valiant few" in the ministry.

JOHN CASE (1783—1867)

This brother was a member of the New York Central Conference, but in 1846, he joined the Erie. He was born in 1783, was ordained at Arcadia, N Y., September 2, 1826, by Elder E. Shaw and others. He then went to Winchester, N.Y. He died on May 14,

1867 at Greenwood, N.Y., eighty-four years old. His writings are lively, spirited, and positive, as if he knew what he was about. Those who knew him well speak of him as a strong defender of the doctrines of the church.

TITUS CASE (?—?)

This minister was a member of the Central Ohio Conference. He was a fine-looking, steady, solemn man, well respected by all who knew him. Like many of our early ministers, he was a farmer, and made a good living for his family by his labor. He was quite liberal with his means. As for his preaching talents, it is not probable that he was a fluent speaker; yet his character was such that he was a firm pillar in the church. In his will, he left part of his property for the use of his own conference.

THOMAS CASON (1793—1855)

Thomas was born in South Carolina, January, 1793. When he was young, his parents moved to Ohio. He was married to Mary Pearson, and soon after, was converted, and commenced preaching among the Baptists. About this time, he moved with his family to Union County, Ind., where his wife died, leaving him alone with six 'children. In 1823, he married his second wife, Amelia Elston, with whom he lived happily for many years. They had fifteen children. In 1841, there was a division in the Baptist Church on the subjects of close communion, total depravity, Trinity, etc. The Elder took the liberal side, and in 1843, joined the Cole Creek (now Western Indiana) Conference. In this conference he continued an active member till 1847, when he moved to Madison County, Iowa, where he soon organized the first Christian Church in that county. September 8, 1854, while in very poor health, he joined the Desmoines Conference. He was conveyed to the church in a bed for that purpose, and made an affecting address, when received. December 27, 1854, he died, in his sixty-second year. His education was limited, but he was very successful as a preacher, and many hundreds were converted through his labors during the thirty years of his ministry.

JACOB CASSETT (?—?)

This brother died in some part of the West before 1826.

OLIVER CASTLE (?—?)

This pioneer minister moved with his family to Hartland, N.Y., and died in the work.

WILLIAM T. CATON (?—1871)

In 1843, this minister announced through the "Palladium" the dedication of a meeting-house at Westbury, N.Y. In 1847, he is settled as .a pastor of the church at Honeoye Falls. In March, 1856, he is at Arcadia with Hezekiah Burnham, assisting in a protracted meeting, with seventy converts forward for prayer. He died March 25, 1871, not far from fifty years of age. At the time of his death, he had been in the ministry for thirty years.

JABEZ CHADWICK (1779—1857)

The subject of this sketch was, in many respects, a peculiar man. He was not a great preacher. Perhaps his early training and his close study had, in a measure, cramped the off-hand delivery so essential to the orator. But what he lacked in rousing the multitude, he made up, fully, in deep research. Naturally, he was a student, a conscientious seeker after truth, and no worldly gain or popularity kept him from following wherever it led him.

The Elder was born in Lee, Mass., August 14, 1779. He embraced religion at the age of thirteen, and commenced preaching with the Congregationalists June, 1800. He was ordained December following, and at the same time settled as a pastor in Salem, Conn. After serving the church faithfully for many years, he moved with his family to Camillus, N.Y., where he was settled over two Presbyterian congregations. A Christian minister, Elder O. E. Morrill first formed an acquaintance with Elder Chadwick in this place, in 1822. His first break from the Presbyterians was his change of views on the mode of baptism. With this change, as might be expected, he joined the Baptists, and continued in their fellowship several years, highly respected as a scholar and a useful minister. In consideration of his learning, Hamilton College confeted on him, during this time, the honorary degree of A.M. Before 1838, Calvinism, Creeds, Trinity, etc. gave him much trouble; so, true to his conscience, he announced his convictions, and, though with a sick wife and in limited circumstances, he left a good salary and went out, not knowing where to find a home. In June, 1838, he joined the New York Western Christian Conference, and continued a faithful member of the denomination to the end.

His sickness was short—only one week. He died at Enfield Center, N.Y., February 20, 1857, aged seventy-eight years. For the last twenty years of his life, Elder Chadwick was one of the most zealous, diligent, and active ministers in the denomination. It is astonishing to see the amount of labor he performed, and this, also, among a people new to him, differing with him in many important particulars. In all the general measures of the denomination, the Elder was ready with pen and tongue to encourage all. It is seldom we open a periodical of those twenty years that he was connected with the Christians but that we find the name of Jabez Chadwick. His articles were often very short, a mere statement of what he desired to say, with no exordium or conclusion. I have no statement of all his published works during this time, but they were many. None were very large. The "Bible Dictionary," a dollar book of about 400 pages, was the largest of his works.

The activity of this aged man was shown by his constantly issuing from the press a pamphlet, a sermon, or a tract, one after the other in quick succession, and this in the midst of parochial duties, missionary work, protracted meetings, and a? ways in limited circumstances.

As stated, he was in perfect harmony with the Christians on the main subject of Theology; but on many side issues, he differed widely from the main body of the denomination; but? with all his mild, clear, and voluminous publications, he never became an authority in matters of a doctrinal nature as Millard, Badger, Clough, and others. He was respected by all, and was considered an able writer and expounder of Scripture, especially was his "Bible Dictionary" considered an able work; but to his views on the "Destruction of the wicked," "The son-ship of Christ," etc. he never carried many away.

Dwelling on the passage in Rev. 3:14, where the son is called "the beginning of the creation of God" the Elder taught that Christ was the son of God by creation, not by derivation, pre-existent as to his spirit, and, in due time, incarnate for man's redemption. He believed, also, in the final destruction of the wicked—Rev. 20:6. It is not strange that he held speculative views not commonly held by the Christian world. All his life, he had been a hard thinker. Speculative and figurative expression had been as tangible to him in early life as the most practical duties of Christ's teaching.

In early life, the Elder had an insatiable thirst for knowledge. He was willing to work at anything honorable to obtain his end. He worked for a mechanic for very low wages to pay his tuition until qualified to teach a common school. When qualified for this, he taught with avidity, and devoted all the proceeds to his own education. When he had acquired a good English education, he studied Greek, Latin, and Theology under Dr. Alvin Hyde, a Congregational minster, in his own parish. He was ordained to preach by the Calvinists of New England, in 1800. Standing upon the premises of his own confession of faith, there is no wonder that the inquisitive young minister should strike right and left to find deliverance. No wonder that in shunning the theory that God punished the little children of the non-elect he should not stop till he had the wicked struck out of existence. It is a consoling wonder, however, to see this aged thinker, scholar, and writer, with views differing materially from those of his new allies, when few of these possessed learning equal to his own, so meek in all his utterances. He was positive in all his declaration, yet, such was his clear understanding of the basis of Christian union, he never imposed his views upon others, nor did he resort to special pleadings in his own defense. One peculiarity of his controversial writings is the candor with which he treats an opponent.

The following are a few of his articles published in our periodicals from. 1838 to 1856. June, 1838. he writes from Medina, N.Y., reviewing an article on the Trinity. In July, the same year, he gives his views of the Christians, his new friends whom he had lately joined. He had visited several churches of the connexion, and gives his impression of their position. In November, he reviews Mr. Myrick of the "Union Herald" for his intolerant spirit in excluding honest Non-Trinitarians from the pale of the church. March, 1839, he replies to Justitia on the nature of punishment. In the same year, in several articles, he gives his reasons for rejecting the Trinity. In 1841, he labors in Union Springs, and reports a good revival there. In 1847, he writes on his return from Oshawa, Canada, where he had been laboring in the office of the *Christian Luminary*. He urges the Christian brethren to return the intolerant spirit of sectarianism with the mild spirit of Christian forgiveness. In 1848, he writes a very sensible article on the support of the ministry, taking the ground that the defect is not so much with the laity as with the ministry. His remedy is, that ministers show themselves workmen and the people will appreciate their worth, and will willingly pay for the labor. June, 1849, he writes to announce to his subscribers how he intends to proceed in the preparation of his "Bible Dictionary" in regard to those doctrines wherein he differs with the church. Generally, his plan is to give both sides of the argument, and leave himself out of the question. In the same year, he appeals to the public in behalf of the small society at Union Springs. In 1852, he has a written discussion with Elder H. Grew in regard to the "Kingdom," and similar subjects. In 1853, he writes a very interesting letter upon the support of learned and unarmed men in the denomination, and especially on the folly of not supporting those of limited education, and thus driving them to other occupation for a living, and crippling them for all future time; whereas, if liberally supported at first, they would acquire knowledge sufficient to become very useful men.

I will here give the substance of an article on "Free Discussion," published in July, 1852,—the necessity and danger of the same. After showing that discussion must be free or else there is an end to all investigation for knowledge, he proceeds to show the great evil that grows from the abuse of this right. "What I wish suppressed," he says, "is too much and unnecessary harshness of expression, severe criticism, imputation of unworthy, and even base motives to one's antagonist,, aspiration of pride and jealousy, fears that others may outdo or outshine us, uncomfortable anticipations of the unfavorable light in which other denominations and the learned public- may hold our acquisition and standing and whatever savors of' boasting, self-confidence, and worldly-mindedness." He then proceeds to show much of that among us at the time, and that in a fatherly spirit, appeals to all combatants to value free discussion too highly to endanger its continuance by indulging in those errors.

In conclusion, it is evident that Elder Chadwick was an unassuming, humble, sincere, pious, and good man. His coming to the Christians, although at the advanced age of fifty-eight years, was a great advantage to the body; and it was equally advantageous to the Elder that he found a body whose views so nearly coincided with his own.

EDWIN CHAFFIN (?—1848)

Elder Chaffin was, a member of the Wabash Conference, and died about 1848.

JOHN MILTON CHALMEES (1820—1852)

This minister was born in Albion, Me., in 1820. He commenced preaching: in 1840. He preached more or less in Skowhegan, Palmyra Dixmont, Plymouth, and Troy, Me., and in Wells and New- Castle, N.H. It was while laboring at the latter place that his health failed, so that he was compelled to retire from active service. He departed this life March 18, 1852.

AMOS CHAPMAN (?—1843)

In May, 1835, Elder Chapman was in Jasper, N.Y., in a great revival, where he was baptizing many. He died about the first of February, 1843, after a short illness. The Sunday before, he delivered a powerful exhortation to the church of his charge at Springwater, N.Y.

S.W. CHAPMAN (?—1875)

S.W. Chapman died in Vandalia, Mich., about 1875.

EZRA CHASE (1783—1873)

This brother was born in .Fredericktown, N.Y., October 11, 1783, was converted in 1796, was licensed to preach in 1808, and was ordained in 1820. At first, he was a minister of the Methodist denomination, but in 1822, he left that body and joined the Christians. For many years, he was pastor of the Christian Church at Enfield, N.Y., then considered by such men as Badger, and Millard as the strongest church in that part of the state; and Elder Chase was one of the most prominent ministers. In April, 1833, Elder Badger gives an account of a conference being held in the church in Enfield, where the pastor's son, John B. Chase, was set apart to the work of the ministry.

Elder Millard speaks of Elder Chase's gray locks and venerable appearance, and that he felt a great reverence for his presence. The Elder died at Enfield Center, N.Y., March 27, 1873, in his ninetieth year.

In addition to the above, we have the following—the substance of a letter from his son, Elder John B. Chase. From boyhood up, Elder Chase was deeply impressed with the leading of the Spirit of God. At one time, when preaching among the Methodists, about the middle of his sermon he was impressed to give an invitation for seekers; but, failing to do so his mind became darkened. At his next appointment, he was similarly impressed; when he obeyed, seven or eight came forward, and great good was accomplished.

Early in life, he married Elizabeth Byington, in West Chester County, N.Y., of whom he had six children. In 1817, he buried her, and some years later married Julia Curry. April, 1820, there was a meeting held in Hector, his home at that time, when he was ordained a Christian minister. The meeting was largely attended, and much stir was manifested on account of several ministers beside the Elder changing their ecclesiastical relation.

Elder Chase moved to Enfield when the church was very weak; but, through his labors, it became a strong body. In 1868 and 1871, when the Elder was eighty-five and eighty-eight years old, respectively, there were reunions held at his house, and in 1872, the New York Central Christian Conference was held in Enfield. The Elder was present, and was addressed, by order of conference, by Elder Keyes Coburn. In all these meetings, the old patriarch looked well in the midst of his brethren. He died in 1873, at the ripe age of ninety years.

<u>ISRAEL CHESLEY (1788—1866)</u>

From a letter of Miss O.G. Chesley, a daughter of the deceased, and from an obituary notice by Elder D.P. Pike, I gather the following items concerning this father in Israel. Israel Chesley was born in Durham, N.H., November 24, 1788. He was the eleventh child of his parents, but the first to embrace religion. In February, 1810, he was converted at the beginning of an extensive revival, and at once became an active worker in the cause. April following, he was baptized by Elder Osborne, in Durham. A journal of his, of that date, reads, "I had such freedom in exhortation and prayer that I could truly say that 'I gloried in the Gospel of Christ.' " October 14, 1812, he was married to Elizabeth Folsom, daughter of Colonel John Folsom, in New Market, of whom he had seven children. His journal of 1814 shows the pressure upon his mind to sacrifice all for Christ. Under these impressions, he exchanged property with his brother at a great sacrifice, and moved with his family to

Rochester, where he labored constantly wherever an opening was made.

July 11, 1816, he was ordained in Lee, and united with the Christian Church. Sermon by Elder Osborne. He was remarkably led by the Spirit, all through life. He remained in Rochester one year, when he moved to Lee. His labors in the ministry were very extensive. During his life, he preached 1,500 funeral sermons—a labor to which he was well adapted because of his sympathetic spirit. He baptized many, and married one thousand couples. He died September 29, 1866.

Elder Chesley was a man of mild and loving spirit. He was benevolent and kind to all, but very unassuming in his acts of generosity. In his early days, he wrote frequently to our periodicals, but in latter years he wrote but little. His labors were mostly confined to the State of New Hampshire, but his name, for years, was well known to the denomination. Funeral sermon by A.G. Morton.

ISAAC CLARK. (?—?)

R.M. Thomas says that this brother died in Fountain County, Ind., a few years ago, aged seventy-five years.

JEFTHA CLARK (?—1836)

This was an aged minister who died in Scott, N.Y., in 1836. He was a devoted preacher for many years, and did much to build up the cause in the field of his labor.

JOHN CLARK (1802—1876)

A *Herald* of February, 1876, states that this minister was born in Broadalbin, X.Y., October 24, 1802, and died at Union Mills January 31, 1876. He was baptized by Elder King October 12, 1817, and, for many years, was publisher of the "Palladium." He was a fine singer, and taught music. Later in life, he became a preacher, and continued to labor till 1874, when his health failed.

RICHARD CLARK (1781—1814)

This brother was a useful minister in the church. He was a man of talent and education, firm in his convictions, of good morals and fine de livery. He was born in 1781, died in 1814, and was buried in West Liberty, O. From 1805 to 1808, he labored in and around Burlington. His home, in the latter part of his life, was in Champaign County, O. He was a strong advocate of system in the work of the church.

SIMON CLOUGH (1793—1844)

The subject *of* this sketch was, in many respects, one of the leading men of his church, and it is a wonder to many that a full biography of his life has not been published long ago. There is material sufficient to compile an interesting book of biography. From a sketch of his life, by Elder Morgridge, I gather the following. Simon Clough was born in Monmouth, Me., March 5, 1793. His father, Benjamin Clough, had three children—one daughter and two sons. Simon was the second son. His early life was spent on the farm with his father, and, like all New England boys, he went to school in the winters. In the fall of 1812, when nineteen years old, he attended the Monmouth Academy one term, and taught school the following winter. While teaching in Augusta, he made a profession of religion. Subsequently, he went to Boston, Mass., intending to engage in business; but he soon returned to Hebron, Me., where he was baptized in 1817, and immediately commenced preaching. In November, the same year, he was ordained as an evangelist, and immediately entered on the work in the vicinity, organizing several churches.

In 1817, he moved to Export, and continued to labor there through the winter. From that place, he went to Portland, then to Boston, Mass., where he became pastor of the church— a position which he sustained about five years. In 1824, he left Boston, went to New York, and organized the first Christian Church in that city. In New York, he labored about nine years. During this time, he was married. His wife, died in a few years. At this time, also, he edited the *Gospel Luminary.* In the autumn of 1833, he settled in Fall River, Mass., where he labored with great success for about three years. From Fall River, he went to New Jersey, where he had great success in his ministry. November 24, 1841, Elder Clough was a second time married, this time to Mrs. Minerva Howell, of New York, which proved a very happy union. He died at his residence, 201 Broom St., New York, May 20, 1844, aged fifty-one years. He had been in the ministry twenty-seven years.

The above is an outline of the labors and removals of Elder Clough. The Elder was a large man, though not tall. His physical powers had been well developed, in his early life, on his father's farm. When twenty-one years of age, his father informed him that, as his older brother was to continue on the place, he (Simon) might choose any pursuit he pleased—he was free. About this time, while a great epidemic was raging in the community, and many were dying, Simon was sitting up with a dying comrade. When about to depart in the morning, the dying man asked him where they would meet next. This made such an impression on Simon's mind that he made up his mind to acquire an education, and devote his entire life to the work of the ministry. With this subject in view, he went to school and taught, alternately. But, while at the Hebron Academy, he overreached the mark; for, while studying hard,—reading the Greek Testament by day and by night,— he injured his eyes so much that it was a long time before he could read. This was the time he went to Boston with the intention of engaging in business; and when, like Jonah, he felt that he was running away from duty and had to return.

From this time, he never turned to right or left, but pressed right along in the path of duty. Still, his path was not a smooth one, as the following circumstance will show. His first sermon, at Portland, was a failure. He was then considered the best educated minister in the connexion, and the report having been circulated that a young man of learning was to address the congregation, expectation was on tip-toe. The Elder took his text and paused. He went on a little longer, then paused again, doing so several times. Then he said, "When I took my text, it was very dark, and it has been growing darker and darker all along. I cannot preach." He then sat down, bathed in tears, and continued so during the entire night.

As a pastor and preacher, Elder Clough had few superiors. Add to this his upright, moral, and devoted life and it is no wonder that great success attended his labors. In Boston, he raised the church from a small body to a flourishing congregation. In Fall River, his success was still greater. From a .small congregation, which he had when he went there, he soon had a full house; and, during his labors-there of three years, two hundred and seventeen were added to the church—firm .and reliable members. In New York, his labors were blessed with the building up of a respectable church in that city. As for New Jersey, all through the churches there were great ingatherings, and many new churches were organized in that state, through his instrumentality.

As a writer, however, the Elder exercised particular power. In early life, he had stored his mind with such knowledge as was taught in the academies he attended. Since that, and all through life, indeed, he was an intense student. His position, .also, in such places as Boston and New York, the head centers of books and papers, was favorable to him in this direction. The *Gospel Luminary* was edited by him, and he made a good periodical of it, though some of the numbers were written mostly by himself. As long as he lived, he was a writer to all our papers. . "The Select Works of Elder S. Clough" is a book so well known to our people that I need say nothing in its favor. Looking upon the entire written work of the Elder, in the short period of about twenty years, in the midst of .pressing parochial duties, we almost wonder at their amount, and especially at their thoroughness in style and matter.

In his social relations, Elder Clough was affable, kind, and sympathetic, though, owing to his studious habits, and entire consecration to his work, on first acquaintance, he had the appearance of coldness. His first marriage was not a happy one, but his goodness and entire self-government, which he had practiced through life, carried him through this period with no diminution of his reputation as a minister. His second marriage, with Mrs. Howell, who had one daughter, and who had been a widow four years when he married, her, was a very happy one. The daughter of Mrs. (dough, Minerva Ann Howell, became at once a great favorite with the Elder, and, as a token of his high regard for this young lady's education mid taste, he willed her his entire library.

In conclusion, I will offer a few thoughts on letters published by him between the year 1834 and 1842. In February, 1834, writing from Fall River, Mass., he gives a vivid account of a great awakening in various places in New England. His descriptions are most lively, as if his whole soul was enlisted. February, 1839, he writes from Boston in regard to a book of .sermons, contemplated to be published at that time, and mentions twenty-five or more sermons of his own production that are at the service of the brethren. November, the same year, he writes from New Jersey, giving an account of hundreds of' conversions in various places through the state—one hundred converted at one meeting. A year later, (November, 1840,) the revival in New Jersey continues unabated. January, 1841, he writes of the failure to debate on the part of a Mr. Fay, who had boasted his readiness to meet these Arians at any time. April, the same year, the revival still continues through New Jersey, and five or six meeting-houses were being built by the Christians in different places. October, 1841, he gives a very full account of a debate between Mr. Mattison, Methodist, and P. Hawk, Christian, where Mattison takes the whole matter in his own hands, refusing a board of moderators. November of the same year, he writes a very interesting communication on the wants of the Christians—a University, a Biblical School, and a Commentary of the Bible suited to the Christian Church. He urges the necessity of a general meeting of the whole denomination for the purpose of maturing plans for the accomplishment of this work. July, 1842, he writes of his declining health, and of consulting a prominent physician who pronounced his disease, dropsy on the chest, but feels hopeful that the disease is yielding to the remedy.

From the above, we see what a loss it was to the denomination when he died in the prime of manhood; and it was s, felt through the entire church.

ELIAS COBB (1776—1838)

Elias was born in Middlebury, Mass., in 1767, and early in life joined the Baptist Church. He was a minister among the Baptists for some time, in Woodstock, Vt. When the first Christian Church was organized in Woodstock, he was one of the first to join it. He continued in that connexion till death, an active, firm, and prominent man in the denomination. At first, his labors were bestowed on the churches around Woodstock; but later, he moved to West Randolph, and, later still, to Braintree, the same state, where he died February 15, 1838, aged seventy-one years.

By trade, he was a blacksmith. He also had a farm, and worked at both occupations. He was social and kind in his intercourse, always urging the claim of religion. His goodness and zeal in the church gave him a leading position among his neighbors.

WILLIAM COE (?—?)

This minister was a brother of J.H. Coe, of New Bedford, Mass. William had been laboring, in his early ministry, at two different times, in the State of New York among the more destitute churches, and there lost his health. In 1834, he writes that he had not seen a well day for five years. He was in Portland, Me., having charge of the church left destitute by the death of Elder Samuel Rand. Elder Coe had been near unto death, but the gospel he had preached made him strong to face the tomb. Elder Moses Howe and others speak highly of this brother as a zealous man. Though often in poor health, he was very cheerful and fond of innocent jokes. Elder Luther Baker and he were well matched in this respect, both jovial but true and faithful men.

Fredrick Cogswell (1792—1857)

This minister was born in 1792, and died in Memphis, Tenn., August 4, 1857. He was married to Hannah Peavy, sister of Elders John and Edward Peavy. His wife, also, was a public speaker, and for many years the two traveled in company, preaching as they went, and doing much for the upbuilding of the cause. Their names are generally signed together, and Elder Cogswell, in most of his letters, uses the pronoun "we," while speaking of the meetings held. They traveled extensively in different places, but mostly in New Hampshire, and their letters were generally dated at Durham, in that state. Great revivals followed their labors, and they doubtless did much to build up the church of their choice.

J.T. G. Colby (1796—1877)

This brother was born in Exeter, N.H., in 1796, commenced preaching at York, Me., was ordained in Durham, N.H., May 27, 1827, and died in Dover, N.H., June 5, 1877. Un till 1832, he preached as an evangelist in New Hampshire and Canada East; at this time, he located at Wolf borough, N.H., where he remained till 1850; then he labored six years at West Milton; then, on account of failing health, he located at Dover. He was a good citizen and a faithful minister.

A. Cole (?—1876)

This brother was an aged minister in the Miami Reserve Conference, Ind., and died in 1876.

Timothy Cole (1806—1866)

Timothy was born at Landaff, N.H., September 6, 1806, was converted in 1826, and was baptized by Elder A.C. Morrison. He commenced preaching soon after, and was ordained at Alton, N.H., in 1828. He .died at Lakeville. N.H., January 18, 1869, aged sixty-three years. For many years, Elder Cole was one of our most prominent ministers in New England. In Lowell, Mass., by his untiring labor, he built a very large church, mostly from the operatives of the mills. In those days, he wrote frequently to our periodicals, and his writings show considerable ability. When the Advent excitement came around, from 1840 to 1843, the Elder went into it with all his might. After the failure of his expectations, he, like many others, seemed at a loss how to proceed. For a while, he did but little, but finally he commenced preaching again; but his mind was divided, his ardor and zeal was, in a measure, gone; yet his death was mourned by his brethren. Elder Cole was considered a good and able man.

GEORGE COLLINS (1787—1852)

This minister 'was a resident of Scituate, R.I., for some time. He was born in 1787, and died February 15, 1852. He is spoken of as a successful and faithful worker.

NATHAN COMER (?—1868)

This brother was a licentiate minister in the Miami Reserve Conference, Ind., and died in 1868

THOMAS CONCANNON (1800— 1856)

Thomas was born in Montgomery County, O., September 2, 1800. He was quite wild, and was a ringleader of comrades like himself. In 1820, he and his gang attended a Methodist camp meeting in the neighborhood, and, to increase the amusement, Thomas proposed that they should go to the altar for fun. By some mysterious influence, they were all converted. Thomas soon after joined the Christians. From this' time to 1841 he had a constant struggle with his own convictions about preaching. In 1821, he was married to Miss Polly Morgan, near Day ton, and soon after, moved to Tippecanoe County, Ind., where he engaged in mercantile pursuits, made money, became security for another, and lost all his property. He moved to Laport, Ind., bought a farm on time, suffered much from sickness, and finally his faithful wife died, leaving him with six small children. He finally lost his farm. During all these afflictions the voice of conscience cries, "Woe is me if I preach not the gospel." He finally yields, and, in his forty-third year, takes up the work of preaching in earnest. He became very successful at once, but the country being new his support was meager and expenses large.

In 1846, he was married to a widow lady, Rhoda Williams, who had four small children. He moved to Pulaski County, Ind., clearing a new farm, preaching to four churches quite distant from each other, supporting a family of a wife and twelve children, and studying by fire-light to prepare his sermons for the ensuing Sunday. In June, 1856, he started to- Iowa, intending to settle in Madison County, that state. While moving, he took a violent cold, from the effect of which he died December 27, 1856, near Winterset, Iowa, in his fifty-seventh year.

WILLIAM CONCANNON (1825—1853)

William, a son of the preceding minister, was born in 1825, was ordained in 1854, and died in 1857. He was a young man of modest and retiring disposition, but was highly respected by his brethren. He was a member of the Tippecanoe Conference, Ind.

ABEL P. CONDRA (?—1869)

This brother was a licensed member of the Spoon River Illinois Conference, and died in 1869.

JOSIAH CONGER (?—?)

Josiah Conger labored for many years in Preble County, O. He was somewhat local in his labors, but was very useful in his day. He died many years ago, leaving an excellent family to perpetuate his name and principles.

JAMES CONKLIN, JR (1817—1841)

This young brother was born in 1817, and died at East Berne, N.Y., April 7, 1841, in his twenty-fourth year. He had been pastor of the church in East Berne for eighteen months at the time of his death. He was highly respected by the church and congregation.

AMMON COOK (?—1869)

This brother was a minister of great usefulness in the Miami Reserve conference, Ind. He was formerly from some of the Eastern States. He died about 1869, not far from sixty years of age. He was highly respected by all who knew him.

BENJAMIN COOK (1807—1842)

Benjamin was born near 1807, began preaching in Canada about 1832, and was quite successful, especially in reformation. He died at Pickering, Canada, about 1842, thirty-five years old. He was a good and useful man.

JOHN COOK (1810—1865)

The subject of this sketch was born in 1818, was converted in 1838, and soon commenced his labors as a minister in Portlandville, N.Y. In 1842, he was ordained, and, in the same year, moved to Cobleskill Center, the same state. He died in Avon, N.Y., February 19, 1865.

M.W. COOK (1788—1869)

This aged brother died in Albion, Ind., December 1, 1869, a superannuated member of the Eel River Conference, Ind., at the time of his death. He was born in 1788, commenced preaching among the Freewill Baptists about 1823, and continued with them about forty years, laboring in Canada, New York, Ohio, and Michigan. In 1863, he joined the Eel River Indiana Christian Conference, in which he labored till death. He was a man of great physical strength, and continued vigorous in his old age.

PETER COOK (1797—1877)

This aged minister was a native of Vermont. He was born in 1797, moved West in 1814, and began to preach in 1823. He continued to preach regularly till 1874, when his health failed. He died June 8, 1877.

JOSEPH GREEN COOPER (1800—1855)

This brother was born near Owensville, Ky., December 10, 1800. He was converted when sixteen years old, under the labors of Elder James Hughes, and was baptized by the same. Soon after, his father's family moved to Wayne County, Ind., where, on August 22, 1822, Joseph was united in marriage with Elizabeth Leonard. In 1826, he moved to Henry County, where he began to preach. In 1833, he moved to Bartholomew County, and, in 1837, was ordained as an evangelist by Elders David Douglass and Jolin Crafton. He labored as an evangelist the greater part of his life, traveling extensively in Bartholomew and adjoining counties in Indiana, and many were converted under his preaching. He was a member of the Central Conference, Indiana. In 1847, he moved to Clark County, RI., in poor health, but labored considerably in the bounds of the Southern Illinois Conference, of which he was a clerk. In 1853, for the purpose of educating his children, he moved to Yellow Springs, O., where he died January 11, 1855. He was gifted in exhortation, and his public labors were blessed in the conversion of many.

AARON CORNISH (1801—1872)

Aaron was born in 1801, commenced preaching in Royalton, N.Y., in 1825, was ordained June, 1830, by Jeremiah Gates, Joel Doubleday, Reuben Fairly, and William Blake, and joined the Erie Conference July, 1824, where he continued his membership till death. He died July 6, 1872, aged seventy-one years. He is said to have been a devoted and useful man.

HENRY CRAFT (?—?)

Henry Craft was a minister in the southern part of Indiana, many years ago.

JAMES CRAFT (1830—1864)

James was born in 1830, joined the Anglaise Conference in 1855, and was ordained in 1860. He went to the War of the Rebellion, and died in Knoxville, Tenn., of smallpox, January 25, 1864. He was a young man of great promise.

JOHN CRAFTON (1788—1838)

John was born June 22, 1788, commenced preaching in 1812, was married to Cynthia Crawford April, 1823, and died December 18, 1838. He labored extensively as an evangelist in Indiana and Kentucky. He was well posted in the Scriptures, and had zeal and good talent. He died of inflammation of the lungs, which was produced by excessive labor in the pulpit.

NANCY GOVE CRAM (1776—1816)

This female laborer's life is inserted among the ministers of the Christian denomination, not because she was a regular member of the body, but because of the prominent part she occupied amongst the people called Christians in the State of New York for the space of four years. It is not certain that this sister ever joined the Christian Church; for when she left Ware, N.H., for New York, she was a member in good standing of the Freewill Baptist denomination. But she was so earnestly engaged in the salvation of souls that she had no time to think of denominational lines. The life of this worthy sister in Christ was singular, successful, and yet sad.

She was born in Ware, N.H., in 1776. Her maiden name was Gove. About 1796, she married a man by the name of Cram, who was thought, at the time, to be a respectable man. In process of time, he turned out to be a dissolute and wicked man, abusing his wife, and finally living with another woman. In all this affliction, Nancy clung closer to her God, and received the approbation of those who knew her. After laboring in the ministry for some time in her native state, having much of the missionary spirit, and being entirely released from all earthly ties, about 1812, she went to the State of New York on a preaching tour. From this visit of Sister Cram, many of the most flourishing churches in the eastern part of the state had their start. Through the same visit, also, Elders Thompson, King, Martin, and others were induced to move from

Vermont to New York, and through it, finally, some of our most prominent ministers were converted and called to the ministry. From the Balston church alone, raised by her labors, Elders David Millard, John Ross, and John Hollister, together with two female laborers—Abigail Roberts and Mary (Stevens) Curry entered the Christian ministry.

Her labor in New York continued some three or four years, after which she returned to Ware, her native town, where she died January, 1816.

COMER CRANDALL (1791—1835)

This Elder was born in 1791, embraced religion and joined the Christians about 1821, and soon after began to preach with great zeal and energy. His health had been poor for some time, yet he continued to preach almost to the end. His last sermon was truly affecting, he being on the verge of the grave, yet so anxious for the salvation of sinners. Soon after this, he took to bleeding at the lungs, and died soon after—December 30, 1835. On his death bed, he requested to be buried by the side of his old friend, Elder John Peavy, in the grave-yard at Milan. He is said to have been a very zealous man, devoted to his high calling.

ELIAS CRANDALL (?—1859)

This Elder was a member of the Southern New York Conference, and died about 1859. Sermon before the conference by Elder J.W. Stearns.

LEWIS CRAVEN (1806—1842)

Lewis was born in 1806, commenced preaching in 1829, and died in Halifax County, Va., October 7, 1842. His labors were extensive and very efficient. Sunday, October 2, 1842, he preached a powerful sermon before the conference, and it was thought that this was partly the cause of his death. The next day (Monday) on his way to meeting, he was compelled to turn to a house on the way for rest. He was perfectly resigned to die. He said. "I feel like going home."

JACOB F. CRIST (1807—1873)

Jacob was born in Hamilton County, O., in 1807, moved to Brown County, the same state, and became an exhorter about 1840. He continued to exhort, the rest of his life. He moved to Missouri, and died there in May 1873, aged sixty-six years. He was a very zealous and devoted man.

THEOPHILUS CROCKER (1761—1853)

This aged man was born in Massachusetts, in 1761, experienced religion when six years old. In the beginning of the Revolutionary War, he entered the army, and continued connected with it more or less to the close. In 1783, he joined the Baptists, and continued in that connexion for some years. He became acquainted with the Christians in their early struggles, and, feeling in harmony with their Hews, joined them. In 1785, he was married to Mary Allen, and, in an early day, moved with his family to Genesee County, N.Y. About 1791, he began to preach, and for thirty or forty years spent much of his time in traveling and preaching, as was the custom of many in those days. In 1830, his wife died. Since that time, he lived mostly with his children. During the last thirty years of his life, he did not preach much until a few years before he died, when he labored more. He died in 1853, ninety-two years old.

He was a man of wonderful memory. It is said that, when eighty-seven years old, he committed to memory the whole book of Revelation, and that he would repeat whole chapters without missing a word. He left five children, two of whom —Allen and Theophilus —became ministers. For many years, he was one of the oldest ministers in the church.

JAMES CROSBY (?—?)

James Crosby was a minister who died near Skowhegan, Me.

SAMUEL CROSS (1780—1860)

This aged brother was a member of the Tioga River Conference. Elder Badger speaks of him, in July, 1847, as an old man with a voice like a lion's and hair as white as wool. He died at North Cohocton, N.Y., near 1860, about eighty years old.

ZEPHANIAH CROSSMAN (?—?)

This Elder was one of the committee appointed to ordain Elder Benjamin Taylor, at Assonet,, Mass., in 1811.

PETER CULPEPER (?—?)

This was a Virginia minister of prominence A.D. 1800. Elder Burlingame, of Rhode Island, says the Elder was an author of some repute, and that he has an able sermon of his in answer to John West on the "Mystery of Iniquity."

MOSES CUMMINGS (?—1866)

Though this Elder occupied a prominent position in the church for many years, yet I have failed to find any considerable account of his life and labors. One letter I see dated at Honesdale, Pa., where he was pastor of the church, and where he continued for several years. His letters at this time show great energy, liberality, zeal, and liveliness. His style is very plain and somewhat given to irony, especially in writing against narrowness and bigotry, which subjects he frequently takes up and handles without gloves.

In March, 1855, he became the resident editor of two papers, the "Palladium" and "Messenger." His editorials are generally very able. It was remarked by many, during his connection with those papers, that he was one of the ablest writers in the church. These papers became quite popular under his administration, at first, but other papers being published in other parts, and the failure of Antioch College taking place at the time, the Central Publishing Establishment, under his care, failed for want of patronage.

The Elder was a member of the New Jersey Conference, and in his latter years, lived at Irvington, N.J. Of his preaching talent, I have no knowledge; but, judging from his success as a pastor in his early years, and his ability as an editor and writer, I should suppose that he was an able preacher. After leaving the office of the "Palladium," for several years, he published a commercial paper and advertising" medium in the city of New York; but he never was prominent in the church after this time. He died in Irvington, N.J., about 1866, but I have not the precise date or circumstances connected with his death.

<u>William Cummings (1785—1847)</u>

From the "Palladium" of 1848, page 592, we gather the following: William Cummings was born in the State of New Hampshire, in 1785, was converted in 1806, commenced preaching in 1810, and was ordained at Bradford, Vt., in 1815. In 1817 or '18, he moved from Rumney, N.H.. to Delaware County, N.Y., where he spent most of his time till death, although he traveled extensively through other states. He died at Lansingville, N.Y., of inflammation of the lungs December 12, 1847.

The Elder was a prominent man in the church. He was also a man of more than ordinary consecration to the great work. His letters, of which he wrote many to the different periodicals of the day, are full of cheerfulness, faith, hope, and confidence in God. When he first embraced religion, he was so full of joy that some of the older members told him he was going on borrowed capital, and that the sorrows of life would have to pay back, etc. The Elder, mentioning this in his last days, said, "They were mistaken; I have been full of glory all the time." At one time, his house took fire and most of his property was consumed; while preaching soon after, referring to the circumstance, he said, "None of these things move me."

<u>Charles Cummins (1780—1850)</u>

Our present subject was born in Augusta County, Va., in 1780, joined the Baptists in Virginia about 1820, but, forming an acquaintance with the Christians, he joined them. He was ordained a minister of the Christian Church in Giles County, Va., by Elders Duncan and Kirk. In 1831, he moved to Henry County, Ind., where he died March 13, 1850, aged seventy-nine years.

R. Cummins (1824—1859)

This was a relative of the preceding, and lived in the same neighborhood. He was born in 1824, in Madison County, Ind., and died in the same county February 3, 1859. He was a young preacher who stood high in the community but was local in his labors. He was a member of the Bluffton Conference. He died lamented, leaving a wife, and children.

William Cunningham (?—?)

This brother was a member of the Central Illinois Conference, which he joined at the time of its organization. He was local in his labors, but faithful and true. He died, full of years.

J.H. Currier (1808—1859)

In the "Palladium," Vol. 29, page 139, J.M. Wescott gives the following items on the life of Elder Currier. He was born in Reading, Vt., May 20, 1808, was converted in Canandaigua, N.Y., in 1825. In 1828, he lost his interest in religious matters, in a great measure; but in 1830, he renewed his covenant, and soon after, commenced laboring in the ministry. In 1828, he attended the Middlebury Academy for some months. When he renewed his covenant, he was teaching school at Lakevillage, N.H. He was ordained at Fairfield, Pa., March 9, 1833, by Elders D. Millard, Seth Marvin, and Daniel Rote. .He was married October 23, 1836, to Emily Campbell, in New York City, by Elder I.N. Walter. He died at West Shelby, N.Y., January 9, 1860.

Elder Currier was a man of great energy and activity. In looking over our periodicals from 1832 to the time of his death, we find articles written upon almost every subject connected with the interest of the church. At one time, we find suggestions for the correction of errors he sees in his traveling; then a commendation of certain things he observes; now a doctrinal article in answer to someone either in his own or some other church. But, whatever it is, the man is always awake to the interest of religion. July, 1832, we find him in Canada West, attending meetings of great interest with Elders McIntire, Bailey, Bliss, and Stump. This was soon after he commenced preaching. May, 1834, he is at Providence, Pa., holding a four days' meeting. He rejoices in the prosperity of Zion. September, the same year, we find him near Philadelphia, holding many meetings with Elders Fleming, Thompson, and others; many are converted, and the prospect is brightening.

June, 1835, he continues his labors at Lawrence, N.Y., for several months, in company with Elders Burges, Thompson, and others. July, 1835, he writes from Camptown, N.J., having left Lawrence, and calling on Elder Cummings in Delaware County, N.Y., he passes through Plymouth, Pa., and other places. He comes to Johnsonburg, N.J., in time to assist at the burial of Elder Joseph Thomas, the White Pilgrim. His reflections on the death of this stranger, whom he had never before seen, far away from family and kindred, of the contagion that prevented friends from administering to him in his last moments as they desired, are solemn and very pathetic, showing the true nature of the man.

April, 1840, he is pastor of the church at Stephentown, where they were building a meeting-house, for a place of worship, and a schoolhouse under one roof. In this same letter, he urges promiscuous sittings in the congregation. In 1845, he is in New York City, with no engagements, willing to serve where needed, and, at the same time, he makes a fair proposition to go anywhere at a moderate salary to teach Grammar, Natural Philosophy, Astronomy, and kindred branches of knowledge in any church that may want him. This work was to be done by lectures, week days and evenings. The same year, he held meetings at Gulf Mills, Pa., New York City, and other places. February, 1846, he became pastor of one of the churches in New Bedford, succeeding Elder J. Black- mar. He commends the loving nature of the union meetings held in that city, where the ministers of all denominations meet together to consult and pray for the prosperity of their respective churches. He was an active man and a great writer, not only on the workings of the church, but on subjects of a controversial character as well.

In 1853, he moved to Dundee, N.Y., where he had himself fixed, as he thought, to spend the balance of his days. But, for some cause, he continued with this church only three or four years. In May, 1859, he moved with his family to West Shelby, N.Y., where he preached with great energy and success till the December following, when his labors were closed by death, in the zenith of his power. He died of a carbuncle on the back, over the spine. He left a wife and four children—two sons and two daughters.

In person, the Elder was a fine looking man, rather short, thick set, with black hair and eyes, very pleasant in his habits, full of life, and always cheerful. He was a thorough grammarian and a good elocutionist, calm but earnest. In fine, he was a man who could ill be spared at his age.

EZEKIEL CURRY (1791-1867)

This brother was born in Athens, Penn., June 6, 1791, and died in the same place, October 26, 1867. He married, for his first, wife, Clarissa Lamphere, August 9, 1812, who died April 29, 1835. February 6, 1837, he married Mary Stevens, a female laborer in the Christian Church, who survived him.

The Curry family belonged to the Methodists. Ezekiel was converted in that church in 1814. He continued an active member of that body for about twenty years, when a certain trouble occurred in the church, and the class-book was burned by one of the ministers. About the same time, some of the Christian ministers preached in Smithfield, Penn., near his residence, which caused him to search the scriptures for himself. His views were changed and he joined the latter body. He had heard of the "Christ-ians," as they were called, before and formed a very poor opinion of them, but when he learned for himself he became a zealous advocate of the doctrine he had hated.

His first public work was in connection with his wife. He being a good singer and an earnest talker he soon became an active lay worker in the church. He was ordained to the full work of the ministry about 1839, and became a member of the New York Eastern Conference. By occupation he was a farmer and acquired a handsome property. He became a very useful man. While limited in education he gained much knowledge in laboring in the ministry.

WILLIAM CURRY (1770—1855)

William was born near Peekskill, N.Y., in 1770. He joined the Methodists and commenced preaching among them about 1795. He continued a minister of that church about twenty-seven years. In connection with eight other ministers, he left that body on account of a disagreement on the doctrine of the Trinity, and kindred tenets. They at first formed an independent body of their own, but finally joined the Christians. He died at Enfield, N.Y., March 25, 1855, in his eighty-fifth year.

The Elder had been a resident of the Western part of New York for many years. He was an active minister of the Christian Church eighteen years. He was a man of respectable ability, of lively conception, and his communications were forcible.

W. CURTIS (?—1870)

This minister was a member of the Southern Wabash Illinois Conference. He died in 1870.

ZARAH CURTIS (1761—1849)

Zarah was born in Plymouth, Conn., May 2, 1761. He entered the army, in the service of the State of Connecticut, in 1778, and continued two years. January 1, 1780, he enlisted in the Continental Army, in Captain John Webb's company, Colonel Sheldon's regiment of Dragoons, in which he served to the end of the war. He served as orderly on the staff of General Howe, with the rank of a noncommissioned officer, and was finally promoted to the grade of sergeant.

His position with General Howe gave him a fine opportunity to study the character of the great men of that trying time— as Generals Washington, Rochambeau, Sterling, LaFayette, Steuben, Parson, Heath, Lincoln, and others, of whom he often spoke to his friends in after years. During the service, he was engaged in the battles of Horse Neck, King's Bridge, Harlem River, and in the taking of the brig "Three Brothers," off Fairfield, in 1783.

After the war, he married a daughter of Aaron Yale, of Hartford Conn., and moved to Vermont. For a while, also, he lived in Champlain, Clinton County, New York, but in 1809, he moved to Newark, Ohio, a journey of more than two months at that time. In Licking and Knox counties, Ohio, he spent the remainder of his days.

About 1798, he joined the Methodist Church, in which connexion he continued for about twenty years, but being convinced that the doctrine of the Trinity was not taught in the Bible, he united with the Christian Church in 1819, in which he continued until death. He was a man and minister of irreproachable character and of acknowledged usefulness, commanding the respect of the conference and all who knew him.

He died near Utica, Ohio, June 9, 1849, aged eighty-nine years.

JOHN DALE (?—1870)

This minister was a member of the Southern Wabash Conference, Illinois. He died in 1870.

JOHN DANIELS (1763—1846)

John was born in 1763, and served some time in the Revolutionary War. He was converted when young, and soon became a zealous, self-sacrificing minister. Many were converted under his preaching. His field of labor was mostly in Genesee County, N.Y. He died in Stafford, N.Y., October 10, 1846, aged eighty-three years.

H.P. DARST (1816—1860)

This Elder was born in 1816, joined the Christians, under the labors of Elder P. Stipp, in 1843, and soon commenced preaching, joining the Northwestern Ohio Conference. He died in Hardin County, O., of milk sickness, October 24, 1860. All speak of him as a good man and a faithful worker.

JOHN DAVIS (1781—1856)

John was born in 1781, was raised among the Baptists, and was ordained by them October 11, 1820. Having embraced the Christian doctrine of the sufficiency of the Bible for a creed, he joined the North-western Ohio Conference, and labored faithfully with that body till death. He died October 8, 1856, aged seventy-five years.

EPES DAVIS (1773—1856)

Epes was born in 1772, and lived most of his time in Gloucester, Mass. He was converted in 1804, and commenced preaching soon after. As was the custom in those days, he supported himself by his own labor, and had conscientious scruples about receiving compensation for his ministerial work. But in his last years, he called in question the soundness of his early views. However, he acquired some wealth, and built a meeting-house, worth about fifteen hundred dollars, at Gloucester, at his own expense. In May, 1856, he moved to Lynn, where he died December 5, 1856.

JACOB DAVIS (1786—1851)

John K. Davis, a son of the deceased, says his father was born in Alton, N.H., February 17, 1786. He was the son of Timothy and Mary (Granville) Davis. His father was a farmer, and the son followed the same occupation till the age of seventeen, when his father sent him to learn the shoemaker's and tanner's trades, in the neighborhood. He followed the latter occupation till he was twenty-one years old. He experienced religion in 1803, was baptized, and joined the Freewill Baptist Church. He was married to

Louisa Kelly, of Gilman ton, N.H. About this time, he had it impressed upon his mind that he must preach, which impression he
resisted for a time. In 1825, he joined the Christian Church, and the
next year gave up the struggle of opposing his call to the ministry.
He was ordained at Alton, N.H., May 31, 1829, Elder Timothy
Cole being ordained at the same meeting. In 1831, he moved to
Barnstead with his family, where he continued to labor till 1839,
when his wife, Louisa, died. From Barnstead, he moved to West
Milton; during his stay there, he married for his second wife Mrs.
Hannah Lambert, a widow lady of that place. After this, he labored
in Dover and Boscawen. He died suddenly at the residence of his
son, at Barnstead, N.H., July 13, 1851. He was ready to depart; for,
to him, death had lost its terror.

JOHN L. DAVIS (?—1837)

This brother lived and died in Chester, S.C. He died February
16, 1837. His writings show much ability and earnestness.

M.F. DAVIS (?—1875)

M.F. Davis died at Stetson, Me., about 1875.

PATTEN DAVIS (1808—1860)

Patten was born about 1808, and was raised in Bethel, Vt. He
was a small and very energetic man, and a great revivalist. For a
time, he labored with a class oi Communists in the State of New
York. After this, he engaged in the business of daguerreotyping,
preaching, whenever he could, in Vermont. He became insane, and
died in a lunatic asylum about 1860.

RICHARD DAVIS (1791—1868)

Richard was born in Rochester, Mass., May 5, 1791, and died in
Milwaukee, Wis., December 28, 1868. He was converted in 1817,
and was ordained in Brutus, N.Y., in 1822. His labors in New England were in the neighborhood of Durham, N.H. He organized the
Upper Gilmanton Christian Church in 1839. He ' also preached in

Franklin, South Hampton, and Andover. Late in life, he moved to Wisconsin, and died there as stated.

He was a large man, with a strong voice, pleasant and prompt, and a ready speaker. His education was somewhat limited, but his quickness of apprehension made up for the defect, in a great measure.

RUSSEL B. DAVIS (1807—1838)

Many of the Maine and New Hampshire brethren have written to me concerning this young minister, and all agree that his early death was a great loss to the church. He was born in 1807, was converted in 1832, under the labors of Elder Henry Frost, and was baptized by the same. In 1834, he commenced his labors in the ministry, and the next year, left all to engage in his sacred calling. His influence and power were felt at once in the region where he labored, and he took a higher stand in the conference and church than could be expected of one so young in the work. In June, 1836, he was ordained at Cornish, Me. During his short life in the ministry, he labored first in Penobscot and Summerset counties.' Afterwards, he went to Kennebunk, Me., Lynn, Boston, Dartmouth, and Westport, Mass., and died in Fairfield, Me., May 13, 1838.

ELIJAH DAWSON (?—?)

This minister was a member of the Central Indiana Conference. He was a faithful minister.

SAMUEL R. DAWSON (?—1846)

Dawson was a prominent man, a Colonel of the Militia. He had a fair education. He commenced preaching about 1816, and died in the bounds of the Deer Creek Conference, O., about 1846.

A.S. DEAN (1820—1860)

This Elder lived and preached in Michigan till 1848, when he entered the Theological school in Meadville, Penn. In 1851, he graduated in the three years course. Soon after, he took charge of the church at Union Springs, N.Y. In this church, he was quite successful as a preacher and pastor.

When the Antioch College enterprise commenced, the Elder was one of its most ardent supporters. In 1851 or '52, he took the New York agency to raise money for the building of the college. He raised a large amount of money, mostly among the Unitarians and other liberal people in New York City. He soon became an assistant treasurer of the college, under Mr. Palmer, of the Broadway Bank, New York City, and located in Yellow Springs, O., where he married Miss Pennel, a niece of Hon. Horace Mann, president of the college.

In June, 1855, in company with his wife, he started for Europe, and traveled considerably through the old world. He wrote some interesting letters to our papers, describing quite vividly the scenes through which he traveled. About the beginning of the war of the Rebellion, he moved to St. Louis, Mo., and soon after died. He was not far from forty years old at the time of his death. He was a man of more than ordinary talent

<u>Isaac Dearth (1785—1869)</u>

This aged servant of God was born near Brownsville, Penn., December 26, 1785. He was the son of Edward and Elizabeth Dearth, who were members of the Methodist Church. In 1801, he moved with his father's family to Warren County, O., where Isaac had such educational advantages as were common in that early day in Ohio. In 1800, he received religious impressions from a Presbyterian school-teacher, which never left his mind. In 1806, he was married to Miss Betsy Newport, who survived him. In 1818, he was licensed to preach in the Christian Church, and was ordained in September, 1820, by Elders David Purviance and John Plummer. He died February 28, 1869.

The field of labor of this brother was mostly in Warren and adjoining counties in Ohio. He carried on a farm during his entire ministerial life; yet, under all the embarrassments of small pay, a large family, and large secular business, at certain periods of his life, he traveled quite extensively, and saw thousands converted through his labors. For many years, the Elder was a prominent man in the Miami Ohio Conference.

WILLIAM DEMERITT (1789—1841)

This Elder was born in Durham, N.H. in 1786, was converted in 1809, and soon began to preach. He was ordained in Lee, N.H., July, 1816. He became pastor of the church in Durham, and joined the New Hampshire Conference at its organization, and continued both relations till death. He died at Durham, December 29, 1841.

This Elder was a man of great energy. His whole heart was in the work. He had undertaken many enterprises for the good of the cause, and was always successful. The last enterprise carried through by his indomitable spirit was the establishment of the Durham Academy of the Christian Church, in his own village. But before the work was finished, he died. He left a mother, wife, and children. The cause of his death was an injury received by being thrown from a carriage.

ELI DENIO (1783—1846)

This brother was born in 1783. In his youth, he was a sailor, and traveled through many foreign countries. He sailed for the East over the Red Sea and Indian Ocean. On one of these voyages, during a severe storm, he was struck under conviction. When he came to land, he joined the Baptist Church; but, through the preaching of Elder J.S. Thompson, J. King, and others, he was led to join the Christians. He commenced preaching among the Christians in 1821, and continued faithful until death. He died at Moira, N.Y., June 23, 1846.

For many years, this Elder was well known in the denomination as a faithful and useful minister. His peculiar gift was that of a revivalist. His delivery was smooth and easy, his zeal knew no bounds, and his piety was deep and fervent. He was a plain, delicate, and slender man, with stooping form, a clear, shrill voice, and rapid delivery. His education was quite limited, and it was a won-

der to many that such an illiterate, rough sailor should be so successful as a minister. But the Elder, in his humility, attributed all
his success in the work to the grace of God. His health, never good,
broke down entirely at the death of his wife, in 1836. His mind and
body sank underneath this stroke. From this time till death, he
lived with his children, generally in limited circumstances. He died
at the house of a son-in-law. His faith continued strong to the last.

JOHN DEPEW (1815—1879)

John was born in 1815 He was early converted, and joined the
Christian Church at Newark, N.Y. In 1848, he began to preach. He
was pastor at Sodus, N.Y., for twenty years. He died at Arcadia,
N.Y., September 6, 1879, leaving a wife and five children.

PETER M. DEVORE (1802—1877)

The Devore family is of German origin. The grandfather of the
deceased came from Germany, from the bank of the river Rhine.
Peter was the son of David Devore, who was a prominent member
of the church at Ripley, and whose children became prominent
members of the Christian Church. Peter embraced religion about
1837, and soon commenced preaching. All the Devores were in
good circumstances, and our brother had a large farm on the bank
of the Ohio River, near the village of Higginsport. With the care
necessary to manage his property and a large family of children,
the wonder is that he devoted so much time to the work of the ministry; yet, in the thirty or forty years of his ministerial life, he did
much to build up the cause in Southern Ohio and Northern Kentucky. He was a man of great zeal, tender feelings, and, as he often
said, he believed in a Holy Ghost religion.

He died in triumph at his own home on the bank of the beautiful
Ohio, June 7, 1877, leaving a mourning widow [who followed him
soon after to the better land] and many affectionate children to
mourn their loss.

JOHN DEWITT (1814—1854)

John was born in Allegany County, Penn., March 4, 1814. He moved with his parents to Meigs County, O., in 1822. In 1835, he was married to Miss Olive Gee, and, soon after, both joined the Christian Church at Dexter, under the labors of Elder Tewksberry. In 1846, he began to preach. In 1851, he moved to Wapello County, Iowa; but, at the request of brethren, he moved to Batavia, the same state, where he labored in the surrounding churches till ill health prevented. He generally had charge of three or four churches. His means were limited, and, with thirteen children, and the pay for ministerial labor small, it was impossible for him to devote much time to the work he loved so much. He died at Batavia, June 29, 1854. His ministerial life was short, and the circumstances under which he labored were very trying; yet all felt that he did what he could in the cause of God.

WILLIAM AND JAMES DICKINSON

In the periodicals of the time, there is some confusion in regard to the history of these ministers. It is stated that two ministers of the above name labored near Williamsport, O., in an early day. Elder Millard, writing from the above place to the "Palladium," in 1834, gives an account of William, who was raised near that place, went to Virginia, and after laboring in that state for a time, died there in 1827. In the *Christian Messenger,* Vol. II, page 47, there is a fuller account of James Dickinson, who was born and raised in Ohio, and afterwards moved to Virginia, where he labored with much success. He also preached in Philadelphia and Baltimore. His health failing him, he undertook the practice of medicine. He died at the home of Brother Joel Ellison, at Cape Capron, Va., October 31, 1827. There is but little doubt that Elder Millard had the same person in view; whether William or James was the one who died in Virginia is unknown.

<u>BAYLES L. DICKSON (1816—1874)</u>

Our present subject was a zealous and energetic man, a member of the Tippecanoe Conference, Ind. He traveled as a conference missionary for many years, and was quite successful in the conversion of sinners.

He was born in Fayette County, Ind., May 5, 1816, and died in Fulton County, the same state, November 3, 1874. In 1836, he moved with his parents to Marshall County, Ind. In 1840, he married Miss Emma Houghton, who survived him. In 1854, he entered the ministry, and at once became a successful preacher. His first pastorate was in Winamack, and his second at Argos, both in Indiana. , In the latter place, by his judicious management and that of his family, he built a strong church, although laboring extensively as an evangelist most of his time. He died lamented by the church and community, and especially by a loving wife and affectionate children.

<u>ELIAS DOBLE (?—?)</u>

This brother died in Etna, Me., before 1875.

<u>REUBEN DOGES (?—1828)</u>

This brother was one of the most devoted and self-sacrificing of men. In early life, he lived in Charleston, Mass., where he worked at the trade of brick-laying. He finally moved to Stowe, Vt., where he continued at the same trade, and preached when he could. He would work hard all day and walk ten miles to meeting and back again the same night to be ready for work the next day. His constant theme was religion, of which he talked much and wisely. He was in limited circumstances, but he raised a fine family of children, some of whom became scholars and teachers. He was an influential man, in his narrow sphere, and was much respected by his brethren. He died about 1828.

John Donachy (1813—1841)

This brother was born in 1813. He was one of the first who joined the Christian Church in Lewisburg, Penn. He commenced preaching in 1836 or '37, and died in Lewisburg, November 22, 1841, leaving a wife and children. In person, he was tall and slim, and had a dark complexion. His peculiar forte was exhortation and doctrinal subjects.

Tiffin Donaldson (1836—1862)

This brother was a young man when he died, and had been but a few years in the ministry; but, from the way he started out, all the brethren expected a great future for him in the Master's work. He was raised in Fountain County, Ind. Very early in life, he joined the Methodist Church. He attended school whenever he could, and made great progress in knowledge. As he proceeded in the study of the Bible, he found that he could not honestly subscribe to some of the doctrines of his own church. He applied and was received a member of the Christian Church. Soon after, he joined the Central Illinois Conference, and was very active in winning sinners to Christ. About this time, also, he was united in marriage to a lady well suited to the high calling which he had espoused. It was his intention to enter Union Christian College; but, when the war of the Rebellion broke out, he enlisted in the service of his country. He died in the service at New Haven, Ky., of typhoid fever, February 23, 1862, leaving a young wife and one child to mourn his untimely departure.

Moses Dooly

This brother was a minister in an early day, in Ohio and Kentucky. He was an old man before 1825.

Reuben Dooly (1773—1822)

Few men of limited education left a deeper impression upon any denomination than did this brother upon the Christian Connexion. He is remembered with affection in all places where he traveled.

He was born in Bedford County, Va., November 14, 1773. His father was an Elder in the Presbyterian Church. Reuben moved with his father's family to Madison County, Ky., in 1781. As it was in the time of the Indian War, the family at first lived in a fort; so Reuben's educational advantages were not great. He had to attend school in perilous times. His first ideas in Theology were in keeping with the Calvinistic preaching he heard—that he was a reprobate. This led him to lead a wild and reckless life. He was finally converted in the Presbyterian Church, under the preaching of Samuel Findley. His temper and zeal at once led him to exhort others. So successful was he in this irregular preaching that many were led to Christ through his exhortations. He could not enter the Presbyterian ministry on account of his limited education. So anxious was he to labor in the Christian cause that he went three different times to the Cherokee Indians to tell them how good religion was. He was well received by the red men. He had David Haggard to visit them too. He lived at this time in Barren County, Ky.

In 1801, he attended the great meeting at Cane Ridge. The work there was just to his liking. He took an active part in the exercises, was soon baptized by immersion, and was ordained by the new party to the full work of the ministry. He now labored in various places with great success. In 1807, he was about to move his family to Preble County, O., where his father had already moved; but death came, his brother and wife died within four days of each other. His children were taken by some relatives and he was entirely foot-loose—and well did he use the opportunity. One time, we find him in Ohio, in company with Elder Barton W. Stone, who, also, was a widower, crossing streams that were over their banks, being carried over a, mill-dam and nearly drowned, tearing garments by their rough traveling, yet so poor that they lacked the means to pay for being ferried over the many streams they had to cross.

In 1810, we see him visiting Kentucky, Tennessee, and Virginia, and, perhaps, other states. At Norfolk, Va., he had a good time with Rice Haggard, one of the pioneer ministers of the O'Kelly branch of the Christian Church. Indeed, he was like Paul, he knew nothing but Jesus Christ and him crucified. About 1811, he took the milk sickness in Miami County, O., from the effects of which he never fully recovered. In 1817, he went on a preaching tour to the State of Missouri. Great success attended his preaching and many souls were converted. On his way back, he and his horse were both sick. He often had to alight from his horse and lie down to rest, thinking, sometimes, that he should never reach his family. His way lay through the unbroken forest, with neither a house nor a clearing for scores of miles. After resting for a while from his fatigue, at home, we find him, in company with his father, visiting Virginia. The same year, he has great meetings in Kentucky. ~ In 1820, his father died. From this time, he felt his iron constitution giving way, and realized that his time to die was not far off.

A short time before he died, when his health was quite poor, there was a meeting held by Elder David Purviance and some others at the Paint Church, Preble County, O., where the Elder lived. In this meeting, he did not speak till toward the close. When he did speak he carried everything before him. His wife said to him, "Reuben, you have killed yourself." His answer was expressive of the man, "If I was to die on the spot, I would not have said a word less." This was his last sermon. He died April 22, 1822, aged forty-nine years, about twenty-two of which he had spent in the ministry. He was married twice—first to Lean Railsback, of whom he had five children, second to Rachael Martin, in 1811. His great power as a speaker was in rousing the people. Elder Barton W. Stone used to say of him that when he built the brush heap Dooly could set it on fire. His powerful constitution was broken down in the short space of twenty years by excessive labor.

JOEL DOUBLEDAY (1766—1858)

Joel was born in Lebanon, Conn., January 12, 1766. He was the son of Joseph and Elizabeth (Phelps) Doubleday. His mother was a pious good woman, and his father was religious, but so set in his Calvinistic Theology that he would hardly consent to examine any other views. In 1782, his mother joined the church during a revival in Lebanon, and Joel was much affected by the act. In 1785, the family moved to Coventry, Conn. Through these years, Joel was much concerned about religion, sometimes concluding that he was a reprobate, at other times cherishing the hope that he might be converted. In 1787, another awakening occurred in the village, and his conviction deepened more and more; but, in the autumn of the next year, while on a visit to a brother in the State of Massachusetts, he met a Universalist, and although he argued strongly against the doctrine of universal salvation, yet, as they both agreed that God had foreordained whatever should come to pass, when he left his Universalist companion, he was more than half converted to his opponent's views. From this time, he argued the Universalist doctrine with many inward doubts of the truth of his theory. It was his peculiar hobby, also, to oppose fatalism and Calvinistic doctrines. About this time, he read the entire Bible through, six times. In 1789, he moved to Windsor, Vt., and, in the fall of 1790, was married to Miss Anna Wentworth. He was now the head of a family, and, being well posted in Bible lore, he was counted by his neighbors a staunch advocate of universal salvation.

Thus he continued till 1802, when, according to his own words, "he heard the first gospel sermon." The preacher's name was Steadman, and he belonged to the Freewill Baptist Church. The man seemed to direct all his arguments at Joel, treating on free grace and God's willingness to save all on the terms of repentance. At this time, Joel had not been to meeting on Sunday for three years, and his thirteen years of Universalism received a heavy shock from that sermon. It is useless to mention here all the exercise of mind through which he passed before he was soundly and almost miraculously converted, or the great struggle through which he passed before he consented to become a minister of the gospel, or the opposition of his father, the encouragement from his wife and mother-in-law, the great disappointment of his Universalist friends. June 12, 1803, at his own home, he and his companion gave themselves to the Lord, and a family altar was reared. He soon after joined the Christians, and became an active and able minister of Christ.

In his thirty-seventh year, in 1803, his autobiography of eighteen pages, foolscap, ends. From this time to the close of his eventful career, we have but little account. After laboring faithfully in Vermont, for a time, he moved, in an early day, to the State of New York, and took for his field of labor all the country from the Genesee River to lakes Ontario and Erie. He labored as but few men labored, and with peculiar success. Many of the churches in Western New York were organized by him.

Through his long life of labor and success, he failed to lay up means of support for his declining years. In his old age, he was very poor. January 13, 1834, his faithful companion died at Barre, N.Y. In 1852, the New York Western Conference proposed that a collection be taken up in all the churches for his benefit. In 1858, the old pilgrim lay off the coil of mortality. When he died, he was ninety-two years old.

<u>David Douglass (1781—1861)</u>

This veteran was born in Shroud's station, Ky., in 1781, in the time of the Indian War. When he was eight months old/his father was killed by the Indians at Gray's defeat, at the Upper Blue Lick, leaving the mother with three small children. In 1763, the boy took a job to quarry and haul stone, by which he laid up money enough to buy two hundred acres of land. Soon after this, he was married to Catherine E. Sidener, with whom he moved on the land. But, as was not uncommon in the State of Kentucky in those days, the title proved worthless, and he had to pay for the land a second time.

He was converted in 1801, and commenced preaching soon after, holding to the Bible to the exclusion of all creeds, and "Christian" alone as a denominational name, not knowing then that any other people held the same views. He was baptized among the Freewill Baptists, but did not join the church.

Such was his energy and success that many of the neighbors fell in with his views. He had a meeting-house built on his own farm, where he preached regularly. There were many who looked with contempt on the "Douglassites," however, and they styled his meeting-house the "Frog pond." The few who joined in this service did not mind the Scoff. They came from far and near, crossing swift streams on rafts, and traveling three or four miles to the prayer meetings on week nights. Mothers with three or four children traveled on horseback many miles, as happy as if riding in the finest coaches, for their hearts were warm in the love of God.

Besides attending to the few congregations around his Kentucky home, the Elder soon traveled far and near through Indiana, Ohio, and other states. He soon formed the acquaintance of Stone, Purviance, Kinkade, Hughes, and other fathers in the Christian Church, with whom he worked faithfully to the end of his long life. One peculiarity of this minister was, that, although he lived in a slave state, as soon as he was converted, he became a strong anti-slavery man, and blacks, as well as whites, were welcomed to his house and church. .

In 1825, he left Kentucky and moved to Decatur County, Ind., where he labored the rest of his days, and where he closed his useful life. And, on the farm he first bought in Indiana, his body was laid by the side of his faithful wife, in a private graveyard, reserved when the farm was sold, a few years before his death. He died at Milroy, Ind., January 23, 1861, aged eighty years.

In moving to Indiana, his trip was quite disastrous; a noble boy, twelve years old, fell under the wagon wheel and was instantly killed. At the same time, one of the finest horses was killed by being stopped too suddenly. As soon as the Elder settled on his new place in Indiana, all hands went to work to clear and burn the unbroken forest; and no sooner was the house put up for the family than a house for education and for worship must be reared also. A schoolhouse, large enough for a church, was put up in which, soon after, the Elder organized into church relation a band of pioneer Christians.

From this time till near the close of his life, no name was more conspicuous in the Central Indiana Conference than that of this brother. His peculiar forte as a minister was his great knowledge of the Bible. His arguments, by the application of passage after passage of the Bible, were overwhelming. His wife, also, was a great help to him—not only by seeing to things at home, when the husband was absent, but also by attending with him all accessible meetings, and bearing a warm testimony with her husband of the reality of religion.

Like most of our early ministers, Elder Douglass went on his own expense. The meetings at his own place in Indiana, as in Kentucky, were carried on almost entirely by himself— some meetings of several days costing him no less than fifty dollars. Besides these, he gave liberally of his own money for the building of meeting-houses at other places. But, to make up for this, he had often to work by moonlight, as well as to travel many a weary mile, after preaching at night, in order to be back to his work next morning. By his thrift and economy, with all his sacrifice, he laid up a nice property. After the death of his wife, he sold his farm and moved to the village of Milroy. He was then worth some nine thousand dollars. He lived comfortably in his new home with his daughter Elizabeth. When first taken sick, he at once said he should not recover. But, with the old veteran, it mattered not. His work was finished, the companion of his youth was gone, and he was at peace with God and all the human family. He died in triumph.

E. DRAKE (1798—1864)

This brother was born in 1798. In early life, he joined the United Brethren Church, became a minister in the same, and continued so for thirty years. At the first session of the Antioch Christian Conference, Ind., Elder Drake became a member, and continued so till his death. He died April 18, 1864.

JOHN DUDLEY (1784—1849)

John was born in the state of Maine, July 19, 1784, and died in Fountain County, Ind., at the home of his son-in-law, Mr. Jonathan Board, July 17, 1849.

Before leaving his native state, he married Sarah Marston. He also joined the Freewill Baptist Church and became a minister in the same. In 1818, he moved to the neighborhood of Cincinnati, O., and soon after, joined the Christian Church at Burlington, O. He preached for the latter, and surrounding churches for some time. In 1822, he moved to Warren County, O., and settled near the village of Red Lion. He preached in Warren and Butler counties, O., and Union County, Ind., for many years, with great success.

August 9, 1838, he and Elder James McKinney organized a Christian Church, on Osborn Prairie, in Fountain County, Ind. He had moved to this part of Indiana, at the above date, and these two veterans preached for this and surrounding churches for years. They were well suited to labor together, McKinney was a good sermonizer and Dudley was equally good in exhortation. Elder Dudley continued to labor in Fountain and adjacent counties in Indiana, till death, highly respected by all who knew him, but not having a very rugged constitution, the exposure to which a pioneer minister is subject, soon broke down his health, and he died as stated, in his sixty-fifth year, full of labor and usefulness.

MOSES DUDLEY (?—1870)

Moses was a son of the preceding. He was a licensed minister of Union Conference, Iowa. He died July 11, 1870, not far from fifty years of age.

? DUDLEY (1808—1849)

There was a minister of the above name who labored in the neighborhood of Randolph, Vt. He was an earnest, faithful worker, and had often expressed a wish that he might die in the pulpit. His wish was granted, for he died while preaching, about 1843, aged thirty-five.

STEVEN DUNBAR (1790—1849)

This brother was born in Chelsea, Vt., in 1790, moved to Woodstock, in 1801, to learn a trade, and was converted in 1809, under the labors of Fredrick Plummer. He was impressed to enter the ministry at once, but rejected the call till after his marriage. Soon after this event he entered the work in earnest, and continued faithful to the close of life. He died at Georgia, Vt., April 27, 1849.

JOHN DUNCAN (1821—1869)

John was born in 1821, joined the church in 1842. Not long after that, he began to preach and joined the Miami Conference, O. During the war of the Rebellion he lost a son. January, 1867, his wife died. After this, he gave up his farm and his entire time was devoted to the work of the ministry. While preaching to a church, which he had organized, in Henry County, Ind., he was taken sick and died after a short illness, September 6, 1869. He was a good man and a fair speaker.

? DUNCAN (?—?)

This brother assisted at the ordination of Elder Charles Cummins, in Giles County, Va., in 1825.

JAMES DUNLAP (1773—1860)

This brother labored for many years, faithfully, in Champaign and adjoining counties in Ohio. He belonged to the Freewill Baptist connexion when he first came among the Christians. He and a brother-in-law, Johnson, by labor, became identified with our people.

He was born in Augusta County, Va., July 10, 1773. He moved with his father to the neighborhood of Lexington, Ky., in 1784, and married Emily Johnson, sister of Elder Johnson, in 1795. Rejoined the Baptist Church in 1800, was ordained a minister, in that church, in 1805, and moved to Pretty Prairie, Champaign County, O., in 1812. He continued to preach at that place till 1844, when he moved to Jacksonville, Ill. He lived there the remainder of his life, laboring but little in the ministry. He died February 28, 1866, in his ninety-third year. While not a regular member of the Christian Church, yet he preached for that body more or less for about thirty-six years; hence the insertion of his memoir. He was a strong and good man.

<u>J</u>OHN <u>D</u>UNLEVY (1771—1824)

This pioneer minister of the church was the son of Antony Dunlevy, originally from Ireland. The mother's name was White, and was of Scotch descent. John was born near Winchester, Va., in 1771; the same year his parents moved to Washington, Penn. His brother, Francis, was a school-teacher and John received his early education from him. John's memory was retentive in those early days. It is said that he and a fellow pupil committed the entire Latin grammar to memory in one week. He became a fine Greek scholar, and a graduate of Cannonsburg Theological Institute, Penn.

He commenced preaching about 1798. In the same year he became pastor of a Presbyterian Church on Eagle Creek, O. His manner of speaking was slow and logical with a slight impediment in his speech During this pastorate, in 1801, the revival which commenced on Cane Ridge, Ky., reached Eagle Creek, O., and Rev. Dunlevy, with several other Presbyterian ministers, was carried away from his mooring in Calvinism and entered heartily into the spirit of the movement. He was an active worker in the organization of the Christian Connexion, and continued a zealous advocate of the same till 1806, when he and all his family joined a Shaker Community near Harrodsburg, Ky. In 1824, a severe epidemic broke out in a Shaker village, at Busro, Ind., and as the Elder was considered an ingenious physician he hurried thither on an errand of mercy. He succeeded to some degree in his mission, but as he was ready to start for his home he took the contagion and died in 1824.

He was a leading man among the Shaker community through life and the books published by him are highly valued by the brotherhood to this day, as standard works. His works were mostly on Doctrinal Theology.

Samuel Dunwoody (1799—1852)

Samuel was born in Virginia, June 5, 1799. In 1801, his father's family moved to Pennsylvania, and in 1809, to Butler County, O. In early life, Samuel followed flat-boating on the Ohio and Mississippi rivers.

In 1819, he joined the Methodist Church, as a probationer, but was never taken into full membership. In 1828, he was married to Maria Lander, of whom he had twelve children, and with whom he lived happily for many years. Soon after his marriage, he and his wife joined the Christian Church, and were baptized by Elder Nathan Worley. About 1841, he was licensed to preach in the Bluffton, Indiana Conference. His first wife died in 1849, and in 1851, he was married to Catharine Hall. From 1842 to 1849 he labored as a licensed minister, but in the latter year, he was ordained at a session of the Western Conference, Ind. at the town of Alamo. He died November 7, 1855, aged fifty-six years.

William Dyer (?—?)

This brother was born in Pennsylvania, previous to 1800, and moved with his parents to Ohio, while young. His mother, who died when he was small, was a member of the Baptist Church, but his father and step-mother were members of the Christian Church. William united with the latter church in early life, and was ordained to the work of the ministry in 1818, by Elder Nathan Worley. He at once took a high position in the church. He was a young minister of excellent character and very promising, but he died early, leaving a young wife and small children to mourn his early death.

John Eastwood (?-1863)

Brother Eastwood was a member of the Tippecanoe Conference, Ind. He died about 1863.

At the ordination of Elder Benjamin Taylor at Assonet, Mass., in 1811, this brother assisted in the work.

JOHN EDMAN (1796—1870)

John was born in Augusta County Va. in 1796, moved to Licking County, O., in 1813, and, in 1828, embraced religion and was baptized by Elder I.N. Walter. In 1850, he began to preach, laboring faithfully in his own and neighboring churches until death, which took place near Homer, Ohio, June 10, 1870.

THOMAS ELLIS (1790—1839)

Old members of the Church in Hamilton and Clermont counties, O., speak highly of Elder Thomas Ellis as a man of God, and a very earnest minister. By trade, he was a bricklayer, and laid the brick for the first brick house in Cincinnati. He had a wooden leg. It is probable that he was born about 1790, and died about 1839. All speak highly of him. He was a man in good circumstances, owning a good farm near South Bend, O. His house was the preacher's home, in those early days, and he was very generous and kind to all his neighbors. His preaching was of the exhortation kind, and he seldom had charge of a church; yet he was counted a very useful man.

WILLIAM D. ELLIS (1820—1865)

William was born not far from 1820, and died about 1865, in Western Pennsylvania. He was a young man of great zeal, with a good education. He wrote much for our periodicals. He was a member of the Erie Conference, Penn. He labored, also, in Eastern Ohio.

JAMES ELLIOTT (1822—1862)

Of all the ministers, whose lives are recorded in this volume, there is none that the compiler has had such advantages to form a thorough acquaintance with, as with this brother. Yet such is life, and its changes, that in his case, after having lived in the same room for three years, I am unable to state the time or place of his birth. James was born in Ireland, crossed the ocean with his parents when a child, became an orphan when quite young, and was brought up by a good Samaritan, a member of the Christian Church, and the boy soon embraced religion, and joined the church of his benefactor. He commenced preaching when about the age of sixteen, and became a member of the Central Ohio Conference. He continued his connection with that body, until 1851, when he joined the Bluffton Conference, Ind.

In early life, he labored with the church in Cincinnati. After a while he went to Ripley, and, by the advice of Dr. Campbell, Brother Ridgeway, and others, he attended a high school in that place. In 1844, at the opening of the Meadville school, he entered as a student, and continued his studies there for more than three years. During his connection with that Institution, he took a high position. He wrote frequently for our periodicals. His industry was wonderful. He was well informed, especially on religion, temperance, and negro slavery. He read every paper that came to the institution. He traveled on foot, far and near to preach, and lecture, on the above subjects. Slavery was his particular hobby in those days.

He left Meadville in 1848, and soon after was married to Miss Sarah Hoover, of Felicity, O., who survived him only a few years. His ministerial life, after leaving Meadville, was not long. He preached a few years in Sidney, and Greenville, Ohio. After this he turned his attention to school teaching, and finally studied law, and became a law-partner of Hon. F. Haussarek, in Cincinnati. He still continued to preach occasionally, in the surrounding churches. In 1862, he became a war correspondent of the Cincinnati "Gazette," in the Army of the Potomac. At Martinsburg, Md., he took the camp fever. His wife hurried to his side and brought him on the way home, as far as Wheeling, Va., but while waiting there for a boat for Cincinnati, he died, in 1862, not far from forty years of age.

Simon Emery (1762—1844)

This aged minister was born in 1762. He labored in the State of Maine, and died there in 1844.

Isaac Emily (1806—1877)

Isaac was born April 21, 1806, was converted in 1849, and was ordained in 1851. He was one of the few ordained ministers at the organization of the Illinois Central Christian Conference, September 24, 1852. He died June 14, 1877, near Danville, Ill.; sermon on the occasion delivered by Elder Clapp. Elder Emily was a very unassuming man, of limited education; but he was very successful in the conversion of sinners.

Shubal C. Evans (?—1860)

Evans was a native of North Carolina. He was an itinerant minister for many years, and was quite successful in winning souls to Christ. He died in 1860, in North Carolina.

Thomas Evans (1811—1879)

This Elder was born in Pennsylvania, October 4, 1811, was married in Butler County, Ind., February 22, 1838, was converted in 1839, and was ordained about 1865. He died at his residence near Danville, Ill., June 21, 1879. His health had been so poor since 1875 that he had been unable to preach.

Benjamin Fairly (?—?)

Elder Fairly was ordained in Milo, N.Y., in connection with Elders Potter and Lamphere, by Elder Badger and others, September 3, 1820. He was a member of the New York Central Conference. In 1832, he lived in Phelps, N.Y., and preached there and at Marion. He subsequently moved to Michigan, and died at the residence of his daughter, at Burroak, in that state.

<u>Rueben Fairly (?—?)</u>

Reuben Fairly was a brother of the preceding; but, though older in years, he was not so prominent as Benjamin. Both had been preachers in the Methodist Church before joining the Christians.

<u>Jonathan Farnam (1805—1874)</u>

This minister was, like many others, impressed with the duty of preaching early in life, but postponed it till he was thirty-seven years old. He was born in Enfield, N.H., May 26, 1805. At twelve years of age, he had serious impressions, and was a praying boy. These impressions wore away for a time, and he made many excuses. The death of a brother brought him back, and he was baptized, September, 1824. From this time till 1842, he labored, to some extent, as a lay brother, and was very successful. In 1826, he was married to Miss Stevens, of Enfield. He also taught school part of this time.

In 1842, he held many meetings of great interest at Enfield, Grafton, Lebanon, and Dorchester, N.H. He was ordained at the latter town by Elders Morrisson, Davis, and Hershey, June 1, 1843. He was engaged as pastor in the churches of Marlow, Washington, Walpole, and other places. In the year 1852, he traveled 1,832 miles, made 131 religious visits, and preached 103 times. When he died, he left an account of his labors, and his report shows him to have been a man of industry. September, 1856, he moved to Illinois, and joined the Northern Illinois and Wisconsin Conference. Two years before—in 1854,—he had buried a wife, father, and mother. He married, for his second wife, Laura P. Fish, of Wilmot, N.H. His labors in the West were abundant—in Illinois, Wisconsin, and Iowa. His salary was generally small, and he had to perform manual labor to support himself and family. He died at the house of his son, at Cornwall, HL, March 28, 1874.

<u>Douglas Farnum (?—?)</u>

Many opinions are entertained as to the real character and standing of this minister, but all acknowledge his talent and magnetism as a speaker. He was brought up in the State of Vermont, ordained by John Rand, Uriah Smith, and Elias Cobb. After preaching to great acceptance in Vermont and New Hampshire, he visited Rhode Island and Massachusetts, in 1813. Great revivals followed his preaching wherever he went. In Providence, R.I., a church was organized as the result of his labors, but his greatest power as a preacher, was manifested at Coventry, R.I. A man by the name of "Sam" Rice, lived in the latter place, who was a noted gambler, and who kept around him a wild set of men like himself. By some means, Farnum was invited to preach in this gambling house. He went, and one of the first that felt the power of the word was Rice. Most of his comrades were converted at the same meeting. Soon a church of hundreds of members was organized. The work spread far and near, and Farnum was idolized by many.

It is impossible, at this distant day, to decide the merits of the controversy that arose in the churches concerning Farnum. Some of the brethren were anxious at this time to organize the churches into conferences; for hitherto, although there were many churches in New England, yet in many places the church was amenable to no other body. Farnum, and his adherents, opposed conferences; but about 1817 he was tried by a general conference that met at Hampton, Conn., for some irregularity. Farnum denied the authority of the body to try him. His plea was, that he was amenable alone to the church, of which he was a member. His church, at Coventry, stood by him almost to a man. Pamphlets were published for, and against him, and the excitement became great.

In 1817, Elder Farnum, in company with a colony of church members, mostly from Rhode Island, Connecticut, and Massachusetts, moved to Darby Plains, O. There were some seventeen or eighteen wagons in the company, and one preacher, at least, beside Farnum—Elder Nathan Burlingame. All the way out, Farnum preached wherever there was an opportunity. In Columbus, Dublin, and all through the Scioto Valley, revival followed revival. Several ministers of other denominations, and hundreds of members joined the church. It is hard to tell how much fanaticism was mingled with these revivals. Farnum made the trip from New England to Ohio and back more than once. The second time he went to Ohio he took his family. The settlement on the Plains was soon visited by a fanatical class of people from Vermont, calling themselves "Pilgrims." These people had a prophet who was implicitly obeyed. Their habits were filthy, believing that in order to be religious they must appear dirty. Elder Farnum opposed them and they finally went away, taking no members with them. These people were traveling in search of Zion under the guidance of their prophet. They finally settled on an island in the Mississippi river, but when the weather became warm, sickness broke out among them, their prophet died, and many of their members died also. The others scattered and the whole company was broken up.

Not long after the Pilgrims, the Shakers came among Elder Farnum's flock, and these were more successful in making converts than their predecessors. Elder Nathan Burlingame, and family, old Squire Samuel Rice, (the Sam Rice of gambling notoriety, of Coventry, R.I.,) and family, and some other members, joined the Shakers. Elder Farnum moved with his family to Upper Sandusky, O. That part of the state then, was very sickly, and ague and fever broke out among the settlers. Many died of these diseases, and Elder Farnum was one of the number. He died soon after his removal. I have not the date of his birth or death.[1] Those who were acquainted with Elder Farnum speak of him as one who exercised the most wonderful power on an audience. He had a musical voice, a fluent delivery, somewhat of a "holy" or singing tone. He spoke with mouth, hands, feet, and, in fact, with the entire body. Many think he was fanatical in acting from a Divine impression in temporal things; others think that he had no more of these than other men of his cast, generally. It is very probable, however that the time and circumstances under which he lived with the "Pilgrims"

---

[1] A gravestone for "D. Farnum," in the area of his death, gives dates of 1780-1822. Other records list 1779 as his birth year. One record says he was "killed by a falling tree," though the source of that statement was not provided.—*Editor.*

and Shakers, spoken of, had considerable influence on the man, and perhaps gave rise to more rumors of the kind than was true.

MARK FERNALD (1784—1851)

Few men exerted a greater influence in the denomination than Mark Fernald in his day. He was a son of Joshua and Elizabeth Fernald. He was born in Kittery, Maine, March 9, 1784. He was the youngest of six children, four sons and two daughters, and was of English descent. His early associates were wicked people, and he partook of their habits. He was sent to school early, but was a dull scholar. At thirteen, he undertook to learn the carpenter's trade. Before he was twenty he spent one year at sea. His mother was religiously inclined, but not converted, still the interest she had in religion was a help to the boy in his youth. His great temptations were drinking, dancing and card playing.

When twenty-one years of age, he read the Bible -and White-field's sermons, which made him sober and serious, but he had great prejudice against baptism by immersion. His theological preference was to the Congregational church, the church to which his mother was inclined. In 1807 there was a great religious awakening at Kittery, under the labors of Elder Moses Safford, of the Christian Church, and Stinchfield, of the Freewill Baptist. In this meeting, some of his own family were converted, and in December, 1807, after being under conviction since the preceding April, and after passing through a rough voyage at sea he was baptized in the Atlantic Ocean. Such was the temper and earnestness of this son of the sea, that to be converted was to become a minister, it is true, it took him some time to come around, but all knew that it could not be otherwise. He soon visited the churches in Kennebec, Hallowell, Augusta, Waterville, and Sidney, Me. In the summer of 1808, he met Elder Elias Smith at Portsmouth, N.H., and the September following he preached his first sermon at Kittery. On September 20, 1808, at the urgent solicitation of Elder Peter Young, who was lame, he was ordained at South Berwick, Me., by Elders Peter Young and Ephraim Stinchfield. From this time, to October

16, 1825, when he was married to Jane Stevens, he traveled and labored, almost constantly. The wonder is that any constitution could stand, under such intense excitement. Even the day of his marriage, he had preached twice to his congregations at Kittery, and at the third meeting on that day, he was married in the public congregation.

Although he traveled through all the New England states, and often beyond their limits, he always retained his connection as pastor with the church at Kittery. From 1807, until 1825, he had no home of his own, and after the latter date, while he had a family, he traveled and preached almost constantly to the end of his days. He died at Kittery, the place of his birth, December, 30, 1851, aged sixty-eight years, and the forty-eighth of his ministry.

The peculiar characteristics of Mark Fernald, were:

1st. Strict honesty. He had no deception in him.

2nd. Boldness. We feel as we look upon his likeness that there is no sign of timidity in that countenance, and we are confirmed in this opinion as we read his fearless combats with bad men.

3d. Sound common sense. There is much of eccentricity in his composition. His whole life is full of oddity and yet under all, and through all, there is a clearness of ideas. His expressions may be odd, but they are wise—they are philosophic. We see these characteristics also in his passing through all the fanaticisms of New England, in his day, without ever being tinctured with them. The Jacob Cochran fanaticism was in his field of labor, so also was the Osgoodites. He fought both, and vanquished them, with the strong weapons of common sense. Then the Mormons, the "Come-out-ists," the Adventists, that turned the heads of so many, never turned him to the right or left.

4th. Great originality, He was always himself. It was Fernald and no one else. He doubtless used the thoughts of other men, but they were always well digested and seemed internalized before they were used as his own.

These, and similar traits, made Fernald welcome to all our gatherings. In 1850, I remember of meeting him at the New England

Christian Convention, at Newburyport. His appearance was very common. He had none of the gloss or diction that many others, in that body, had. He was plain, and somewhat uncouth in appearance, yet when he spoke all listened. His words had weight in them. The most of those present had measured arms with him before, and they knew his strength. Similar receptions were accorded him everywhere. The name of Fernald was a tower of strength among the churches in New England, for his goodness ability, and zeal were acknowledged by all that knew him.

<u>ALPHUS FIELD (?—?)</u>

This man was a younger brother of Lebbeus Field, whose information is below. He commenced preaching in New York, went to Michigan, where he labored successfully for some time, and died in that state many years ago.

<u>LEBBEUS FIELD (1780—1879)</u>

Elder George S. Warren, sent me an excellent biography of this veteran. It would be a great pleasure to insert it here, word for word, but as it is too lengthy for my present purpose, I will here give the substance.

Elder Field was born in Woodstock, Vt., February, 2, 1780, and joined the Methodist Church, in 1803. He soon began to labor in public, and in 1813, he was licensed to preach in the Methodist church. He had two brothers who were ministers. Hezekiah, with the Methodists, and Alpheus with the Christians. Lebbeus was married to Eunice Warren, an excellent woman, and a suitable helper to a minister. In 1807, he moved with his small family, of wife and one child, from Woodstock, Vt., to Watertown, N.Y. His father and family had moved to the same place before, and-, as they were pioneers, the place is called the "Field Settlement" to this day, by the neighbors.

Before leaving Vermont, Elder Field met Abner Jones and Elias Smith, and was favorably impressed with their liberal views, but when he gave up his Methodist doctrine, he had considerable opposition, and was tried for heresy. When he moved to New York the country was new, and the settlers were poor like himself. January, 11, 1813, he re-organized the church at East Houndsfield, where he had previously removed. He preached to this church steadily, until 1860. At the latter date, his voice failed, when his meetings became less frequent; still he continued to labor in the settlement to the extent of his ability to the end of life. The church at Houndsfield, was the first Christian Church, and Elder Field the first Christian minister in Northern New York. This church celebrated its sixty-third anniversary, January, 11, 1880. His faithful wife died in 1865 at the age of eighty-eight years. He died, September, 6, 1879, at the great age of ninety-nine years, seven months and four days.

In his habits, he was social and generous. His sermons were mostly of the textual kind, delivered with great earnestness, and full of Bible proofs to sustain his points. He was a man of strong constitution, and it required great strength to perform the double labor of preaching to so many churches, and to support his family by the labor of his hand. For many years he was quite deaf, and about one year before he died, he became almost blind. Thus shut out from the world by sight and sound, and the weight of almost a century resting upon him, yet he was patient, and ever cheerful. His funeral was largely attended. Sermon by Elder J.E. Hayes, from Rev. 3:12, and the old patriarch rests sweetly in the Lord.

ISAAC AND JOSIAH FISHER

Father and son, were ministers in the Christian Church near Worthington, O., about 1820. Both died many years ago.

EBENEZER S. FLEMING (1803—1850)

From Miss A.A. Fleming, a daughter of the deceased, I gather the following: Ebenezer was born November 22, 1803, in Chapinville, N.Y. His father died when Ebenezer was young, and the boy was raised by his maternal grandfather. He worked on a farm, and learned the tanner's and currier's trades. In 1825, he was married to Miss Margaret Hannah, who became a great help to him in the acquisition of knowledge. In 1830, a young child of theirs was drowned in a tan-vat—which so affected the minds of the parents that soon after, they were converted, and joined the Christian Church. Such was the interest of Brother Fleming in this new life in Christ that he at once took a public position in the church, and in 1832, was. received a member of the conference. The same year, he moved with his family to Genesee County, N.Y. Here, while living on the bank of a stream, the house and furniture were carried away with the flood, the family barely escaping with their lives—and even this was effected by the restlessness of a traveling minister who was kept awake by the sound of the water.

July, 1834, he was ordained, and the same year, moved to East Sparta, where, in the following year, a great ingathering took place. In 1837, he moved to Steuben County, and the year following, to West Sparta. In 1839, he moved to Cohocton, where he continued to labor with great success until 1843. Many were baptized by him during these years, both in Steuben and Livingston counties. In 1843, he traveled as a colporteur through New England, North and South Carolina, and as far west as Indiana. In 1844, he was taken sick at Greenville, N.C., where he was confined a long time. While convalescing, he received a letter that his family was sick, and that one was at the point of death. He started for his home, though hundreds of miles away, but took a relapse; after a long and anxious delay, he reached home in safety and found his family recovering.

In 1845, he moved to Searsburg, where he took charge of the church and, the same year, began the practice of medicine. In 1848, his oldest daughter died suddenly, which was a great shock to the family. His last move was to Benton, N.Y., where he had a large practice as a physician, and labored in the ministry when he could. He died June 5, 1850, in consequence of being thrown from his gig.

<u>Lorenzo D. Fleming (1808—1867)</u>

This was a younger brother of the preceding. From some of his letters, I learn that his father was drowned before Lorenzo was born, and that his mother died while he was young. There were four children in the family beside himself. He was born October 9, 1808, commenced preaching in 1830, and was ordained at Starkey, N.Y., February, 1832. He was a member of the New York Central Conference. From 1830 to 1840, he labored extensively in the New England States, New York, Pennsylvania, New Jersey, and Canada. In 1838, he took charge of the church in Portland, Me. In 1840, his voice failed, and in 1841, he resigned his charge in Portland. He died in Rochester, N.Y., June 16, 1867.

The Elder was a man of great energy. During the thirty years of his ministry, few men traveled and wrote more than he. He had studied medicine early in life, and his education was quite good. He had many revivals in all the places where he preached, especially in Philadelphia, New Jersey, and Portland; yet, while he was a pathetic and sensational speaker, he was no less an advocate of education and a thorough organization of the churches. His letters throughout show a mind entirely consecrated to the work of the ministry. Being used to writing, and his mind constantly planning how to advance the interest of the church, he immediately penned his thoughts on paper and sent them to one of our periodicals for publication.

He often visited Elder I.N. Walter in the city of New York, and at one time, he gave instruction to his children in certain branches, to the thorough satisfaction of his employer. In 1834, he met Alexander Campbell in Philadelphia, and compared notes with him in regard to the two branches of the Christian Church. Another time, he talks with Abner Kneeland; then, with a leading Atheist. These conversations, no matter where occurring—on steamboats, stage coaches, or railroads,—are reported by him through our periodicals, to the edification of the readers. If the published letters of this Elder were gathered together in a volume today, they would make a book of great value to the Christian world.

The Elder was a man of ready wit, fluent in conversation, of pathetic address, of an active and earnest spirit in the promotion of truth, and, withal, conscientious and firm in his convictions. Still, when the Advent wave of 1843 swept over the land, he entered into it with all his energy, and labored hard to convince others—what he doubtless believed with all his heart—that the world would soon come to an end. His voice having failed, his ministerial labors, in the latter years of his life, were limited, and his attention was devoted mainly to his medical profession, in which he succeeded well.

JOHN C. FLEMING (1843—1876)

Brother John was born in 1843, and entered the ministry in early life. He was ordained in the Central Conference, Va., in 1873, and had charge of churches in Rockingham and adjoining counties. A short time before his death, he moved to Pennsylvania, and labored most earnestly in a series of meetings at Mt Hope till God called him from earth to join the ransomed above. He died January 31, 1876.

RICHARD FLINT (1773—1830)

This Elder was born in 1773, labored mostly in the State of New York, and died of jaundice in Delaware County, N.Y., May 23, 1830. It was thought his disease was brought on by hard labor.

LEONARD JACKSON FOOR (1815—1866)

Leonard was born May 31, 1815, was baptized by Elder Daniel Long in 1834, and joined the Valley Virginia Conference, in 1844. In 1847, he was ordained by the Rays Hill Conference, Penn. After laboring for some years in Pennsylvania and adjoining states, in 1852, he moved with his family to Poesy County, Ind., and in 1855, to Cedar County, Iowa. He died in the latter place, of inflammation of the brain, February 2, 1866.

In early life, he had a strong impression to be a preacher. His struggle, before yielding to the call, was great. His first efforts in the ministry were also attended with peculiar opposition and persecution, not only from the unconverted but sometimes from members of the church. In his early ministry, he kept a record of his travels. In 1847, he traveled 500 miles, preached fifty times, and received ten dollars. In 1848, he traveled 2,115 miles, preached 126 times, received fifty-one persons into the church, for all of which he received ninety dollars. The highest amount received by him for any one year was $189.00; but his average salary did not exceed $100.00—yet his labors were immense. At times, he felt like giving up the work, but these thoughts were momentary; for while he saw souls sinking to perdition, as he expressed it, no power on earth could keep him still. It is doubtless true that the Elder shortened his life by excessive labors and exposures —but, to him. it was a cheerful sacrifice.

<u>DAVID FORD (1778—1868)</u>

David was born in 1778, was converted, and commenced preaching, while young, among the Methodists, with whom he continued to preach for about twenty years. But, on account exchange of views on doctrinal subjects, he joined the Christians. Being a strong man, he soon took a high position among his new brethren. He joined the Eastern New York Conference, where he continued a worthy member till death. He died December 1, 1868, in his ninetieth year. By his will, he donated $500.00 for the benefit of the church in Canaan, N.Y.

<u>E. FORD (?—1840)</u>

This brother was a member of the New York Eastern Conference. He died about 1840.

<u>MORDECAI FORD (1806—1867)</u>

This Brother was a quiet, good, but local man, living most of his ministerial life in Darke County, O. During many years, he was pastor of the church at DeLisle. He was born in 1806, was married to Miss Mary Tillman, March 27, 1839, was converted, and commenced preaching soon after. In 1831, he was ordained. He continued a member of the Miami Conference, O., till death. He died November 23, 1867.

HIRAM FORTNER (1812—1878)

Brother Fortner was born in Montgomery County, Ky., January 17, 1812, moved to Indiana in 1829, and settled in Vigo County.

He was converted, in 1831, and soon after joined the Christian Church. In 1833, he was married to Susanna Lamaster. He began to preach in Indiana, but soon after moved to Iowa, where he made a full proof of his ministry. For many years he was a leading spirit in the church there, not so much for his talent, as a speaker, but for his promptness and zeal. A few years before he died, he moved to the village of LeGrand, for the purpose of education. He died there, December 18, 1878, greatly lamented by the churches.

LEWIS FORTNER (?—?)

Lewis Fortner was a Christian minister in the State of Kentucky, about 1825.

JONATHAN FOSTER (?—?)

Jonathan Foster was a minister, living in Winchester, Va., in 1808. He was then a correspondent of the *Herald of Gospel Liberty.*

JOHN FOSTER (?—?)

John Foster was born about 1780, and preached near Mechanicsburg, O., in 1814, where he baptized Elder Daniel Long. He moved to the west some years afterward.

NATHAN FOSTER (?—?)

Nathan Foster was one of the ministers that labored in the church about 1808.

ROBERT FOSTER (?—1835)

Brother Foster was a lay, not a clerical minister, yet he was a faithful public man for more than twenty-five years. For a time he officiated as pastor to the Christian Church in the city of Portsmouth, N.H. But the great life work of Brother Foster, was as editor and publisher. When Elias Smith left the Christian Church in 1818, Robert Foster undertook the publication of the *Herald of Gospel Liberty,* and other publications, and continued the same most successfully, until 1835. During this period he was one of the leading men in the church. From the testimony of his contemporaries, he must have been a man of rare gifts, great reliableness, and energy. Soon after discontinuing the publication of the *Herald,* he died of typhoid fever, at his home, in Portsmouth, N.H., October, 14, 1335.

THOMAS J. FOWLER (?—1878)

Brother J.D. Gunter speaks of this Elder as being a very successful itinerant minister for many years, in North Carolina. He was a member of O'Kelly's Chapel, and married a granddaughter of Elder James O'Kelly. He raised an interesting family of children, and did a great service to the church. He died November, 1878, full of faith.

JEFFERSON FOX (?—1875)

This young minister died in Starkey, N.Y., February 23, 1871.[2] Though not advanced in years he was ordained, and had a family. He had been a student at the Meadville Theological School, Penn. At the time of his death, he was a teacher in Starkey Seminary. He died very suddenly. There was great lamentation at the time of his death, by teachers and pupils; for he was liked by all. He was a young preacher of great promise.

---

[2] The original edition had a discrepancy in the year of death. I have been unable to locate information to validate or invalidate either year (1871 or 1875), and thus have left this obvious discrepancy in the text of this book.—*Editor.*

JESSE FRAZER (?—?)

Jesse Frazer was a member of the Central Conference, Ind., and died several years ago.

SAMUEL FREEMAN (?—1857)

The ministerial labors of this brother were mostly confined to Miami and Darke Counties, Ohio. He was inclined to the Disciples in his views on baptism. He died February, 18, 1857.

HENRY FROST (1786 - 1857)

For many years, Elder Frost was a prominent man, and minister in the State of Maine. He was born in Kittery, Me., in 1786, commenced preaching in Waterville about 1808. He soon became' a talented and very useful preacher. He spent most of his time with the churches in the vicinity of the Kennebec river. For several years before his death, he had been failing in body and mind. In 1848,Ihis wife died. October 2, 1857, he died and was buried at Cornville, the place where he labored for many years.

Elder Frost was a writer of some note. In his ministerial work, also, he filled a wide sphere, for many years, but I have no materials for a longer biography.

SILAS O. FULLER (1823—1859)

Silas was a native of Connecticut. He was born in 1823, was converted in the Christian Church, in 1841, commenced preaching in 1846, entered the Meadville Theological School, Penn., the same year, and continued his studies there about one year and a half. He was married to Miss Emily G. Elliott, of Sag Harbor, N.Y. His labors in the ministry were at Wernersville, N.Y., North Dighton, Mass., Milford and Little York, N.J. At times, he taught school and preached in the same place. He was very active and energetic, but under this double work, with a constitution not strong at best, his health failed. He died in his native state, June 20, 1859, aged thirty-six years.

The Elder was a small, slightly-built man, of very active and lively temperament. During his stay at Meadville, he was quite industrious, and was considered a good student. In his ministerial labors, he was quite successful. If his life had been spared, he would, doubtless, have become a very useful pastor.

<u>William Furness (?—1868)</u>

This brother was of Quaker origin, and was considered one of the best of men. He was a preacher of talent, but was local in his labor. He lived many years at Pleasant Hill, O., and filled a wide sphere as a minister and a physician. He was a member of the Miami Conference, O. He died about 1868, being not far from sixty years of age. But few better men left the walls of Zion; yet I have not been able to find items or dates of his life and labors.

<u>Jeremiah Fuson (?—1863)</u>

During many years, this Elder filled a prominent position in the ranks of the ministers of the Miami Conference, O. He was a man of unblemished reputation, with a clear head, a warm heart, and was, withal, a master speaker. Such are the reports I receive from those that knew him.

Jeremiah was born in Virginia. His father was a Revolutionary soldier. Jeremiah was one of seven brothers, five of whom became ministers—three of the Christian Church and two of the Baptist. All the schooling he had was thirteen days. When he was quite young, his father moved to Champaign County, O. Jeremiah was converted early in life, and was married when quite young. Soon after his conversion, he began to exercise his gift, and soon became a preacher. His first settlement as a pastor was with the Mud Run Church, near West Liberty. After that, he lived in West Liberty, and labored with the church as long as he was able to preach. He died in the latter place about 1863.

Elder J.B. Robertson says that as late as 1824, the Elder had to spell part of the hymns before he could give them out intelligibly; and yet the man of thirteen days' schooling, by diligent study, became one of the most intelligent men in the community—a man who charmed the best educated by his public addresses. About 1838 or '39, he lost his voice, after which he was appointed Justice of the Peace—in which capacity he served with honor for many years. His zeal, in early life, was wonderful. At one time, he and one of his brothers traveled sixty miles, on foot, to attended a religious meeting at Williamsport, O.; and he felt well repaid for the journey by one sermon that he heard, from Elder Palmer, a mere stripling at the time. His argumentive powers were great. At one time, he got into a controversy with a minister of another church concerning some matter in Theology. This brother, feeling that he could not hold his own in the debate, called on another and an abler brother of the same church to come to the rescue; and the answer he received was, "If you are fool enough to have an argument with 'Jeremiah Fuson' you must get out of it the best you can; you can't get me to meddle in the affair."

His appeals to. sinners were sometimes most powerful. At one time, when he was making one of those strong appeals, Elder Nathan Worley, than whom none understood an appeal of that kind better, grasped the arm of one sitting by him and whispered. "How can a poor sinner, stand that?" In appearance, the Elder at first seemed awkward and homely, with a loud, coarse voice; but as he grew in intelligence, he became a fine-looking man, venerable in appearance, and with a soft voice.

<u>WILLIAM FUSON (?—1862)</u>

This was a nephew of the preceding. He was a member of the Spoon River Conference, Ill., at the time of his death. He was licensed to preach by the above conference in 1855, was ordained in 1856 or '57, and died of consumption April 5, 1862. He is spoken of as a man of good talent, efficient in conference, and greatly lamented at his death.

? GAHER OR GAHE (?—?)

This man was a minister who died some years ago, a member of the Southern Wabash Conference, Ill.

? GALLANT (?—?)

This brother is said to have been one of the charter members of the Miami Conference, O., in 1814. He lived on Rattle Snake Creek, near Deer Creek, O.

SAMUEL GALLOWAY (?—1821)

Galloway was one the first Christian ministers that preached in the church at Marion, N.Y. He moved from there to Darby Plains, O., where he bought a farm and lived and preached in that neighborhood for some time. While on a visit to his old home in New York, after holding several meetings among his old acquaintance, he was taken sick and died there, July 16, 1811. It is said that he was impressed on his journey back, and so remarked while crossing the Scioto river that he should not return to his home. It is said that he was a zealous and very devoted man.

E.D. GALUSHA (1818—1858)

Elder Galusha was born in 1818, and was brought up in Cayuga County N.Y. He was converted in 1838, and in 1855 he commenced preaching in the State of Michigan. In 1856, he was ordained and became at once an efficient minister, and a pastor of two churches in Barry County, Mich. He died very suddenly, in 1858, after forty-eight hours of sickness, in Olivet, Eaton County, the same state. He left a wife, five children, and many friends to mourn.

THOMAS GALUSHA (?—?)

Thomas was a member of one of the Christian Conferences, in the State of Maine, and died many years ago.

Mathias E. Gammon (1864—1865)

Mathias was born in 1804, was an accomplished and zealous minister, for many years. He died in Westport, Mass., January 24, 1865. He was a member of the Rhode Island and Massachusetts Christian Conference.

Seth Gard (1775—1845)

Few men filled a wider station in life, in a plain unostentatious way, than "Uncle Seth," as he was familiarly called by his neighbors. He was truly a frontiersman. He was born near Morristown, Ky., March 14, 1775, moved to Ohio, near the mouth of the Big Miami river,, in 1788, and was married there in 1796. In 1809, he went as Captain of the Militia, to the relief of Fort Wayne. In the same year, he joined the Christian Church, not far from Cincinnati, O., and soon after commenced his labors in the ministry. From this to the close of his eventful career, he never wavered in his holy calling, though, as it was customary, in those early days in the West, men of talent were called into many secular positions and so was Elder Gard.

In 1814, he moved to the State of Illinois and settled near Mt. Carmel, Wabash County. In 1816, he was elected judge of the county court, and the same year he was sent to the Legislature. In 1818, he was elected as member of the convention, appointed for the formation of a state Constitution. The great question in that convention was whether the state should be free or slave; for in spite of the clause of freedom, inserted by Thomas Jefferson in the act of organizing the "North Western Territory," there were great efforts put forward, by the settlers from slave states, to make the states comprising that territory, slave. Elder Gard, knowing the deleterious influence of slavery on the people, and being a strong believer in the "rights of man to freedom" whether white or black, worked with all his power, to make his adopted state a free one, and as he was a chairman of that body, his position gave him a great power in bringing about the desired result. It is said that he was offered two thousand dollars, a large sum in those days, to give his influence in favor of slavery, but whoever made the offer, was mistaken in the man. Plain Seth Gard was not a man either to offer or receive a bribe.

Although a prominent minister, for many years before, yet such was his sense of the sacredness of a minister's work, and such were his own secular callings that he never would consent to be ordained until 1836. Among his acquaintances, many anecdotes were related of him. All these go to show a man of great originality and wit, with no pride or pretention. He dressed very plainly. He was a man of the people—a real pioneer. His sayings were treasured up by his neighbors, as something not to be doubted. A Methodist minister once observed in his presence, that he was going to heaven by the way of "Wesley;" Uncle Seth said, "I do not want to go that roundabout way, I want to go straight."

For some time before his death, he was troubled with "gravel," and died of that disease, July 25, 1845. For many years he was an authority in politics and religion, in South-eastern Illinois and South-western Indiana—the field of his labors.

<u>MATTHEW GARDNER (1790—1873)</u>

The "Autobiography of Elder Gardner," published by Dr. N. Summerbell, is so full of events that I can here give but a summary of the prominent ones.

Matthew was born at Stephen town, Rensselaer County, N.Y., December 5, 1790. His father was of English descent, and of Quaker stock. His mother's maiden name was Hawk, and she was the second wife of his father. When six years old, Matthew had very serious impressions. In 1800, the family moved from Rensselaer County, N.Y., to Brown County, O. In 1809, Mathew ran away from home, went to New Orleans on a flat-boat, and was taken sick while there, suffering much from poverty and disease. When his health began to mend, he started for home, on foot—a distance of 1,500 miles. At Natches, at a horse race, he made his first and last bet, and won five dollars. He bought a mule—and it was taken from him by a ruffian. He spent some time among the

Indians, and found them kinder and better than the rough whites he met in that country. After a long and tedious journey, he reached home, having made the distance on foot, in poor health most of the time. During that time, he tried hard to believe the Universal doctrine.

After his return, Elder Archibald Alexander, of Kentucky, held meetings at his father's house, and some of the family, as well as Matthew, were converted. In 1820, he began to preach, and two years later, joined the Kentucky Conference. May 20, 1813, he married Sally Beasley, and, the same year, was drafted to serve in the army, and spent some time in Northern Ohio, in the war against England. In 1818, he organized the Union Church near Higginsport, O., and in 1819, the Bethel Church, Clermont County. In 1820, the Southern Ohio Conference was organized, he became one of its leading members, and continued so for fifty-three years. In the same year, he had a bitter controversy with McCalla, a Presbyterian minister, which resulted in a lawsuit, a certain Methodist minister, Thompson, siding with McCalla. About 1832, he organized the churches of Bethlehem, Georgetown, and Pisgah, Brown County, O. In 1823, the peculiar views of Alexander Campbell were embraced by some of the ministers of the Christian Church, and the Elder opposed them with all the power of his strong nature. In this year, he published a Christian hymn book. In 1824, '26, and '29, he published respectively the second, third, and fourth editions of the same. From 1825 to 1835, there is no event of note, though he was an active, energetic preacher to as many churches as he could supply, organizing new ones, and especially battling the sects around him; and, withal, carrying on a large farm, supporting a large family, and laying up money continually. In the latter year, while preaching at Jamestown, O., he was challenged to debate the issue between the Disciples [the followers of Alexander Campbell] and the Christians, by Dr. Winans, who finally failed to appear; but in 1839 and '40, he had two debates on this issue with Elder John B. Lucas, a master debater at that time—the first at Jamestown, the second at Lebanon, Warren County.

In 1836, the trouble with the Disciples came to a crisis, and in many of the churches, they had a stormy time. In 1841, he had a debate with Thorp, a Universalist minister, at Aberdeen, O., when Thorp was so badly beaten that he renounced the doctrine of Universalism at the time. In 1841, he published a periodical, "The Christian Union," and in 1849, he issued a small volume on the subject of Masonry— "An exposure of Masonry, with an account of the abduction of William Morgan." Between 1849 and 1857, he published several pamphlets on subjects of Differences between himself and others, Concerning secret societies, Rights of the minority in conferences, and, in the latter year, one treating on the same subject, with the additional idea of Antioch College.

September 20, 1869, his beloved wife, Sally, died. From this time to that of his own death, though he preached, traveled, and wrote much, yet it was evident to all that the end was not far off. In 1873, he made one of his yearly visits to New York. July 10, he arrived at the camp-meeting, at Hyannis, Mass., where, on the 29th, he had a fall from the platform of the hotel, fracturing the thigh bone. He was taken by friends to the home of his daughter, Mrs. Hopkins, at Bentonville, O. He suffered a great deal, and was aware that he- was crippled for life; yet he went to different churches, and spoke—for it was not his nature to lie idle. The session of the Southern Ohio Conference—of which he had been a member fifty-three years—was the last meeting he attended. He delivered an affecting sermon to the conference. He died October 10, 1873, aged eighty-two years, ten months, and five days.

Such is an outline of this Elder's wonderful career. He was- a noted man, and would have been, in any other position he might occupy in life. Few men have had more true friends and bitter enemies than he, and, as such is the case, it is difficult to state the merits and demerits of the man. The Elder was the last man to desire an indiscriminate eulogy of himself or friends, as is often evinced by his criticisms in our papers when unwarrantable eulogies were pronounced on deceased persons. Some of his leading traits of character were:

1st. Determination. He never gave up on account of difficulties.

2d. Promptness. He never was a half-way man, but whatever he believed, he believed and practiced with all his might. He was always on time to all his appointments, and bitterly censured those that failed. He had one of the best watches, regulated for the purpose of being on time.

3d. Activity. He was never idle. He engaged in the ministry with great earnestness and continuance, as if he had nothing else to do; for, at one time, he virtually had charge of the whole conference. At the same time, he published periodicals, books, and pamphlets, held debates with giant opponents, carried on a large farm, raised a large family of children, and made so much money as to become a leading director in one or two banks.

4th. Order was a large element in his composition. Everything with him was in its own place. The large, rough pigeonholes in his desk were full of documents, so arranged that he could take hold of any one in the dark; and woe to the intruder that should mislay one of them.

5th. Concentration. He was a constant thinker. The theme of his meditation was turned over and over in his mind till it was viewed from every side.

6th. Economy. While he gave largely for benevolent objects, yet he wasted nothing if it could be avoided.

7th. Controversy. The whole life of our subject, apparently, was in a whirl of discussion. In public gatherings, where difference of sentiment occurred, the Elder was always the leader on his own side. Sometimes he would face a whole congregation alone. He fought the strong elements of Disciplism, Freemasonry, Universalism, and many other opponents for long years; indeed, it seemed as if controversy was a food to him.

8th. Self-control. While he seemed greatly excited in his debates, he did not bold malice. Some of his best friends, he used to say, were of the Masonic fraternity—which he did so much to condemn.

Jesse S. Garwood (1848—1873)

Jesse was born in Allen County, O., April 7, 1848, and died at Lynnville, Jasper County, Iowa, November 26, 1873. He joined the Bethlehem Christian Church, in Allen County, O., under the labors of Michael Mertz, in 1861. During the war, he became indifferent, but in 1866, on the death of a beloved sister, he joined the church at Swan Creek, and from this time until 1868, when he preached his first sermon, his mind was constantly exercised on the subject of the ministry. For several years previous to 1868, however, he had been studying hard, and had acquired a good education, not knowing then that the Lord was preparing him for the gospel work. February 28, 1867, he was married to Miss Sarah E. Watkins, who became a co-worker with him in the ministry, and who to this day, (1880), is a faithful and efficient minister in the church. After he began to preach, he at once entered heartily into the work, and organized several churches in Fulton and Wood counties, O. His whole time was occupied, and the work prospered in his hand.

On account of poor health of himself and wife, in 1872, he moved with his family to Kansas, where they continued about four months, then to Iowa, and settled at Quarry, Marshall, County. He now had his name transferred from the Northwestern Conference, O., which he had joined and where he was ordained October 13, 1869, and joined the Central Conference, Iowa, in 1872, where he continued until his death. During the short time he labored in Iowa, he had charge of the churches at Quarry and Le Grand, in Marshall County, Walnut Valley and Fairview, in Poweshiek County, and Lynnville, in Jasper County where he died.

Elder Garwood's career was short, but it was very hopeful. He was prompt to every call of the denomination. While collecting materials for this volume, several years ago, I had but few correspondents who wrote so well and took such interest, as our deceased brother. Little did I think then that his name would appear among the number of those gone before us.

JEREMIAH GATES (?—1831)

Brother Gates was born and brought up in the State of Vermont, moved to the State of New York, commenced preaching in 1812, and died in 1831.

HENRY GAULT (1829—1875)

Henry was born in Pennsylvania, May 22, 1829, moved to Ohio with his parents, in 1822, was converted in 1848. He moved to Indiana, and began to preach in the Church of God in 1852. Moving to Wisconsin he labored as a minister in the United Brethren Church until 1867, when he joined the Christian Church. He died of consumption at Buckland Center, Wisconsin, January 2, 1875, leaving a wife and two children, with many friends to mourn his departure.

? GIFFORD (?—?)

There was a minister of this name that preached in the Christian Church, in Milford, N.J., for some time. He has been dead for many years.

JOHN GILMORE (1789—1863)

This good man was for many years a prominent member of the Ohio Central Christian Conference. He was a farmer by occupation, and was in good circumstances, but he labored quite extensively in Licking and adjoining counties in central Ohio. He was a smooth, easy speaker, somewhat given to doctrinal subjects, both in speaking and writing. He was well respected by all that knew him and considered as a man of excellent character. His education was limited, but his natural talent was good.

He was born in 1789, heard the first Christian minister in 1815, tried to be a Universalist. He died, not far from Columbus, O., in 1863. The Elder, like many of his contemporaries, felt it his duty, as a minister, to do all he could in the name of Christ With this feeling, he went far and near, preaching with but little, if any compensation, built a meeting house in his own neighborhood, defrayed most pf the expense himself, but in his later years he felt that his policy was a mistaken one.

WILLIAM GILMORE (1791—1868)

The subject of this sketch was an evangelist for a great part of his ministerial life. He was one of seven brothers, that were all preachers. He traveled and preached through seventeen states of the Union. He was born in Chelsea, Mass., August 7, 1791. His parents moved to the State of New York, and from there to Clark County, O., when William was young. He was converted in the latter place, in 1806, began to preach in 1816, was ordained in 1819, and was married the same year to Jane Ramsey. He died in Bowling Green, Wood County, Ohio, September 22, 1868.

The Elder was a small man, heavy set, with dark complexion. In his intercourse, he was a little distant at first, but on further acquaintance, very sociable. He was a strong believer in the "Advent" doctrine, as to the speedy coming of Christ, for a time

WILLIAM GLENDEMING (?—1816)

William was originally from Munford, Scotland. He was a minister in the Methodist Church, until the separation on account of the appointing of bishops, when he left in company with James O'Kelly and others. He was engaged in the mercantile business in Raleigh, N.C., before his death, and died there in 1816, having partially lost his mind before.

NEWCOME GODFREY (?—1857)

This brother labored in New York, Canada West, Northern Indiana, and Michigan. He commenced preaching when forty years of age. He moved from New York to Canada West, and preached there in 1833. He moved from the latter place to Northern Indiana in 1837, and to Vergennes, Mich., in 1839, where he organized a church in the sparsely settled country, and labored so faithfully, that, through his instrumentality, the Grand River Conference, Mich., was organized.

In 1848, he was taken with rheumatism, and was confined to his room, and mostly to his bed, for three years or more; yet such was his zeal that, when thought -to be at the point of death, he gave out an appointment to preach at his own house. The people came in crowds, and on his bed he preached with great power. He finally, contrary to the expectations of all, recovered his health, in a measure, and labored faithfully to the close of his life. He died at Vergennes, about 1857.

Jedediah Goodwin (?—?)

Jedediah Goodwin was a good man and minister, and lived, preached, and died in South Berwick, Maine.

Joshua Goodwin (1788--1862)

This brother was born in 1788, lived in York, Me., was converted in 1807, commenced preaching in 1827, and died of dropsy in York, Me., January 2, 1863.

George L. Goolet (1817—1862)

This Elder was born in Vermont, in 1817, began to preach in 1837, laboring mostly in Bradford, Vt., and died about 1862. He was a useful and good man.

Hiram Gordon (1830—1866)

When this young minister died, in the beginning of his ministerial work, at Fall River, Massachusetts, there was great lamentation all through the denomination. Our papers were full of the sad loss we had sustained as a church, in his sudden departure, and great sympathy was expressed toward his young wife, and small children. He was considered a young minister of great promise.

He was born in Charleston Four Corners, N.Y., in 1830, joined the Christian Church in that place, under the labors of Elder John Ross, in June, 1840. He attended several schools in the State of New York, was at Antioch College, Ohio, from 1853 to 1855. In 1856, he entered the junior class at Union College, N.Y., and graduated in 1858. From 1859 to 1860, he taught in a school in Kentucky, after which he returned to Union College as tutor and at the same time, to study theology, but from there he went to Andover, Mass., and finished his theological course there.

In 1863, he was ordained as pastor of the church at Haverhill, Mass., where he continued for two years. From there he took charge of the church at Fall River. His prospects were very bright, but before closing his second year in the latter place, he was called from labor to reward. He died October 20, 1866. His body was taken for burial to his native place, Charleston Four Corners, N.Y.

WILLIAM GORDON (?—?)

The late Elder Levi Purviance wrote: "William Gordon was born in North Carolina, and went to Tennessee in early life, professed religion and united with the Christian Church. He moved to Ohio in 1816, and settled in Preble County. He lived with a maiden sister, and afterward bought a small farm a few miles east of Richmond, Ind. He was a very interesting preacher; modest, unassuming,-and diffident. In preaching, his premises were generally well laid, his conclusions fair, his arguments logical, and his discourses very entertaining and instructive. He had a retentive memory and his quotations were correct and properly placed. He preached several years in and about New Paris, Eaton, Paint, and many other places. His gift was calculated to instruct and teed the lambs and sheep, to convince the skeptic, and shut the mouths of gainsayers. He was never boisterous, but always calm, lively, and spiritual. He was a man of unblemished character and of excellent spirit, a fit representative of the beloved disciple." As he was gaining in talent and efficiency as a minister, his sister lost her mind, and his care of her almost paralyzed his labors as a minister, for many years. He lived on his own place almost as a hermit. When the sister died, he re-commenced his ministerial labor again, but his career was short. He died soon after.

<u>Cyrus Gordy (1816—1878)</u>

Gordy was a minister of the Deer Creek Conference, O. He was born in Pickaway County, in 1816, converted under the preaching of Elder Daniel Long, and was baptized by him, in 1834. He began to preach in 1838, and became a member of the Deer Creek Conference in 1837. He was married to Miss Sarah Hornbeck in 1838. For several years he was quite active in the ministry and had a prospect of becoming quite useful, but affection of the throat kept him from speaking, and he turned his attention, mostly, to secular affairs. He died at Philo, HL, in 1872.

<u>Forgus Graham (1768—1830)</u>

This brother was converted at the time of the Cane Ridge revival, in Kentucky. He moved to Ohio, and settled in Madison County. He bought a large quantity of land on the Pickaway Plains, and was in good circumstances. For many years, he occupied an important position as a local, but efficient, preacher in the early settling of the country. Forgus Graham and George Alkire were neighbors, and often labored together. The Elder was a tall, heavy-built man, energetic and zealous, living on his own farm, and having plenty, he, in a great measure, supported the church. Immense crowds would gather at his house for a protracted meeting, and the Elder gladly fed many of the congregation. It was a curious way to carry on church enterprise, but he felt it was right. Thus his time, talent, and property went freely to support the cause.

He finally moved to the State of Indiana, and died there about 1830. In a letter of Elder Joseph Badger, who visited his house in 1825, I find the following: "At Pleasant Township, Madison County, O., we were kindly received by Forgus Graham, a man of fifty-seven years of age, who had just returned from a preaching tour of six weeks, in Indiana. He had had a good journey, and felt encouraged. I surveyed with admiration his gray hairs, his smiles and tears while he gave an account of his journey. He visited the poor cabins in the wilderness, lay on the ground in the great prairie, where the wolves were howling around him, passed through hunger and fatigue, but found God to be with him. His spacious plantation at home, on which he had more than one hundred head of cattle, with other stock in proportion, reminded me of the ancient profession of Abraham, Lot, and Jacob.

JACOB GRAHAM (?—1874)

Jacob Graham was a member of the Eastern Ohio Conference. He lived in Athens County, O., and died about 1874. He was local in his labors.

DANIEL GRANT (1812—1879)

Brother Grant was a member of the Eastern Conference, N.Y., was born in 1812, and died at Delhi, Delaware' County, N.Y., October 30, 1879. He embraced religion from a sense of duty, and with no excitement, in 1832, was baptized by Joshua Howard in 1837, and began to preach the same year. He was ordained in 1842, and the same year he was chosen pastor of the Delhi church, where he was a member, continued his pastorate of that church until 1876, when on account of failing health he resigned. Beside the Delhi Church, where he was pastor for so many years, he preached, also, for the churches of Otego, Portlandville, North Harpersfield, Summit, Delaney, South Franklin, Roxbury, as well as churches in Delaware and Otsego counties. He was married to Miss Sally Tresly, in Delhi, in 1837. The Elder was a very useful man and filled a large field of usefulness for many years. At his death he left a wife and three children.

JOHN GRAY (?—1826)

John Gray died in one of the Western States, about 1826.

<u>JOHN GRAY (?—?)</u>

John Gray was a minister, living in Fairfax County, Va. In 1813, he wrote several letters of interest for our papers. His writings show him to be a man of ability.[3]

<u>SAMUEL GRAY (?—1865)</u>

Samuel Gray was a member of the Southern Ohio Christian Conference, lived in Clermont and Brown counties, died near Hamersville, the latter county, about 1865. He carried on a farm, was in good circumstances, but devoted considerable time to the work of the ministry. He was successful as a pastor and had fair preaching talent. He was not far from sixty years old when he died.

<u>WILLIAM H. GRAY (?—1825)</u>

William H. Gray died in Indiana, March 5, 1825.

<u>CURTIS GREEN (1802—1861)</u>

This Elder was born in Madison Comity, N.Y., in 1802, converted in 1812, and commenced preaching when quite young. In 1826, he was married to Miss Mary Bickford, and in 1841, he joined the Northern Christian Conference, and in 1843, was ordained. He was a hard word working man and followed the occupation of a farmer as well as preacher. He was a faithful minister in his field of labor. He died in Lewis County, N.Y., June 8, 1861.

<u>? GREEN (?—1855)</u>

S.G. Worly, of Henry, Ill., speaks of a Christian minister of the name of Green that died in Galesburg, Ill., in 1854 or '55. He was traveling through Indiana and Illinois as agent for the *Gospel Herald,* and preaching through the churches generally. He was a faithful, good man.

---

[3] It is possible that the two "John Gray" entries are actually the same person. *—Editor.*

JARED GREEN (1805—?)

This Elder was born in 1805, converted in 1826, began preaching in 1828. He was tall and graceful, a good singer and speaker. He traveled with Elder Josiah Knight. In early life he was rather timid and easily discouraged. He died several years ago.

JOHN GREEN (?—1838)

This young brother had a short but brilliant career. He was the son of Thomas Green, of Grassy Point Church, Madison County, Ohio, converted about 1830 under the labors of Elder Daniel Long, and soon commenced preaching with great earnestness. He was a member of the Grassy Point Church, and the Deer Creek Christian Conference. He died about 1837 or '38 in his prime, lamented by all of his brethren.

LEWIS GREEN, (?—1852)

This was a brother of the preceding. He was converted early and commenced preaching at once. He joined the Deer Creek Christian Conference, O., and was ordained in 1843. This young brother was zealous, and would doubtless have made an able minister, could he have devoted his entire energy to the work. He died in Madison County, Ohio, December 20, 1852.

HENRY GREENSLIT (1873—1869)

From the different accounts given in our periodical at the death of this aged veteran, we gather the following: Henry was born in 1793, became wild in his youth, with very limited education. He was converted under the labors of Elder Levi Hathaway, and commenced preaching soon after. At this time, he felt the need of education, and it was lucky for him that he had selected, and won a good scholar for a wife, in the person of Miss Mary Wheeler, who taught her willing pupil useful knowledge. He soon became a well-informed man and minister.

The peculiar gift of the Elder, was as evangelist. He was ordained on wheels—in a wagon, in 1833. It was observed by many, that this circumstance was a true index of the Elder's life and movements. He was a fine speaker and very useful as a minister of the Gospel. He organized the church at Providence, R.I., with many others, who stand up as pillars of honor to the faithful and' efficient labor of the founder. He died at Scotland, Connecticut, October 25, 1868, aged seventy-six years, after spending more than forty years in the ministry.

SAMUEL GREGORY (1818—1869)

Samuel was born in Darke County, Ohio, December 2, 1818. His father, Deacon James Gregory, moved with his family to Montgomery County, Ind., in 1831. In 1832, Samuel joined the Pleasant Hill Christian Church. He continued a member of this church, and for many years he was pastor of the same. He was a member of the Western Conference, Ind., and was ordained in 1843. The Elder was married twice, first to Miss Jane Hall, who died in 1856, leaving him four children. He married for his second wife, Miss Abigail McGilliard, who survived him. For many years he had the care of an invalid father, crippling, to a great extent, his ministerial labors. His education was limited, but yet the activity of his mind enabled him to acquire considerable knowledge, especially in history, which was his particular forte. He was a great friend of education and one of his greatest desires, next to that of true conversion, was to see the youths of the land enjoying this boon. On account of his local position, he was not so much known to the church at large as his talent and zeal would entitle him.

He was an active and useful man in his own Conference. In 1863, he was elected a member of the Legislature of Indiana, where he performed the duties of his position with honor to himself, and to the satisfaction of his constituents. He served two terms as legislator. Soon after this, his health began to fail. In accordance to his accustomed energy, he tried every means to put off the fatal - stroke. For this purpose he took a long trip through Kansas and Nebraska, in a private conveyance, returned with encouragement, but financial difficulties and other troubles aggravated the complaint.

He sold his farm-in Montgomery County, and moved to Thorntown, Boone County. Soon after, he was confined to his room and finally to his bed. He died of consumption, July 11, 1869, aged fifty-one years.

HENRY GREW (?—?)

Henry Grew came to us from the Baptists, though, perhaps, he never joined any of our conferences. He was a great writer for our periodicals for many years. He agreed with no denomination entirely, but he was nearer the views generally held by the Christians, than any other, hence his identifying himself with the denomination. He wrote continually for our periodicals, for many years, with great ability, on the various topics of the day. His home was in Philadelphia, for several years. From 1838 to 1842, he wrote from the above city. In 1838, he criticized Mr. Kay in regard to the influence of the Spirit. In 1840, on the superiority of the name "Church of God" to the common names adopted by the various denominations. At another time, against the practice of allowing unconverted persons to sing in the church. Another time, on the immortality of the soul, and yet another on the evils of American slavery. Doubtless, Elder Grew was a good man, with many hobbies, but in the main his views were in harmony with those held by the Christians.

DANIEL GRIFFIN (1814—1864)

This brother, who filled an important position for many years in the bounds of the Central Ohio Christian Conference, was born in Ross County, O., May, 1814, moved to Union County, the same state, in 1831, converted about 1840, and commenced preaching in 1844, and was ordained by the Central Ohio Conference the same year. It was but a short time after this that he took a high position in the church and conference, so much so that he became one of the leading members. His preaching talent was good, his earnest, plain, and pathetic appeals to the sinner had their effect on the people, and revivals followed his preaching. Elder Griffin's gift, how-

ever, was not so much in rousing the feeling, as it was in instructing the intellect. He became a student of the Bible and other good
books, and being entirely reliable in all his intercourse with the
people, he reached the position mentioned above. His first ministerial labor was in Union, but in 1855, he' moved to Madison, and
for many years, thereafter he labored there, and in Clark, living a
part of the time near Plattsburg, the latter county. For the purpose
of educating his children, he moved to Yellow Springs, Greene
County, Ohio. In January,-1864, he went to Chattanooga, Tenn., to
visit a son who was sick in the army hospital; while there, he was
taken sick, and died among strangers.

WILLIAM GRIMES (?—?)

William Grimes was a minister that labored in North Carolina
and Virginia in an early day, and died many years ago.

AARON C. GROVER (1802—1871)

Elder Grover, for many years, was a prominent minister in
Northern Ohio, and Michigan. He was born in the State of New
York, in 1802, commenced preaching in 1834, died at the house of
his son, in Wood County, O., October 24, 1874.

WILLIAM GUIREY (?—?)

William Guirey[4] was one of the most talented of those ministers
that left the Methodist Church in 1793, with James O'Kelly. In October, 1811, he was a resident of Carolina County, Va., near
Chilesburg, living near his father-in-law, George Phillips, where
Elias Smith visited him. In all the general meetings of the day,
William Guirey was always considered one of the leaders. He was
the author of several pamphlets, and of at least one book, of 331
pages—"The History of Episcopacy," divided into four parts. It is
a pity that the lives and labors of such men are not to be had. He
died many years ago.

---

[4] The original edition of this book says "Guirey," but it was spelled "Guirey,"
as can be seen Guirey's only published book.—*Editor.*

<u>Richard Gunter (1766—1831)</u>

This brother was originally a member of the Calvinistic Baptist Church; but from conviction left it, and joined the Christians in an early day. He was a minister among the latter people about thirty years, highly respected for his kindness, zeal, and faithfulness. He was born in 1766, and died October 22, 1831, in his sixty-fifth year, in consequence of swallowing a piece of bone which settled in his throat. He was pastor of two churches at the time of his death, and was greatly lamented by the people of his charge. He was a member of the North Carolina Christian Conference, and his labors were mostly in Moore and Chatham counties, that state.

<u>? Hafferty (?—?)</u>

Elder Hafferty lived in an early day, and was a member of the North Carolina Conference. It is said that he was the first to propose the platform, "The Bible alone for the rule of faith and practice." His suggestion was at once adopted by the brethren.

<u>David Haggard (?—?)</u>

All I find of this brother is that he was a minister connected with the Christians in Kentucky, in an early day.[5]

<u>Rice Haggard (?—?)</u>

We have but a meager account of this brother; but from what we have, it is clear that he was a leading man in the Reformation of the nineteenth century in promoting Christian liberty. Elder Haggard was a resident for a large part of his life of Norfolk, Va. Elders Joseph Thomas and Reuben Dooly visited him there. He is spoken of by all, not only as a good man, but also as an able leader. He was the author of several productions on the doctrine of the church, one of which, in particular, published in 1804, created quite an excitement among friends and foes. This was on the sub-

---

[5] Scant information exists on David Haggard, but a slightly more informative sketch is found in *Early Christian Preachers,* edited by Kyle D. Frank and Bradley S. Cobb.—*Editor.*

jects of "Union of all the followers of Christ in one church."[6] In this he proposed the name "Christians." His other measures of union were such as had already been adopted, and such as continue to be the platform of the Christian Church to this day. He died before 1826, as I find from the "Christian Almanac."

HIRAM HALE (1805—1874)

From an excellent letter of Elder Young, of Romeo, Mich., we obtain the following: Hale was born in Leominster, Mass., July 13, 1805. He was brought up in the Episcopal Church, moved to Erie County, Penn., about 1825, and experienced religion about 1838. Soon after this, he united with the Christian Church at Fairview, the same county. After this time, he preached occasionally up to the time of his ordination, which occurred in the winter of 1842-43, in Cuyahoga County, O. After this, he united with the Erie Conference, Penn. After eleven years labor in Pennsylvania, he emigrated to Omro, Wis., and preached occasionally until 1866, when he engaged in regular pastoral work, which he continued till near the time of his death. He died at the home of his son, Quintus Hale, May 20, 1874. He was married twice. Two of his sons died in Southern prisons. He was a man of more than ordinary intellect. While his delivery was not the best, his ideas were clear and logical. His funeral sermon was preached by his friend and co-laborer, Elder Young, of Romeo, Mich.; a paper of the deceased brother, against pomp and ostentation at funerals, was also read at the time.

ISAAC HALL (?—?)

Isaac Hall was a minister in the State of Connecticut, where he lived, labored, and died.

JOSEPH HALL (?—1861)

Our present subject was, for many years, a prominent man in the western and middle sections of the State of New York, as a minis-

---

[6] This work appears in *Forgotten Soldier of the Restoration: The Life and Writing of Rice Haggard.—Editor.*

ter, physician, and writer. He was a man of great energy, and of more than ordinary information. August 1830, he was pastor of the church at Union Vale, Dutchess County, N.Y., where he was ordained, at a general meeting held about that time, by Elders Abner Jones, John Spoore, David Ford, and Simon Clough. From Union Vale, he moved to West Bloomfield, N.Y., and was the right hand man of Elder David Millard, in the church there, for many years. His principal occupation at that time was as a physician; still he labored to some extent as a minister. He was especially useful in the business arrangements of the denomination. In 1859, he moved from New York State to Effingham County, Ill., and died there, February 14, 1861, lamented by the entire denomination—for he was generally known and appreciated.

<u>ELI H. HALLADAY (1811—1867)</u>

Eli was born in the town of Groton, Tompkins County, N.Y., March 14, 1811, was converted in 1830, commenced preaching in 1834, near Seneca Lake, and was ordained at Sempronius, by Elders D. Wade, D. Dodge, E.J. Reynolds, M. Wescott, and C.T. Butler, October 1, 1837. He was married to Miss Janet Fisher, of Harmon, Chautauqua County, N.Y., February 14, 1840. He died in Fluvanna, N.Y., August 30, 1867.

In the commencement of his ministerial life, the Elder had great success, sinners were converted at all his meetings, and his school-house appointments increased on his hands so that, in a short time, he had four organized churches, raised, mostly, by his own labors. In 1841, he went from Tompkins County, and labored in Virgil and other places in Courtland County; but as his salary was not sufficient to cover expenses, he sometimes taught school in this neighborhood. Many of his pupils were converted under his labors, and some of them have since become useful ministers of the gospel. In 1843, he moved to Chautauqua County, N.Y., and soon became one of the leading members in the Erie Christian Conference. In this region, he continued to labor till death. With the exception of a short period, he preached for the churches at Parma, N.Y., and Washington, Penn.

The Elder was a tall, sandy complexioned man, and was an earnest, fast, and emphatic speaker—as if his whole nature was enlisted in his message. All acknowledged his integrity, and his zeal in his Master's cause was unwearied. A widow, one son, and a host of brethren were left to mourn his departure.

ISAIAH HALLEY (1809—1869)

Isaiah was born in Kittery, Me., October 27, 1809, and moved with his parents to York, the same state, in childhood. When about five years old, he felt that he was called to preach, and he retained that impression through life. August 15, 1828, he united with the church, in 1841, he commenced preaching, and in 1842, was ordained in Swansea, Mass. In his early ministry, he labored in Massachusetts and Rhode Island; but in his latter years, he labored mostly in New Hampshire and Maine. He died in Kittery, Me., July 20, 1869, aged fifty- nine years.

Elder Josiah Knight, who was his pastor in Lynn, Mass., in 1841, speaks highly of him as a man and as a valuable private member in the church—a man of large soul. He never married, but labored from place to place on a small income.

W.D. HALLEY (?—?)

W.D. Halley came from England, joined the Christian Church, and attended the school at Meadville about 1854. While there, he published a magazine. He preached in Washington City, for the Unitarians. Though not firm, he was a talented man. He died while young.

ABRAHAM HALSTED (?—?)

Abraham Halsted labored near Williamsport, O., about 1800, and was ordained by George Alkire, Isaac Cade, and George Zimmerman at the above place, in 1806. He died in Indiana many years ago

ABIJAH HAMER (1800—1860)

Abijah was born about 1800, in North Carolina, moved to Indiana about 1835, was converted, and joined the Christian Church in Henry County, Ind., in 1846. He began preaching soon after, and continued a faithful minister till death. He was a member of the Bluffton Conference, Ind., and was a; good farmer preacher. He died in Henry County, Ind., January 14, 1860.

WILLIAM HAMIEY (1803—1837)

This brother was horn in 1803, and died in King, Canada West, November, 1837, aged thirty-four years. H. Wilson, who wrote his obituary, said that he was one of the best of men.

EBENEZER HAMLIN (1779—1847)

Ebenezer was born in 1779, and died November, 1847. He labored mostly in the states of Maine and New Hampshire.

JOHN HAMRICK (?—1838)

This Elder lived, for some time, in Highland County, O., and, for twenty years, he labored as a minister of Christ. For some years before his death, he was almost alone in that part of the .state. April 2, 1838, I find a letter from him, in the "Christian Palladium," calling for information of John 3:5, and Acts 2:38—passages used by the Disciples as he states it, "to prove water salvation." Elders David Roberts and John 'Green had been to visit him a short time before, and together they had organized a flourishing Christian Church in the neighboring county of Clinton, of which the Elder was pastor. On the 24th of November following, he died in the triumph of Christianity. The account of his death is sent to the "Palladium" by Elder James Smith, who remarks that "his reputation as a Christian was unsullied, and was of good report with his brethren and those without."

LEWIS R. HAMRICK (?—?)

Lewis R. Hamrick was a minister in the State of Kentucky, in an early day. He was warm and very pathetic in exhortation, and quite successful in winning souls to Christ.

LEWIS HANCOCK (1813—1868)

Lewis was born in Monongalia County, Va., February, 1813, was converted, joined the Christian Church in Fayette County, Penn., in 1834, and soon after commenced preaching. In 1846, he moved to Gallia County, O., and joined the Eastern Ohio Conference, in which he continued a member the rest of his life. He died in Gallia County, December 20, 1868, aged fifty-six years.

MAJOR HANCOCK (1792—1879)

The subject of this sketch was born in Patrick County, Va., March 13, 1792, was married to Mrs. Elizabeth Adams, 1811, and the same year moved to Champaign County, O. He joined the Christian Church in 1821, soon began to preach, and became a member of the Miami Conference, laboring mostly without compensation in his own locality. He died of dropsy, at the home of his son-in-law, Mr. Moore, of Bellefontaine, O., September 20, 1879.

W.B. HAND (1802—1869)

The subject of our present sketch was born in 1801, was converted in youth, became a preacher, and joined the Deer Creek Conference, O. During his labors in this field, the "Campbellite wave," as it was called, came through, and the Elder being a strong advocate of immersion, came near sinking. Writing to the "Palladium" from Pendleton, O., June 20, 1838, he says: "I am still on the shores of time, and not quite drowned by the new reform. About five years ago, I was traveling the circuit of Clinton, Madison, Fayette, and Pickaway counties, in this state, and the people who called themselves Disciples attended my meetings regularly, in many places, and pushed me into the water till I could find no bottom. I then got alarmed and began to look around, but could see no shore. I felt disturbed in my soul." Afterward, he joined the Auglaize Conference, O., and lived in Putnam County. About 1853, he moved to Story County, Iowa, and joined the Rock Creek Conference, where he continued the remainder of his life. He died in the above county, October 9, 1869.

WILLIAM HANSON (1845—1875)

William was born in England, August 15, 1845, was converted there in 1861, and joined the Primitive Methodists. In 1872, he came to America and joined the Christian Church at Newton, Iowa, under the preaching of Elders Sullivan and Jones. In 1873, he united with the Central Conference, Iowa, as a licentiate, and died October 3, 1875.

SAMUEL HARDESDY (?—1873)

This brother died in Randolph County, Ind., February, 1873. He was married and began to preach in Shelby County, O. He moved to Illinois and became a member of the Central Illinois Conference, in which, and the Western Indiana Conference, he labored with great success. About 1868, he moved to the neighborhood of Lima, O., and became a member of the North-western Ohio Conference. About 1871, he moved to Randolph County, Ind., where successful revivals followed his labors everywhere. He was limited in education, but was a warm friend of the same, and any improvement in the church. At the time of his death, he had charge of several churches, and was highly respected by his congregations, and was lamented when he died. He had been married twice, the second wife and several children survived him.

JOHN HARDY (1779—1819)

John was born in Dinwiddie County, Va., November 17, 1779. When he was quite young, his parents moved to Kentucky. In 1801, during "the great revival," he professed religion, and soon after, was impressed with the duty of entering the ministry. Being a timid man, he found this a great cross, but found grace to overcome his timidity. March 1, 1803, he was married to Rachel Downing, and in the fall of 1808, he moved with his family to Preble County, O. During these five years, he had been a faithful lay brother in the church; but he felt the "woe unto me if I preach not the gospel."

After moving to Ohio, a new country, it was harder still to break loose from the care of a family to enter the great work before him; but by the persuasion of ministering brethren, especially Elder David Purviance, who saw that he had a peculiar gift for public speaking, he consented to enter the field as a minister. In the summer of 1810, he was ordained by Elders David Purviance, Hugh Andrews, and Richard Clark. In a short time, he became pastor of several very respectable churches. His education was limited, but by industry and studious habits, he soon became an able minister. His gift was more for building up the cause as a pastor than as a revivalist; yet he was instrumental in turning many to Christ.

In the preparation of his sermons, he was methodical and systematic. He had a pleasant voice, and his gestures were natural. Generally, he labored in Western Ohio and Eastern Indiana, with an occasional visit to his old home in Kentucky. At the time of his death, he was pastor of the Christian Churches in Eaton and Burlington, O. He was what might be called a natural orator. Though not having the advantages of education, yet he was not deficient in knowledge. He and his fellow-workers of that day had to encounter difficulties unknown to those of the present time; but they met them manfully, and conquered. He died in the fall of 1819, in his fortieth year, lamented by all that knew him.

? HARRICOFF (1835—1875)

A minister of this name died in 1875, aged forty years.

CALEB HARRIMAN (?—?)

It is probable that this brother was not an ordained Elder, and, perhaps, never was a member of any conference; but he was a great worker in protracted meetings. And those who were converted under his labors considered him one of the best and most devoted of men. His field of labor was York, Wells, Kennebunk, and Kennebunk Port, Me.

JOHN HARRIMAN (?—1866)

John Harriman lived a long time in Newton, N.H., and was considered a very useful minister, though his principal gift was that of exhortation. About 1866, he died, an aged man.

MOSES HARRIMAN (?—?)

Moses Harriman or Herriman was a New Hampshire minister. Though very informal, yet he was a good man. During his sermons, he would often pray two or three times. In his ministry, he was quite successful.

ABRAHAM S. HARTSHORN (1795—1869)

This brother was born in Vermont in 1795, lived for a time in Calais, and then in Belvidere, Vt. It was middle life before he commenced preaching. He was limited in education, and followed farming as an occupation. He moved to the State of New York, a short time before his death, to live with one of his sons. He died in Franklin County, N.Y., April 23, 1869, aged seventy-four years.

ENOCH HARVEY (?—?)

Enoch Harvey was a man of great physical frame, with an intellect in proportion. In his old age, he was a man of massive appearance, with a head apparently large enough for two. Such a man could go nowhere without being noticed.

He was born not far from 1788, for when he died in 1870 or 71, he was something over eighty years old. What his early education or religious training was, we have not been able to find out. Many years ago, the Elder was a prominent minister in the Deer Creek Christian Conference. He was for many years a co-worker with such men as John and George Alkire, Fergus Graham, James Smith, Daniel Long, Joseph Baker, and many others, who had studied so well the Son- ship of Christ that the Trinitarian, who had the temerity to attack this strong hold of the faith, departed a wiser, if not a better man; and well was it for them that this point of their creed was well fortified, for they lived in stirring and perilous times. The Elder was not the least of those giants. So well rooted were these ideas in his large head, that to the day of his death it was difficult for him to preach a sermon without introducing the doctrine of the "Son-ship." On this, "Total Depravity," "Vicarious Atonement," "Election," and the "Sufficiency of the Scriptures for a rule of faith and practice," there was not an idea that the Elder had not mastered in all its minutia. Doctrinal preaching certainly was the forte of the old veteran, but this was not all; when presenting the claims of the Gospel, and a loving Savior to perishing- sinners, he forgot his dogmatism and was often as tender as a mother.

Many years ago, the Elder left the Deer Creek Conference, moved to Hardin County, O., joined the Auglaize Conference, and for many years, was one of its leading members. He died a member of that Conference at the age of more than four score years, having retained his vigor to the last.

I should judge that two peculiar traits in the character of Elder Harvey were firmness and perseverance. When his mind was once made up on a subject, one might as well change the current of the Mississippi, as to change his purpose. Popularity, interest, and ease had no power to influence him, where truth was at stake. His conscientiousness being- added to the traits already mentioned, and we have a man that would rather suffer martyrdom than to swerve one iota from what he considered as truth.

He was married twice, his last wife having survived him. He traveled quite extensively in other states beside Ohio.

Rufus L. Harvey (1795—1876)

This Elder was born in Lyndon, Vt., April 25, 1795, and died in Preble County, O., February 14, 1876. In early life, he was converted, and began to preach among the Christians, in the State of Vermont. In those days, the Christians and Freewill Baptists were working together in many places, so that they labored often in each other's churches. For many years, this Elder was a member of the latter church. He was chaplain of the Vermont Penitentiary for about fifteen years. In 1840, he moved to New York, and, in 1845, to Woodstock, O., where he re-united with the Christian Church. He joined the Miami Ohio Conference, and continued in the same connection until death. In 1850, he buried his first wife; in a few years he married again, an excellent companion, who survived him. After 1846, the Elder served and labored as pastor in Mainville, Warren County, Russellville, Brown County, Concord, Preble County, and, likely, other places. He was an able preacher, with clear delivery, and systematic arrangement of his sermons. In his latter years, he became quite deaf, so that it was difficult for him to understand common conversation; so for several years he did not preach regularly, but his interest in the work never ceased.

ROYAL HASKEL (1787—?)

This Elder lived in the State of Vermont, and was born about 1787. He was a better exhorter and evangelist than preacher and pastor.

DAVID HATHAWAY (1792— 1845)

This Elder was born about 1792, labored in the ministry in the neighborhood of Cabin Creek, Ky., in 1833, and preached through Northern Kentucky and Southern Ohio, for many years. Later in life, he changed his field of labor to the Central part of Ohio. He died in the village of Catawba, Clark County, O., in 1845, thirty miles from home, while returning- from a visit to his daughter in New Lisbon, O., of congestive fever.

LEVI HATHAWAY (1790—1867)

Levi was born in Middleborough, Mass., February 6, 1790. His father became deranged the year following Levi's birth. He was the youngest of thirteen children. In 1797, when the boy was nine years old, his mother died, leaving him, at that tender age, an orphan indeed. After this sad event the family was broken up, and Levi was taken to live with his oldest brother, who was a professor of religion, to Welton, Me. He continued with this brother until 1808, when he visited his native place. At this time, he engaged to go as a deck hand on a voyage to the West Indies and Europe, and started from the port; but the vessel being crushed in a storm, he gave up the idea of sailing. All this desire to travel was in order to quiet his mind, and banish his convictions. For the same purpose he started, on foot, to visit the distant Ohio. On this journey he was caught in a violent thunder storm in the Alleghany mountains. During the tempest he despaired of his life, cried mightily to the Lord to save him, and vowed that he would go back to his home, embrace religion, and serve the Lord to the best of his ability. When the storm was over, he thought of the disgrace and derision heaped upon him if he returned, after going so many hundred miles without seeing the majestic Ohio river. He finally proposed a compromise with the Lord, that if he was allowed to travel as far as Pittsburg he would then return and pay his vow made in the thunderstorm. In Pittsburg, he was offered a fine chance by a gentleman from St. Louis, Mo., to go to that distant city. He concluded to go. but finally remembering his vows, he dared not. He returned on foot, and traveled as far as the State of New Jersey, where his money gave out. He found a silver dollar and some coppers, where he was sitting under a tree. He considered this a sign that the Lord would provide, but by a certain sign he felt that he had the consent of the Lord to stay and work for a short time. He engaged to work for a man by the name of Halzy, of Morristown, N.J. After this, he attended school for a while, and worked for another man by the name of Hemingway, at East Haven, Conn. For, several months after, his conduct was most exemplary, and all the people were kind to him, but he finally joined the youth in their sports, and the darkness of despair gathered around him. He was one of the most miscrable of sinners. All hope was gone. He became sick. Death was just before him, and hell was keen for its prey. Finally, he became willing for anything and hope revived, when he received the evidence of pardon, and was baptized by Elder Daniel Hix, September 22, 1813, and soon joined the Christians, a people that he never heard of until a short time before, but found, on meeting them that they were the very people he could approve of fully.

Soon after his conversion, the impression to preach came back (he had these impressions when eleven years old), and with small resistance, for he was now completely in the hand of God. In December, 1815, he was ordained. At first, he labored as an exhorter, but soon ventured to take a text. After his ordination, he entered the work with peculiar energy and zeal. He was very successful as a revivalist from the beginning. Sinners were converted by the hundreds. Reformation followed his labors in Massachusetts, Connecticut, New York, Pennsylvania, New Jersey, and Vermont. He traveled extensively, and wherever he went his preaching was blessed with the conversion of souls.

In searching for the cause of his great power over the people, we may mention good sense and pleasant delivery, combined with great earnestness in his intercourse with the people. In addition to all these, however, there is one peculiarity in the Elder that we seldom find in others: that leading of the spirit that he always felt in his early ministry. In sleep and in prayer he was impressed where to go, and would, under no consideration, disregard these impressions. If his heart was sad and a burden was resting upon it, he felt that he was in the wrong place and he hurried to change his course; but on the other hand, if the indications were favorable—if his heart was reaching out after sinners—God was in the work and reformation would follow. With him, these impressions seldom failed. It is said by those who heard him speak when in the spiritual mood, that his eloquence was irresistible. The congregations were spell-bound, and so absorbed were they for the time, that they were insensible of surrounding objects. It is related, as an illustration of this, that at one time, when describing the "resurrection", in one of these flights, a blind horse, which happened to stumble into the meeting house, advanced well toward the stand, but none of the congregation were sensible of the presence of the animal.

In 1837, he moved to West Mendon, N.Y., and had a great reformation there. In 1841, the Elder lived in Royalton, N.Y., where he acquired a competency in worldly matters. He died of cancer, July 9, 1867. He was a man, in many respects, peculiarly adapted for the work to which he was called. His very experience, before and after conversion, made him what he was in his active ministry—irresistible in his appeal to sinners. His son Warren is yet an educated and talented minister in the same church. His father, seeing the necessity of education in a minister, encouraged his son to obtain what he himself had been unable to acquire because of the circumstances in which he was placed.

PHILIP HATHAWAY (1756—1839)

In 1756, this brother was born, and in 1789, was ordained, likely in the Baptist Church. In 1811, he was pastor of the church at Assonet, Mass., and was a prominent actor in the reformation that gave rise to the Christians in New England, in connection with Abner Jones, Elias Smith, Daniel Hix, and others. He died at Freetown, R.I., June 14, 1839.

NORMAN HAWK (1814—1839)

At Lewisburgh, Penn.. November 6, 1839, at the age of about twenty-five, this brother died. Elder E.J. Holland, who was with him in his sickness and preached his funeral, spoke highly of him as a man and minister.

ROBERT HAWKINS (1778—1850)

The subject of this sketch, was born in 1778, moved to the neighborhood of Brownsville, Penn., in 1802, began to preach in 1812, and was for many .years a prominent minister in that part of the state. By occupation he was a farmer, and in good circumstances, occupying a position somewhat isolated, as several of the churches in his vicinity were mainly dependent upon him for preaching. He was well versed in the Scriptures, and made free use of this weapon in his sermons. Those that knew him, regarded him as a man of more than ordinary talent as a minister, but that his secular affairs, which were large, kept him from devoting his entire time to the work of the ministry. He died about 1850.

GEORGE H. HAYDEN (1788—?)

George was born in Virginia in 1788, began to preach in 1808, traveled in the State of Kentucky for eighteen months, moved to Washington, Ga., where he labored faithfully for many years, writing to our periodicals frequently. He died some time ago.

CALVIN HAYES (1818—1862)

In the early part of his ministry, he was a member of the Mt. Vernon Christian Conference. He was born in 1818, lived for some years in the neighborhood of Martinsburg, O., commenced preaching in 1840, moved to Union County, O., and died there, June 2, 1862. The Elder was a studious man, and became well informed in Biblical and other literature. He was more calculated for a pastor than a revivalist. He was a man of excellent moral character.

DAVID HAYES (1814—1873)

David, the son of James Hayes, was born September 21, 1814, and died in Merom, Ind., February 23, 1873. He was converted when quite young. March 11, 1834, he was married to Eliza Dearth, and in 1836 he began to preach. June 23, 1839, having become a widower some time before, he married Olive McKinney, daughter of Elder James McKinney.

In his early ministry, he lived in Butler County, O., but moved to Indiana and labored for many years in Clay and adjoining counties in that state. About 1856, he moved to Sullivan County, for the purpose of educating his children in Merom. He was very active in the work of securing the location of Union Christian College to Merom. He was very zealous in the ministry, and was successful in organizing many churches, as well as in the conversion of sinners. At one time, the writer was holding a meeting of days, in connection with this brother, at Fairbanks, Ind. The prospect for a revival was very discouraging, but Elder Hayes was not discouraged. That night, about one o'clock, on waking up, I heard my brother at my side, in earnest prayer to God for the success of the meeting. He spoke very low, but earnest, and continued for some time. I went to the meeting the next day with the firm conviction that the meeting would be a success, and so it was. Many were converted and a church was organized there as a result of that meeting. It was generally observed by those that knew him, that he was so persistent in his appeals, that he hardly ever failed of success.

DAVID HAYES (?—1862)

David Hayes was a faithful and talented minister in the Deer Creek Christian Conference, Ohio, from about 1810, to 1839. He died in Gallia County, in 1862.

HENRY HAYES (1786—1845)

This Elder was a brother of John and an uncle of H.B. Hayes. He was born in Wake County, N.C., June 3, 1786, was converted in 1802, was ordained December 22, 1810, and married Mary Burnham, in his native county, in 1813. He spent five years itinerating in North Carolina, but finally moved to Tennessee; and not finding any Christians in the neighborhood, he labored with the Protestant Methodists. September 17, 1845, he died in Carrol County, Tenn.

JOHN HAYES (1767—1840)

This was an older brother of the preceding and father of Elder H.B. Hayes, at one time editor of the "Christian Sun." John was born in North Carolina, March 27, 1767, was converted, and commenced preaching among the Methodists. He was present at the Methodist Conference when O'Kelly and others objected to the system of Episcopacy, and was one of the members that withdrew from that body. He was a member of the North Carolina Conference, and did a good service in the Christian Church during his long life. August 4, 1840, he died, aged seventy-three years.

<u>J</u>AMES <u>H</u>AYES (1811—1866)

The subject of this sketch occupied a prominent position in the church, in Central Ohio, about twelve years. In 1811, he was born in Smithfield, Jefferson County, O. When he .was quite young, his parents moved to Dublin, Franklin County. In 1827, he was converted, under the labors of Elder I.N. Walter, at Dublin. The impression that he should preach immediately came upon him; but not receiving proper encouragement, he put it off till some years later. In 1834, he was ordained at Dublin, O., and at once took a high position both in the church and conference. All acknowledged him to be a young man of more than ordinary ability. Though limited in education, yet by industry in the use of books, and by the peculiar grasp of his mind, he soon made up, to a great extent, for early deficiency.

In 1838 or '39, he visited Elder Walter in the-city of New York, and labored there some time. The same year, also, he made an extensive tour through several states, east and south. Wherever he labored, his talent, energy, and usefulness were acknowledged. Before and after this journey, his labors were confined principally to Knox, Licking, and adjoining counties in Ohio. In those days, when every inch of ground had to be fought for, among the Christians, the Elder was not only a successful pastor, but became, also, one of the champions in the controversies of the day. In this, he was peculiarly gifted. As Elder J.W. Marvin, than whom none knew better, observes, in writing his obituary, "His mind was not only comprehensive and grasping, but was also peculiarly quick to see the drift of an argument." In truth, the Elder was a natural logician and reasoner. Friends never feared the issue when he took part in a debate. Still, he was not given to controversy in his preaching so much as many others, less adapted to this peculiar work. Generally, his preaching was practical, and many were converted under his labors.

In 1843, he was called to the pastoral care of the church in Cincinnati, O. That year was a peculiar period throughout the

United States. Many people were convinced that the world was coming to an end that very year. Many had become wild on the subject, and had specified the day and hour when Christ should come. Some of this class were in the Cincinnati church. The Elder was not a man to lay idle nor to float on the current at such times. The man's whole soul was roused, he made a thorough examination of the whole subject, and to him, the one expression of Jesus. "Knoweth no man the day nor the hour," was of more weight than all the prophesies put together. He worked with all his energy to prove that no one knew, or could know, the time. These efforts were too great even for his powerful frame. He broke down in the work, and though he gained strength in a measure, he never was the same man, physically, that he was before. He labored faithfully and efficiently, though for two or three years with wasted strength, till near the close of life. December 13, 1866, he died of consumption, at his own home in Miller Township, Knox County, O., lamented by all the, church.

Physically, the Elder was apparently a perfect man, six feet tall, proportionally full, with blue eyes, of a florid complexion, with a sandy beard; and to see him in the pulpit, with his keen eyes and peculiar energy, one would have thought that nothing but age and long labor could have broken down such a frame, Beside his ministerial labors, the Elder was engaged, to a considerable extent, in writing. Many articles of his appeared in early volumes of the "Gospel Herald." Beside this, he was a member of the executive committee of the Western Book Association, and was one of the most active members in that body in the production of the "Western Christian hymn book." His death, in his prime, was a great loss to the denomination.

JAMES HAYNES (1789—1844)

This brother was born in 1789, was baptized by Philip Sanford, lived for a time at Lakeville, N.Y., and died in Sandusky, O., in 1844.

Joshua Hayward (1782—1840)

This brother was born in Massachusetts, in 1782, and moved to the State of New York, when quite young. In 1806, he was married to Miss Lydia Barker, who survived him. In 1809, he moved to Canada, and settled on the borders of Lake Quanto. Being loyal to his native country, during the war of 1812 against England, caused him much trouble. He finally, in company with three others, embarked in a boat on the lake to cross to the American side, and being perceived by the British, a galley of twelve oars was sent in pursuit, but it being very foggy they eluded their pursuers,, and landed safely in the American camp. In three months his wife joined him on this side.

During his youth, the Elder, by reading many deistical works, such as Paine, Volney, and others, became strongly tinctured with their doctrine. After which he fell on Universalism as more reasonable of the two, but in 1818, he abandoned all speculation and sought a godly life in Christ, as his future portion. Soon after his conversion he felt impressed to preach, and on June 22, 1820, he preached his first sermon in Rutland, Jefferson County, N.Y. From this time, to the day of his death, the Elder was an earnest working Christian minister. His talent was not the brightest, yet the matter and manner was so original and natural that he never failed to leave a deep impression on his hearers. From 1824 to 1826, he labored in Hartwick, Otsego County, N.Y. In that place and the vicinity, he spent the remainder of his life. In 1826, he moved his family to Laurens. In 1833, he writes that he is almost home, that his health was failing. He had labored in Otsego County, nine years, and before that period he had labored in Jefferson, Oneida, and Delaware counties. In the same year, writing from Unadilla, he said: "There are openings all around, but I am almost alone to travel in a region of country nearly sixty miles north, and south and about thirty east and west. There are now seven churches that claim my labors." When broken down in health, we understand that he traveled extensively, his wife accompanying him, mostly, and preached the Gospel to thousands with good effect. He was filled with zeal to the last. A short time before his death he preached a powerful sermon from the word, "I am now ready to be offered." He died in Laurens, Otsego County, N. Y,, May 17, 1840, aged fifty years. In 1845, a biography of his was published in pamphlet form by his widow. Several of the sons and grand-sons of this brother are yet in the ministry of the Christian Church.

LEONARD HAYWARD (1823—1873)

This was a son of the above, and died in Otego, N.Y., March 18, 1853.

J., DAVID, AND WILLIAM HAZE

J., David, and William Haze were ministers in the Deer Creek Conference, Ohio, about 1830.

SARAH HEDGES (1791—1843)

This sister was born about 1791, was converted among the Methodists when about eighteen years old. She labored with the Methodists nearly twelve years. In 1821, she joined the New York Eastern Conference, and was a worthy member of that body until her death, which took place in Chenango County, N.Y., March 15, 1843, aged fifty-two years.

She was married when young and had one daughter. Her husband was abusive at first, and finally abandoned her. The sorrow-stricken and deserted wife, sought consolation in religion, and devoted all her energy to the great work of the salvation of souls. In this, she was very successful, many tracing their conversion to her earnest labor. The tongue of slander was used against her, but those that knew her best speak highly of her pure and devoted life.

JEHIAL P. HENDEE (?—?)

This brother was born in Randolph, Vt. In 1837, he lived in Gilsum, N.H. At a certain period of his life, he published a paper—either the "Gospel" or "Vermont Luminary"—in Stowe, Vt, He was a man of considerable wit, always on the move, calm and deliberate in his utterance, and always possessed of good nature. He was of poor parentage, and was in limited circumstances himself. He had a clear head, was rather metaphysical in his reasoning, was a good writer, and an able preacher.

THOMAS HENRY (1798—1879)

Ireland gave us this faithful man, he having been born there February 2, 1798. After a long, active, and useful life, he died at Oshawa, Canada, September 20, 1879. In 1811, he came to America with his father's family, landing in New York in June. In 1813, he served in the British army, and at the close of the war, settled in Oshawa, where he continued during the remainder of his life. In 1816, his mother died, and in July, 1817, he was married to Elizabeth Davis, who died in 1829, leaving him with five motherless children. November 7, 1830, he married, for his second wife, Laurinda Abbey.

In 1817, he joined the Methodist Church on probation; but soon after, he met Elder Joseph Blackmar, on his way to Toronto, was converted under his preaching, joined the Christian Church, and was baptized by J.T. Bailey, September 24, 1825. The same year, he attended the first session of the Canada Conference, and never missed a session from that one till the one of 1879, during which he died. June 20, 1829, he was licensed to preach, and in 1832, was ordained at Darlington. For more than forty years, he was a representative minister of the church, in Canada. His home at Oshawa became the home of Christian ministers 'from the States and Canada. He was pastor of the church at Oshawa for fifteen years. Although he labored on his farm, and made money, yet he was constantly at work, visiting churches as a preacher, both on Sundays, week days, at funeral occasions, and as committee man. He visited the States quite frequently to attend Conferences, general meetings, and as trustee or director of our various institutions. Firmness was a prominent trait in his character, for he never turned to the right or left to follow any of the wild theories, such as Millerism, that carried so many away. Our brother was a bluff, blunt Irishman, bold, honest, and unyielding in the advocacy of what seemed to him the truth, yet with a heart as tender as a child. Among his many acquaintances none felt like doubting the truthfulness, sincerity, and ability of Thomas Henry, the Irish Canadian Yankee, for he was cosmopolitan in his Christian sympathy.

ALVA HERMAN (1814—1859)

Our present subject died about 1859, in Henderson, Texas. At one time, he lived near Providence, Penn.

JOHN N. HIATT (1812—1845)

John was born on North River, Hampshire County, Va., about 1812. About 1835, he was converted and joined the Christian Church, and soon after, commenced preaching. He was ordained in his own church by Elders Sine and Ferguson, and soon after became pastor of that and neighboring churches. About 1838, he was married to Miss Emma Parks. In 1844, he moved to Missouri and died there of fever in 1845. His wife and infant child died within thirty hours of his own death, leaving two orphan children. He was a sympathetic, able, and energetic preacher.

JOHN HIBBS (?—?)

John Hibbs was raised in Williamsport, O., in early times, and died in Fountain County, Ind.

JAMES HINKLIN (?—?)

James Hicklin died in one of the Western States.

EZEKIEL HILDRETH (1806—1879)

Brother Hildreth was born in Chesterfield, Vt., September 4, 1806, moved with the family to Bangor, N.Y., in 1821. In 1828, his father died, after which, Ezekiel had the care of his mother and two small children. The family was quite poor, in a new country, and the boy had to work very hard. The same year that his father died, Ezekiel embraced religion and became an earnest worker in the church at once. He was baptized by Elder John Smith. January 5, 1841, he married Miss Mary Joy, of Brandon, N.Y., and the same year, was licensed to preach. July 21, 1854, he was ordained at East Dickinson, by Elders Allen, Berry, and Moffat. He traveled extensively as a minister, and labored in the churches of Stockholm, Potsdam, Moria, Dickinson, Bangor, and others. November 18, 1869, he was struck with paralysis, but improved and preached some for several years. In 1873, however, he was taken worse, and for six years was helpless, but cheerful to the last. He died May 8, 1879.

The Elder was an earnest man, wholly devoted to the work of the ministry. He was limited in education, but his tenderness gave him great power over the people; especially in sickness and on funeral occasions was his presence in great demand.

JOSEPH HINTON (1800—?)

Joseph Hinton was a minister of eminence, who lived for many years in Raleigh, N.C. He was born about 1800, and died, in the time of the war of the Rebellion, at his home in Raleigh. He was a man of education. He also practiced medicine, and stood high in the church and conference as a minister of ability, zeal, and earnestness.

DANIEL HIX (1755—1838)

There is not, in all the annals of the Christian ministry, a more noted man than Daniel Hix. He was born November 30, 1755, and died March 21, 1838. Rehoboth, Mass., was his native place. He was the youngest son of Elder John and Hannah (Galusha) Hix— born respectively May 10, 1712, and April 17, 1713. The father was a minister in the Baptist Church for more than forty years. Daniel was a farmer and cooper. He also served nine months in the Revolutionary War. During this time, he was unconverted and reckless; but at times he was subject to solemn thoughts. In 1777, he was married to Mary, daughter of Captain John Kelton. This union lasted over sixty years, his wife dying September 26, 1837, aged eighty-two years, and the Elder, as stated, died March 21, 1838.

Two years after his marriage, he was converted under the labors of his brother Jacob. March 5, 1780, he preached his first sermon. At that time, he joined with eleven others in the organization of a church in Dartmouth—a branch of the church at Rehoboth, of which his brother Jacob had charge. July 12, the same year, he was ordained, and the year following, was regularly installed as pastor of the, at that time, Baptist Church of Dartmouth. He held the pastorate of this church till death.

During his ministry, he received into membership more than 1,000 persons, preached 8,000 sermons, conducted more than 1,000 funerals, and baptized 1;500 persons. His connection with the Christian Church began about 1802 or '3. Elias Smith, on some of his preaching tours, went to Dartmouth, and was received by the Elder as a brother in Christ. For this he was censured by his brethren of the Baptist Church, and was finally tried. But when the appeal was made to his own charge, they stood by him almost to a man. And so, though persecuted, the pastor and people united in a body with the obnoxious Christians. This added much to the strength and efficiency of the Christian Church in that part of Massachusetts—for Daniel Hix was not only a strong man, but his exemplary life gave him an influence that few possessed. As stated before, the Elder followed farming and coopering for a part of his living, and consequently it is not likely that he was a man of much reading; yet his peculiar good sense, independence, and energy gave him an influence with his brethren that no book knowledge could give. He was a leading man in the denomination to the last? In all the general meetings of those days, the Elder's very presence gave an influence to the body, and his advice had power in it. He preached many ordination, as well as dedication, and funeral sermons.

It was said that he was quite eccentric—and there is some truth in the statement if it means the absence of formality. The Elder had but little of the conventionalism of the day, but was natural, always with his wit and bluntness. Many anecdotes are related of him. The following is one: The celebrated John Leland, a man much like himself, on a certain journey in that part of the country, went to see his friend Daniel; for, though they had never seen each other, they had had frequent correspondence, and by this had become strong friends. Leland, finding where the Elder lived, went into the house without knocking, sat down in the corner opposite Mrs. Hix, and began to smoke, uninvited. Mrs. Hix was afraid, and hurriedly sent for her husband. When he came, he asked the stranger, "Who are you?" Leland answered, "I am John of the wilderness. And who are you?" The Elder answered at once, "I am Daniel from the lion's den." After parrying thus for a while, they became known to each other, and embraced and wept on each other's breasts, so glad were they of the privilege of a personal acquaintance.

JOHN HIX (?—?)

John Hix was a minister of the Western Indiana Conference. He died in Carrol County, Ind., when about forty years of age.

J.N. HODGDON (?—?)

J.N. Hodgdon labored in Harrison, Ah., and died there before 1875.

ELLIS HODGESON (?—1872)

This brother was a licentiate in the Bluffton Conference, Ind. He preached about three years, and died April 30, 1872.

JOHN HOFFMAN (1791—1854)

John was born in 1791, and died from the effects of an accident, in 1854. He had not devoted his life wholly to the ministry, and expressed sorrow for it in his last hours; but his life was an exemplary one.

<u>Elihue G. Holland (1817—1878)</u>

The name of E.G. Holland is well known in the church, east and west, as an eloquent preacher, fine scholar, attractive writer, and an able author. He was born in 1817, was a student in Courtlandville, N. A\, joined the Christians, in his youth, and began to preach quite early. He was very ambitious and determined to acquire education, but he studied too hard and became an invalid, the effect of which he felt the remainder of his life. His mind was very active, but he was inclined to be absent minded. He acted as pastor in some of the leading churches of the denomination, and served in the same capacity for some time in the Unitarian Church in Aleadville, Penn.

Several books and tracts were published by him. Among the number are the "Life of Joseph Badger," essays on various subjects, tract on the "Christian Name," and others. In 1872, he went to Europe, and visited Germany, France, and the British Isles, lecturing on various subjects—Theology, Science, and especially on the History of America, with great success. After his return, his health being yet poor, he was engaged, for a time, in the manufacture of Rhus Wine for medicinal purposes. He died of dropsy, in the town of Canandaigua, N.Y., December 13, 1878. For many years, Brother Holland was a prominent man in the church. In the general gatherings of the churches, he was generally called upon to preach. On such occasions he seldom failed to give good satisfaction. He was never married, so he had no permanent home. He was always well dressed, and made a fine appearance, but as he was quite absent-minded, it amused his friends to see how careless he was as to his surroundings, sitting down in a blacksmith or butcher's shop, regardless of how his fine clothes were soiled. Many men of far less talent, were more useful than he in the general work of the church, but he had his place and filled it well. With all his variety of thoughts and tastes, he was always true to the church of his first choice.

LAZARUS HOLLOWAY (?—?)

Lazarus Holloway was a Christian minister that lived in Georgia. He traveled in North Carolina, in 1824, and died soon after.

ZACHARIAH HOLLOWAY (?—?)

Zachariah Holloway was converted under the labors of Elder Joseph Thomas, in 1810. He traveled much. It is said he was a successful itinerant minister.[7]

THE HOLTS. JACOB HOLT (1790—1844)

Vermont was the native state of this brother. He was born in 1790, was converted, and commenced preaching in early life. He embraced the doctrine of Universalism in 1840, but returned to the Christian Church in two or three years. He died in 1844.

JOHN R. HOLT (1812—1870)

John was born and raised in Alamance County, N.C. Early in life, he was converted under the preaching of Elder Lewis Craven. He attended school, and graduated at the University of North Carolina. For some years, he was President of Graham Institute, the same state. The Elder was a man of ability, and of great usefulness in the church. In 1878, he died in Randolph County, N.C., leaving a widow and a large family of children.

MASON B. HOPKINS (?—?)

Mason B. Hopkins was born in Rhode Island, and preached in Foster, in the same state. He is said to have been earnest in the work and to have lived an exemplary life. He died many years ago, in his prime.

ISAAC HORNBECK (1773—1856)

This brother was born in Virginia, in 1773, was married to Margaret Funk, in Kentucky, in 1793, soon after moved to Ohio, was

---

[7] Joseph Thomas, "the White Pilgrim," references "Z. Holloway" twice in his autobiography, each time calling him "my son in the faith."

converted, joined the church at Williamsport, in 1806, and soon after commenced preaching. In 1821, he, with Abram Halstead and John VanBuskirk, was ordained at the above place, by George Alkire, George Zimmerman, and Isaac Cade. He died July 27, 1856, from the effect of a fall.

JAMES HORNBECK (1810—1869)

This Elder was born about the year 1810, and is supposed to be the first white child born in Madison County, O., where he spent his life, and died there in 1869, having spent thirty-four years in the ministry.

ELIAS HORNER (?—?)

Elias Horner died in Fountain County, Ind., about the age of fifty years.

RACHEL HOSMER (THOMPSON) (?—?)

Rachel Hosmer (Thompson) was a female laborer, that had great success as a preacher in an early day in Vermont. She went there from New Hampshire. Her married name was Thompson, but as she was generally known by her maiden name, Hosmer, it is inserted here. She is said to have been tall, with a calm delivery, earnest, logical, and very searching in her description of sinners. In 1827, she went to Stowe, Vt., where she continued for some time, having joined in the work, with another female laborer by the name of Sabrina Lambson. The date of her death is not given.

BENJAMIN HOWARD (?—?)

Benjamin Howard was a minister in the State of New York, in an early day. In 1825, he had an extensive revival in Cayuga County, N.Y.

JAMES HOWE (?—?)

James Howe was a prominent minister in the time of the withdrawal of Elder O'Kelly and others from the Methodists, in 1793.

He continued to labor in the Christian Church for some years, as a talented and useful man. Perhaps Peter Cartwright is right in his memoirs, when he says that he went back to the Methodists, as we have no account of his latter years.

R.D. HOWEY (?—1860)

R.D. Howey was a minister in the State of New York, and died there in 1860.

GERSHOM HOWLAND (1776—1847)

This Elder was born in Boston, Mass., in 1776, moved to Hamden, N.Y., in 1892. He was a member of the Methodist Church for forty years, and for thirty years was a minister. He still continued in the ministry after joining the Christians, and was an earnest, useful man. He preached a funeral sermon a week before he died and said at the time, that this was the one hundred and nineteenth funeral sermon he had preached and that it would be the last. He died triumphantly in 1847, his wife having died a few hours before.

JESSE HUBBARD (?—1776)

Jesse Hubbard was a member of the Southern Wabash Conference, Ill., and died in 1776.[8]

WILLIAM HUBBARD (1792—1876)

Our present subject was a minister that exerted considerable influence as a leading man, for some years. November 13, 1792, he was born, was converted in early life, in Franklin County, Ind., and soon began to preach. After his ordination, he baptized his own father. During many years, he was a constant worker in the ministry, and when he was old, and could not stand up to- deliver the message to the people, he preached sitting down. Two of his sons,

---

[8] Considering the Christian Connexion/Christian Church (as defined denominationally) did not exist prior to James O'Kelly's departure from Methodism in 1793, it is difficult to believe this is the proper death date for this man.—*Editor.*

George and Thomas, became ministers in the same church. He died April 6, 1876.

JAMES HUDSON (1872—1855)

This brother was born in New Hampshire, was converted when young, commenced preaching, and was ordained soon after. He labored successfully in Lempster, N.H., and in 1839, moved to Shrewsbury, Vt., where he continued to labor eight years. He then moved to Will County, Ill., where he ended his days in 1855. In Illinois, he was successful in building up the cause in his new home, although he met with opposition. At the time of his. death, the church numbered forty members. His sermons were well prepared. He depended more upon reason than feeling, in the conversion of sinners.

BENJAMIN HUFFARD (1805—1865)

This brother was a native of Pennsylvania, and joined the church while in that state. In 1851, he moved to Indiana, and soon joined the Bluffton Conference, of which body he was a highly esteemed member till his death. He was born in Burke County, Penn., and died in Henry County, Ind., in 1865, aged sixty years.

JOHN HUGG (1815—1871)

Elder Hugg joined the church, began to preach, and, in 1868, was ordained. He was local in his labors, although active and very successful. He died in Dexter, Meigs County, O., in 1871, aged fifty-six years.

JAMES HUGHS (1773—1833)

James was born in 1773, in Kentucky. He labored in Kentucky, Ohio, Indiana, and Illinois, and was highly respected for his goodness and devotion to the cause. Many of the old brothers and sisters have written to me of this good man, and all bear testimony in regard to his moral and Christian worth. He died December 10, 1833.

JESSE HUGHS (?—1845)

This Elder was a leading man in the Central Indiana Conference for years. He died in Bartholomew County, Ind., in 1845.

R. HULTZ (1819—1879)

The subject of this sketch was a member of the Miami Reserve Conference, Ind. He lived in Pulaski County, and died in 1879, not far from sixty years of age.

D. HUMPHREYS (1821—1880)

Brother Humphreys was born in December, 1821, and died in Rowen County, Ky., February 19, 1880, having spent thirty-five years in the ministry of the Christian Church. He was a zealous worker in the church and his death was greatly lamented by his fellow laborers.

JAMES HUMPHREYS (1810—1870)

Elder Humphreys was a native of Kanawa County, Va., and was, for many years, a member of the United Brethren Church. He joined the Christians in 1867, under the labors of Oscar Kendrick. July 18, 1870, he died at Cleveland, Ind. He was a zealous and devoted man.

JOHN HUTCHINS (1800—1844)

Brother Hutchins was born in 1800, and commenced preaching in 1828. He was very zealous in the ministry, although his health was poor for thirteen years before he died. He died in Troy, Me., in 1844.

AUSTIN HUTSON (1832—1869)

Austin was the son of William Hutson, and was born September 20, 1832, in Madison County, O. The family moved to Jasper County, Ill., in 1837. During the first sixteen years of his life, Austin attended school but three months, during which time he learned to read the New Testament—that being his school book and favorite companion. In time, he became very familiar with the Scriptures, to which familiarity he attributed much of his success in the ministry, in after years.

From 1846 to 1848, he was in Rush County, Ind.; during that time, he attended school three months. After returning home in company with William Markwell, the companion of his youth and his associate in the ministry, while engaged in secret prayer in the woods, he gave his heart to God. In a few months, he began a ministry which he laid down only with his life. He was ordained at Sugar Creek, Richland County, Ill., October 8, 1854, by Elders Foor, Hole, and Wood. He began laboring energetically, preaching wherever and whenever opportunity offered. In 1855, he moved to Indiana. He was pastor of the church at Sumner, ill., for nearly eight years, during which time he received 137 members into the church. He preached to the New Liberty Church, Ind., fifteen years, and received into the-church 153 members. But these were not the only churches for which he labored. Among others was the Bethsaida Church, in Posey County, and the Bethany Church, in Gibson County, Ind. As a preacher of the Word, the Elder was everywhere liked. Punctual to his appointments, faithful but kind in his admonitions, sound in doctrine, liberal and progressive in his principles, and eloquent and earnest in his appeals to both saint and sinner, he fully commanded his congregations, and carried his hearers whither he chose. When the Union Christian College enterprise was started, he became one of its most efficient and earnest supporters. He served as trustee from its opening till his death. He wrote much, though chiefly for his own improvement. His sermons were full of Christ. He seemed to delight in portraying the glories of the cross, the riches of heaven, the joys of the redeemed. He strove to make his hearers acquainted with Jesus.

He was married twice—the last time, September 18, 1861, to Miss Lou W. Wason, who survived him. He died October 16, 1869, at Fort Branch, Ind.

Gardner Hyck (?—1871)

Gardner Hyck died at Palmyra, Mich., in 1871, after devoting twenty years of his life to the ministry.

Roger T. Ingalls (1821—1861)

This brother was born in Windham, Conn., in 1821, was converted in 1836, began to preach in 1841, and went to the State of New York in 1845. He labored with great success in Columbia, Montgomery, and adjoining counties. He was a man of great ability, and an excellent writer. He wrote a great deal for our periodicals, and was always interesting. He never was married. He became insane before his death, and died in a lunatic asylum in Pennsylvania, about 1860 or '61. He was a member of the New York Western Conference. From his writings we judge him a man of fine spirit, strong and clear in his mind.

Andrew Ireland (?—?)

Andrew Ireland was a native of Kentucky. He afterward moved to Ohio, and died in Preble County. He never was ordained, but was a good exhorter. He and John Purviance, David Kirkpatrick, and William Caldwell, went out, two and two, in a short time after the Cane Ridge revival. Kirkpatrick and Caldwell were ordained, but the other two were not.

W.H. Ireland (?—?)

W.H. Ireland for many years was an active minister in Corinth, and Newport, Me., but during the Advent movement, he worked for this cause with great zeal. He wished to continue in the Christian Church all his life, but to the last he expressed a belief that the millennium was Close at hand. In the year 1850, he moved to Rye, N.H., where he labored with great success. He was an excellent man. I have not been able to find the time of his death.

ALFRED ISELY (1814-1878)

Alfred Isely was born in Alamance County, N.C., about 1814, and died in the same county about 1878. He was a member of the North Carolina Conference about forty years. He was a self-made man, an excellent preacher and a good pastor. He left a son in the ministry of the Christian Church.

ABRAHAM JACKSON (1791—1871)

Elder Jackson was a conscientious man, and his long life is a singular one. He was born at Plymouth, Mass., in 1791, was converted among the Congregationalists in 1812, was educated for the ministry at Bangor College, Me., and was installed pastor of the Congregational Church at Machias, Me., in 1821. In this field he had great success, and continued in the same pastorate until 1840, when he settled in Kingston, Mass. He then moved to Walpole, N.H., where he continued for eight years, then to South Deerfield, Mass., then back to Machias, Me., and then back to Walpole, N.H., where his wife died in 1858. After more than thirty years of uninterrupted pastor's work in the Congregational and Presbyterian churches, he embraced more liberal views. He examined Unitarianism, but found it lacking in spirituality, when he became acquainted with the Christians, and found them a people of his own taste and doctrine. At the age of sixty-seven he joined the latter body and labored faithfully the rest of his long life in that connection. With the Christians he labored at Freedom, North Fall River, Rochester, and other places in Massachusetts. He was a strong advocate of the Christian doctrine. He was not a fluent extempore speaker, not having practiced that kind of speaking in his early ministry, but he was a strong, clear-headed reasoner, and well-informed on the subject of Theology. He died April 12, 1874, aged eighty- three years.

JAMES JACKSON (?—?)

This brother was one of those who joined the Christian Church at the time of the separation from the Methodists in North Carolina, in 1793, and died where he had lived for years, in Cumberland County, N.C.

JOSEPH JACKSON (1774—?)

Joseph Jackson was born in 1774, and for many years before his death labored in Western Indiana and Illinois. He was considered a good man.

J. JAMES (?—1852)

Elder James was a member of the Kentucky Christian Conference, and died in 1855.[9]

BENJAMIN JANER (?—1800)

Benjamin Janer lived in North Carolina. He died about 1800, soon after joining the Christian Church.

AMOS JANNEY (1779—1809)

Elder Janney was born in Lowden County, Va., in 1779, and lived there until manhood, when he moved to Ohio, where he united with the Christians. In 1837, he moved to Indiana, where he lived until his death, July 28, 1859. He was a faithful minister, preaching by both precept and example, for nearly forty years.

JOHN JANNEY (?—1868)

Elder Janney was a member of the Bluffton Conference, Ind., and died in 1868.

ABSALOM JENKINS (1794—1874)

Absalom was born in Preston County, Va., July 1, 1794, was married to Elizabeth Board in 1816, moved to Warren County, in 1819, and was baptized by Elder Daniel Call, in 1839. Not long after the latter event, he moved to Fountain County, Ind., where he

---

[9] The original edition of this work contained two different years for his death. As we have no real way of determining which is correct, we have left both in place.—*Editor.*

became a leading member of the Osborn Prairie Christian Church, and soon after began to speak in public. He was ordained in 1852, and moved to Roseville, Ill., in 1865. He continued to labor in the bounds of the Central Illinois Conference until death. In his old age, he had one of his lower limbs amputated. He suffered much, but he was very patient under all his afflictions. Elder Jenkins was not a talented preacher, but being a good man, by his example he exerted an influence for good wherever he labored. He died at his home at Roseville, March 8, 1874, his excellent wife having preceded him two years before.

ISAAC JESSUP (1789—1848)

Isaac was born in 1789, commenced preaching in 1823, being one of the first Christian preachers in South-eastern Indiana. His labor was principally in Ohio, Switzerland, and adjoining counties in Indiana. He had a large family and was in limited circumstances, but for all these disadvantages, he labored extensively and successfully. He was limited in education but well acquainted with the truths of the Bible and ever ready to use them. He died near Allensville, Ind., November 5, 1843. He was well thought of by his neighbors, and even those who opposed his doctrine had great respect for his Christian character.

JACOB JOHNSON (1799—1879)

This brother was born in Whitchurch, Canada, June 26, 1810. In early life he was quite an opposer of religion, but after his conversion, he became very zealous. He did not believe in stated salaries being paid to ministers, but was liberal to those whom he considered faithful ones. He died February 20, 1876, leaving a wife and eight children.[10]

---

[10] The original edition had two different birth years and two different death years, and the only graves we could locate in the same time period don't match either year.—*Editor.*

JACOB JOHNSON (1775—?)

Jacob Johnson was born in 1775, and was ordained in the Methodist Church, by Bishop Asbury, but he afterward rejected creeds and discipline, and hence could not work in that church. In 1828, he was living in Covington County, Ala., and had organized three Christian churches. Fifteen months before this he had met Elder McGaughy, and had then united with the Christians. Of his death and last years, we have no definite account.

J.L. JOHNSON (1799—1872)

This minister was engaged in preaching for about thirty years. For many years he was a member of the Southern Wabash Conference, Ill., but for the purpose of educating his children, he moved to Merom, Ind., about 1860. He was married three times, his last wife surviving him. He was born October 18, 1799, and died in Merom, Ind., December 17, 1872. He was not a very great preacher, but an exceedingly well-posted man, especially in the general measures of his own church. He wrote a great deal for our periodicals. Few of our ministers sent me as much material for this volume as Elder Johnson. He did his life work faithfully and died in the triumph of faith.

JAMES JOHNSON (?—1840)

James Johnson was far advanced in years in 1828, when preaching on Darby Plains. He was a brother-in-law of Elder James Dunlap, both belonging to the Baptist Church, but they preached for the Christian churches on the Plains for several years. Brother Johnson was a good and faithful worker until his death, which occurred about 1840, being at that time about seventy years old.

JORDAN JOHNSON (1815—1861)

This brother was born near Lynchburg, Va., October 25, 1815, but was brought up near Liberty, Ind. His parents were Quakers. In 1835, he joined the Silver Creek Church, and was baptized by Elder Thomas Carr. In 1849, he commenced preaching, and was ordained in two or three years after, in the Western Indiana Conference, by Elders Wilkins, Gregory, and Thomas. He was married three times, and had six children. He was a good, earnest, zealous man, but with moderate education. He always had charge of two or three churches, and was a faithful, energetic, and successful pastor. He died in Boone County, Ind., July 23, 1861.

<u>ABNER JONES (1772—1841)</u>

This Elder was born in Royalston, Mass., April 28, 1872. His parents were members of the Baptist Church, his father being a leading man, and quite Calvinistic in his views.

When Abner was eight years old, his parents moved to Bridge water, Vt., where he remained until the death of his father. Several years passed before he enjoyed the evidences of conversion, as during the illness of his father, an ungodly brother had returned home, and was the means of leading Abner astray, but his brother dying in great fear, influenced our subject then, to turn entirely to God, and take an active part in the church. At the age of twenty-one, he went to Hanover, where he continued two years, preparing himself for the practice of medicine, although since his conversion, he had felt that it would be his duty to preach at some time. He finished the study of medicine, and after remaining in several places for a short time, he finally settled in Lyndon, Vt., in the year 1796. He was also married about this time to Miss Damaris Prior. He was very successful as a physician, but he was continually goaded by the thought that he had neglected the intimations of Providence, and was constantly impressed with the idea that he should have to preach, but in doing this he knew that he should receive the reproach of the world, and seal forever the bond which would hold him to poverty and trials. After a long struggle with his own reluctance and his wife's opposition, he made up his mind to preach, but found that his views were not in harmony with the prevalent doctrines of the day. After long and serious thought, he finally decided on the present views of the Christian Church, and with this understanding, he was ordained by the Freewill Baptists in 1802. The of-

ficiating clergyman being Elders Buzzell, King, and Brown. But
the year before, in 1801, he had organized the first Christian
Church in New England, at Lyndon, Vt. It consisted of eight or ten
members, but rapidly increased in numbers. From this time forward, he devoted himself wholly to the cause, regardless of the opposition of wife (who, after becoming reconciled to the change, became an earnest worker and helpmate), patients, neighbors, friends,
and all. He had now given up the practice of medicine, and had
moved his family to Lebanon, N.H., traveling far and near, wherever there was a call, or wherever he could get a hearing. In 1802,
the second Christian Church was formed in Hanover, N.H., and
soon after the third was organized in Piermont, the same state. In
the course of his travels, he met Elias Smith, who had renounced
the Baptists, and had gone into this work with all his energy. They
worked together at Portsmouth for some time, after which, Elder
Jones went to Boston, where he did a mighty work, as he had taken
his family, and was devoting nearly all of his time to preaching.
During these years, his work was excessive, preaching thirty or
forty sermons a month, regularly, baptizing from ten to fifteen
'persons at one time, and often traveling over two hundred miles
during the month.

After he left Boston, he moved to Bradford, afterward to Salem,
Mass., and from there to Portsmouth, N.H. He was there when the
port was blockaded and the town nearly consumed by fire. An incident which occurred here, will show, in some degree, his benevolence and perfect trust in the Lord. He says there was never a day
when he or his family went hungry, but one Saturday his wife
came to his study, and told him "there was really nothing to eat."
He had but one dollar in his pocket, and the prospect seemed quite
dark. While thinking of this, a stranger came in, asking for help
and the Elder soon found there was one at least in a worse condition than himself, so he gave the stranger the last dollar. After the
stranger had gone, he began to doubt the propriety of the act of taking the bread from his children's mouths, but it was now too late to
repent. While thinking over the bitterness of the situation, the old

trust in the Lord was revived, and just at this time a neighbor came and said, "Mr. Jones, a laborer is worthy of his hire, and as my family and I have been attending your meeting, I now ask you to accept this trifle as part of the pay towards the debt I owe you." It was a five dollar note. In 1815, he moved his family to Hopkinton, N.H., and here he stayed for several years, as two of his married daughters lived there. Soon after coming to this place, the spotted fever, or cold plague, made its appearance, and by this means, he obtained extensive practice, although much against his will. During his residence at Hopkinton, he traveled less than at any other period of his ministry, as his practice was very large and his pastoral cares were heavy. He laid by some money, and might have made a fortune, had he continued there, but other churches, less fortunate than the one here, were calling on him for aid, and he felt where duty called, there he must go. He moved to Salem in 1821, and when he started on his journey to the West in 1829, he left the church in a prosperous condition. He had gone as far as Mayfield, N.Y., when he was stricken with the rheumatic billions fever, and for weeks his life was despaired of. He was confined to the house for three months, but during his suffering he showed great fortitude.

The destitute condition of the church at Milan, N.Y., touched his heart and he consented to stay some time with it as a pastor, although when he left Salem, he fully intended to return, as the church and brethren were very dear to him. During his pastorate at Milan, in 1836, his faithful wife, Damaris, died. This noble woman was subject to some of the greatest trials as a wife and mother. Although opposed to her husband entering the ministry, yet when the trials came, she stood ever ready to share the burdens. She showed herself to be a person of strong attachment for home, children, and friends, but all through her life she was continually called upon to give up these, when there was work to be done for the Master. Before his wife's death, Elder Jones had given up the pastorate at Milan, leaving it in a very prosperous condition, and had taken charge of a church at Assonet, Mass., which he found in a much worse condition than the one at Milan. Under his labors, the church speedily revived, and was now united, at least, if not as prosperous as it might be. But he felt he must go on, there was work for him at other places. His wife having died before this, he felt a great desire to be among old friends.

In 1839, he was married again, and now hoped to live in comfort and quiet for the rest of his life. He took charge of the church at Exeter, N.H., and moved there with his family. When he married the last time, his life was full of great purposes but in less than two years, he was called on to follow the dear ones who had preceded him to the land of rest. He died May 29, 1841. Funeral services in the Christian Chapel, at Exeter. Sermon by Elder Elijah Shaw.

The above is a mere outline of the vast labors of Elder Abner Jones, the founder of the Christian denomination in New England. He had not the versatility of talent of his co-laborer, Elias Smith, but was a man of more stability. The two men were well adapted to work together: for one supplied what the other lacked. Each was a pioneer in his way. Each suffered much from opposition, persecution, and poverty, but each bore well his part of the work in the establishment of an independent body of Christians.

WILLIAM A. JONES (?—1849)

This brother was a native of Virginia. His life was spent in that state, principally in Nansemond County. His ministry was instrumental in doing a great deal of good. His death, which occurred during the summer of 1849, was caused by drowning while endeavoring to cross a stream.

JESSE JUSTICE (1811—1877)

Brother Justice was a man of good character. He was born in 1811, was converted in 1829, was ordained in 1840, and became a member of the Deer Creek Conference, O. Several years before his death, he moved to Champaign County, Ill., where he died suddenly, of heart disease, in 1877.

W.N. KEILEY (1828—1867)

This brother was a young man of promise, and had already done a great deal of good before he died. He preached for a time at Liberty, Ind., but afterwards removed to Illinois. He was an active business man, and a ready and interesting writer. He was born in 1828, and died in Illinois, in 1867.

GEORGE KELTON (?—1862)

This Elder was a native of Rhode Island. He died in 1862, at Providence. He preached quite often, but never traveled far from home. He was the father of George N. Kelton, now (1880) living in the State of New York.

GEORGE W. KELTON (?—?)

George W. Kelton was a pious, prudent, and very useful minister. His father lived in Taunton, Mass., where George was born. He labored as a minister for some time in Salem, Mass.; but he traveled extensively through New England, doing a good work. In 1834, he left Salem for Plymouth, where he continued for years. He also became pastor of the church at Eastport, Me., from which place, he went to Providence, R.I., and took charge of the Sailors' Bethel Church, where he died several years ago. The Elder was a good writer, and wrote much for our various periodicals. His death, so early, was a great loss to the denomination.

JEREMIAH KENARTON (1828—1868)

Our present subject was born in Caledonia County, Vt., September 3, 1828, and died in Jefferson, Mich., May 3, 1868. He commenced preaching in 1848, and was ordained in the Ohio Central Conference. He labored extensively through the Western States, especially in Michigan, where he died.

OSCAR KENDRICK (1820—1868)

Brother Kendrick was born February 23, 1826, in Preble County, O. He was converted early in life, and joined the United Brethren

Church; but desiring, as he deemed it, more liberty in religion, he joined the Christians. He felt himself called to preach, and early in life became a minister. He had no sympathy with dogmatic theology and proscribed no man for his honest convictions. He regarded as a brother and loved as a Christian, all who loved God and kept his commandments. His preaching was full of justice, mercy, and practical piety, insisting that to do right, is more important than to believe right, and that moral duty is of higher obligation than ceremonial observance. His public discourses were characterized rather by clearness of thought and cogency of reasoning than by flights of eloquence. And the earnest, loving manner he used gave his sermons a force and influence which no rhetoric could equal. His life was a constant and faithful effort to mitigate human misery and promote human happiness. For many years, he lived in the city of Indianapolis, and worked faithfully as a minister in the churches near his home. During the war of the Rebellion, he served, for a time, as Pay Master in the army, performing the responsible duty with honor. He suffered much with bronchitis, which finally terminated in consumption.

A few days before his death, he said to a friend: "My dear brother, I am looking death steadily in the face. I must soon rest in the grave. My faith is not orthodox. Trinitarianism I never believed. My belief is that the Father only is God, and that Jesus is his son. In this faith I have long lived; in it I am ready to die. I die confident that it is the great central truth of Christianity. I expect eternal life, and have a blessed hope of soon being in heaven, where there shall be no more death, neither sorrow and crying."

In this confident hope our brother continued till the 5th of March, 1868, when he closed his eyes without a struggle, and quietly passed away.

J.B.H. KENISTON (1831—?)

J.B. H. Keniston was born about 1831. He labored for some time in Northern Indiana and Southern Michigan. He was an easy and fluent speaker. He organized several churches, among which the one at Jefferson, Mich.

Daniel W. Kerr (1800—1850)

This Elder was editor and founder of the "Christian Sun," and was born in Virginia in 1800. He spent the most of his active life in North Carolina. He was a companion of Elder O'Kelly, and one of the first preachers of the day. He was a man of great learning, and good business talent. He founded the "Christian Sun" in 1844, and continued as editor and publisher until his death. He died in May, 1850, at his residence, in Pittsborough, Chatham County, N.C. The Elder was a self-made man. In early life he studied hard, as he thought then, for the legal profession, but when converted he devoted his talent, energy, and education to the work of the ministry. For a time, he was the Principal of Junto Academy, Orange County, N.C. It seemed a great loss to our Christian brethren in the South, when this faithful minister, scholar, writer, and leader in the church died in the zenith of his life.

Josiah Kerr (1791—1869)

Josiah was born in 1791, in Butler County, O., where he united with the Christian Church. He was ordained in 1849, and continued to take an active part in the ministry until his death, January 2, 1869. Elder Kerr's talents were not remarkable, but his mild disposition, earnest zeal, and holy life were sufficient passports to the hearts of the people. During the latter part of his life, he was in good circumstances, as he had a large farm in Fountain County, Ind. He never received much, if anything, for his work as a minister; therefore, his places of preaching were mostly with weak and desolate churches. But he filled an important place in the church for many years.

William Key (1805—1860)

William was born in 1805, was converted in 1825, began to preach in 1850, and became a member of the Western Indiana

Conference. He .afterward moved to Iowa, where he died in June, 1860,

Reuben Kedner (?—1870)

Reuben Kedner was a member of the Bluffton Indiana Conference, and died in 1870.

John Kempton (?—?)

John Kempton was born not far from 1791. He lived and labored in Hartwick, Vt., and was a good pastor, though local in his labors. He died some years ago.

W.A. Kidwell (1806—1876)

William was born in Hampshire County, Va., December 19, 1806. He was converted early in life, but did not continue steadfast at first. He moved to Ohio, and settled in Athens County. He renewed his covenant with God, soon after began to preach, and joined the Eastern Ohio Conference. He was a zealous, faithful minister to the end of his days. He died of heart disease, on Monday, after preaching on Sunday, July 10, 1876.

Jabez King, Jr (1791—1844)

This worthy brother was born in Woodstock, Vt., in 1791. His parents were persons of very respectable standing in that place, and early implanted the seeds of virtue and morality in the minds of their children. He received, what was then considered, a sufficient English education, and was apprenticed to the shoe-making and tanning business. When about twenty years of age, he was converted under the labors or Elder Frederick Plummer, and soon became impressed with the idea that it was his duty to preach, but the sacrifice seemed too great, and he refused to obey the promptings of the spirit. After a severe illness he became reconciled to God and prepared to do his duty. He spent that season, and a part of the next, in his native state, exhorting and inviting sinners, and performing the duties of a lay brother with Elders Plummer, Putnam,

Smith, and Rand, until 1813, when, in company with Elder J. Thompson, he left his native state and went to Charleston, N.Y. Here, these two young brethren encountered the prejudices of sectarians and the malevolence of the enemies oi the cross. Yet nothing daunted, they warned sinners, invited them to Christ, encouraged the saint, and God gave them success wherever they labored.

In 1814, he returned to his native place, and was ordained at the recommendation of the brethren in Charleston. -From this time forward, he was permanently located in New York, and his labors became widely extended during the three following years. His labors were principally in Montgomery and Saratoga counties, and being blessed with a good constitution, he was enabled to endure his hardships with cheerfulness. His associates here, in the cause, were Elders Thompson and Martin, and under their united labors, many were raised up to assist in the work of the Lord, among whom were Elders Koss, Milliard, Capron, Mosher, Rider, Hollister, Sanford, Spore, Allen, and others. It will be remembered that the period alluded to was not only one of continued reformation, but of great conflict. The new sect, as the Christians were called, were everywhere spoken against, and were opposed, not only by the infidel, but by the bigoted sectarian as well. But the brethren, and foremost among them was Brother King, united themselves only the closer, firmly met the storm of opposition, and a rich harvest was the consequence.

In 1816, he was married to Miss Ruth McOmar, a pious lady, and one well qualified to share with him the trials incident to the self-denying life of a minister of Jesus Christ. He gradually became more local, as the care and wants of a rising family required, and the circle of his ministerial labors became necessarily more contracted; yet he never seemed to lose the ardor of his youth, or the zeal of his missionary spirit, making frequent journeys, when he could, into new, as well as former scenes of labor. As a public speaker, he was energetic and often graphic; his discourses were usually warm, often abounding with incidents; without ornament, plain and pointed. But his worth cannot be known in the character of a public speaker. As a pastor, he was gentle and kind to all, always ready to counsel and advise, never boisterous or severe; more ready to forgive than to criminate. He was charitable to a fault. He was patient and kind, never troubled with jealousy, and always rejoicing in the prosperity of others. But of all his qualities, none shone more brightly than his benevolence; the poor, the sick, the bereaved, and the mourner always received his deepest sympathy. As a husband and father, he was strong in his attachments, familiar in his intercourse, [and instructing much by his own example. He died in Northampton, N.Y., November 14, 1844.

THOMAS KING (1809—1850)

This Elder was a member of the Eastern Ohio Conference, within the bounds of which he labored for some time. He died April 20, 1850, aged forty-one years.

FRANK KINGSLEY

Frank Kingsley was a native of New York. He was converted when sixteen years old, and commenced preaching about four years later—attending school for three years before as a preparation for the work. In company with Elder Ira Allen, he went to the Northern New York Conference, intending to move to Ohio at once, but the church at Leroy prevailed on him to remain with them for a time. He spent the following year at Leroy and Pamelia, and a great reformation followed, greatly reviving the brethren of the different churches. He remained with these churches about six years, when he took charge of the church at Lawrence, N.Y., where he remained three years, then, he resumed charge of the churches at Leroy and Pamelia. In 1854, he moved to Pennsylvania, in which state he remained for a year, when he moved to Wisconsin. Soon after, he began to labor for the Hampden and surrounding churches of Columbia County, Wis. He remained here until 1864, when he moved to Iowa. While staying there temporarily, he died from the effects of an accident. He was always spoken of as a talented, zealous, and really useful man in the cause.

<u>Mary (Herr) Kingsworth (1829—1879)</u>

This was a female laborer who had a short but earnest career in the ministry of the Christian Church. She was born in Westmoreland, Penn., June 3, 1829, married John Kingsworth in 1852, and moved to Illinois in 1855, where she united with the Christian Church. In 1865, she returned to Pennsylvania, was licensed to preach by the Western Pennsylvania Conference, was ordained by the same body in 1872, and died September 26, 1879.

<u>William Kinkade (1783—1832)</u>

This Elder was born in the backwoods of Pennsylvania, September 22, 1783. He moved with his parents to Kentucky in 1786. He was raised in the Presbyterian Church, and was converted in that church in 1802, when he immediately began to preach. He determined to hold to the Bible and right of private judgment, though he had no knowledge of any one holding similar views. These views he held unto the last. At the beginning of his ministry, the Elder was ignorant of even the rudiments of education; but he did not long remain so. For being possessed, of an active and inquiring mind, he soon became proficient in the acquisition of knowledge. After he had preached the gospel for some time, he commenced a regular course of study under the tuition of Dr. Stubbs, then under different teachers till he became well versed in the Greek and Hebrew languages. As an evidence of his attainment in that direction, it is said that all the criticisms of those languages in his "Bible Doctrine" were made from memory, and without the assistance of either a Greek or Hebrew lexicon; and even without the aid of a Greek or Hebrew Bible. And all these criticisms were found, on critical examination, to be generally correct.

The principal field of this Elder's labors was in the Western States, he having spent twenty years of his life in that part of the country. During that time, his labors were abundant and his exertions untiring; and, in some instances, he endured incredible hardships. He frequently addressed assemblies in the open air, and generally preached two hours. On some occasions, his sermons were three or four hours long, and on one occasion, he preached for five hours. Sometimes he would be compelled to ford rivers and travel for hours without change of garment, and that, too, at the cold season of the year, when the icicles would hang to his garments like fringes. Oftentimes he would be overtaken by night, in a dreary forest; and then, like Jacob, he would lay himself on the cold ground, with the heavens for a covering and a stone for a pillow. He possessed a strong and robust constitution, but the frequent occurrence of these hardships gradually undermined it till he at length sank under the weight of disease, and, at forty-five years of age, he presented the appearance of a man of sixty.

For several years, he resided in the State of Illinois, near Lawrenceville. While there, he was elected a member of the Convention. He was a fearless champion of freedom, and probably did as much as any other man in redeeming the state from slavery. He spoke of this political campaign as among the most happy and useful days of his life, and always appeared to reflect on it with a great deal of pleasure and de light, feeling that he had rendered to his fellow-citizens a lasting and great blessing. In the fall of 1828, he visited some of the Eastern States for his health, and went as far east as Boston, Mass.; but the disease bad become so firmly seated that no change of climate could benefit him. But during this •time he was able to preach, and his name will long be remembered by the brethren in that part of the country.

While in New York, he wrote and published his book "The Bible Doctrine." This book contains his views of divine truth, as taught by the great founder of Christianity; but it was not written as the sentiment of any people or party of Christians. He was as tenacious of the language as of the sentiment, being desirous that the author should be recognized by old friends on reading the book. Hence the reason why some of its peculiar phraseology was retained. It is a work of highly original characteristics. The Elder had no books of reference except the Bible and concordance. He consulted no author, counseled no friend, but committed his own thoughts to writing, in his own language. All his references to authors were from memory, or from notes that he had taken at some former period of life. He might have received aid from others had he wished any; but he did not choose to retail the sentiments and opinions of others, wishing to give to his friends an original book—and it was done. Very few books have been presented to the world so highly original in character, and under such peculiar circumstances.

The Elder's talents were of a high order, and he was original in every sense of the term. Although he took a comprehensive view of any subject, yet he often came to wrong conclusions, and there were but few as capable of vindicating their sentiments as he. He was a man of great honesty, frankness, and decision of character; and since he was honest in forming his convictions, he was very tenacious of them, and' ever ready to defend them. As a public speaker, he was always interesting, and at times very eloquent, never failing to command the attention of his audience. He was generally grave and serious in the pulpit, but sometimes indulged in wit, to the great amusement of his hearers.

He returned to the Western States in 1829, as his health failed and his infirmities increased. His sufferings were long and severe, but he bore it all cheerfully. His only desire to recover was that he might be about the work of the Lord but when he found that his work was well-nigh done, he told his friends that they should not object to God's will. During his last illness, he gave this opinion, "That little doctrinal preaching is requisite in our day; but simple gospel preaching such as is calculated to lead to experimental and practical religion is more necessary." The doctrines that are published in his book he held to the last, and seemed pleased to think that he should leave that book as a legacy to his friends and the world.

His wife having died some years before, leaving no family, he had no nearer relation than a sister to minister unto him in his last days. But his memory will ever be dear to those who were with him both in a ministerial and social capacity. He died at the residence of his sister, near Burlington, O., in the forty-ninth year of his age, after a long and very painful illness.

Thus died William Kinkade, at the early age of forty-nine years. As we may see from this short sketch, he was a man of great independence, which was increased in him, doubtless, by the perilous times in which he lived—among blood-thirsty Indians, daring pioneers, and ferocious wild beasts. From a religious mother, he early received solemn impressions, so that, he resorted to secret prayer at the age of six. The Bible became very .precious to him, in his youth. He read it at home and at the day school; and after he began to preach, he worked five days, grubbing briars, for the first copy he ever owned. For many years, he was very poorly clad, and his exposures, in constantly traveling through the newly-settled country, were very great. In the midst of all, his courage never failed, nor did his mind ever become sluggish; whether on foot or on horseback, in the deep forest or by the cabin fire, he was always studying his little pocket Bible.

In the territory of Illinois, he was elected a member of the Convention to form the State Constitution—and nobly did he work there to make his adopted state free from slavery. When threatened with death by his rough pro-slavery colleagues, his answer was, "I would just as soon die in this cause as any other, and heaven is as near Illinois as any other place." In connection with Elder Seth Gard and others, most of them raised in slave states, and well acquainted with the blighting influence of slavery, he succeeded in his noble effort, and free Illinois has reason to thank him and his colleagues for its present great prosperity. He always considered his labors in that convention as the most 'useful of his whole life.

There is an anecdote related by the early settlers of Butler County, O., regarding the Elder's views on baptism, and why he changed from a believer in infant to that of adult baptism, that is worth mentioning here. During one of his meetings in the above named county, the Elder was called upon to christen two or three children of a pioneer. The smallest of the children could be managed tolerably well as they had not strength sufficient to resist. But the oldest boy, disliking the preacher's treatment of his little brothers, got angry, climbed a sapling, and swore most wickedly that he would not be baptized by that ugly old preacher. The Elder told the father that he did not think it was right to force a swearing boy to be baptized. After a serious consideration of the subject, he concluded never again to baptize any but voluntary candidates.

The Herculean work of the Elder is his "Bible Doctrine." As stated, the work is the product of his conviction alone, with no help from others—neither concordances nor commentaries. The work is doubtless a copy of what he had preached all over the west, in his pastorates, general meetings, and debates. We may imagine how the little pocket Bible, his constant companion, was marked through and through, so that, when he began to write, all arguments and illustrations were ready to his hand. The work was written in a great hurry. Much of the time, the author had to be on his knees, as the pain in his side would not allow him to sit down or stand up. Some oi the doctrines in regard to the Sonship of Christ were not endorsed by our leading brethren; otherwise it was read and studied for years, as among the ablest productions of any of our writers. There is no gloss in the style. It is the Elder throughout, strong, clear, logical, and so natural and forcible in the argument that it drives conviction on the mind of the reader, whether he will or not.

<u>CHESTER D. KINNEY (1817—1878)</u>

The following is the substance of a letter of Elder A.J. Welton: Chester was born at Wayne, N.Y., June 21, 1817, was converted February 27, 1835, was baptized by Rev. G.A. Hendrick, commenced preaching at Hornby, October 12, 1840, was ordained July 9, 1843, and died at Lawrence, Penn., August 25, 1878. His principal field of labor was in Steuben County, N.Y., Tioga, Bradford, and Potter counties, Penn. His last labor was in Lawrence. He had preached between 800 and 900 funeral sermons. He was an excellent preacher, a successful pastor, and was highly esteemed for his labor of love in the ministry of Christ.

R.O. KINNEY (1830—1879)

This brother was born in Sullivan County, N.Y., February 5, 1830, joined the Baptists in 1847, was married to Miss Sarah E. Cox in 1857, moved to Saline County, Ill., in 1858, joined the Christian Church in 1863, buried his wife in 1877, and died in October, 1879, leaving two orphan children. He joined and labored with the Christians because there was no Baptist Church convenient. He was a faithful, and good man.

JOSEPH KIRBY (1802—1876)

Elder Joseph Kirby was born in New Jersey, March 31, 1802, was brought to Warren County, O., by his parents in 1806, joined the Christian Church at Westville, in the same county, under the labors of Elder George Shidler in 1818, was baptized by Elder John Dudley in 1821, and joined the Miami (then Mad River Conference), in 1822, Elders L. Purviance and A. Snethen uniting at the same time. In 1828. he moved to Champaign County, O., where belabored as a licentiate, and in 1830, he was ordained by Elders Samuel Kyle and Caleb Worley. He was married first to Miss Margaret Gustin, by whom he had ten children, three of the sons becoming ministers in the same church. In 1854, he married again, a Mrs. Sherwood. He died at his home in Champaign County, O., October 10, 1876. The Elder was a man of systematic mind, was faithful and earnest in his calling, for many years, but the infirmity of age, and the care of a farm, kept him at home, in latter years.

JOHN MARK KIRBY (1823—1869)

This was a son of the preceding, was born in Champaign County, O., April 17, 1823, was converted under the labors of Elder Matthew Gardner, in 1841, joined the Miami Christian Conference, and soon after, was ordained by Elders Simonton and Baker. His labors were confined principally to Miami, Champaign, and Shelby counties. In 1843, he was married to Miss Ruth Egbert, who, with four children, survived him. In 1856, he took charge of a church at Careysville, where he continued until death. During his pastorate at Careysville, he organized several churches. He died at his home, January 3, 1869. Elder Kirby was a man of energy, had a good command of language, and was successful as a pastor.

GRANT KIRBY (1834—1863)

This was a younger brother of the preceding and also of J. 0. Kirby; the father and three sons being acceptable ministers of Christ. Grant had been a licentiate member of the Miami Conference, for seven years, but had never devoted himself fully to the work. As he was teaching, he would preach whenever opportunity offered. He was away from home at the time of his death, which occurred in Warren County, in 1863, at the age of twenty-nine.

JEREMIAH KIRK (1791—1872)

Jeremiah was born in Virginia in 1791. He united with and began to preach in the Baptist Church, in 1822, and continued in that connection till 1852, when he joined the Christian Church. He continued to preach until his health failed. He died at his son's residence in 1872, at the advanced age of eighty-two.

DAVID KIRKPATRICK (?—?)

David Kirkpatrick was one of the converts of the Cane Ridge revival, and soon after commenced to preach, having been appointed to the work by Elders Stone, Purviance, and the two churches of Cane Ridge and Concord. He had had great success and seemed to devote all his time and talent to the work, but was stricken down in his usefulness, while comparatively young.

JOHN KIRKPATRICK (?—?)

John Kirkpatrick was also a native of Kentucky, but nothing can be known with certainty, but that he died before 1826.

JAMES KNIGHT (?—1850)

James Knight was at one time a Freewill Baptist, but in 1829 he joined the Christian Church. Sometime afterward, he joined one of the New York Conferences, and labored there with great success. From New York he went to Michigan, where he remained for several years, then returned to New- York for his health and labored among the churches to good advantage. He preached in Jackson and Calhoun counties, Michigan, for several years before 1829, in which year he writes to the "Palladium," giving a full account of his labor. He was a man of fine appearance, and of considerable talent. He started to California in 1849 or '50, and died on the way.

HERMAN D. KNOWLES (1823—1869)

Herman was born in the State of New York in 1823, was converted, and joined the church while young. He moved to Jackson County, Iowa, and in 1864, joined the Northern Iowa Christian Conference, and was ordained in 1867. He was an earnest student of the Bible, and was likely to become a strong and influential minister, but he died in 1869, leaving a wife and six children.

EBENEZER KNOWLTON (1783—1842)

Ebenezer was born in 1783, brought up in the Baptist Church, began to preach, and for many years was pastor of the Baptist Church' at Pittsfield, N.H. Afterward he joined the Christians, in which connexion he continued until his death. His sound faith, untiring perseverance, and strong sense combined to make him a very successful minister. He served several terms in both the Maine and New Hampshire Legislatures. His father, brother, and son, were all acceptable ministers of the gospel. He died in Montville, Me., in 1842.

D.J. KNOWLTON (1814—1869)

This brother was a son of the preceding. He was born in 1814, was ordained in 1838, and soon took charge of the church at Lynn, Mass. After leaving Lynn, he lectured on Adventism for a time. He died in Boston, in 1869. He was well spoken of by those that knew him, and his kindness of heart was the subject of frequent remark.

LEWIS KOMER (?—?)

Lewis Komer was an Ohio minister, and preached on the Darby Plains for some time.

SAMUEL KRATZER (?—1829)

Samuel Kratzer was a minister in an early day, living in Edgar County, Ill., for some time previous to his death in 1829.

SAMUEL KYLE (1785—1836)

Samuel was born in Monongahela County, Penn., in 1785, moved with his parents to Woodford County, Ky., when quite young, was converted in 1805, and joined the Christian Church at the same time his parents did. Soon after his conversion, he commenced preaching, although some thought that he had not sufficient talent; and on his first application for ordination, was objected to for this reason. He was ordained by the Miami Conference in 1807 or '8, and at the time of his death, was one of the most accomplished ministers in the denomination. Before his ordination, he had married, and soon after moved to Ohio. At one time he served in the Legislature of the state. His wife possessed about $4,000 worth of slaves, which they brought with them from Kentucky to Ohio and liberated, although at the time they were quite poor. He determined to devote his last days to the ministry, but in 1835, he had a stroke of paralysis, from which he recovered sufficiently to preach for a few months, when he received a second stroke in April, 1836, and never recovered. His physicians, one a Presbyterian and the other a Methodist, having told him that he could not live, asked him if he felt reconciled. He answered, "You have not held me as a brother on account of doctrine, but I am now willing to inform you that I die fully confirmed in the faith and doctrine that I have preached for more than twenty-five years." He died April 8, 1836, leaving an affectionate wife and twelve children, several of whom had openly espoused that faith which the father had defended so nobly for many years.

The Elder presented a very grave and interesting appearance in the pulpit, and, although he was rather slow of speech, his voice was pleasant and harmonious, his manner agreeable and impressive, and his discourses able and instructive. He was the means by which a great many churches were organized all through the state of Ohio, especially in Miami County. The Cove Spring Church was organized through him, and in it he lived and died, having served as its pastor for several years. Although he labored principally in Ohio, yet he traveled through many other states. The last trip be made was through Indiana, preaching a great deal, and encouraging those that were weak and cast down.

THOMAS B. KYLE (1779—?)

This brother was born in Pennsylvania in 1779, and came with his parents to Woodford County, Ky., when quite young. He was Converted in 1804, and soon felt it was his duty to spread the gospel, but feeling his unworthiness, he delayed going until urged by his friends, when he left his work (he was a mechanic), and gave his life to the work of an evangelist. He soon after left Kentucky and came to Ohio, traveling and preaching on the frontiers to the scattered and destitute inhabitants of the wilderness. In 1808, he married an amiable and accomplished young lady, a daughter of Judge Barbee, of Miami County, O. But he did not live long after to enjoy the society of his happy family, being cut down in the midst of his usefulness, when life seemed the brightest, not in his full prime, being not more than thirty years of age. He was possessed of more than ordinary talents, a profound student of the Bible and a deep and logical theologian. His manners and appearance were pleasing, and he was pronounced by some as. one of the best orators of the day.

<u>Derostus F. Ladley (?—1858)</u>

Elder Ladley was born in Chester County, Penn., April 10, but the year is unknown. He came to Hebron, Ohio, in 1832, about the time the church was organized there, and served as deacon of the church for several years before he began to preach. During this time he wrote much for the "Palladium" and was an instrument by which much good was done in his own church. There was a great revival in 1834, by which the members were increased to seventy. In 1835, he began to preach and soon after traveled with Elder Walter, visiting the churches of Hartford and Bennington, and others of Ohio. In 1826, he traveled through Maryland, New York, and Pennsylvania. While in New York he was ordained by Elders Walter, Currier, and Badger. On his return, he visited different churches in Southern Ohio, assisting in the organization of one church, and the revival of several. He continued in Cincinnati for some days, in company with Elders McClain, Morris, Carr, and Worley. In 1837, he took the pastoral charge of the church in '.Cincinnati, and although there was considerable division in the body on doctrinal subjects, yet there was great good done. In 1838, he again visited New York, New England, and Pennsylvania, in company with Elder Long, preaching and organizing churches wherever opportunity offered. He returned the same year, but in 1839, he moved to Enon, Clark County, O., and took charge of the church there, and during the same year organized the Ebenezer Church. He remained there until 1842, when he moved to Miami County, O. During the six years he remained in this field he had charge of several different churches, staying at Sidney and Rocky Springs, perhaps, the longest. In 1848, he moved to Ripley and labored for that church until his removal to Yellow Springs, in 1852 or '53. Soon after his health began to fail, and this prevented his taking an active part in the work of the church, as he had done heretofore. His disease was consumption, and although lingering and painful, he bore himself with patience and cheerfulness until the last. He passed away October 16, 1858, leaving a small family.

Elder Ladley had been twice married, but his first wife did , not live long, and he afterward married Miss Griffith, in Licking County, a lady in every way worthy, as she proved herself a faithful and willing aid in his noble work.

Elder Ladley's greatest talent was in organization and pastoral work, although his discourses were able, effective, and full of good sense. For many years he had the name of being one of the best pastors in the church in Ohio. His wife was a great help to him in his fields of labor. Enon and Ebenezer, in Clark County, Rocky Springs, in Miami County, Sidney, in Shelby County, and Ripley, in Brown County, O., were the churches where he spent the most of his ministerial life, and in all of which he succeeded well as a pastor. Besides his pastoral work, Elder Ladley was an active business man in our conferences, and in all enterprises organized for the purpose of carrying on our general measures. Missionary societies, publishing associations, and especially our great effort for the building of Antioch College, had his sympathy and co-operation. In all these he rendered valuable service.

Though not a rugged man in his physical structure, yet he labored faithfully, and endured many privations for years. His writings are characterized throughout, with good sense, clear expression of thought, and fervent zeal for the prosperity of the cause. As a general thing, his articles to our periodicals were Very short, sometimes not more than four or five lines, but they appear often, almost in every issue of the paper, with a mere statement of how the cause is prospering in his own and neighboring churches. His education at first was limited, but as he became active in the ministry, his knowledge increased, and his mind became more and more expanded. He was a man of taste, precision, and order. He had acquired a respectable library of well selected books, which he used to great advantage. Elder Ladley would have been a useful man to any church, and his loss, a little past his prime, was deeply felt by the church in which he had been so faithful a member.

JACOB LAMB (?—1850)

Jacob Lamb was a member of the Eastern Ohio Conference. He died in 1849 or '50.

SABRINA LAMBSON (1799-1833)

This sister was a female laborer in the church. She was born in Vermont, in 1799. For years, she was a helpless cripple, from scrofula. In 1823, John Pratt, of Walpole, N.H., a healer of the sick, was sent for to visit a neighbor of Mr. Lambson. He was called in to see Sabrina, as her case was very peculiar. Her disease had been pronounced incurable by the physicians, and Pratt said that he himself could do nothing by medicine; but he believed in the efficacy of prayer in the restoration of the sick. These means were used, and soon she declared, with a shout, that she was cured. Physicians made an examination, and gave the decision that the cure was genuine. The circumstance was published in the papers at the time as something very mysterious. In 1824, Sabrina began the work of the ministry in earnest, working in revivals chiefly, and assisting others. Wherever she went, great revivals followed. She was tall, dark-complexioned, and thin in appearance, possessing great command of words. Her deportment, both in the pulpit and out, was calm and serious. She was a member of the Vermont Conference, but never was ordained. She died in Randolph, Vt., in 1833, in her thirty-fourth year.

WILLIAM LAMPHREE (?—?)

William Lamphree was a Virginia minister. In 1808 and '9, he wrote to the *Herald of Gospel Liberty,* giving an account of the spreading of the gospel in Virginia. He was one of the earliest ministers of the Christian Church in that state.

WILLIS LANE (?—?)

It is said that a minister of this name died some years ago, in Tippecanoe County, Ind., about the age of thirty-eight years.

JOHN LASON (?—1858)

This brother was one, among many others, who organized the New York Southern Christian Conference. He continued a respected and honored member of the same till death. He was the father of Rev. A.A. Lason. He labored mostly in Southern New York and Northern Pennsylvania. He was an earnest, zealous, and useful man, and died March 12, 1858.

WILLIAM LAUER (1793—1870)

Elder Lauer was born in Pennsylvania, in 1793, joined the Mount Zion Church at Philadelphia in 1814, was ordained in 1829 by Elders Proctor and Ferguson, and soon became an earnest, active worker in the vineyard. Having received the idea that it was wrong to accept compensation for preaching, he conscientiously refused to receive anything beyond his traveling expenses. This made his work double, as he labored extensively in the ministry in early years, and supported himself and family by his manual labor. He organized several churches in Pennsylvania, and afterward became a member of the New Jersey Conference, and labored in that state. In 1838, he organized the church at Carversville, which bad ninety members at the end of the next year. In 1839, he labored with Elder Porter in Philadelphia, and in Carversville, Penn., and at Milford, N.J., with Elders Clough and Mellick with great success. Sometimes there would be forty conversions at one meeting. He was at this time in his prime. In 1855, he held a great meeting in New Jersey, where many were converted, among the number, four of his own children. During the latter part of his life, he was not actively engaged in the ministry; and as the infirmities of life increased he laid aside the work entirely. He died at Lambertville, N.J., July 18, 1870.

JONAS LAWRENCE (1808—1834)

Jonas was the son of obscure and humble parents, who lived in the hills of Southeastern Ohio. He was converted early, and soon began to preach, traveling in company with Elder H.B. Miles. He soon took a high stand as an efficient minister of the gospel. At the age of twenty-five, in less than two years after the commencement of his ministry, he writes to the "Palladium" that he had traveled 5,606 miles, preached 411 times, organized three churches, and baptized 152 persons.

In June, 1853, he writes from Gerry, Chautauqua County, N.Y., telling of a glorious awakening there, many being converted, and the church greatly revived. In March, 1836, he writes from Conneaut, in a very earnest manner, exhorting ministers to more faithful study; ignorance, he says, being a pest in the church. He continued for two years at Conneaut as pastor of the church, it having been, during that time, brought from a weak to a strong and flourishing condition. Before this he had traveled principally as a missionary, for which work he had a special talent, through the greater part of New York, and was on his way to the Eastern States, when the church at Conneaut prevailed on him to remain with them awhile. He did so, and had just returned from a visit to his friends in Ohio, when he was stricken down with bilious fever, and died September 12, 1834, at the age of twenty-six, having been in the ministry but a little more than three years.

The Elder was one of those young men, who, with untiring zeal and grasping intellect, make such rapid strides, as soon to leave all competitors behind. He was of medium size, with a musical voice, easy delivery, copiousness of language, logical arguments, and above all, with a heart burning with zeal for the salvation of sinners. He died, mourned by an entire denomination. The short period of three years was long enough for the obscure boy, from the hills of Meigs County, to leave a lasting impression on the church East and West; for among all the ministers and leading members of the church a few years ago, the name of Jonas Lawrence was a household word, everywhere. What he would have been, had he lived longer, is not for us to know. He was buried by the side of Elder Blodget, and one or two other ministers, in the old graveyard at Conneaut, O.

<u>J.G. LAWSHEE (?—1853)</u>

This brother was a young minister at the time of his death. He wrote very often for our periodicals, and from his writings we may suppose that he was a good scholar, and well read on the subject of Theology. His home was in New Jersey. He was converted, began to preach early, and afterward became the pastor of the church at Bristol, R. I, In June, 1852, he wrote that he was compelled to give up the charge of the church. He soon after returned to his father's home in Hunterdon County, N.J., and died there in 1853.

<u>JOHN L. LAWYER (?—1865)</u>

The Elder was of German parentage. The Lawyer family left Durbach on the Rhine, in 1709, and settled in Schoharie County, in 1713, on a tract of land purchased of the Indians. David Lawyer married Mary Sternberg, daughter of Judge David Sternberg, so famous in the early history of our country, and their first born is the subject of this sketch. He had a liberal education, going to school in Albany at the early age of nine, where he remained until twelve years old, preparing for a college course, when he found he could not, according to the by-laws, enter until fourteen. He spent the intervening time studying all the Latin authors that could be found. He graduated at Union College in 1814, and immediately commenced the study of law and was admitted to the bar in 1817. He practiced law for several years, proving himself an able counselor and an eloquent advocate, holding, during the time, very many political offices. While in this profession he was brought to see his duty to God, and a call to the ministry was one that he could not put aside.

He began the study of Theology with George A. Linnter, D.D., pastor of the Lutheran Church in Schoharie, N.Y., and in 1827, he was ordained a minister of God at Albany, N.Y., attaching himself to the Lutheran Church. His first •charge was over Stone Arabia, N.Y., and subsequently various other charges, the last in the Lutheran Church being the church at Hartwick. In 1834, a new light dawned on his mind. He was engaged in translating from the

German, "Rambach's Treatise on Infant Baptism," when the words, "He that believeth and is baptized shall be saved" came into his mind and would not be put out, and, to use his own words, "While progressing in my task of translating from the German, I was compelled from powerful convictions of mind, and the force of divine light, to leave the work unfinished: for it had no foundation in scripture. I now begin to speak the language of God." About this time a small volume of David Milliards came into his hands, which he carefully read, and thus his faith in the Trinity became unsettled.

In 1848, he moved from Hartwick to Norwich, N.Y., engaged in the printing business, and became the editor of the "Chenango Free Democrat," the advocate of free democracy, free speech, free labor, and no more slave states. As an editor, he was quite successful, and his paper never failed to speak out plainly for truth and liberty. His was never a doubtful patriotism. He was an advocate for freedom for all, when such advocacy cost a sacrifice. He lived to see slavery overthrown, and while the nation rejoiced, with old Simeon he exclaimed, "Now lettest thou thy servant depart in peace, for mine eyes have seen thy salvation."

In the spring of 1855, he was appointed Chaplain of the State Prison at Auburn, a position he filled with great success, for he witnessed a great many conversions among the convicts, and baptized fifty of them, a thing which had never taken place in that prison before. He had retained his connection with the Lutherans heretofore, but in 1857, he united with the Christians, and was received into the Central New York Conference. He now became the pastor of the churches at Hartwick and Freehold. His last work was accomplished at Medway in a lecture entitled "Bible Translation," delivered at the Eastern Conference. On his return, he immediately took his bed and gradually declined until March 31, 1865, when he calmly fell asleep.

EBENEZER LEAVITT (1770—1843)

The subject of this sketch was born March 2, 1770, was ordained at Hampton Falls, N.H., July, 1808, being one of the first ministers ordained in the Christian Church. He labored faithfully for many years, and died in North Hampton, N.H., December 14, 1843, aged seventy-eight years.

JOSEPH LEE (?—1853)

This Elder joined the church in 1827, and, in 1834, was ordained. After organizing several churches in Southern Ohio, he moved to Missouri, where he was very successful in his labors. Among others, he organized a large church in Wright County, the pastoral charge of which he held at the time of his death, December 22, 1853.

PHIDELO LEE (1811—1849)

Phidelo was born in Jefferson County, N.Y., in 1811. But while he was a child, his parents moved to Chautauqua County, N.Y., where he was converted, and was baptized by Elder Joseph Bailey. He soon felt that it was his duty to preach the gospel, but was prevented by his lack of education. After spending some time in preparation, he became a member of the Erie Conference, and was ordained in 1841. He became a very useful member of the conference, and organized several churches, making a very successful pastor. In 1849, after a lingering illness, he died at the age of thirty-eight.

SIMON LEE (?—1870)

Our present subject was a member of the Eel River Conference, Ind. He died in 1870, just as he was entering on what seemed at that time a prosperous ministry.

G.D. LEVELL (?—?)

G.D. Levell was a member of the Bluffton Conference, Ind. He was a man of good education, and was well informed, especially on scientific subjects; but he was not a successful preacher. He was pious, cheerful, benevolent, and pleasant in all his relations, both to family and neighbors. He frequently lectured on literary and scientific subjects. He died some years ago, when not far from fifty years of age.

<u>Edward Lewis (1801—1837)</u>

This brother professed religion under the labors of Elder Walter, and was baptized by him in 1830. The same year, he began to preach, and the following year he spent in traveling with Elder Walter through Kentucky. August of the same year, he was ordained at Dublin, O. He spent the next year, also, in Kentucky, his labors resulting in great good. The following year he spent in Ohio. On the first day of 1833, he was married to Miss Julia Stevens, a pious and faithful member of the church. In 1836, he moved his family to Maryland, on the Alleghany circuit. He continued in his new field but little over a year, when he was called away, in the midst of his usefulness, at the age of thirty-six.

He had been instrumental for good among these last churches, for he found them very weak, and much divided on account of the doctrine of baptism and similar subjects; but he, by his deep piety and consistent Christian life, had united, revived, and started many of them anew.

<u>John B. Libby (1821—1870)</u>

John was born in 1821, and was, for many years before his death, in 1870, a successful minister. His last pastoral charge was at Goshen, N.H. He died at Newport, the same state, at the age of fifty-one.

<u>Jonathan Lineback (1823—1873)</u>

This Elder was a member of the Bluffton Conference, Ind., and died January 8, 1873, aged fifty years.

ELI LINSCOTT (?—1863)

Eli was born in Trumbull County, O., of poor but pious, Methodist parents. In 1834, the family moved to Knox County, in the same state, and there reunited with the Methodist Church. But his father being of anti-slavery opinions his connection with the church was unpleasant, and in about four years after coming to this county, he left the Methodists. A year later, he united with the Christian Church, in which he continued until his death, in 1849. In 1842, his son Eli, our subject, was converted, and joined the Christian Church at West Liberty, in Delaware County, whither his parents had moved some time before the death of his father. Eli's education was limited, before this, he having received only what could be obtained at the common schools of Ohio. But he now took a greater interest in books, especially the Bible, and made 'considerable progress in his studies.

In 1847, he joined the Mount Gilead Conference, but was not ordained until the year following. Immediately after his ordination, he began to labor as a self-constituted missionary in Central Ohio, Indiana, and Michigan. He labored in this way for four or five years, when he moved to Ogle County, Ill., laboring as he had done previously, and with good success. In September, 1853, soon after going to Illinois, he was married to a worthy member of the Washington Grove Church, Miss Elizabeth Tilton, one in every way capable of assisting in the good work. He soon joined the Northern Illinois and Wisconsin Conference, of which body he continued an active and earnest member until death. He had under pastoral charge, at different times, the churches at Washington Grove, Union Prairie, South Branch. Industry, Blackberry, and other places. He labored with these churches until 1863, when he accepted a college agency. He had made his arrangements to that effect, when, on the twentieth of May, in company with several others, he. went on a fishing excursion. During the day, being an expert swimmer, he endeavored to swim from an island to the shore, but the cramp seized him and he sank, thus closing what had been, and what might have continued to be, a very useful life. The Elder was a faithful, zealous, bold, and fearless defender of the faith, possessing more than ordinary talent.

SHUBAL LITTLE (1790—1847)

This Elder was a native of Vermont. He was converted at Hartwick, in 1807. He moved to New York State, and joined the Northern New York Conference, of which he continued a member till death. He was a very active and industrious man, working continually with his hands for the support of his family, even when performing pastoral duties. He was opposed to the education of ministers and the salary system, and in one of his last letters to the "Palladium," he urges the brethren to follow the old plan, and not send to seminaries for ministers, as they were doing, and hedging them in by salaries. He died in Dexter, N.Y., October 3, 1847, after a long and painful illness. but supported by Christian patience and resignation.

JOSHUA AND JOHN LIVESAY

The two brothers, Joshua and John, were members of the Virginia Conference, and traveled over a great part of that state as missionaries. Joshua was well known as a writer, as he wrote several articles on the support of the ministry, also concerning the constitutions of conferences. These two were at times pastors of the Cypress Chapel Church, in Virginia. They were opposed to conference constitutions, and for some time there was an able discussion carried on in our papers between Elder Joshua Livesay and Mills Barrett, on the subject. The Elder was an able writer and so was his opponent. From some of these letters we gather that Joshua was born in 1786. He labored in three places in Virginia, and in two in North Carolina. For about seven years after he began to preach, he devoted nearly his whole time to the work of preaching. From the time his health failed to the close of his life, he only preached on Sundays. He was an able man.

We have not as full an account of John as of his brother; hence they are given in the same paragraph.

JOHN LOCK (?—1850)

This Elder was a native of New England. He moved to Ohio in 1811, was converted in 1842, and soon after began to preach, having joined the Central Ohio Conference. He was married in 1844, to Miss Louisa Harrington, of whom he had nine children. He labored very earnestly in the cause until his health failed him. He died in 1850, his career in the ministry having been short, and his labors mostly local.

Ward Lock labored among the Christians in Maine, in the early days of the Christian Church. He was originally a Freewill Baptist minister, and may have continued his connection with that church, as, in those days, the ministers of both denominations labored together without distinction of party. The Elder was not only an earnest, successful preacher but a frequent and interesting writer, taking an active part in all the discussions of the day. He took a prominent part in the General Christian Conference held in Hampton, Conn., in 1816. He also traveled with Elder Abner Jones, preaching to crowds of people. In 1818, he preached in Portland, Me., but we have no explicit account of his ministrations after this. We know that he is spoken of with respect, and that he lived to be quite old.

DANIEL LONG (1789—1873)

January, 1873, in a conversation with Elder Long, then a hale old man in his eighty-fourth year, we gathered the following: He was born in Alleghany County, Md., was the son of Ransomond and Margaret (commonly called Peggy) Long. The mother's maiden name was Devault. She was the first wife of his father, who married for his second wife, a widow Denyer, and for his third wife, widow Rhetts. His father had, in all, fifteen children. Daniel had a twin brother, and was the youngest of nine children. His mother died when he was two years old. His second step-mother died in 1825, and his father in 1831. Daniel's father was a farmer and a deacon in the Baptist church. The boy's education was limited. He attended school for about one year at a school house- three miles away. His main teacher was William Shaw, a Methodist preacher. Some of Daniel's recollections of his religious thought in his youth was his bitter opposition to the doctrines of Calvinism, as preached in his father's church, and his wonder that churches of different denominations did not rejoice in the success of each other.

The following from the pen of Elder Josiah Knight, long a co-laborer of our subject is so full that I insert it here in his own language: "Elder Daniel Long was born in Alleghany County, Md., August 9, 1789, and died in Union County, O., November 26, 1873, aged eighty-four years, two months, and seventeen days. He emigrated to Ohio in 1808, and two years later he married and settled in Union County, where he resided until his death. He was converted to the Christian religion, joined the Christian church in July 1809, and commenced preaching in 1811. He enlisted in the war of 1812, and was one of the victims of Hull's traitorous surrender. Immediately after returning home, he resumed his ministerial labors, was ordained to the work of the gospel ministry in 1820, and continued an earnest and efficient worker in the Master's vineyard until his death. Only the evening before his death, he started to go to church to preach, but was suddenly taken ill on the way. He attended the services, however, and returned home, feeling better, ate his supper, and retired. During the night, he was taken worse, sank rapidly, and died at ten o'clock. Thus passed from labor to reward, another of the old pioneers of the Christian Church, gathered home to the garner of the Lord, ripe in years and labor, having been engaged in active labor in the Master's work for sixty-two years. Elder Long was a member of the Central Ohio Christian Conference, but his ministerial work was by no means confined to that conference, nor to the state, but he traveled and labored in several other states in the Union. He was noted as a fine sermonizer; his sermons were clear, forcible, and marked with deep thought. The conference of which he was a member, and one of the founders, will greatly miss his zealous labors and wise counsel. He was ever mild and courteous, yet firm as adamant in defense of right."

From what has been said of his education and training, it is easily seen that Elder Long was a self-made man. When he began to preach, he felt the importance of his position and at once prepared himself for the work, though under great disadvantages, in a new country, when a terrible war was near his own cabin in the forest. His knowledge of books, except of the Bible, was always limited, but he studied nature, humanity, sin, and righteousness thoroughly. He bad proper ambition and courage, and soon became a tower of strength to the small denomination in which he labored. In the Central Ohio and Deer Creek Conferences, plain, courageous, energetic, and fearless Daniel Long was, for many years, a prominent figure. Elder I.N. Walter, more polished in his address, always looked upon Long, if not as a superior, yet as a full equal in the work. Elder Long made several visits to Pennsylvania, Maryland, and Virginia, for the purpose of preaching. Generally, he and another minister would start on horseback, preach almost every night. During these trips he organized many churches, fought the enemies of the denomination, and generally came out conqueror. During one of these visits, also, he went to New. York City to assist his friend Walter in a meeting. Some of the fashionable members of that city church, seeing the backwoodsman, Long, in the pulpit with their pastor, felt scandalized at first, with .his appearance, but when he spoke with such ability and clearness, they wondered how such a plain man could have so much power. Little did they know the large soul that burned under the plain garb, nor the many battles he had fought for Christ, in the far West. In his intercourse, he was plain, but rigid. Had he been a member of a sectarian church, he would have been a stern one himself. All acknowledge his goodness and purity of character, and for many years he exerted an influence second to none in the spread of the principles of his own church.

JAMES LONG (1790—1852)

Our present subject was a member of the Virginia Conference at the time of his death. He was born in Orange County, Va., in 1790, was married to his first wife in 1810, began to preach in the Christian Church in 1820, and died December 10, 1852, aged sixty-two years. His labors were confined, mostly, to the Shenandoah Valley, and to Orange, Culpepper, Rockingham, and adjoining counties in Virginia.

STEVEN LONG (1798—1854)

This minister was the father of Elder Albert Long. He was born in Kentucky, September 8, 1798, moved with his family to Marion County, O., when young, moved from there to Jacksonville, Darke County, in 1834, was converted under the labors of Elder Hallet Barber in 1841, and soon after, began to preach. He was ordained in the Bluffton Conference by Elders Robertson, Brandon, Fowler, and Penrod, in 1846. His labors were confined principally to his own church at Jacksonville, Darke County, O. He died December 31, 1854.

THOMAS LOOMIS (?—1856)

Thomas Loomis was a member of the Bluffton Conference, Ind. He died about 1856.

DANIEL LORD (1748—1825)

Daniel was born in Brunswick, Me., in 1748. He was at one time a Freewill Baptist, and he preached in that denomination six years. He was ordained in North Durham, Vt., in 1793. His eyesight had been affected from his youth, and for many years he was entirely blind, but he retained his memory to the last. He died in Genesee County, N.Y., in 1825, after a ministry of twenty years.

? LORING (?—1852)

Brother Loring was a member of the Huron Conference, O. He died about 1852.

<u>James Lothridge (?—?)</u>

James Lothridge labored in Kentucky about 1825.

<u>? Louton (?—?)</u>

Brother Louton was a minister in Pennsylvania in an early day.

<u>Samuel Lowe (?—?)</u>

Samuel Lowe died in Clinton County, Ind., some years ago, aged eighty years.

<u>William Lowe (1797—1843)</u>

William was born in Nelson County, Ky., in 1797. His parents were quite poor, and his education was very much neglected; yet he possessed ordinary capacity, and during his ministry, he did a great deal of good. He was, in every sense, a pioneer preacher. He moved to Carrol County, Ind., in 1829, at that time a howling wilderness. Here he cleared a farm, and raised a family of seven children, preaching all this time for mere nothing. He was converted in 1828, soon after commenced preaching, and was ordained in 1835. From this time till death, although laboring under great disadvantages, he continued an active and earnest preacher of the Word. He was a small man, of pleasing address, very firm in his convictions, and consistent in his daily life. He was not a great preacher, but was a very successful pastor. From exposure and hard labor, he was afflicted with chronic sore eyes for about four years before his death, which occurred in March, 1843, he being forty-six years old.

He had an appointment to preach with Elder Isam Adkin- son, some distance away, on the Sunday preceding his death; when Elder Adkinson called for him, not knowing of his illness, he was told to go and fill the appointment, and to stop on his return and preach at the house, but that he (Mr. Lowe) would not be there. It was so—Elder Adkinson did preach there, with the dead body of his friend and co-laborer before him.

EMERY LOWMAN (?—?)

Emery Lowman was a resident of Michigan, in which state he died.

? LOWMAN (?—1860)

This brother was a member of the Bluffton Indiana Conference, and was an excellent man, but was local in his labors. He died in Delaware County, Ind., in 1860, aged nearly sixty years.

BENJAMIN LUMBARD (1822—1850)

This brother was born in Mendon, N.Y., in 1822, was raised in the Christian Church, and embraced religion in 1839. In 1841, he moved with his parents to Michigan, attended a select school at Jackson, for a year, when he began to preach. In 1845, he returned to New York, taught school in Livonia and preached through the neighborhood. In 1846, he married Miss Frances Burr, a highly esteemed member of the Livonia Church, and afterward attended school at Starkey Seminary. While there, pursuing his own studies, he served as an assistant teacher, and also taught vocal music, preaching on the Sabbaths. In May, of 1850, his health failed him to such a degree that he was compelled to give up his place, much to the regret of both officers and students. He died October 10, 1850, resigned to his destiny, though greatly lamented by a young wife, and numerous friends.

CHILDS LUTHER (1779—1859)

This Elder was born in 1779, was converted in 1809, began to preach, and was ordained a year later by Elders Elias Smith, Daniel Hix, and J. Crossman. He was a prominent minister in the church for many years and also served several terms in the Legislature of Massachusetts. He died in Rehoboth, Mass., July 3, 1859.

? LYBURTIS (?—?)

This brother was a colored Christian minister of great ability. He labored as a pastor for some time, at Drayton, Canada, and died many years ago. He is said to have been a man of talent, both as a preacher and a physician.

J. MACE (?—1872)

J. Mace lived in Delaware County, Ind., and died there in 1872.

JOHN MACKLEN (1799—1877)

Elder Macklen was born in Pennsylvania in 1799, moved with his parents to Youngstreet, Canada, in 1802, and to the Sixth Concession of Whitchurch, Canada, in 1803, where he remained until death, June 24, 1877. In 1818, he was married to Miss Mary A. White, by whom he had six children, was converted in 1826, began to preach in 1835, and labored in the ministry till 1875, when his health failed.

NELSON MADDOX (?—1875)

Elder Maddox was a self-made man of ordinary education. He lived near Danville, Ill., the latter years of his life, and was an active member of the Illinois Central Conference. His labors were mostly local. He died September 12, 1875, aged about sixty.

PATRICK MALLORY (1802—1868)

Patrick was born in New York in 1802, and was of Irish parentage. He was converted while young, and although impressed with the idea that it was his duty to preach, he did not enter the ministry until his mind became so wrought upon, that he would preach in his sleep. Crowds would assemble to hear him, so peculiar was the case. His discourses at such times were clear and logical, more so than they would have been, perhaps, had he known of what was going on around him. In 1830, he removed to Huron County, O., and there began his career as a minister. He was ordained in the Central Ohio Conference, in 1836. In 1842, he assisted in the organization of the Huron Conference, and continued an active member of that body until his removal to Jackson County, Iowa, in 1853, where he preached the gospel until a short time before his death, which occurred at Earlville, Delaware County, Iowa, August 22, 1868. His education was not extensive by any means, but there were few more correct preachers than he at the time of his death. His . sermons were clear, logical, and he never failed to be understood by his hearers.

Elder Mallory had many excellent qualities, and not the least of these was his affectionate solicitude in the encouragement of those young men who felt "woe is me, if I preach not the gospel." Having suffered so much himself, from a sense of duty, he was ready to encourage and strengthen those who felt impressed with the same.

<u>HORACE MANN (1796—1859)</u>

The name of Horace Mann is inserted among the ministers of the Christian Church, on account of his prominent position as an educator in the connexion, and his frequent speaking in the pulpit during his presidency of Antioch College.

He was born in Franklin, Mass., May 4, 1796, and his youth was spent in earnest study; all his pursuits centering upon the improvement of his mind. At an early age he graduated from Brown College, Rhode Island, and soon entered on the practice of the law. The years he spent in this profession were very successful, and during this time, he served several terms in the Legislature of Massachusetts. He resigned that position that he might become the Secretary of the Board of Education, of Massachusetts, in which prominent position he devoted himself with singular zeal to his duties, and with wonderful success in his work. In this capacity, he visited Prussia and other parts of the Old World, and soon after gave to the people his Annual Report, a part of which was published separately in 1843 under the title of "Report of an Educational Tour in Germany, Great Britain, &c." This was afterward republished in London, and has attained the rank of authority • in its class of work. Among other volumes that he published may be mentioned "A Few Thoughts to Young Men," and a companion volume under the caption of "A Few Thoughts on the Powers and

Duties of Woman." In 1836, he resigned his post as Secretary of Education, and was soon after elected to the Senate of Massachusetts, and in 1848, was appointed to the place in Congress made vacant by the sudden death of John Q. Adams. This position he Billed with great honor to himself, and to the satisfaction of his constituents. During all this time, while he faithfully attended to his duties as a statesman, he never lost sight of the cause of education, and during a long and active career, his interest never relaxed.

In 1853, Mr. Mann accepted the presidency of Antioch College, and from this time forward, he became identified with the interests of the Christian Church. Probably one of his ideas in accepting this position was his hope of realizing there a larger and nobler theory of education than had before been put into practice, for among other innovations was the equal privileges given to both sexes, and this, Mr. Mann heartily endorsed. With him the ruling principle was, that every person, possessing a human soul, should be educated. He died at Antioch College, Yellow Springs, O., in 1859. His connection with the Christian Church was brief. It was a surprise to many that the well-known Horace Mann, should accept a position so obscure as the presidency of a new college under the control of a small and unpopular denomination, but he accepted, and entered upon his mission with his accustomed energy. For a while the prospects were very flattering, many hundreds of students entered the institution, many induced to attend, doubtless, by the attractions that the name of Horace Mann gave unto it. The finances of the college were not sound, and Mr. Mann, with all his talent, could not make that a success. He labored incessantly in his college work, delivered many lectures on the subject of education, and other themes; and while not a professional preacher, he often spoke in public in our churches. In the midst of his Herculean efforts to sustain a failing institution, he died at the age of sixty-three years.

John Newton Manning (1833—1880)

The substance of the following is from the "Christian Sun." Elder Manning was born in Rockingham County, Va., in 1833, professed religion in his youth, and after a careful study of the merits of more than fifty of the various denominations of the land, he decided to cast his lot with the Christian Church, though at the time he was not personally acquainted with a member of the body. He started from his home on foot in search of the denomination of his choice. He visited the Christian Church at Antioch, in the Valley Conference, was cordially received by the brethren, united with the society at the time, and continued a member until death. At an early age he manifested great fondness for books. A prominent and wealthy member of the above church observing this, and knowing the young man was poor, generously offered to educate him. With profound gratitude he refused the offer, as his independent spirit would not allow him to accept, though at the same time he determined to educate himself. At his own home, by hard study, he acquired considerable information, and soon began to teach, which enabled him to earn sufficient money to take him through college. He became a student in the Virginia University at Lexington, and graduated in several departments. From there he went to North Carolina, united with the North Carolina and Virginia Conference, where he was licensed and ordained a minister of Christ. He became the pastor of Union Church, Halifax County, Va., teaching also, a part of the time. He served other churches in the same capacity with success. During this time he matured and recommended the pastorate plan to the churches of his conference, and had it adopted.

After the war of the Rebellion, when his native state, civil and religious, was in a condition of utter confusion and desolation, a convention of Christian brethren was called to consider what to do with their prostrate denomination, and Elder Manning presided over the meeting. A plan of operation was drawn up in the form of a "Declaration of Principles and Form of Government for the

Christian Church." The idea, the plan, and the arrangement, is said to be his. After this he labored faithfully in Virginia, striving to build up the wasted churches. He was also associate editor of the "Christian Sun," during the most active years of his life. In all respects, Elder Manning was an able man—a fine writer, a successful pastor, and an eloquent preacher. It is said that in his best mood he had few equals as a speaker, moving, stirring, and convincing. He died in the city of Norfolk, Va., February 14, 1880, in the prime of life.

<u>JACOB MARINO (1803—1857)</u>

Jacob was born in 1803, was converted and baptized in 1840, and joined the church at Dundee, N.Y.. Soon after, he moved to Steuben County, and united with the church at Riker Hollow, where he commenced preaching, and was ordained by Elders Chadwick, Buzzell, Wescott, and Ward. Soon after his ordination, he became pastor of the church at Springwater, where he continued until his death. He died January 10, 1857.

<u>WILLIAM MARTIN MARKWELL (?—1876)</u>

Elder Markwell was a member of the Southern Wabash Conference, Ill. He was an early companion of Elder Austin Hutson, and they were co-laborers for years. These two young men entered the church and ministry about the same time. Both possessed more than ordinary talent. They died while young. Elder Markwell was pastor of the church at Mackville, Ill., at the time of his death. He died at his home in 1876.

<u>AMOS MARSH (1766—1842)</u>

Our present subject was born in 1766. He became a member of the regular Baptist Church, and for many years, preached for that body. He was pastor of the Weybridge Baptist Church, in Vermont, for some time. He moved to Massena, N.Y., and joined the Christian Church and the Northern New York Christian Conference. He continued an active minister in that church till his health failed. In 1842, he died in Massena, N.Y.

JOSEPH MARSH (1802—1863)

This minister was a nephew of the last mentioned. He was born in 1802, at St. Albans, Vt., and commenced preaching in 1818. He was editor of the "Palladium" five years, taking charge of it in 1838, and keeping it until 1843, when he embraced the Second Advent doctrine. At that time, he moved to Rochester, N.Y., where he published several pamphlets containing his views on the new doctrine. He moved his family to Oshawa, Canada, and shortly before his death, reunited with the Christians, laboring for them and preaching their doctrines until his death. He died in Tecumseh, Mich., in 1863, in his sixty-second year, while on his way home from Tennessee.

The Elder was an able and good man, and for many years, stood high in the estimation of his brethren in the church. Like many others, for a time, he seemed to have lost his balance on the Advent doctrine, so sure was he that he was right.

ORIN MARSH (?—?)

Orin Marsh was a younger brother of the preceding. He became a talented preacher in the Christian Church, in which connection he continued until his death, with the exception of one year, when he was a Universalist. After his return to the church, he was a zealous and earnest worker until, in consequence of becoming deranged, he committed suicide.

IRA MARSHALL (1795—1823)

This brother was born in Stowe, Vt., in 1795, and left that place while a rude, uncultured boy; but he returned in a few years, not only an accomplished gentleman, but a talented preacher. He was converted in Henrietta, N.Y., and was baptized by Elder Badger in 1816. He commenced preaching, and the following year, traveled with Elder Hathaway through Otsego County, N.Y. In 1819, he was ordained in New York, and spent the next year traveling with Elder Hathaway through Connecticut. He married a young lady in Hampden, Conn., a daughter of Elder Burnham. He settled there, preaching very successfully until his health failed. January 23, 1823, he died of consumption.

JOB MARSHALL (?—?)

Job Marshall was a New York minister. He died several years ago.

ROBERT MARSHALL (?—?)

Robert Marshall was one of the five ministers that left the Presbyterians during the time of the Kentucky Reformation, and assisted in the organization of the Christian Church in that state. He and Thompson returned to the Presbyterians, McNemar and Dunlevy went to the Shakers, and Stone partially to the Disciples—the whole five leaving the church they had started.

CHRISTOPHER MARTIN (?—?)

Christopher Martin was a son of Richard Martin. He was a native of Vermont, and assisted a great deal in the spread of the gospel in that state. He was a man of great power as a speaker, and was as bold and ready as he was able. He came to New York at the time of the introduction of the Christian cause in that state, and traveled extensively with Elder Millard through the eastern part, exhorting sinners to repentance, and organizing churches. In 1816, he traveled with Millard through Delaware County. About this time, he was married to a Miss Camp. He returned to Vermont from New York, but we have no definite account of his labors until 1830, at which time he had charge of the church at Stowe, Vt. In his early life, he was one of the most devoted and able pioneers of the day; but the latter part of his life, to a considerable extent, was spent in secular pursuits—probably from want of support in the ministry.

RICHARD MARTIN (?—?)

Richard Martin was a minister of the Freewill Baptist Church before the Christian Church was organized in New England. And after joining the Christians, he still continued in the ministry. He was the father of Elder C.W. Martin, and father-in-law of Elder William Blaisdell, in whose ordination he assisted.

JOHN P. MARTIN (1794—1849)

John was born in 1794, and spent his youth in Williamsport, O. He was converted in 1819, and was ordained some fifteen years later. He was pastor of the Graham Creek Church for some years, and finally died in that pastorate, May 27, 1849. He was a small man, of fair complexion, very energetic in his preaching, more inclined to the emotional style than to reasoning, and very firm in his convictions.

EZRA MARVIN (1806—1871)

The subject of this sketch was born in Laurens, Otsego County, N.Y., in 1806. While he was young, his father moved to Genesee County, where Ezra remained till manhood, helping to clear the forests and cultivate what was at that time a wilderness. During that time, a Christian Church was organized by Elders Millard, Badger, True, and others, of which his parents soon became members. Deacon Marvin and wife will long be remembered as true and earnest workers in that part of the vineyard, and it will not seem strange that, under the training he received, Ezra early chose the good part. He commenced preaching in 1827, and was ordained the same year, traveling a great part of the time with Elder Chase, of Enfield, chiefly in that part of the state.

In 1827, he married Mrs. Huldah Ink, a widow with one daughter, a daughter of Elder Ezra Chase. The result of this union, which lasted nearly forty years, was six daughters, five of whom survived him. He married a second time, a Mrs. McAlpine, a worthy woman who was with him in his last hours. From the time of his first marriage, in 1827, until the winter before his death, he superintended a farm; yet he was pastor of several churches, acted as itinerant, and traveled extensively. Twenty years of his life was spent as agent for Starkey Seminary. He died at Olean, N.Y., while on his way home from a trip among the conferences in favor of Star- key, October 1, 1871. He was buried in Dundee, N.Y., by the side of the wife of his youth, and in the community where he had spent the greater part of his life. Funeral services by Elder Austin Craig.

The Elder, though not a great scholar, was a friend of education, and was one of the greatest workers in the carrying on of the seminary at Starkey, N.Y.

<u>SETH MARVIN (1807—1843)</u>

Seth, a brother of the preceding, was born in Otsego County, N.Y., in 1807, where he lived until the removal of his father, Deacon Marvin, to Covington, Genesee County, where he experienced religion in 1824. He began to pray and exhort soon after his conversion, but never fully consecrated himself to the ministry until 1828. At this time, he gave up all for Christ, and until the day of his death, as much as health and strength would permit, his energies were wholly devoted to the building up of truth and the advancement of the Redeemer's kingdom. He spent about two years in Upper Canada, after he had begun an active ministry, and twice returned to that place with Elder Millard, great success attending both visits. He labored successfully in different parts of his own state and spent some two years in Pennsylvania, principally in Lewisburg and Plymouth, in both places witnessing extensive revivals.

April 17, 1836, he was married to Miss L.E. Badger, daughter of Elder Joseph Badger, an intelligent and efficient helpmate for the work to which he had devoted his life. But this union continued but seven years, when it was broken by the death of the husband. He was a man of dignified and pleasing appearance, of a light complexion, slenderly built, bland and agreeable in his manners. He had but few enemies, and his piety was so constant and conspicuous that his praise was truly in all the churches. His preaching was of the first order, correct and methodical in its arrangements, clear and impressive in its illustrations. His gestures were easy and natural, and his manner pleasant. To him the word of God was all in all, and while describing the vastness and glory of the great redemption through Christ, his whole soul was absorbed in the subject, and his strains of eloquence were powerful. But towards the close of his ministry, his voice was so much injured by bronchitis, brought on by hard labor and exposure, that he could preach but very little. In 1842, he was elected to the office of book agent of the Christian General Book Association, a position he filled satisfactorily until his death, at which time he had the "Palladium" under his control. The paper was of so much interest to him that, at the very last, he would ask of its welfare, and if it was approved. His death occurred September 4, 1813, amid a host of weeping and sympathizing friends.

<u>MATTHEW MARVIN (1777—1827)</u>

Our present subject was born in Pennsylvania, in 1777, moved to Ohio about 1807, and settled in Hocking County. From there, he moved to Delaware, and thence to Knox County, where he died September 13, 1827, aged fifty years. He was one among the first Christian preachers in that part of Ohio, where he traveled very extensively, and with good success.

His talent for preaching was quite good, possessing an easy, smooth style of delivery. He had a very good voice, both for speaking and singing, being peculiarly gifted in the latter respect. His son, Elder J.W. Marvin, says of him: "He was of a fine, portly build, and possessed great physical strength; had fine blue eyes, and to me, his child, he had a mild, beautiful countenance. At any rate, he impressed upon my young and tender heart religion so effectually that I think I was by this means led to a religious life." He was buried on his own land, in Bloomfield, Knox County, O. Three of his children entered the Christian ministry, one of whom, James W., is yet (1880) living, and has been a prominent member of the Christian Church for many years.

<u>Samuel B. Marvin (1799—1837)</u>

Samuel, a son of the preceding, was born in Pennsylvania, in 1799, and moved with his parents to Hocking County O., in 1807. He was converted in 1819, and soon after began to improve his gift as a public speaker, but was not regularly ordained for the work until 1822, after which time, he traveled very extensively as a missionary, and was a successful pastor of several churches. He was for many years a prominent member of the Ohio Central Conference, and was always considered an able and wise counselor. The firmness of his belief was evident to the last, as during his last sickness, when a skeptical neighbor came in, he said with a bright smile, "Have you come to see with what composure a Christian can die?" He died at Bloomfield, July 21, 1837, in the prime of life, greatly lamented by the church, leaving a wife and three children.

The Elder died comparatively young. During his life, education was not general, even in the cities, much less in the rural districts of Ohio, where he lived. From what we can gather, he had a mind of great power, and no matter what lie undertook, he would investigate to the utmost. He taught school, and during all this time he was studying diligently, reading and digesting such books as came within his reach. Much of the preaching of that day was of a doctrinal nature, and the Christian ministers were compelled to arm themselves for this kind of a struggle—for the liberal views held by the Christians were bitterly opposed. The Elder was one of these champions,—and a very successful one, too, possessing a calm, deliberate manner and the power of adapting himself to his hearers,—and was surpassed by none. In church polity, his views were in advance of many of his brethren. While he was earnest in his appeals to sinners, and sound in the doctrines held by his church, he plead for order, education, and system in the entire work of the denomination. The death of such a man, at that early period in life, was a serious loss to the small and imperfectly organized body with which he was connected.

SAMUEL S. MASON (?—?)

Samuel S. Mason.—The death of this brother is recorded in the *Herald of Gospel Liberty.* We have no further account, but his record is on high.

JAMES MATTHEWS (?—?)

James Matthews lived in Lauderdale County, Ala., and was a leading man in his conference in 1827, '28, and '29. He wrote frequently to the *Christian Messenger* and *Gospel Luminary* on various doctrinal subjects, especially on baptism, of which he was quite an advocate, but not to the extent of A. Campbell and his followers. In 1831, he expressed a strong conviction that he was near his end, as his health was then very poor, having been broken down by excessive labor.

WILLIAM MATTHEWS (?—?)

William Matthews was a traveling companion of Elder William Lane about 1824. He was then about fifty years old.

ROBERT MATHIS (?—1840)

This Elder was a member of the Strafford New Hampshire Conference. He died at his residence in Milton, N.H., March 13, 1840.

JOHN MAVITY (?—1826)

This brother was a member of the Indiana Central Conference in 1826. He died the same year. He was a zealous and earnest preacher and a faithful pastor.

? MAXWELL (?—?)

A minister of this name died a few years ago in the West. He had labored in the states of Illinois and Ohio. He was pastor at Carlisle, O., a few years before his death. He was a person of considerable ability as a preacher and pastor.

ANDREW MCBRIDE (?—1826)

Of the McBrides, there were four brothers. They were from Tennessee, originally. We know but little of any of them but Isaac, who traveled extensively in in Ohio and Pennsylvania, and other states in the West, in an early day.

Andrew was a native of Tennessee, and at his death, in 1826, was a member of the conference in that state.

ISAAC MCBRIDE (?—1824)

Isaac McBride began his labors in the ministry in Tennessee, but traveled extensively for five or six years in Ohio and Pennsylvania. About 1818, he and Elder R. Hawkins had great revivals near Brownsville, in the latter state. In 1822, his health failing him, he returned to Tennessee, and died there about 1824.

He was of a dark, swarthy, complexion, medium sized, of a slow and deliberate delivery, with some fondness for argument. He was always highly spoken of, both for his zealous work and consistent life. Doubtless hundreds were converted under his preaching.

JOSEPH MCBRIDE (?—1826)

Joseph McBride was a member of the Tennessee Conference, but we have no account of him farther than that he died previous to the session of conference in 1826.

THOMAS MCBRIDE (?—?)

Thomas McBride was a brother of three ministers mentioned in the preceding sketches, and a member of the same conference in Tennessee, but he moved to Missouri.

SAMUEL MCCANN (?—1872)

Samuel McCann was a member of the York and Cumberland Conference, Me., and died in 1872.

William McCaslin (1793—1852)

This brother was of Scotch descent, was born in Bedford County, Penn., December 19, 1793, was converted under the labors of Elder Kilwell, in Pennsylvania, and joined the Christian Church in 1817. He commenced preaching, and was ordained by Elder B. Miles and others in 1828. He was a strong and faithful supporter of the Christian Church in its early days. He was also one who stood firm at the time when many left the denomination and joined the Disciples, as the followers of Alexander Campbell were called at that time. He and Elder John McDonald, and a few others, were unshaken in their adherence to the doctrines of the church, and their firmness, doubtless, saved the Ohio Eastern Conference from being broken up at that time. The Elder, like many of his co-workers, would receive no pay for preaching. He Organized the churches at Bear Run, Island Run, Oakfield, Blackfork, and others. His labors were mostly in Perry and adjoining counties in Ohio. He had good native talent, and had great success as a preacher. He died in Perry County, October 11, 1852.

Alexander McClain (1797—1856)

This brother was born in Pennsylvania, October 14, 1797. His parents were of Irish and Scotch descent, and were members of the Presbyterian Church. In 1808, he moved with his parents to Nicholas County, Ky., where, in 1816, he was converted among the Christians and soon began to exhort. When he joined the Christians, his parents were much opposed to him, and promised to educate him for the ministry, if he would join the Presbyterians. This he refused to do, and was ordained for the work in 1823, by Elders Rogers, Longley, and others. He labored, after this in Kentucky for several years with occasional trips to Ohio and Indiana, but, 1829, after six years of faithful and successful work in Kentucky, he moved to Russellville, O., where he remained until 1850, when he moved to Carlisle, Clark County O., staying for two years, and then moving to Dayton, where he died, in the triumph of a living faith, August 30, 1856, in the sixtieth year of his age.

The Elder was a well-made man, of medium size, and great activity, with keen black eyes. His zeal for the cause knew no bounds, and as he was a very popular preacher, he received calls from many churches to hold protracted meetings, and seldom refused to go, although the remuneration for ministerial labor in those days was small. He had accumulated some property, but in a mercantile transaction he lost all. This was a hard trial, but he determined that he would pay the last dollar, which he did, some little time before his death. His great power for good among the people lay not in his: preaching, simply, but in his daily actions, and his power of simplifying gospel truths. His prayers in families were often as effectual for good, as his sermons, as he presented the condition of each member of the family—father, mother, sons, daughters, hired persons, strangers—to the loving Father. Not one was forgotten. Each one felt there was something to do, to be worthy of the blessing. He wrote frequently for our periodicals, but the articles were usually short, treating upon the one theme of his life, the salvation of sinners. While we have had better logicians and more comprehensive minds, few if any, were more efficient workers in the salvation of sinners, than he. In 1817, he was married to Miss Elizabeth Caldwell, of Nicholas County, Ky., who proved herself to be an efficient and faithful helper in the years of trials and hardships- that came with a growing family. They had seven children. Several of these and his companion survived him.

The Elder's field of labor, during his prime, was in Southern Ohio. He preached to the churches of Russellville, Sycamore,. Carlisle, Knob Prairie, and many others, as a pastor. For many years, indeed, he was one of the leading men in his field of labor. He and Elder Gardner were neighbors. Two such men in the community would be a power in any denomination. It is difficult to tell which was the most talented, although they were as different in their talent as two able men could be. Gardner was the more intellectual, while McClain was the more sociable and pathetic.

R.H. McClain (?—1863)

This minister joined the Deer Creek Conference, March 13, 1860, at a called session. He died at Louisville, Ky., in 1863, while in the army. He was a single man about twenty-seven years of age. He came to Ohio from one of the provinces of British America. He is spoken of by those that knew him as a young man of fine spirit and great promise for the future. Though a comparative stranger, his death was a great sorrow to many.

John McClure (?—?)

John McClure labored a part of his life in Canada. He died some years ago.

William McClure (?—?)

William McClure died in the State of Indiana when about forty years of age.

Samuel McCormick (?—?)

Samuel McCormick was a member of the Northern Kentucky Conference in 1826. He died many years ago.

John McCreary (1771—1857)

This brother was born in Iredell County, N.C., August 7, 1771. His educational facilities, being the time of the Revolution, were limited; but through the energy of his father, he received what would now be a common school education. Being of a studious mind, he was not content with this, but endeavored to increase his knowledge to the end of his public career. He was brought up under the influence of the old school Presbyterians, joined that church, and had taken the first steps in the ministry when he began to doubt and therefore investigate some of the articles of faith in that church. He continued that investigation until after his marriage to Ruth Warren, and till he had two children. These were christened according to the practices of the Presbyterian Church, although with some reluctance on the part of the parents. When he declared his views on this subject, there was a great deal of remonstrance made, but with no avail. Soon after, he moved to Tennessee, joined the Christians, and became a co-laborer with Kinkade, Dooly, Stone, and others who wished a free church and had separated themselves from other churches at the time of the Cane Ridge revival.

About 1812, he removed to the Indiana Territory, locating about eighteen miles from the site of the present city of Evansville. Notwithstanding the many privations incident to settling in a new country and the unfriendly relations of the Indians during the war of 1812, he was not unmindful of the cause of Christianity. He and Elders Wasson, Palmer, Miller, and others gathered together all who were willing to take the Bible as their rule, and organized churches in their respective localities, holding meetings in private houses till they could get suitable buildings for the purpose. He remained here nearly thirty years, and preached in nearly every county in the south-western part of the state. He was in the prime of life when Indiana was admitted into the Union, in 1816, and took an active part in making it a free state. Soon after, he was elected Associate Judge. At one time, he represented Vanderburg County in the legislature.

But during a greater part of this time, he was preaching regularly in the different counties near him—Gibson, Poesy, Warrick, and others further north. In 1835, in company with his three sons and an only daughter, he left this place and located in McDonough County, Ill., where he remained two years, when he moved to the territory of Iowa. Although far advanced in years, he labored there until he had organized a church on the DesMoines River, in Van-Buren County. He kept his appointments until near his death. He died September 19, 1857, at the advanced age of eighty-six years. He was very successful as a minister, was a good reasoner, and was so familiar with the old and new testaments that he was never at a loss for a proof text. As an exhorter, he was warm and sympathetic, and did not fail to get the attention of his hearers.

JOSIAH MCCULLOUGH (1815—1859)

This Elder was horn about 1815, in Alamance County, N.C., and died in 1859. He was an educated man, very devoted in the cause, and a fine orator. He acted for a time as agent for the Graham Institute, N.C., and exerted a good influence in the church.

JAMES MCDANIEL (1793—1873)

James was born in Bedford County, Penn., October 11, 1793, united with the Christian Church in 1815, moved to Ohio about 1843, and soon after, united with the Eastern Ohio Conference, of which he remained a member till death. He died in Vinton County, O., March 23, 1873.

DAVID MCDONALD (?—?)

David McDonald, one of the leading jurists of Indiana at the time of his death, was, in earlier years, a faithful and zealous Christian minister. At the time of his conversion, he determined to preach the Word, and with this determination, he commenced traveling, preaching as he went. He labored through all Southern Indiana, and was quite successful in winning souls to Christ. During a part of this time, he was in company with Elder Daniel Roberts, one of our leading ministers, who, at that time, did not believe in receiving pay for ministerial work—and it is likely that David partook of the same idea. At least, he received little of the small contributions that the older ones did when the brethren came to the "shaking hands" part of the service; and he soon found that he could not live in that way. At the last conference he attended, he made a statement of facts, asking members to continue his name on the conference record. He taught school for a while, little by little studied law, was admitted to the bar, moved to Indianapolis, became a leading lawyer, and published a digest of the laws of Indiana. He married, acquired considerable property, and soon became a Judge of the United States Court in Indiana, in which position he continued till death. With all this honor, he expressed to the compiler of this volume, a short time before his death, much regret that he ever left the ministry of the Christian Church. He thought that it would have been much better had he battled with poverty in what he considered duty than to gain the great honor he did by his profession as a lawyer. He was always a pious man, and did much good in the church. He joined the Methodist Church, but in his latter years, he was a great support to the small Christian Church in Indianapolis.

JOHN MCDONALD (1789—1864)

John was born February 12, 1789, in Maryland, moved to Cainsville, O., when a boy, was married to Sally Dew, March 26, 1812, moved to Monroe, Perry County, in 1814, served in the war, was converted under the labors of Elder B. Miles in 1819, and joined the Christian Church—he had joined the Methodists before. He soon began to preach, and for several years, was a leading-member of the Eastern Ohio Conference. He was very successful in the accumulation of property, but was noted for his benevolence, having erected a comfortable house of worship on Sunday Creek, near his own house. This church was organized about 1820, and was donated to the Christian Church. The Elder nearly supported those ministers who came there to preach. He was injured by cattle in the road, and died September 22, 1864. He received no salary for preaching, though he paid others. He moved all his effects to Perry County, O., on a horse, blazing trees to guide his way back; and for some time, he went to Zanesville, thirty miles, to mill and market.

WILLIAM MCDOWELL (?—1850)

This brother was quite an old man in 1834, out we have no further account of him except that he died in 1850. Elder Carns says he was a minister in the Eastern Ohio Conference.

DAVID MCGAHE (1771—1851)

This minister was born in Pennsylvania, in 1771. He moved from Pennsylvania to Guilford County, N.C., thence to Georgia, and in 1801, he professed religion in the Presbyterian Church. The next year, he moved to Wilson County, Tenn. Although brought up in the Presbyterian Church, he was very liberal in his views. The doctrines that arose from the, Cane Ridge revival were fast spreading through the country,, and the Elder readily received them; and, after some mental struggle, determined to advocate them publicly. There were some misgivings, however, that he was not acting in strict accordance with Presbyterian rules. But, under the impression that the Presbyterian Church was about to renounce creeds, he attended the Presbytery at Red River, Logan County, Ky., and there found himself more closely bound by creeds than ever. And then and there, he determined to declare himself independent of the Presbyterians. There had been a church built by the efforts of the revivalists, and when the division came, the majority retained the church property. Thus the Elder and others, by their earnestness and zealous work, started the first Christian Church in Kentucky.

Although they had a church and congregation, there were really no ordained ministers. To remedy this, Elder Pope, one of O'Kelly's co-laborers, was sent for, and McGahe was ordained for the work May 1807. He now started out to travel, laboring under the disadvantages of delicate health and stinging poverty; but his labors were wonderfully blessed, and the church was strengthened, help coming from Ohio, Kentucky, and other states. In 1815, he moved to Crawford County, Ill., where he labored faithfully as a pious preacher, resisting everything that had a tendency to shackle the mind or divert it from its proper course. Not only did he preach a free salvation, but he wrote much, never hesitating to do what duty demanded. He was twice elected to the legislature, and served several years as receiver at the Land Office in Palestine, Ill. During all this time, his interest in the good work never abated, but he kept up an active ministry. William Kinkade, Seth Gard, and himself, of the Christian, and Daniel Parker, of the Baptist Church, were four of the most active men in keeping slavery out of the constitution of Illinois. Old age came on, however, and for several years, he did not attend the sessions of his conference. But he was at the last one before his death, and was called upon to preach, which he did in an able manner—from Titus 2:7. He died September 29, 1851, at the age of eighty years. His aged companion preceded him a few years.

WILLIAM MCGAUGHY (1804—1830)

This brother was born October 10, 1804, was converted in 1820, and began to preach in the following year. His labors were mostly confined to his native state, Georgia. He was a very earnest man and zealous in the cause, but he died July 19, 1830. at the early age of twenty-six, after being nine years in the ministry.

JAMES MCGREGOR (1786—1852)

This Elder was born in 1786, embraced religion in Cayuga County, N.Y., under the labors of Elder Shaw, and began his work in the ministry before leaving New York. In 1837, he moved to Michigan, where he organized several churches, one very fine one in his own neighborhood, of which he was the chief support while he lived. He was peculiarly gifted as a pastor, and was very zealous in the support of the cause. He died March 17, 1852.

THOMAS MCINTIRE (1789—1861)

This brother was born in New York in 1789, was converted in 1821, and commenced preaching soon after. In 1825, he moved with his family to Canada, and was ordained at Mendon, N.Y., the year after his removal, by Elder Shaw and others. In 1838, he wrote that he had labored in Canada, for eight years. His co-workers, during a part of this time, were Elders Seth Marvin, A.C. Morrison, and others, and great success attended their work. In 1841, he left Canada, after having lost all his property in the rebellion, going to Marion, N.Y., where he remained two years, organizing several churches during the time. About 1857, he moved to Michigan, and died at Independence, May 1, 1861, aged seventy-two years.

He devoted his whole life to the work, often times neglecting his own interests that he might advance the cause. His principal labors were performed in New York and Canada, and very often under very great disadvantages of poverty and opposition. He was a talented, zealous, and self-sacrificing man, , but like Elders Daniel Call, Joel Doubleday, and other revivalists, he was often destitute of earthly comforts. In Canada and New York, his name was familiar in all the families of the Christian denomination, and many hundreds, if not thousands, were converted under his preaching.

JOHN MCINTURF (1815—1847)

This Elder was born in Licking County, O., in 1815, was converted in 1832, was ordained the year following, and from this time forward he devoted his time, talents, and all to the work of the ministry. He traveled extensively through Ohio and some other states. His talent was best exercised in revival work, and being a very eloquent and earnest preacher, revivals followed his labors every-where. His trust in the Lord was complete, and his zeal for the salvation of sinners knew no bounds, therefore it is not wonderful that he often taxed his physical powers beyond endurance. Still his health was quite good. He was a fine-looking man, very pleasant and agreeable in his manners. He was married in the Christian Church in Hartford, Licking County, O., by Elder J.W. Marvin, where nine years afterward the same minister preached the funeral of both husband and wife. He died January 29, 1847, and his wife just two weeks before, leaving two small children.

JASON MCKEE (1800—1876)

Our present subject was born in Manchester, Conn., November 17, 1800, moved with his parents to Adams, Jefferson County, N.Y.', in 1803, was converted in 1818, and was baptized by Elder Lebbeus Field of the Christian Church. He became well versed in the common branches of education, taught school, and preached as a licentiate until 1831, when he was ordained in the Northern New York Conference. His labors were continued within the bounds of his own conference through life, with the exception of three years that he preached in Ohio and Western Pennsylvania. He was a frequent writer to our periodicals, reporting the doings of the churches in the field of his labor. He was a plain, pointed writer, clear in all his statements, and his suggestions were timely and wise. He was a progressive man, a lover of education, system, and enterprise in the churches. He died of paralysis in Watertown, N.Y., at the house of his daughter, August 2, 1876, his faithful companion having died six years before.

The Elder was a tall, spare man, having a quiet and grave countenance; in his old age he had quite a venerable look. He devoted more of his week days to the work of the ministry than was common with the ministers of his conference, and as the pay for ministerial work was small, he was in limited circumstances. After the death of his wife, he lived among his children, visiting and preaching what he could to the churches of his neighborhood. When he had the first stroke of paralysis he was staying at the house of a son in Brooklyn, N.Y. He recovered sufficient strength so as to be brought to his home in Watertown, where he passed away, as stated, in peace and triumph.

<u>James McKinney (1789—1872)</u>

James was born in Washington County, Penn., July 17, 1789. He was of Scotch and French ancestry. In 1791, his father moved his family to Cincinnati, afterward settling in Campbell County, Ky. They remained there for some time, then moved to Clark County, O., where James received such education as was commonly given in those days. In 1818, he was married to Mary Flynn, and in the same year he was converted.

In 1812, he enlisted for the war against England, and remained a year. During this time, however, by exposure, he contracted the sciatic rheumatism and was severely afflicted by that disease for two years. When he had partially recovered, he taught school, and farmed on a small scale. He now began to preach and took a strong stand on the Bible as a creed, and the belief 'in the union of all believers. In 1829, he moved to Montgomery County, Ind., where he soon took a prominent place as a minister in the Christian Church, and retained this until his death. He continued for over forty years a prominent member of the Western Indiana Conference, and during the last years of his connection with the conference, he was considered the father of it, as the early members were all gone except himself. He was always expected to open the conference, as no one was willing to take the place of the worthy patriarch. He wrote a great deal for the different papers of the church, informing the denomination at large of the events transpiring in his part of the country. In 1843, he wrote to the "Palladium" at two different times; in one, he mentions a revival in one of the churches of his charge, and of the addition of seventy members, and in the other letter, he tells of the death of his son Watson, in his twentieth year, a heavy stroke to the parents, but borne in the triumph of faith. The Elder was a bold defender of the doctrines held by the church of his choice; the circumstance of his position, together with his peculiar promptness and ability making him, for many years, a leader in his field of labor. Many were the difficulties encountered by our pioneers, in an early day, in Western Indiana, and Elder McKinney had his full share of these, but he met them all manfully, and came out victorious. Some of his companions in labor were Elders Dudley, Jackson, Lowe, Snethen—all men of sterling worth as pioneers. He preached but little for the last three years of his life, but his interest in the church never lessened, and all looked upon him as a safe and able counselor. He died November 3, 1872, in Merom, Ind., in his eighty-fourth year. The Elder raised a large family of children. Elder A.L. McKinney has been for many years a leading minister in the same church. His youngest son, Moses B., was a promising young minister, but he passed away several years ago. Watson, who died in 1843, had the ministry in view. Three of his daughters married ministers, one daughter married a Methodist minister; the other two married respectively, Elders Leonard Shoemaker, and David Hayes. Thus, from one family there was, at one time, seven ministers serving the Master. His companion, who died many years before him, was a faithful helpmate to him in his ministerial work.

MOSES MCKINNEY (1828—1866)

Moses, a son of the preceding, was born in Clark County, O., April 6, 1828, was converted while quite young, and joined the Western Indiana Conference in 1848. He attended school at Antioch College for some time. His ministerial labors were confined principally to Montgomery and Sullivan counties, Ind., although he had preached some in Ohio. He was drowned in the Wabash river near Merom, while fishing, June 1, 1866, in the prime of life, after laboring twelve years in the ministry. He left a wife and two children.

ALLEN MCKINSEY (?—1875)

Allen McKinsey was raised at Alamo, Montgomery County Ind., embraced religion, began to preach early, and joined the Western Indiana Conference. He moved to Merom to educate his children, and labored in that vicinity for some years. Later in life he moved to Pulaski County, Ind., joined the Tippecanoe Conference, and died in Star City, Ind., about 1875.

DAVID MCKOWN (1820—1846)

David was born in Jackson County, Va., in 1820, moved with his father's family to Knox County, O., about 1823, where he remained until manhood. He was converted in 1840, under the labors of Elder John McInturf, and the next year, became a member of the Ohio Central Christian Conference, but was not ordained until two years after. From this time forward, he traveled extensively in different parts of Ohio, Indiana, Maryland, and Virginia. In 1846, he entered Meadville Theological School, for the purpose of fitting himself more fully for the work in which he had been engaged for six years. He labored here very hard as a student, and there were few that made a more rapid advancement than he. But his constitution was not. strong enough for the strain put upon it, and he was obliged to leave school. He went to Spring, Penn., where he died May 22, 1846, at the house of one of the brethren, in his twenty-seventh year.

DANIEL MCLAUGHLIN (1807—1867)

This brother was born in 1807, moved to Iowa about 1865, and died in Cedar County, in 1867. He was a successful preacher and a good man.

JOHN MCLEAN (?—1836)

John McLean had been in the Christian ministry for about five years at the time of his death, which occurred in Upper Canada in October, 1836.

WILLIAM MCLUCAS (?—?)

William McLucas was an Indiana preacher, and died at the age of forty.

WILLIAM MCMASTERS (1785—1855)

This brother was born in Pennsylvania, about 1785, and moved to Ohio, near Cincinnati, with his parents in 1803. In 1807, he united with the church, and in two years he began to exhort. Such was his success that many were astonished, and a certain Judge remarked that "the illiterate man speaks like a learned minister." After his ordination in 1813, he took charge of the church at South Bend, Hamilton County, O., and during this pastorate he organized a church across the river in Kentucky, many of the members being from the fishermen along the banks of the river. He served as a pastor of the church at South Bend for five years, after which he removed to Kentucky, where he remained until his death in 1855.

ANDREW MCKEES (1816—1872)

This brother was a native of Tennessee, being born in Washington County, January 21, 1816, moved to Randolph County, Ind., in 1829 o "30, married Miss Jane McIntire in 1835, and joined the

Methodist Church in 1836. In 1839, he joined the White River Christian Church, at the time of its organization under the labors of Elder Brumfield, the first church of our denomination in the county. Soon after, he joined the Bluffton Conference, and was ordained by that body. His principal field was Randolph and adjoining counties in Indiana and Ohio, though he labored for some time in Illinois. He was quite successful as a minister, especially in general meetings, organization of churches, and revivals. He baptized a great many. He spent twenty-nine years in preaching the gospel, and died September 9, 1872.

RICHARD MCNEMAR (1769—1839)

McNemar's name is inserted in this book from the fact that he was one of the founders of the Christian Church in Kentucky, although he did not labor long in the body. He was born in 1769, and commenced his religious life in 1790. He was educated for a Presbyterian minister, and labored successfully as such until the Cane Ridge revival in Kentucky, when he cast away creeds and confessions of faith, and with others, took the Bible alone as the foundation of faith. With the people of this faith he labored for several years, until the Shaker element arose, when he and John Dunlevy embraced this doctrine, and became zealous workers in that body. The Elder possessed great talent both as a speaker and writer, and was very successful as a minister in the Presbyterian Church. As a leader, he became quite prominent among the Shakers, and died in one of their villages many years ago.[11]

DANIEL MCPHERSON (1759—1839)

Daniel was born in Scotland, in 1759, was converted, and preached for some years in the Methodist Church, but on the entrance of the Christian ministers to Delaware County, N.Y., he was among the first to receive them to his house. He soon partook of their sentiments, and for this reason, his connections with the

---

[11] Note: Death date is taken from the book, *A Sketch of the Life and Labors of Richard McNemar* (Charleston, AR: Cobb Publishing, 2014).

Methodists were severed in 1818, when he identified himself with the Christians, and for twenty years, continued a faithful and zealous worker in that church. The latter part of his life was consecrated to one object—the conversion of sinners—and he was greatly blessed in his purpose. He died September 8, 1839, aged eighty years.

STEPHEN MERRIHEW (1827—1863)

This brother was a native of New York. He was a member of both the Baptist and Methodist churches before he joined the Christians, having joined the former in 1847, and the latter in 1849. Sometime after joining the latter body, he began to preach, and was ordained by Elders Welton and Tyler. At first, he lived at Halsey Valley, Tioga County, N.Y., but soon after moved to Boone County. He was a pious, devotional man, and an earnest believer in the faith in which he died. He enlisted in the War of the Rebellion, but was sick nearly all the time while in the service, and died May 23, 1863, aged thirty-six years.

CHARLES VAUGHN MERRILL (1800—1846)

Charles was born November 21, 1800, was converted under the labors of Jasper Louis, and joined the Christian Church at Worthington, Me., in 1829. He afterward moved to Dover, Me., organizing several churches in that part of the state, and one at Exeter. In 1837, he moved to Fulton County, O., and joined the Southeastern Michigan Conference. From this time until his death, his labors were confined to Northern Ohio and Southern Michigan. During this time, he was active in the work, and especially was he called for on funeral occasions. He was a very devoted man and was blessed with a perfect trust in God. Sometimes he would get out of his bed to baptize at midnight. Having dreamt one night that his eldest son had died, he was so affected that he prayed with and for his children, whereupon four of them were converted. He died at his home in Fulton County, January 4, 1846. One of his sons died a prominent minister of the United Brethren Church.

JOSEPH MERRILL (1779—1860)

This brother was born in 1779, and was ordained in 1827. He was a member of the Maine Christian Conference, and spent the greater part of his life in that state. He was a very successful minister in revivals, and enjoyed that kind of labor, greatly. He died in Canaan, Me., in November, 1860.

The Elder was not a great preacher, but he was so good and kind that all had confidence in him. To illustrate his kindness and wit: An anecdote is related of him in the case of receiving into church a young girl about fourteen years old, who had been brought up by religious parents, and as such, had but little experience in sin. As was customary in Maine in those •days, the little maid was called upon to give her experience. She gave a good one, but did not say much about her feeling of guilt. An old brother, a member of the Calvinistic Baptist Church, who had been back and forth from sin to holiness, frequently, but more in the former state, expressed himself as not satisfied with the experience given, as it did not show the sense of sin prominently enough. The Elder promptly answered, "Good reason, good reason, Brother F., for she never had the experience that you have had in sin and crime."

ABRAM MERRITT (1779—1847)

This brother was a member of the Cincinnati church and the Miami Conference. He died January 18, 1847.

BARZILLAI H. MILES (1797—1833)

This Elder was born in Otsego County, N.Y., in 1797. He was converted when quite young, began to preach in 1818, moved to Ohio, and labored in the neighborhood of Rutland, Meigs County, O., for many years, with great success. In May, 1831, he started on a preaching tour through Indiana, traveling through the country as far as the Tippecanoe Battle ground. His letters, describing the events of the journey, are very interesting. In the same year, he started on an eastern tour through Ohio, Pennsylvania, and to the city of New York. From the city to his native place in Otsego

County, back again to New York City, going from there to New Jersey, thence to Monroe County, N.Y., and from there to Onondaga County, where he remained until 1832. He was a welcome visitor, not only in the families of the different churches where he preached, but was gladly received in other families, being very agreeable in his manners and liberal in his views, while he lived a consistent life, and one full of good works. In his journal, he speaks of his trip in the East, saying "that in the counties of Jefferson, Tompkins, Cayuga, and Otsego, I have formed the acquaintance of at least forty ministers, and a thousand worthy brethren of the Christian Church." From the East he returned to his home in Meigs County, O., and soon started on his last journey— the one to Louisiana. The principal object of this journey was to visit a brother living in Natchez, but during his stay in the Southern States, he labored as usual in the ministry, and with great success.

On his return, he took the cholera and died on the steamboat, 105 miles below Louisville, Ky., May 29, 1833. He was an active, strong man, who devoted his whole life and energy to the cause. He was a regular correspondent and Assistant Editor of the "Christian Palladium" at the time of his death. The circumstance of his death, from the contagion, on the steamboat, with no acquaintance near, and buried on the bank of the river, all alone, added to the sadness of the event, which was considered a great calamity to the denomination.

Nelson Millar (1798—1825)

This minister was born in 1798, in Gosport, Va., where he lived until he had grown to manhood. He embraced religion while quite young, began to preach soon after, and was ordained in 1819. He was a fine speaker, and such was his zeal and earnestness in the work, that he traveled through Virginia, North Carolina, and some of the Northern States, everywhere rousing the people by his eloquence and enthusiasm. He was the means of bringing many to a knowledge of their fallen state, and leading them to a better life. His education was quite good, his preaching full of energy, and his delivery pleasant. In 1824, he was elected to the Virginia Legislature, where he took a prominent position as a speaker, and filled his place so satisfactorily that he was re-elected; but he died September 13, 1825, a short time before the legislature again convened. His death was a great loss to the denomination, and much regret was expressed by his co-laborers in Virginia, and those places he had visited the most. A fine eulogy on his life was delivered by Elder Reuben Potter, at the time, which was read with great interest in all parts of the denomination, as the Elder's reputation was well known throughout the church.

DAVID MILLARD (1794—1873)

There is not a minister, probably, whose life is recorded in this volume, so well-known to the denomination in all parts of the country as David Millard, by his publications, his travels, and his poetry. He was a full man, naturally, his education, in the beginning, was respectable, and his activity unlimited. Being blessed with robust health, generally, it enabled him to accomplish a great amount of labor in the fifty-eight years of his ministry. I doubt if he was as brilliant as his friend, neighbor, and co-laborer, Badger. He did not possess the learning of Clough, the eloquence of Walter, nor the peculiar special gift of many others of our ministers, but in many respects, he surpassed them all.

The following is a summary of his various changes in life, taken from the excellent volume of biography compiled by his son, Elder David E. Millard, and published in 1874: Two brothers by the name of Robert and Nathaniel Millard came from England to Rehoboth, Mass., about 1650, on account of religious persecutions. David Millard is a descendant in the sixth generation of Robert, who was a Baptist minister. He was the son of Nathaniel Millard and was born at Glenville, Schenectady County, N.Y., on November 24, 1794. His mother's maiden name was Mary Hunter. The place of his birth was near the battle-ground of Burgoyne's defeat. He had education enough to teach common school. His education and good behavior gave him a respectable position among the youth of the neighborhood. Nancy Cram, whose name is recorded in this volume, came from Vermont to preach in his father's neighborhood at a time when David was one of the directors of a fashionable New Year's ball. The young man went to hear the woman more, perhaps, from curiosity than anything else, but her appeals were so powerful that he gave up his management of the fashionable dance, absented himself from the same, and consorted with the humble few that attended the meeting.

After some struggle of mind, he determined to give himself entirely to the Lord. Almost from the time of his conversion, he felt that he must preach, and on March 16, 1816, he left his home to devote his time and talent to the service of God. He first joined his labors with Elder C.W. Martin, of Vermont, and the two young men had great success through Green and Delaware counties. He was ordained in Ballston, N.Y., August 4, 1816. From this time, his talents and zeal were acknowledged, and he at once took a leading position. He held meetings in various places with Elders William Cummings, Badger, and others. In 1817, he baptized Elder Hollister, at Ballston.

His labors were constant from this time until June 27, 1819, when he married Miss Celia Hix, of Taunton, Mass. In September, the same year, he went to New England to visit his wife's relations and preach in various places while there. In 1818, he published the "True Messiah." In 1824, in company with Elder Morrill, he made a long tour through the Southern States, especially Virginia. In 1825, he published the *Gospel Luminary* at West Bloomfield. He continued the publication of this monthly periodical until the third year, when Elder Clough became associated with him and the paper was moved to New York City, the management falling upon Elder Clough. In 1825, he visited Canada, in company with Elder Joseph Badger. In 1831, the "Millard and Badger Hymn Book" was published, and the same year, he held debates with those that differed with him. He held one that year with Elder Hoag, on the Trinity. In 1832, all the periodicals of the denomination were united in the "Gospel Palladium," edited by Elder Joseph Badger, our subject being one of the most prominent managers. In 1833, he made an extensive tour through Ohio and Kentucky. Here I would observe that when Elder Millard visited a section of country, he did it to preach every day, to report the particulars of churches and ministers, and so ably that his letters became historical. From the latter date until October, 1841, when he started for Palestine and Egypt, he was sometimes pastor at West Bloomfield, N.Y., Portsmouth, N.H., Portland, Me., or traveling as missionary in Pennsylvania, Michigan, and New York. In the East, he spent nearly one year, during which time he visited Malta, Egypt, Palestine, the peninsula of Sinai, and Arabia Petrea. He also spent several weeks a quarantine prisoner in Smyrna.

In 1844, he was elected professor of the Meadville Theological school, where he continued for years, giving great satisfaction in his lectures on Jewis11 customs. The book he published on the subject of his journey in the East, under the name of "Millard's Travels" etc., is so well known, both in and out of his own denomination, that it is useless to mention the subject here.

On his return from his long tour, he entered into his ministerial work with the energy and zeal of youth. Beside regular preaching to his own church at West Bloomfield, and others in the State of New York, he traveled extensively, lecturing on Palestine. These lectures were exhibited by magic lantern, and that, connected with his happy faculty of describing the scenes of his journey, made them very interesting. In 1852, he visited Ohio, and in 1854, Indiana, on lecturing tours, at the request of churches. In 1868, he moved to Jack- son, Mich., where his son, David E., was pastor of the church in that city. He continued to reside there to the last, doing what he could in the great work of preaching, and doing much good by his wise counsel in his ripe years. He died at his home in Michigan, August 7, 1873, in the seventy-ninth year of his age and the fifty-eighth of his ministry.

From what has been said of Elder Millard, we see that his career was quite exceptional. As seen from the account given, education, wealth, family connection, or denominational prestige gave him no position; nor did the surroundings in a large city give him any advantage in this respect. Yet we see the boy from the rural district of Ballston battling with poverty, preaching week days and Sunday for next to nothing, and rising, in a few years, from an obscure boy to a national man, his- writings on Theology, Politics, and Travels read by thousands that never knew the man or his church. Many persons reach distinction through fine personal appearance, ready wit, great eloquence, or brilliancy of conversation; but plain David Millard possessed none of these. The following may be some of the gifts that made Millard what he was:

1st. Bodily strength. Working on his father's farm, in the rocky region of Saratoga County, N.Y., had developed every muscle, bone, and organ in his body, so that, although his system became deranged by excessive labor, a little rest or change of climate and scenery set him all right again. When he left for the far East in 1841, his health was poor; but a few months rough sailing on many seas, a ride through the sandy waste of Sinai, and a few weeks confinement in the filthy Lazaretto, of Smyrna—that would have killed many a weaker man,—set David Millard on his feet, and gave him a new lease of life.

2nd. Entire consecration to the work of preaching. With less of this, with the talents that were soon developed in him, the temptation to turn aside to some more lucrative profession would have been almost irresistible; and, like many others, his talent would have been lost to the church of his first choice, and would have graced some state legislature, the United States Congress, or, perhaps, a seat on the Judge's bench. He never swerved. Many of his comrades turned aside to medicine, law, or speculation, but he, with more talent, lived and died in the work, with no higher title than simply David Millard.

3rd. Readiness in composition as a writer. With Millard, this faculty was developed quite early. He had been in the ministry but two short years when, on account of misrepresentation of his views, he ventured to take the field as an author. "The True Messiah Exalted" was published. This pamphlet of thirty-eight pages was read far and near, and many were converted to the doctrines advocated therein. Soon after, the "Gospel Luminary," a monthly periodical, was published in West Bloomfield, a small village in Western New York. It was dependent for its support upon the brethren of the scattered and poorly organized churches in the then new country. But under the ready and graphic pen of Millard it succeeded.

4th. Great and fearless activity, combined with strict economy. Without these, the other gifts would fail to carry him through. In reading the life of our brother, we see him constantly on the move, not only in places of apparent safety, but in places of real danger as well. We find him in 1823, with Elder Morrill as a companion, on his way to Virginia in a frail sailing ship, on the tempestuous sea, and nearly shipwrecked. Soon after, he traveled through Ohio and Kentucky, swimming his horse across strange and overflowing streams, subject to the deadly malaria so dangerous to unacclimated persons on the great rivers of the West in an early day. The same activity prompted him, with small means, to undertake the long and dangerous journey to Palestine, before the days of ocean steamers and systematic arrangements, with dragomen, to ascend the river Nile in an Egyptian sail boat, and cross the perilous peninsula of Sinai with untamed Arabs. The same activity, also, enabled him in seven weeks to prepare the volume of 4'Millard's Travels," and to keep up a vivid description on paper of all he saw in every country, and have them correctly recorded in print. All these with the proceeds of the small and uncertain salary of an itinerant Christian preacher.

5th. Poetical genius. Though this does not enter largely into the work of his life, yet it is doubtless true that a poetical mind can see and arrange objects more graphically, and hence more attractive to the majority of readers, than one that does not possess that faculty, though no effort be made to throw the composition to a poetical form.

Such are the views of the compiler of Elder Millard. It was my privilege to have quite a thorough acquaintance with him, by being a student under him at Meadville, Penn., while delivering his lectures to the students on Jewish Antiquity and' Sacred Geography, in the above Institution, by frequent correspondence at different times, and by personal intercourse at various occasions during the last thirty years.

Elder Millard was one of the noble army of pioneers that fought the first battle for Christian liberty in the organization of the denomination. Among these were Jones, Smith, Plummer, the Peaveys, Badger, Shaw, Hathaway, and others, in the East, and not less brave warriors in the West and South. There were giants in those days, and our subject is not the least of these mighty and valiant men who fought the battles of the Lord in those trying times; for when the ministers of the Christian Church gave out an appointment to preach, it was not, as now, kindly received by other denominations.

ISRAEL MILLARD (?—?)

Israel Millard was a member of the South-eastern Michigan Christian Conference, at the time of his death.

ABRAHAM MILLER (1803—1872)

Abraham was born in 1803. He had preached for some time, when he joined the Rayshill Pennsylvania Christian Conference in 1847. His education was limited, but he was a man of great piety and earnestness, and success attended his labors. He carried on a farm while engaged in the work, but frequently went from home, oftentimes traveling a great distance. He assisted in the ordination of Elder B.A. Cooper, who traveled with him for some time. He died January 11, 1872, aged sixty-eight years.

FREDERICK MILLER (1809—1844)

Frederick was born in Alleghany County, Md., in 1809, was converted under the preaching of Elder Walter in 1827, and was baptized the year after by Elder Long. He soon became an active lay brother, and was ordained in 1830. He began to travel, preaching with great success. In 1833, he married Miss Rebecca L. Chaney, of Ohio, in Cumberland, Md., where she was visiting with her brother. In her he found a helpmate in the great work. The year after their marriage, they visited Ohio, preaching as they went. Soon after, he received a call to Cincinnati, where he labored very successfully; the church revived and the cause prospered under his administration. He was, for some time during his stay here, affected by the views of Alexander Campbell on baptism, but soon after his removal from the city, he abandoned these views and returned to the old ground. In 1837, he removed to Rockingham County, Va., and took charge of the Antioch Church, where he soon became an influential minister and a great favorite of the people.

As a minister, he was eloquent and powerful in his appeals to the heart and conscience of his hearers. He was persevering in his purposes and untiring in his studies and pursuits to obtain knowledge. He was of a cheerful disposition, always ready to assist those who needed aid, and there were many to deplore his death in the midst of his usefulness. He died at his home in Rockingham County, March 11, 1844, in his thirty-fifth year.

<u>REBECCA L. MILLER (1814—1844)</u>

Rebecca, wife of the preceding subject, was born in Greene County, O., in 1814, and was converted under the labors of Elder Isaac N. Walter, at Williamsport, O. She commenced preaching soon after her conversion, and traveled much before her marriage in 1833. Her life, from this time forward, was so closely allied with that of her husband, Elder Frederick Miller, that the history of one is the history of the other. She was a very pleasant speaker, a fine reasoner, and a good historian. Thousands were called together to hear the gospel from her lips, from the novelty of seeing a woman stand up and preach the word. She would often chain the attention of the most skeptical for hours, with her flow of eloquence, and at no time was she ever at a loss for words to express her views on any subject that was brought up in the pulpit. She died March 14,

1844, just four days after the companion whose toil and care she had shared on earth, and whose triumph and reward1 she went to share in a brighter world.

JAMES MILLER (?—?)

James Miller was a native of Maine, but his ministerial labors were confined principally to Tennessee. He was a minister of the Tennessee Conference in 1832, and great revivals were the result of his labors there about that time. He was the author of "Trinitarianism Unmasked."

JONATHAN MILLER (?—1817)

This brother was a minister of the Calvinistic Baptist Church at New Bartholomew, N.Y., in 1812 or T3, when Elder Jasper Hazen, the first Christian minister in that part of the country, came to his house. He had been dissatisfied with the doctrines of partial salvation for years, and had repeatedly told his family that a people holding more liberal views would rise, and that he should finally find a home among them. On the coming of Elder Hazen, he told his wife that "this was one of the persons of whom he had spoken" and when a Christian Church was organized, he and all his family united with it, and from that time forward, he labored as a minister in the church until his death. He died in 1817, in the triumph of faith. One of his daughters married Elder Levi Hathaway.

SAMUEL MILLER (?—1877)

Samuel Miller was, for many years, a minister of considerable influence in the State of Indiana. He labored in Randolph, Wayne, and adjoining counties in Eastern Indiana. He was then a member of the Bluffton Conference. After this, he moved to Tipton County, and joined the Miami Reserve Conference. He died in 1877, not far from seventy years of age. He was a zealous man, of limited education, but quite successful in winning souls to Christ.

THOMAS MILLER (1812—1877)

This brother was born October 17, 1812, and died near Evansville, Ind., February 19, 1877. He commenced preaching in 1847. His education was limited, and his principal strength as a speaker consisted in his application of Bible quotations to the reformation of sinners.

WILLIAM MILLS (?—?)

William Mills lived on Ludlow Creek, O., and died many years ago.

SAMUEL MILNER (1817—1858)

This brother was born in Indiana in 1817, and was brought up under the influence of the Methodist Church, which he joined when quite young. In 1843, he united with the Christian Church and was ordained two years later, in Franklin County, Ind. In 1847, he removed to Huntington County, and in 1852, joined the Bluffton Conference. His education was limited but his zeal and faith in the work was great, and his labors were greatly blessed. He died February, 1858.

? MITCHELL (?—?)

This minister was present at the organization of the Miami Conference in 1814. He lived on Rattle Snake Creek.

AMRI MITCHELL (?—?)

Amri Mitchell was a well-known minister in the Christian Church from 1810 until 1815.

LEWIS H. MITCHELL (1828—1868)

Lewis was born in Ohio, February 15, 1828, but moved with his parents to Indiana when quite a small child. He lost his mother at the age of twelve, and in 1844 went with his father's family to Jefferson County, Iowa. In 1819, he married Miss Elizabeth Carr, and in 1852, they both united with the Christian Church under the labors of Elder W.H. Phillips. He now felt that it was his duty to preach, but failing to do this he backslid, but renewed his covenant some time after in a United Brethren meeting, and began to preach for them, but on his return to the Christians he continued to preach in that church, and remained in that faith until death. He now devoted his time to the work, and joined the Des Moines Christian Conference, in which body he soon became a prominent member. In 1864, he joined the 7th Iowa Cavalry and continued in the army for over a year. In 1866, he joined the Union Christian Conference, and labored in Washington County, until 1867, when he was appointed an evangelist in the bounds of the conference, a position for which he was well adapted. He continued to hold this position until his great exposure threw him into lung fever, from which he never recovered. He died January 6, 1868, at the age of forty.

B. D. MOORE (1809—1834)

This Elder was born in 1809, moved from Compton, Lower Canada, to Niagara County, N.Y., in 1832, where he died May 1, 1834, in his twenty-sixth year.

EPHRAIM MOORE (?—?)

Ephraim Moore was a co-laborer with John Miller and others in Tennessee, in 1806, and was quite old at that time.

JAMES MOORE (1785—1839)

This Elder was born in 1785. He spent the last years of his life in Darien Centre, Genesee County, N, Y., where he died January 24, 1839. From a letter he wrote some weeks before his death, we find that he had joined the Christian Church some ten years before, and that he was still firm in that faith and ready to battle for the truth to the last.

PETER MOORE (1751—1835)

Peter was born in Candia, N.H., December 3, 1751. He was converted in 1767, had began to preach about 1791, being ordained for the work among the Baptists, in Deerfield, N.H. He remained in this place until 1817, when he moved first to Winthrop, Me., then to Vienna. About this time, he became convinced that Calvinism was not the true doctrine, and asked for dismission from the Baptist Church. Soon after this, he joined the Christians. He continued in this faith, preaching regularly every Sunday until three weeks before his death. He died September 9, 1835, aged eighty-four years, leaving an aged widow with whom he had lived happily for more than sixty years.

In some doctrinal points he differed somewhat from the majority of the church; but in the most essential point—salvation to all who repent and believe—the union was perfect.

George Morrill (?—1843)

This Elder was a young man, with a wife and one child, at the time of his death, December 22, 1843. In 1839, he became a member of the Rockingham Conference, at York, Me. In 1843, he had moved to Hope, N.J., in order to take the pastoral charge of some of the surrounding churches. But death came before he had really begun the work, and he departed in the triumph of faith.

Obadiah E. Morrill (?—?)

Obadiah E. Morrill began to preach about 1816, and moved to New York about the same time. He remained in that state until his death, and was one of the most useful and talented ministers in the state. The first years in New York were spent at Cato, from which place he wrote several very able letters. He did not write much for the papers before 1838, but after that time, he wrote frequently, some years, writing for nearly every number. These letters were full of interest, some of them relating to the progress of the Christian Church, and its increase in the different places where he had traveled; others are on different doctrinal points, showing him to be a deep thinker and an earnest searcher after truth. In 1842, he was elected to the position of Chaplain of the State Penitentiary at

Auburn, N.Y., one that he was well able to fill, not more from his talent than his deep sympathy and unostentatious piety.

After leaving Auburn, he took charge of the Second Christian Church in New Bedford, Mass., where he remained until 1846, when he removed to Portsmouth, N.H., becoming a minister at large under the patronage of some wealthy persons in that city. In 1851, he lived in Finsville, N.J., and in 1856, in Plainville, N.Y. He was a member of the Executive Committee of the Publishing Association of New York. His name was on the record of the New York Central Conference as late as 1862. He continued to take a leading part in the enterprises of the church to the last.

In person, the Elder was tall and dignified, with a keen eye and very intelligent countenance. He was sociable, and able to please any number of auditors. His attachment to friends and relatives was very strong. The Christian Church and its ministers were subjects of which he never tired, having, as he did, such an interest in the welfare of both. He was truly a denominational man, holding that the interest of his own church was always of the greatest importance, although he was very liberal and pleasant in his relations with other churches. In an argument, he displayed not only his reasoning powers, but wit and appreciation of his opponent's powers; and, above all, a kind and gentlemanly spirit. It is a wonder that, with all my inquiries, I could obtain no connected history of Elder Morrill. In 1823, he made an extensive tour, in company with Elder Millard, to Virginia, by sea. During the journey, he preached several able sermons, not only in the. churches but also in the seaport towns and on the vessel.

<u>PETER MORRIS (1795—1835)</u>

Peter was born in 1795, and died October 9, 1835. He was one of the early Christian ministers.

<u>ROBERT W. MORRIS (1831—1864)</u>

Robert was born in 1831, and spent the greater part of his life in Tipton County, Ind. He joined the Miami Reserve Christian Conference in 1858, and was ordained the year following. He labored faithfully within the bounds of this Conference until death, and his work was greatly blessed. He died in Tipton County, Ind., September 30, 1864.

SYLVESTER MORRIS (1775—1865)

This Elder was born in Wilbraham, Mass., in 1775, but moved to New York in 1796, where he was married in 1797. He was converted in Watertown, N.Y., in 1807, and united with the Methodists, although differing with them in several doctrinal points. He also began to preach while among them, but in 1814, left them, and after his removal to Victor, Ontario County, N.Y., he, with a number of brethren, worshipped agreeable to the views of the Christians, but no church was formed, and on his removal to Henrietta, Monroe County, he labored on the same platform as before, and organized a church, although they, as yet, knew of no such body as the Christians. Elders Shaw and Badger visited them some time afterward and informed them of the Christian denomination, when they united themselves formally with the church. He joined the New York Central Christian Conference in 1841, and continued a member of that body until his death at Conesus, Livingstone County, April 9, 1865, in the ninetieth year of his age.

SYLVESTER MORRIS (?—1876)

Sylvester Morris, a son of the preceding, was a member of the New York Central Conference, and died the year preceding the annual session of that body, June, 1877.

T. MORRIS (?—?)

T. Morris is mentioned by Elder Joseph Thomas in his travels through Virginia, as an aged man in 1810.

ASA C. MORRISON (1797—1848)

Asa was born in Sanbornton, N.H., July 8, 1797, was converted in 1809, and commenced preaching at twenty-two but was not ordained until two years after. He devoted his time, talents, and all wholly to his calling, and in the early part of his ministry, traveled extensively. Soon after entering upon his new duties, he left New Hampshire and went to the western part of New York, where he was ordained, from there to Canada, where he was very successful. From there he went to Pennsylvania, then to Ohio, laboring with all his energies wherever he went and his work was greatly blessed. But his constitution, though naturally strong, could not stand such a strain, and his health failing him, he was obliged to limit his field of labor.

In 1838, he was chosen pastor of the church in Ogden, N.Y., and sustained this relationship for four years. Here he lost his wife, with whom he had lived happily for thirteen years. This great loss so affected him that he yielded to the wishes of his friends and returned with his daughters to New Hampshire, leaving a community strongly attached to him, and full of regret at his departure. He spent about five years in New Hampshire and Massachusetts, and while in this part of the country, married again, thus securing a companion who was a source of great comfort to him in his declining years, by her kindness and deep piety. In 1847, he returned to New York with his family and settled in Parma, where he remained until his death, May 1, 1848. Here belabored with great success, for while his health was failing slowly, the church was becoming strengthened and many additions were made during his pastorate.

As a minister of the gospel, the Elder occupied a high standing. He possessed a clear mind and sound judgment. His preaching was full of scriptural references, and his reliance strongly on the present, direct influence of the spirit to give success to his labors. He was liberal and generous in his actions toward all sects, and for those who were out of the church, his heart seemed to yearn, his work manifesting in a great degree by its ardor, his great interest in their salvation.

? MORROW (?—?)

Morrow was a minister in Kentucky, and died many years ago.

CALEB MORSE, SR (1795—1872)

A minister of the above name was born in Rhode Island, May 5, 1795, and was married to Huldah Arnold in 1815. He was converted about the same time, under the labors of Elder Douglas Farnham, and in 1817, was set apart for the work of the ministry by the same preacher, in connection with others. About 1820, he moved to the Darby Plains, and settled near Irwin Station, where he remained until his death, in 1872.

CALEB MORSE, JR (1824—1869)

This Elder was a son of the preceding. He was born on the Darby Plains, September 4, 1824. He was brought up under the influence of the Christians, was converted early, began to preach in 1845, and was ordained in 1847. December 5, 1848, he was married to Chloe P. Wells, of Hartford, Licking County, O., with whom he lived happily till death. He died in Montgomery County, O., August 16, 1869, aged forty-four years, eleven months, and twelve days. Having successfully preached as a missionary for a few years, and feeling a desire to acquire more education, in September, 1852, he entered Antioch College as a student, and continued there until his graduation, in 1859. His pastorates, after leaving college, were Cincinnati, Ebenezer, Waterloo, Clark's Run, Antioch, Williamsport, Grassy Point, and Shiloh in all of these he succeeded well. During his time in college, he labored under many disadvantages, for at this time he supported himself and family, having charge of some churches during the whole time. But his studies did not end with his graduation—he read whenever opportunity offered. Thus an already varied and liberal stock of information was being continually enlarged. He was a prominent member of the Christian Publishing Association, and, as such, transacted the business of transferring the *Herald of Gospel Liberty* and the "Denominational Hymn Book" from New England to Ohio. In 1867, he accepted the traveling agency of the Ohio State Association, and devoted all his time to this work until his death, and for this purpose removed to Springfield, O.

As a minister and pastor, he had few superiors in the pulpit or in any of the many qualities which constitute an able, acceptable, and successful ministry. His style of speaking was deliberate and clear, and as he progressed in his sermons, he grew animated and became so earnest that sinners felt, in spite of themselves, there was truth in all that had been said. His sermons were always filled with this earnestness, no matter what the size of the congregation or the surrounding circumstances were, he always felt that he was laboring for Christ, for the good of souls, and that he ought in no wise to slight his work. In revival work, he was very successful; being strong, he could endure the fatigue attending constant preaching. The earnestness and warmth that characterized his usual sermons seemed to be doubled when he saw the seeker praying or venturing from the ranks of the unconverted. There were very few who could withstand his powerful appeals, for he spared the feelings of none, but showed the teachings of Christ in the plainest manner. Hundreds there are in this state who refer to this brother as the instrument, under the blessing of God, by which they were brought to a knowledge of their perilous condition, and to a means of saving grace.

Elder Morse had gone to attend a meeting near Dayton, O., and while in the pulpit, not being well before, the fatal illness, of which he died, seized him and he died in a little more than a week after the first symptom appeared. From the church he was taken to the house of a brother, where he continued until death. His family was with him from the beginning.

JOTHAM MORSE (1792—1878)

Jotham was born in 1792, and died at West Shelby, N.Y., September 18, 1878. He moved to Orleans County, when the whole country was a forest, and was ordained in 1824. For sixty-five years, he was a faithful minister of the Word. He was entirely blind and greatly afflicted some time before he died.

<u>SQUIRE MORTON (1797—1867)</u>

This Elder was born in- 1797, and was converted under the labors of Elder Allen Huntley, the first minister of the Christian Church who- preached in Canada. Elder Morton was one among the first converts in Canada and joined the first church, which was organized near Lake Simco by Elder Huntley, in 1821. He bought a farm in 1835, near Union Street Christian Church, with which he united, and after his ordination in 1835, by Elders Henry, Spooner, and Smith, he became the pastor of this church, and continued this relation until death, March 3, 1867. He left behind a wife and nine children. He was highly esteemed and greatly beloved as a pastor, as his long pastorship will testify. His worth in preaching was his great knowledge of the Bible. In this he was perfectly at home. In this, also, he was a close reasoner of far more than ordinary ability. He has a daughter, Sister Jenny Thompson, who is an able minister of the same church at the present time (1880).

<u>CALEB MOSHER (?—?)</u>

This Elder was formerly from Galway, N.Y., and was baptized there by Elder Rider in 1842. In 1843, he settled with the churches in Sodus and Alton, Wayne County, where he also organized several churches in the same vicinity. After laboring in the latter place for three years, he moved to Vermont, Chautauqua County, N.Y. In 1855, he moved west, and settled with a new church at Sylvania, O., in the bounds of the South-eastern Michigan Christian Conference, where he died soon after.

<u>CALVIN MOSHER (?—?)</u>

Calvin Mosher was a minister who was brought up in New York, moved to Michigan, and died there.

<u>CHARLES MOSHER (?—1871)</u>

Charles Mosher was a. member of the South-eastern Christian Conference of Michigan, and died the year previous to its session in 1871.

<u>Edward H. Mosher (1816—1855)</u>

Edward was born in 1816, was converted and began to preach when young, and was ordained in 1841. He labored with much success at Marion, Cicero, and Greenville, N.Y., before 1846, when he took charge of the church at Royalton, the same state, where he continued until 1852. His health was always poor. On leaving Royalton, he moved within the bounds of the Erie Christian Conference, and labored for a short time as a missionary, but his health failing him, he gave up that work and moved to Jackson, Ind., where he died April 16, 1855, at the age of thirty-nine, leaving a wife and two children. Although his health was quite poor all through his ministry, he was very active and accomplished a great deal in the vineyard of the Lord.

<u>Edwin Mosher (?—?)</u>

Edwin Mosher was a minister in Michigan, and died in that state.

<u>Maxon Mosher (?—1852)</u>

Maxon Mosher was born and brought up in Galway, Saratoga County, N.Y. He was converted early in life, and was .set apart for the work of the ministry in 1820. He was a member of the New York Eastern Christian Conference, and in connection with Elder Rider, held the pastorate of the church at Galway from the time of his ordination until his death, which occurred about 1852. He was one of those quiet, steadfast men, who do no brilliant deeds by which they are remembered, but his memory will always be fresh in the minds of his parishioners at Galway, where his life was spent.

<u>Peter Mosher (?—?)</u>

Peter Mosher labored in Kentucky, and died there at the age of forty.

RICHARD MOSHER (?—1860)

Richard Mosher was brought up in Galway, N.Y., began to preach there in 1832, moved to Ballston in 1835, and continued there one year. In 1836, he labored in Charleston Four Corners, supplying for Elder John Ross, and 1841, he had charge of the churches at Hunterland and Reedsville, where he continued for several years. He died about 1860.

WILSON MOSHER (?—1876)

Wilson Mosher was a Christian minister, who died near Belding, Mich., about 1876. He had been laboring in and around Otsego, the same state, since 1847.

AVERY MOULTON (?—1829)

This brother was one of the pioneer ministers of Canada, and spent a long life in the ministry. Elder Joseph Badger was baptized by him, and the relation between them, for years, was like that of father and son. His life and ministry have been highly spoken of. He died at Stanstead, Lower Canada, July 14, 1829, at an advanced age.

T.C. MOULTON (?—1871)

T.C. Moulton was a native of Canada. In 1850, he entered the Meadville Theological School, and graduated with honor three years later. During his course of study, he preached very often and held a high position in the esteem of both teachers and students, both as a man of talent and of great moral worth. After his graduation, he preached a few years for a Congregational Church of liberal people, in Ashtabula County, O., but his life work was with the First Christian Church in New Bedford, Mass. During his connection with this large church, he not only performed the duties of pastor and preacher with satisfaction to all, but in the meantime, did much denominational work in the preparation of the "Denominational Hymn Book" for the press, writing for the different periodicals, etc. This constant and wearing labor for twelve years, however, shortened his life. Before leaving New Bedford, his nervous system gave away, and he lay at the point of death for some time; but his strong constitution and temperate habits, with the blessing of heaven, overcame the disease and he recovered in some degree. At this time, he received a call from the church at Franklin, where he nearly regained his health, and the future seemed brightening before him. In the summer of 1871, he accepted a call from the Yellow Springs Church, and had started to the place, when he became prostrated with his old disease, and quietly passed away in four or five days, leaving a wife and two children, with a whole denomination, to mourn his loss. He was a man of excellent character, and was beloved by all.

JAMES MOULTRY (1766—1828)

James was born in North Carolina in 1766, was baptized, and joined the Baptist Church in 1804, in which body he began to preach, and was ordained in the same connection. In 1809, he moved to Indiana, and settled in Salem, on the Wabash, and was pastor of the church there for some time. When the Christian ministers came to that place, he invited them to his house and opened the doors of the church to them, for which he was tried and expelled from the Baptist Church in 1814. He then united with the Christian Church, devoting all his time and energies to the spread of the faith, and was the means of accomplishing a great amount of work. His manners and address was plain and unaffected, and his piety and usefulness universally acknowledged. His excessive labor brought on a pulmonary disease, which prevented his preaching for several months before his death, September 21, 1828.

DAVID MUDGE (1748—1841)

This Elder was born in 1748, was preaching near South Waterloo, N.Y., in 1809, and died near Elmira, the same state, in September, 1841, aged ninety-three years.

Larkin Mullen (1813—1865)

The subject of this sketch was born in Licking County, Ky., August 7, 1813, moved to Indiana in 1819, was married to Martha Beard February 4, 1834, being converted, was baptized by Elder John Hull February 4, 1841, and joined the Bluffton Conference, Ind., soon after. He was a man of far more than ordinary talent as a speaker, especially in revival meetings, where hundreds were converted under his labors. His education was limited and his support scant, hence he followed his trade of blacksmithing, and never devoted his whole time to the ministry. His labors were confined mostly to Randolph and adjoining counties in Ohio and Indiana. He died at his home in Randolph County, October 11, 1865. As a revivalist, he had few equals, scores being added to the churches by conversion where he preached during many of his protracted meetings.

Samuel Mulner (?—1858)

This minister was converted when nineteen years old, was ordained in 1845, and died in Huntington County, Ind., March 12, 1858.

William Munroe (?—1879)

William Munroe was a member of the Eastern Michigan Conference. He died about 1879.

Joseph Murray (?—?)

Joseph Murray died in North Carolina several years ago. He was a good man, and, on account of his great knowledge of the Scriptures, was called "The Walking Bible."

F.R. Muse (?—1879)

F.R. Muse died about 1879. He was a pioneer minister of the Kentucky Christian Conference.

JOHN MYERS (1791—1866)

This Elder was, for many years, a resident of Licking County, O., a member of the Sylvania Christian Church, and of the Mt. Vernon Conference. In 1844, he had been in the ministry but a few years, although he must have been, at that time, over sixty years old. "Uncle John," as he was called, was very zealous in the cause, and had become a useful preacher, feeling that no sacrifice was too great for such a glorious work.

He was a large man, with much of the German brogue, quite eccentric in his expressions, but always full of good sense. He generally had good congregations, and many date their conversion to his influence as an exhorter. He moved to Illinois between 1852 and died in that state in 1866, not far from seventy-five years of age.

NICHOLAS MYERS (1817—1867)

Our present subject was a native of Germany, and carried with him through life many of the ways of the Fatherland, speaking with a great deal of brogue to the last. He settled near Peru. Ind., and, in time, became quite wealthy After his conversion, he began to preach, and was ordained in the Tippecanoe Conference, in the business affairs of which he always took an active part. He was a trustee of Union Christian College from the first, and there were few who could give better counsel than he, or were better able to transact business. His death, which occurred at his home, near Peru, in 1867, at the age of fifty, was a great loss to the Christian cause in that part of the country.

CLEMENT NANCE (1757—1828)

Clement was born in Virginia, in 1757, joined the Methodist Church in 1776, and commenced preaching in 1782. He left that church and joined the party of O'Kelly in 1793. On moving to Kentucky, some years later, he joined the Christians in that state in their formation as a distinct body. He lived in the territory of Indiana as early as 1812, and at the time of his death, July 21, 1828, was a member oi the Indiana Central Conference. Elder Barton W.

Stone, speaking of his death in the *Christian Messenger,* gives him great praise, not only as a good man, but as a very useful and efficient minister. Elder Stone had been intimately acquainted with him for many years.

SAMUEL NASON (1818—1865)

Brother Nason was born May 9, 1818. Early in life, he learned the saddler's trade at Levant, Me., and became interested in religion by reading "Baxter's Call" and other books of the same nature. He joined the church, was baptized when fifteen years of age, and commenced preaching before he was twenty, being ordained two years later. About this time, he married a daughter of a Baptist minister,-Miss. Hannah Seavey, who died in 1863. They lived, for a time, at Stetson, but in 1839, moved to Albion. Here the Elder was very successful baptizing 100 persons soon after his arrival— some of whom became ministers. During all this time, he was working at his trade, sometimes going thirty miles to a night meeting. He labored at Bangor for some time, going from there to Penobscot and adjoining counties. After his wife's death, he took charge of the church at Green Point, N.Y., but when his health began to fail, he returned to Bangor, where he died, July 3, 1865. He willed $2,300 of his property to the Christian Church in Maine.

W.H. NASON (1804—1877)

Elder Nason, an elder brother of the preceding, was born at Sanford, York County, Me., June 3, 1804, received a common school education, was converted in 1814, and in 1825, was baptized by his uncle, Elder Henry Frost, when he joined the Second Christian Church in Monmouth, the same state. Soon after, he began to preach, but became discouraged with his success and abandoned the work, in a measure, for five years, but finally, after having lost two sons, one by drowning, which the father considered a divine visitation for not doing his duty, he entered the work with new vigor, was ordained in 1842, and continued faithful until death, doing much for the advancement of the cause in his fields of labor.

He labored as pastor in East Newport, Me., Rye, West Springfield, Walborough, Newton, Sanbornton, Colebrook, Columbia, Andover, Marlow, and Mason, N.H., and West Mansfield, Mass. He died in West Springfield, N.H., March 28, 1877.

Elder Nason was a decidedly pious man. He held views on the subject of Sanctification that differed, in some degree, from the majority of his brethren of the Christian Church, and it grieved him sometimes that others did not see as clearly as himself, that Christ made his disciples free from all sin. He was a frequent contributor for our periodicals, and his articles always bore the mark of deep piety. In his last illness, he suffered much, but his mind was calm under the affliction, for he realized that he was in the hand of a loving Father. He occupied a prominent position in his field of labor for about forty years, and for twenty-five years of this time, he was Secretary of the Merrimac Conference, New Hampshire. He was more noted for deep piety and zeal than for intellectual greatness.

JOSEPH NESMITH (?—?)

Joseph Nesmith was born in Virginia, in which state he labored and died.

B. NEWHOUSE (?—1867)

B. Newhouse was a member of the Bluffton Conference, Ind. He died about 1867.

JABEZ NEWLAND (1785—?)

This minister was born about 1785, and had lived and preached in Lower Canada before he moved to Hyde Park, Vt., where he labored for many years. He was a plain, moderate preacher, and limited in education. He carried on a farm as a means of support.

F.R. NEUSE (?—1879)

F.R. Neuse was a prominent minister of the Kentucky Christian Conference. He lived at Plummer's Landing, Ky., and died May 23, 1879.

J.P. NICHOLSON (?—1878)

J.P. Nicholson was a member of the New York Southern Conference. He died about 1878.

WILLIAM NOBLES (1809—1874)

William was born in Herkimer County, N.Y., March 11, 1809, moved to Canada in 1822, embraced religion and was baptized by John F. Baily in 1826, and became one of the seven chartered members of the Haldeman Christian Church. He commenced preaching in 1829, and after traveling as an evangelist a year or two, he settled as pastor with the Haldeman Church, which position he occupied about thirty years, until failing health compelled him to resign. He died in Hope, Mich., February 25, 1874.

Elder Nobles was not a fluent speaker, but he possessed a sound mind, a fair education, and a very extensive knowledge, both of sacred and secular history, which he obtained by extensive reading that made him quite interesting, both in public speaking and private conversation. He published the first religious periodical that was ever issued in Canada. He spent the latter part of his life in Michigan, though not in the regular work, on account of poor health, yet doing much on funeral occasions, Sunday-schools, and such work, where he was very useful.

MARK NORRIS (1768—1832)

Our present subject was born in 1768, and died in Hartwick, Vt., May 12, 1832. He was one of the first settlers of that place. He professed religion in the Christian Church. He was an able worker, and was the means of doing much good.

BOWMAN NORTH (1809—1839)

This brother was born in 1809, and was ordained in 1836. He had just entered upon the duties of pastor of the church at Clinton, Me., when he died, June 3, 1839.

SAMUEL NUTT (1784—1872)

This Elder was born in 1784. He entered upon the work of the ministry when quite young, and for a great many years, was one of the most energetic of the ministers of the time. He traveled extensively in different parts of the United States and one of the Provinces of Canada, and was truly called a "pilgrim and a stranger." In 1842, he lived in Troy, Me., but his last charge was in Franklin, N.H., where he died September 18, 1872, aged eighty- seven years, having been for some time superannuated on account of age and infirmity. He began to preach in the Baptist Church, but in 1806, he joined the Christians, and from this time forward, his labor was not confined to any one place or state. Wherever he went, from Maine to Ohio, reformation followed reformation. He baptized about three thousand converts, but the number converted under his labor was much larger. He was one of those ministers well known in all parts of the country, on account of his travels, success, and the long time he continued in the ministry, but for the lack of a biographer, we have but detached sketches of his life and labor.

JOHN NUTTEK (1790—1872)

This Elder was born in N.H., in 1790, and began to preach in 1828. He spent a long and useful life in the ministry, and died at North Barn- stead, N.H., July 11, 1872.

JAMES O'KELLY (1753—1829)

Although James O'Kelly was the first man in America to plead tor the principles of the Christian Church as it now stands, and although his name is one familiar to the members of every Christian family, yet in all my searching, I have not been able to find a full biography of this great man. It is probable that he was born in

1753, and therefore about seventy-six years old at the time of his death in 1829, and was about forty years old when he opposed the Episcopizing of the Methodist Church. He was converted, and became a leading minister among the Methodists of Virginia. After the close of the Revolutionary War, when the Methodists of America had separated from their brethren in England, John Wesley wrote from Bristol, England, September 10, 1784, to Dr. Coke, Francis Asbury, and others, advising them how to proceed in the future. Asbury and Coke desired to Episcopize the church in America, and made an announcement to that effect in the conference; and for the purpose of deciding the matter, a General Conference was called to meet in Baltimore in 1792. Preparatory to this meeting, James O'Kelly, too, had been studying concerning this subject, and came to the conclusion that the Bible was sufficient as a standard of faith. During the discussion, he arose with the Bible in his hand, and cried out, "Brethren, hearken unto me. Put away all other books and forms, and let this (holding up the New Testament) be the only criterion, and that will satisfy me." This, with other propositions of the same nature, was bitterly opposed by many, and the majority voted against him, Francis Asbury was made Bishop, the first in the Methodist Church, and James O'Kelly, with about one thousand others, left the body and organized the Christian Church. They called themselves at first, "Radical Methodists," but the name Christian was soon proposed by Rice Haggard, and adopted by the entire body. It is said that Elder O'Kelly ruled the body, which was soon numbered by its thousands, by his personal presence and talent, as completely as Francis Asbury ruled the Methodist Episcopal Church. This could not last, however, for in 1809, Elder O'Kelly taught that baptism by sprinkling should be the rule in the new church, to the exclusion of all other modes. This was in consequence, likely, that many of the members, untrammeled by creeds, had begun the practice of immersion. This proposition of Elder O'Kelly was not received very cordially by the majority, although many adopted it, and thence arose a division that lasted some time.

Elder O'Kelly was a strong believer in sprinkling, and that Christ, in his divine nature, was God, but denied the doctrine of the Trinity. He impressed his views to a great extent on the body called for some time, by his name, as O'Kellyites. In a free, untrammeled church, however, it is impossible for any one man, however strong, to rule a body long. The Elder soon learned that. In a conference, where the subject of baptism was discussed, and being strongly opposed, he asked William Guirey, who was one of the strongest of the opposers, "Who rules this body, you or I?" The quick response was, "Neither of us, brother, Christ rules here."

In the Methodist Church, James O'Kelly stood as high as either Asbury or Coke, being a Presiding Elder, the highest office in the original Wesleyan Church, and hence when he opposed these brethren in conference on the question of the appointment of Bishop, it was "Greek meeting Greek." Beside the quality of strength and boldness, however, Elder O'Kelly had other traits that we love better to dwell upon. He was a pure, good and holy man, to the day of his death, and even to the present time, the name of this good man is held with peculiar veneration by thousands of his fellow church members. Meeting houses and other things of sacred association are named after him. He was a writer of considerable ability. The following are some of the works he published: "Annotation on his book of Discipline," 1809, "Apology for Rejecting Episcopacy" 1802, "Vindication of the Author's Apology with reflections on the reply and remarks of Bishop Asbury," "The Divine Oracles Consulted, or an Appeal to the Law and Testimony," 1820, "Church Government," in which he opposed American Slavery.[12] There are several other works of his, whose titles I have not.

The following, from the pen of Brother J.D. Gunter, of the North Carolina University, although a repetition of some of the items in the above, is so full and to the point, that I insert it here: "James O'Kelly was born, brought up, and educated in Virginia. He was a

---

[12] "Church Government" and "Annotation on his book of Discipline" are not titles of O'Kelly works, but sections in other works. One of his works was entitled "An Essay on Negro Slavery."—*Editor.*

classmate of Thomas Jefferson and Patrick Henry. He was a member of the Methodist Episcopal Church, was one of the leading divines in the Virginia Conference, and was strongly in favor of an injured preacher; i.e., one appointed to a weak circuit by the Bishop, and that the preacher should have the right to appeal to the conference from such an appointment, and it was argued in such a masterly manner that no one in the conference could meet his argument, whereupon the Bishop, in an abrupt manner, said it should not be allowed. Then it was that Mr. O'Kelly picked up his hat and left the conference, and was followed by fifteen or twenty other ministers, among whom was Mr. McKendra, who went back to the conference, was made Bishop, and settled in the West. When Mr. O'Kelly's death was announced to him, he was silent for a time and exclaimed: 'A great man in Israel has fallen.' Mr. O'Kelly spent a day in Washington, while Congress was in session. He went to the Capitol to see his friends, Jefferson and Henry, who were to speak the next day. Mr. Jefferson told O'Kelly that after the speaking, he must preach. He tried to excuse himself, but his two friends would have no excuse, so he consented. The next day, the speaking being over, Mr. Jefferson moved an adjournment to give Rev. Mr. O'Kelly an opportunity to preach. Congress was adjourned, and he preached one of his best sermons to the Congress of the United States, in the Capitol. After the sermon, Mr. Jefferson arose with tears in his eyes and said he was no preacher, but he believed that James O'Kelly was one of the greatest divines living.

After Mr. O'Kelly left the Methodist Church, he became a leader and. established the Christian Church, then moved to Chatham County, North Carolina. Colonel H.B. Guthrie, from whom this information is received, says he heard a very eminent divine of the Presbyterian Church say, that Mr. O'Kelly preached to five different congregations in one day, and there was no sameness in one of the sermons—all different. Mr. O'Kelly was a strong advocate of infant baptism, was virtually opposed to immersion, and would not baptize by immersion. He was a man of deep piety. He breathed his last near O'Kelly's Chapel, in Chatham County, N.C., in the midst of his children, grand-children, and friends, and was buried at the church which bears his name. He is quietly waiting for the resurrection morn."

As Jones and Smith in the East, Stone and Purviance in the West, so O'Kelly, Haggard, Guirey, and others stood up for the Bible alone in the South. Each party left its impress upon its own section. The brethren in the East, to this day, show more or less of Baptist proclivities, those in the West have many Presbyterian features, and those in the South very much of the Methodist tendency. O'Kelly exerted a greater influence during his life than any one man in the section where the Christians took their rise. Either he was an abler man than his comrades, or more positive, or his previous leadership in the Methodist Church gave him a superiority that continued for many years. There can be no doubt as to his talent or his goodness—all agree to give him these traits. In his position of opposition to Episcopacy in the Methodist Church, he had the strong backing of John Wesley, the father of Methodists, and all the denomination in England. No one in that day opposed Episcopacy in the Wesleyan Church more than John Wesley. The pungent letter written by the leader of the body in England to his brother, Francis Asbury, the leader of the same body in America, is well known. Calling Asbury by his given name, as was customary with the early Methodists, "Francis," says the great John Wesley, "call me thief, scoundrel, or anything else, but for the cause's sake call me not Bishop," etc. But when O'Kelly began to examine the nature of church government for himself, he went beyond the liberality of the Wesleys; for he not only saw the great injury that the ministerial class had done, but also the injury, creeds, Und forms, in binding peoples' minds to religion; but such was the nature of the tithes, that he, who fought so manfully against the tyranny of others, was not willing to allow his brethren to be baptized by immersion; yet with these few and small inconsistencies, which were owing more to the times and circumstances than to himself, Elder O'Kelly was a good and great man.

ABEL OLIVE (?—?)

Abel Olive was a native of North Carolina, living in Wake County. He moved to the West in 1807. and died there before 1826. He was a contemporary of James O'Kelly and the dissenters from the Methodist in 1793.

JOHN ORCOTT (1796—1846)

This Elder was a member of the Vermont Conference, and his principal field of labor was within its bounds, although he preached in New York for a year or more. But he moved back to Vermont, where he died in 1846, when about fifty years of age. He was a farmer, but he faithfully performed his pastoral duties; and although he did not travel extensively, yet he did good work wherever he labored.

JOHN ORRELL (1820—1876)

As I sit here, writing a short biography of my intimate friend and school-mate, tears come unbidden to my eyes when I remember the many happy seasons we spent together in talking about our early lives in the old country. Brother Orrell had more than ordinary gifts in conversation, and he especially delighted to talk over his life and adventures in the cotton mills of England and Pennsylvania. The remembrance of these enables me to record a part of his adventurous career.

He was born in Bolton, Lancastershire, England, about 1820. He continued to live in that city, working in the cotton mills from early life. After working at his trade till his majority, as he had some relations in America, the young man decided to try his fortunes in the new world. After tramping for a while in search of work, he found employment at Gulf Mills, and under the preaching of Godfrey Hawk, joined the Christian Church. It was soon observed that the factory boy had more than ordinary gift as a speaker in social meetings, and his zeal was commensurate with his talent. He attended Dr. Robertson's school in Philadelphia. Under the tuition of the good Scotchman, who, also, as a rarity, was a zealous member of the Christian Church, Orrell grew in knowledge and zeal with great rapidity. Through the influence of Dr. Robertson and others, be was induced to apply for admission to the Meadville Theological School. He entered the school in 1846, and continued there four years. As his knowledge in the common branches was limited, and as the writer of these lines had been in the institution one year,- it was his privilege to become a voluntary, teacher and director of the new student; and a better pupil than John Orrell no one ever had. He at once grew in knowledge. During his first year, he read "Rollin's Ancient History," "Gibbon's Rome," and "Hallam's Middle Ages," with many other works, beside mastering the studies of the year equal to the best student in the class.

In 1850, he graduated in the four years course, and after "candidating" a while in the Middle States and in the West, he settled in Providence, R.I., with the Sailors' Bethel Church. From there, he took charge of a church in New Bedford, where he became acquainted with our excellent brother, Crapo, who was afterward elected Governor of the State of Michigan. Elder Orrell married a daughter of Brother Crapo. His last regular work was as teacher and preacher of the Freedmen of the South during, and perhaps after, the war of the Rebellion. He finally settled down in Flint, Mich., being engaged in the lumber business with some members of the Crapo family. He died in Flint, in 1876.

Few of the students of Meadville possessed better talent than Orrell. He had a fine delivery, with a slight English accent. He was quick with the pen, and his composition was deep, easy, and sprightly. In our correspondence, in later years, when deploring his absence from the active ministry, he always acknowledged his interest in the work of preaching the gospel. After an intimate acquaintance of many years, I consider Elder John Orrell a good and able man. He left a wife and several children to mourn their great loss.

JOHN ORTON (?—?)

John Orton was a native of North Carolina but spent a great part of his life in Tennessee. He was converted in the Methodist Church, but joined the Christians, and was baptized by Elder John Miller in 1807. He could not read and was very ignorant of everything except the Bible. His ministry was chiefly spent in going from one place to another, starting great revivals. It is said that he returned to the Methodists, but nothing definite is known of his later days.

JOHN OSBURN (1769—1832)

This brother was a prominent minister as early as 1810, as in that year, he baptized Elder Israel Chesley, two years later, performed his marriage ceremony, and four years after this, preached his ordination -sermon. Elder Osburn was converted in the Congregational Church, and was educated for the ministry of the same. He •continued a prominent minister of that church for many years. During the war of 1812, he gave up his state pay, to which he was entitled as a minister, because of the hardness of the time. Several years before he died, he became a teetotaler—a strange thing for a minister in that day. His principal field of labor was in New Durham and Lee, N.H. In 1829, he held a great revival in Exeter, N.H., and organized a church of over forty members. His last charge was in Lee, where he died in 1832.

WHEELER OVIATT (1797—1879)

This brother was born in Milford, Conn., in 1797, and died in Oregon, Lapeer County, Mich., January 20, 1879. In 1820, he was married to Miss Rhoda Cornish at Oil Creek, Penn., and was converted the same year. In 1824, he moved to Royalton, N.Y., and joined the Christian Church under the labors of Elder Joseph Badger. Sometime after, he was ordained to the Christian ministry at Cambria, N.Y., and traveled extensively through the Eastern States and Canada. He moved to Michigan in 1854, and settled in Lapeer

County, where he labored faithfully till within one year of his death.

George Owens (1794—1855)

This minister was of Welsh descent. He was born in Virginia, October 27, 1794. His mother died in 1806, and in the same year, he moved to Xenia, O., to the home of Mrs. Harris, a married sister, and was married to Deborah Marsh May 11, 1811. September 8, 1825, his wife died. They had two children, but both died while young. June 8, 1826, he married Malinda Boiles, who survived him, and of whom he had three children. He was converted in the old Baptist Church soon after his first marriage, and commenced preaching in the same church about 1822. He joined the Christian Church about 1829, through the influence of Elder Nathan Worley, and joined the Miami Conference. He labored extensively through the bounds of that conference, though mostly in Greene County. He died December 26, 1855, aged seventy-one years. He received but little for preaching, and in early life, was opposed to the pay system. He acquired a large property, though he devoted one-third of his time to his pastoral duties. His knowledge was quite limited when he began his ministerial work, but, by diligence, he became well informed in the Scriptures. He attended the school of Mr. Steele, in Xenia, three miles away, when he had the care of a church, a family, and a farm.

Benjamin Page (?—?)

Benjamin Page at one time had charge of the church at Calais, Vt. He died many years ago.

George Palcher (?—1834)

George Palcher was a resident of Maine. He died at Saco about 1834.

Bennet Palmer (?—1851)

Bennet Palmer was converted at Calais, Vt., in 1823, and commenced preaching in 1829. He was in Washington, N.H., in 1859, and at this time he favored the doctrine of the final restoration of the wicked, but in a year or more he returned fully to the doctrine of the Christians on that subject. In 1840, he was elected to the New Hampshire Legislature from Marlow, and the next year found him in Springfield, the same state, where he remained until 1846, when he moved back to Calais, Vt., where he held the pastorate of the church until death, about 1850 or '51.

Elder Palmer was a tall, fine-looking man, a ready speaker, possessing fine talents, and always considered one of the first- class ministers of the Vermont Conference,

Ezekiel Palmer (?—?)

Ezekiel Palmer was converted and began to preach among the United Baptists; but about 1824, he united with the Christians, and began to labor earnestly in the central part of Ohio. In 1826. he moved to Steubenville, where he was very successful; fifty or more were converted in a short time, and a strong church was soon organized there. He traveled with Elder Long for the first three years after uniting with the Christians. After his removal to Steubenville, he and Elder Secrist were co-laborers together for some time. While in this place, he began the study of medicine, and practiced this profession ever after, preaching when opportunity offered. After finishing the study of medicine at Steubenville, he moved to Licking County, where he died very suddenly of apoplexy.

The Elder's talents were of a high order, and during the early part of his ministry, he devoted all his time and energy to the work.

H.D. Palmer (?—?)

H.D. Palmer, while a young man, was a co-worker in the ministry with Elder Kinkade and others. His labors were greatly blessed, and good results followed. He lived in Kentucky for some time, working energetically through the south ern part of the state. He removed to Illinois, where he remained until his death.

BELA PALMER (?—?)

Bela Palmer was a Vermont minister that was very successful in revivals. After traveling extensively in Vermont, he died in the State of New York some years ago.

WILBER PALMER (1792—1877)

This brother was a member of the Erie Conference for many years. His home, in the latter part of his life, was in Sherman, Chautauqua County, N.Y. He was born in 1792, and died in Sherman, N.Y., January 1, 1877. His preaching talent was not great, but his goodness and zeal in the cause, enabled him to fill a useful position in the master's service.

LEVI PARKER (1791—1827)

Levi was a native of Kentucky, in which state he died May 28, 1827.

LYNDON PARKER (1802—1840)

This Elder was converted when very young, and was baptized by Elder James Burlingame in Foster, R.I., where he was born in 1802. He soon moved to Cortland County, N.Y., where he began to preach in 1829, in the midst of a great reformation, both in that place and adjoining counties. During this time, he was not connected with any church as there was none of his early choice near him, but in 1831, he assisted Elders Ambrose Burlingame, and David and Ebenezer Wade in organizing a Christian Church in Lapeer, Cortland County, N.Y., of which he became a member. In the same year, also, he was married to Miss Anna Sexton. From this time forward, all of his energies were devoted to the work. He joined the Central New York Conference in 1833, but was not regularly ordained till 1837. He was a zealous, successful worker and an active member until his death, July 5, 1840.

SILAS PARKS (1806—1857)

This Elder was born in Butler County, O., in 1806, but was raised in Preble County, where he was married in 1828 to Miss Sarah Frame. He was converted, and joined the Freewill Baptist Church, but stifling his conviction, that it was his duty to preach, he lost all his interest. He moved to Grant County, Ind., where he was re-converted under the labors of Elder Hallet Barber, soon after began to preach, and was ordained in the Bluffton Indiana Conference. He continued an active member of this body until his death, October 27, 1857.

STEVEN PARNELL (1820—1844)

Steven was called away in the commencement of what he had hoped would be his life work, and when there seemed to be so much usefulness in store for him. He was converted in 1842, and commenced preaching at once in Parnell, Laporte County, Ind. He was married in May, and joined the Laporte Indiana Conference June, 1844, and was accidently killed just ten days after, June 18, 1844.

EDWARD PEAVY (1788—1856)

This preacher was an elder brother of the following, although his junior in the ministry. He was born in Farmington, N.H., February 13, 1788, was married twice, the first time in 1814, and the next time in 1834. This latter union continued until his death, in Exeter, N.H., June 22, 1856, at the age of sixty-eight years.

He became concerned about his spiritual welfare very early in life, and continued under conviction, more or less from the age of seven until about the age of twenty-six. He began to preach in his native place in 1818, at the age of thirty, and was ordained four years later in the State of New York. He was a man of great zeal for the work, and faith in its ultimate success, and like many of the New England ministers of his time, was influenced to a great extent by the impressions made upon his mind, as he felt, by the spirit of God. His sole object in life was the salvation of sinners, and while in the active work of revival or reformation he was happy, but when away from the excitement and influence of the meeting, he was often miserable. He began his ministerial career at home and labored there for some time, but from 1818 to 1823, the greater part of his time was spent in New York, three hundred miles from his family. He often spent from six to nine months in a continued revival, preaching as often as once, and sometimes twice, a day during the whole time. One of these long and glorious revivals was held in Laurence, Otsego County, N.Y., and the other in Dutchess County, both resulting in the strengthening of the churches in the surrounding country, by the addition of great numbers. While on his way to New York at one time, he met a young woman, and immediately became impressed that it was his duty to ask her if she loved Christ. He did this, and on her returning an answer in the negative, he rode on and nothing was said by either party, but a year later, as he was passing through the same section of country, he heard of a great revival going on in the neighborhood. He visited the place and found that it had been started by this woman to whom he had spoken in reference to her love for Christ, and that she had been converted and was now earnestly at work for the salvation of others. He wrote a long and very interesting autobiography, giving a detached account of his work for many years. Had it been published at the time, it would have thrown a great light on the work in his field of labor, in New Hampshire and New York.

JOHN L. PEAVY (1793—1829)

Few men have stood higher in the estimation of the brotherhood than Elder Peavy. He was the son of Captain Anthony Peavy, was born in Farmington, N.H., in 1793, was converted when quite young, and soon uniting with the Christian Church, commenced preaching and was ordained, March 28, 1816. In the same year, in company with Elder Shaw, he left New England and went to New York, where he remained, laboring constantly, until his death, nearly thirteen years later, and his labors were blessed in the conversion of hundreds of souls. When he began to labor in the eastern part of New York, he was not only young in the ministry, but young in years, and full of enthusiasm for his chosen calling. No weather was too disagreeable, no opposition too strong, but that he was always at his post, and no matter what the call of duty was, he was ready to obey. His family were all interested in the religious work. His father and mother were active members of the Christian Church in New Hampshire. His brother Edward was a minister of some prominence in the same church. One of his sisters had married Elder Joseph Badger, and another, who was herself a public speaker, was the wife of Elder Frederick Cogswell, all active workers ill the church.

He died at Milan, N.Y., June 9, 1829, at the age of thirty-six years, while in the midst of a great field of labor and when the harvest was great, but the laborers few. His death was hastened by the arduous labor he was called upon to perform; for in those days, the manner of conducting religious services was more laborious than now, protracted and general meetings were held through all seasons of the year, and additions to the church were expected at every meeting. He v as a great revivalist, and the people were always ready to hear his defense of the new faith, although he was violently opposed by the different sects in some parts where he did the most successful work.

<u>Benjamin Peckham (1753—1836)</u>

This brother was born in 1753, and was converted, uniting with the Baptists about 1783. He commenced preaching among that people in 1788, but was pastor of the Christian Church at Tiverton, R.I., for thirty-five years. We have no certain account of the time when he united with-the Christian denomination, but all his latter years were spent in that church. He was a man of great moral worth, and a good, useful preacher, his greatest good being accomplished by his successful pastorate. His most prominent characteristic was his desire for peace between all men and God. He died where he had lived for so many years as a beloved pastor, at Tiverton, R.I., March 13, 1836y at the advanced age of eighty-three.

ORSON PEMBERTON (1808—1876)

Orson was born in Richmond, Ontario County, N.Y., June 16, 1808, and died in Tioga County, Penn., February 15, 1876. He became an orphan at the age of ten years, and two years later, he moved to Tioga County, Penn., where he continued the most of his long life. He embraced religion and became a minister in the Methodist Church, but later in life, he joined the Christians. One of his sons became a minister and labored in the West, and one of his daughters married Elder Kilbourne. Elder Pemberton was a good man, an able preacher, and an excellent singer.

JOSHUA PERKINS (?—1842)

This minister was a native of Sterling, Conn., and was ordained in that place, June 3, 1816, by a conference of Elders, consisting of Mark Fernald, Ward Lock, Asa Foster, Levi Hathaway, Joseph Badger, and others. Elder N. Burlingame was ordained also at the same time. He died in his native place, in June 1842. He was not known extensively through the denomination, his labors being confined chiefly to his native place, where he was well respected, both for his consistent life and his successful ministry.

RANSOM PERKINS (?—?)

Ransom Perkins was an uncle of the preceding, and was also a native of Sterling, Conn., where he spent a useful life, and finally died in the triumph of a living faith. He was ordained at Coventry, R.I., in 1813, by Elders Hicks, Smith, Hathaway, Colby, and Farnum.

WILLIAM PERRY (1811—1876)

William was born in Schenectady, N.Y., March 24, 1811, commenced preaching in 1846, was baptized by Elder Seldon in Alleghany County, N.Y., and ordained soon after. He moved to

Michigan and was pastor of Vergenes and other churches in that state. He was a good preacher and a very conscientious man. He died at Lowell, Mich., June 8, 1876.

SIMON PETTERSON (1796—1837)

This preacher was a member of the Northern New York Conference. When young, he lost the greater part of his left hand, and in "consequence of an injury, was compelled to have it amputated a year previous to his death. He died in Hermon, N.Y., July 20, 1837, at the age of forty-one years, from the effect of a cancer in the hand. He had never devoted his whole time to the ministry but had been the means of strengthening many churches by revivals, in which he was very successful.

HIRAM PETTEYS (1805—1864)

Hiram was born in Montgomery County, N.Y., in 1805, was converted, united with the Christian Church in 1840, commenced preaching soon after, and was ordained at Camden, N.Y., in 1843. He moved to Wisconsin, where he labored for some time, and then to Illinois. He died at Annawan, Henry County, Ill., August 2, 1864, in the fifty-ninth year of his age.

JOHN T. PETTEYS (?—?)

John T. Petteys was raised in Chatham County, N.C. He labored in that and surrounding counties for some years, with good results. He moved to the State of Mississippi, where he died after a faithful ministerial work. He is said to have been a devoted man.

SENECA PETTEYS (1806—1845)

Seneca was born in 1806, commenced preaching when about thirty years of age, and was ordained about three years later. He continued a faithful and devoted minister in the cause till his death, which occurred at Corunna, Shiawassee County, Mich., in the thirty-ninth year of his age.

<u>William Petro (1826—1863)</u>

Our present subject was an earnest and devoted minister of the gospel, and although his ministerial career was short and full of obstacles— such as limited education, poverty, and a large family,— yet the course was well run and the results are lasting, great numbers dating their conversions to his earnest appeals. He commenced his ministry in the Western Indiana Conference about 1856, at the age of thirty, and was ordained September 24, 1859. His appointments were filled until about a week before his death. He died near Attica, Ind., February 17, 1863.

<u>Isaac Pettingill (?—?)</u>

Isaac Pettingill was a member of the Christian Brethren Church, but united with the Christians in Danville, Vt., where he spent most of his life, when that body became a part of the Christian Church. He long refused to preach, feeling that his talent was too feeble; but he was led to the calling of the ministry by a dream; i.e., He was told to water an orchard with a small cup, but after expressing his doubts as to whether he would be able to do so, he commenced, and soon watered a large orchard without refilling his cup. This he felt was an intimation from the divine spirit that he was to preach, and he soon after began the work of the ministry. He was a fluent and ready speaker, and would have made a successful minister but he was a poor financier, and was always hampered with his great poverty.

<u>Gideon Phebus (1817—1867)</u>

Gideon was born in 1817, and was converted at Williamsport, O., in 1835. Commencing his ministerial career soon after, he spent several years in earnest and laborious work. During this time, he was married twice. In 1849, he lost his health, and was compelled to give up his calling. He spent the last years of his life in Jackson County, where he died May 24, 1867.

<u>EPHRAIM PHILBRICK (?—1863)</u>

This Elder spent the greater part of his ministerial life in or about Rye, N.H., where he died in 1863. From Rye, he wrote many letters to the early papers. His writings were of a very practical nature, treating of the current subjects of the day, and expressed in language that is plain, familiar, and definite. From some of these letters, we find that he was converted in 1810, lived many years in Rye, and was ordained in 1826.

<u>IRA PHILLIPS (?—?)</u>

Ira Phillips was a New England minister. He was present and assisted at the ordination of Benjamin Taylor in 1811,

<u>JOHN PHILLIPS, SR (1811—1868)</u>

This Elder was born at Broadalbin, Fulton County, N.Y., September 13, 1811, of humble parentage. He died near Merom, Ind., September 18, 1868, aged fifty-seven years. The following is a synopsis of the various changes and removals of his life:

In 1826, he became an apprentice to the carpenter trade. In 1827, he was converted, and in 1830, joined the Christian Church at Union Mills, N.Y. In 1832, he entered the Kings- borough Academy, where he studied hard, living an abstemious life for the want of means, having begun to preach about the time he entered the school. He continued his connection with this school about three years. In 1835, he went to Mason, N.H., where he preached for some time, and the fall of the same year, he settled as pastor in Westport, Mass. He continued in the above place until 1837, and during the time, was united in marriage with Miss Gifford of that place, a young lady of excellent character and of good family. In the latter year, also, he moved to Ohio and settled with the Pisgah Church, in Brown County. After laboring in the southern part of Ohio two or three years, he returned to New England. At this time, he settled at Russells Mills, Mass., and then, in 1844, moved to Ohio the second time. His first labors in Ohio were as before, in Brown and Clermont counties, but in 1845, he began his labors in

Warren and Hamilton counties. In 1848, he moved his family to Warren County, near Lebanon, the county seat. He continued in this place until 1861, then moved to Sullivan County, Ind., in the vicinity of Merom, the location of Union Christian College. During his stay in Lebanon, he served as pastor of the churches of Bethany, Fellowship, Red Lion, Gentown, in Warren, Sycamore, in Hamilton, and Miamisville, in Clermont County. During the same time, also, he served as agent for Antioch College. After his removal to Indiana in 1861, for some years, he did not labor much in the ministry, owing to the care of a large farm, the war times, and his own poor health. A few years before his death, he renewed his labors again, and was quite as successful as before. His death was caused by falling from a horse, close to his own house, bursting the skull slightly, and, perhaps, causing internal injuries, from which he died in a few hours.

Such is an outline of the external life of the noted John Phillips. We now proceed to offer a few thoughts on the internal man as seen in his work.

As stated above, Elder Phillips was the child of poverty and toil, hence, in the commencement of his active career, being ambitious for knowledge, he had to endure great hardships to obtain it. Elder J.O. Wait, his school-mate and fellow church-member, speaking of this time, says: "I have known him to board himself on smoked herring and crackers for weeks. He knew what hard fare and scanty wardrobe were." From this rough fare, in the beginning of life's labor, we trace much of the rough side of the Elder's life. In his religious and emotional element, he was sound. When converted in his sixteenth year, he was converted all over. There was no halfway work about it. In his darkest moments, it is not probable that he ever doubted the genuineness of religion, or his own call to the ministry. The whole man was filled with such convictions, and as such, when he addressed his congregations, he addressed them as one having authority from above.

Another prominent feature in the Elder's life is apparent in all his labors; viz., his wonderful imagination, together with his readiness of mind to express himself in exaggerated figures. This faculty of his mind was sometimes so strongly expressed that it seemed to border on blasphemy or fanaticism. At one time, at Fincastle, Brown County, O., when in the midst of a very able sermon on "Benevolence," wishing to show his congregation that this was a divine attribute, with a peculiar look, such as he alone could give, he said: "Talk of benevolence I why this bump on the head of God Almighty, is larger than ten thousand mountains." The expression was so odd, so sudden and unexpected, that it thrilled his audience with a peculiar feeling.

Many blamed Elder Phillips for the glowing pictures of Antioch College, and the wonderful profit that would accrue to those who would be so fortunate as to own a share of stock in the Institution. His queer phrases, in those days of excitement, will never be forgotten—such as "The great Antioch telescope will be placed on such a high tower, that we can see Lake Erie, and the people in the streets of New Orleans, La." And also, that this Institution was to "beat the whole world and the Islands of the sea beside." No other man could use such a phrase without being counted a fanatic, but to John Phillips there was nothing unnatural in the expression, and yet in his common conversation, he was as logical as other men. These traits were doubtless born with him. His mind was of that peculiar type.

In his agency of Antioch College, he did a work at which all wondered. His descriptive power was so great, and the excitement he aroused was so high, that many, doubtless, subscribed much more than they were able to pay, and when the day of reckoning came, blamed the Elder with misrepresentation, when, the truth was, both speaker and hearer, for the time, were oblivious to everything but the glory of Antioch that was to be.

The same feature of his mind was manifested more strikingly in connection with Union Christian College in the small village of Merom, Ind. This college was to be located in the State of Indiana, in the town that would donate the largest sum of money for its location, raised by the people of that community, provided other considerations were equal. Many large towns were competitors for the institution, and some smaller ones; among the latter was Merom, the smallest of them all. But there were choice spirits in that village that were determined to have the college, if possible. Among these was Dr. J.N. Halstead, who knew John Phillips and his peculiar adaptability for canvassing in such enterprises. A small subscription of fifty dollars was raised to employ the Elder for two weeks. At this time, he lived in Lebanon, O. He consented to serve, arrived in the village, and delivered a lecture on education in general and the advantage of having such an institution in their village, in particular. In his first lecture, he gave his experience in acquiring education in his youth, his hardships, and the advantage it had been to him since. The people cried, they shouted, they were charmed. From that time to the end of four weeks (he was employed a second term of two weeks), there was nothing thought of in the village, or for miles around, but education and this new institution of learning. A four-horse team and a band were equipped, and some ten or twelve men, with the Elder as their speaker, traveled far and near, almost day and night. Persons of all ranks and conditions in life subscribed largely; many that had no money subscribed houses, land, horses, cattle, and labor at a fair stipulated price. At the end of four weeks, $37,500 were subscribed, 35,000 of which was vouched for by twelve or thirteen responsible men; and Merom, through John Phillips, obtained the college.

In a word, the Elder was a peculiar man. His preaching was powerful, but not always logical. There was something in the very appearance of the man that gave him power with his congregation. He was large, tall, swarthy, and homely in his appearance, and careless in his dress. His voice was powerful, and his intonations were peculiar to himself. His education, though not extensive or thorough, was yet sufficient to make him at home upon almost every subject. His social qualities were like himself—various. Sometimes he was a very interesting conversationalist and a most pleasant companion; at others he was moody, crusty, and, for hours together, would not utter a word. The reasons he assigned for the latter trait was, that his mind was so occupied with other thoughts that he could not disengage it.

Such is an imperfect sketch of John Phillips—the poor boy, the striving student, the successful pastor, and the powerful agent for our institutions of learning. He filled a wide place in the church of his choice, sometimes blamed, sometimes praised, but died regretted by thousands that knew him intimately in his life and labors.

Many anecdotes are related of him. Here is one showing his contempt of the practice of sprinkling babies. Being at a meeting at Pisgah Church at one time, when a Pedo Baptist was about to administer the above rite, the Elder became thirsty. There was no well or spring within a considerable distance, but on the table there was a basin with water prepared for the ceremony, The Elder took up the basin and drank all its contents. When the time for the christening came, and not a drop of water left, the Elder observed, in his peculiar way, "In my thirst, I drank your entire Jordan?'

OLIVER PHILLIPS (1799—1876)

This minister was born in 1799 and died in 1876. He labored near Wilkesbarre, Penn. He was a good, plain man and did a good service in his day.

WILLIAM H. PHILLIPS (1810—1875)

William was born in Fayette County, Penn., November 27, 1810, moved with his parents to Wooster, O., in 1821, and married Miriam DeGroot at Fort Wayne, Ind., May 23, 1830. He moved to Jamestown, Greene County, O., in 1831, joined the Christian Church at that place, and was baptized by Elder Matthew Gardner in 1836. August 19, 1841, he was licensed to preach, and joined the Deer Creek Conference. ' In 1843, he was ordained, and the same year, moved to Bloomingsburg, Clinton County, O., where he lived on a farm. In September, 1849, he moved to Jefferson County, Iowa, where he lived the balance of his days. He joined a Conference in Iowa August 18, 1851, organized the Ebenezer Church, near his home, in 1853, and joined the Union Conference at its organization, in 1857. His field of labor, in Iowa, was in Jefferson, Washington, Van Buren, Davis, and surrounding counties.

He died suddenly, of heart disease, at his home, eight miles from Fairfield, Iowa, March 8, 1875. He was a faithful Christian, a good preacher, and his labors were greatly blessed in the building up of the cause and in the conversion of sinners. The Elder had twelve children, three of which died before the father.

E.G. PIERCE (?—1875)

E.G. Pierce was a member of the Miami Reserve Conference, Ind. He died about 1875.

WILEY T. PIERCE (?—1865)

This young preacher lived for many years at Centreville, Clinton County, O. He commenced his labors in the ministry as early as 1852, but was engaged in the mercantile business and devoted but a small portion of his time to preaching. He was ordained in the Deer Creek Conference in 1861, and died in Bentonville, Adams County, O., about 1865.

NOAH PIPER (?—1865)

This brother filled a wide sphere in the Christian Church in New England for many years. He was what is called an old-fashioned preacher, wielded a sharp pen, and wrote much for our own papers. He had a great abhorrence to applying the title Reverend to ministers of the gospel, considering that title as exclusively belonging to the Deity. He united with the Christian Church in its early days, about 1809, and, as he says in one of his letters, when he took that step, he "renounced all human creeds and all inventions of men." He continued that advocacy through a long and active life. He lived for many years at Stratham, N.H., and died not far from 1865.

<u>ABRAHAM PLEW (1813—1875)</u>

Elder Plew was born in Ohio, June 3, 1813, and died October 8, 1875, near Parsons, Kan. He moved to Indiana, joined the Christians in 1830, and was ordained in 1855, by Elders Quillen and Bannon, by order of the Western Conference. He moved to Kansas, assisted in the organization of the South-eastern Conference in that state, and labored faithfully until death. He left a wife and seven children, with many friends, to mourn his departure.

<u>FREDERICK PLUMMER (1785—1854)</u>

In many respects, Elder Plummer was one of our most talented ministers. Having started out in the ministerial life when a young man, in a new denomination, thought by most people to be heretical, meeting with opposition wherever he labored; being a natural orator, gifted with a comely appearance and a mild and lively disposition, he soon became, not only a noted preacher, but a leader, in many places, of the people he so ably represented.

He was born in Haverhill, Mass., not far from 1785. His father, at one time, was the only man in town that would receive-Elder Elias Smith, and other Christian ministers, to his house. In January, 1805, he was baptized in the Merrimac River, and at once commenced his labors in the ministry. In 1807, he left his home as a traveling minister, never to return except on occasional visits. His first public labors were in the State of Massachusetts, in the neighborhood of Dartmouth. In this, and neighboring towns, he met the venerable Elder Daniel Hix, and others, and a great many were converted under their joint labors. The Elder, though a young man, not much over twenty years of age, took a high position at once as an able minister of the New Testament.

In 1810, he went to Woodstock, Vt., where he baptized five hundred converts in a short time. In this revival, the Christian cause received an impetus in that meeting, which has not died out to this day. Many able ministers and leading members were converted, during his labors at that time. There is an anecdote connected with the above meeting that is often repeated by our Vermont brethren.

It shows vividly the character of young Plummer in those early times. Being at a tavern in Hartland, a neighboring town, the conversation soon was started about the wonderful meeting at Woodstock. The landlady expressed herself freely of the heresy and bewitchery of the strange man who was deluding the people. After a while, when alone in the room, the Elder started up one of his favorite hymns, being a beautiful singer, and the tune being new, the landlady listened until he was through, then starting into the room excitedly, she asked, "Who are you? Are you the new preacher at Woodstock?" The next day the landlady was at the meeting in that town, and was converted, with several other members of her family.

In 1815, he went to Philadelphia, Penn., where his earnestness and eloquence drew crowds of people together, and many were converted under his ministry. As he, at that time, did not contemplate the organization of a Christian Church, a fine Baptist Church was organized from the converts of these meetings. From 1817 to 1843, his labors were confined to the city of Philadelphia and the surrounding country. Many churches were organized by him during these years, and generally, he supplied them as pastor. But one thing he neglected, with alibis talents—to teach the churches of his charge to become self-supporting in financial matters. Having started in the ministry in the early days of the denomination, his great object was the conversion of sinners, regardless of"- the future influence of the church as a nursing mother to the converts. Many strong churches in the field of his labor did as they chose in the support of the ministry. If they paid anything, it was all right, and if not, it was all right—with him. The result of this policy was, that when Plummer ceased his labors many of the churches ceased to exist.

He married Catharine Burkloe, a wealthy lady, and a true helpmeet for her husband in his work. His first wife died, and he was married again, to a lady of excellent character, who survived him at his death. In his family relation, he was affable and kind, and was equally fortunate in the selection of his companions. He was a man of great talent, whether as a preacher, a lecturer, or a debater. In early life, he was a fine singer. He was easy in his manners, having a kind word for all. In his public addresses, he seemed always ready, speaking as if it were no effort for him.

He died at Assonett, Mass., May 6, 1854, of hemorrhage of the bowels, not far from sixty-nine years of age. His death was most triumphant. Being in his right mind to the last, he called each one of his family by name, and gave each a parting word of advice, appropriate to their age and condition in life. Beside his ministerial labors, he was the author of several publications of ability. In every department of life, he showed a strong mind and a good heart.

HENRY PLUMMER (1794—1869)

This was a brother of the preceding, and, like his brother, was born and brought up in Haverhill, Mass., but unlike his brother, he continued in the same town through life. In his youth, he learned the baker's trade, which he followed for many years, as in those days, ministers of the Christian Church generally followed some other occupation for a living. He was born in 1794, was converted in 1810, was baptized by Elder Douglas Farnum, August 2, 1826, and was ordained at Haverhill, by Moses How, Mark Fernald, and others. He soon after became the pastor of the church at the above place, where he continued in the same relation the most of his life. He was a large man, candid and substantial, but had not the attraction of his brother Frederick, as a speaker. In his intercourse with others, he was social and friendly—in all, a man well suited to the office of a pastor.

In 1842, he became a firm advocate of the doctrine of the speedy coming of Christ, and held the same views to the last, though he never joined the Advent Church. He died in his native town, Haverhill, falling at his own door, of heart disease, January 27, 1869, aged seventy-five years.

<u>John Plummer (1786—1846)</u>

The following, in substance, is from the pen of Elder Levi Purviance, who was an intimate acquaintance of our subject: He was born in North Carolina, about 1786, moved to Ohio in 1809, and was married to Miss Hawey, in 1811, who proved to be a true helpmeet to her husband. He professed religion after his marriage, and moved to Union County, Ind., where he cleared a farm. In 1815, he began to preach, and soon became a useful minister. Having lived in Ohio, and being then a leader in the sports of the youth there, he felt inclined to visit the same place as a minister, and, if possible, lead them to Christ. In this he was successful beyond his expectation. He also organized the church at Hannah's Creek, Union County, Ind., and labored for it for many years. He was ordained by Elder David Purviance and others.

About 1840, he moved to Kosciusko County, Ind., where he labored faithfully in building up the Christian cause in that new country. By this time, as he was still growing in ability, he had become a powerful preacher and took a leading position in the Eel River Conference. While his manner of delivery was not so attractive as some, his good, sound sense and exemplary deportment gained him friends and adherents everywhere he labored. He was struck with death in the middle' of his sermon, and died in twelve hours after, in September, 1846.

<u>John Poff (1818—1878)</u>

John was born in Clinton County, O., March 12, 1818, In 1828, he moved with his parents to Delaware County, Ind., was married to Eliza Miller in 1838, and sometime after, moved to Wells County. In 1839, he professed religion, moved to Howard County, was ordained in 1850, joined the Miami Reserve Conference in 1851, and continued in that body until 1865, when he moved to Wisconsin. In 1860, he helped to organize the Richland Union Christian Conference. He died July 6, 1878. He had eleven children, eight of whom, with his wife, survived him.

<u>Donoughson Potter (?—?)</u>

Donoughson Potter was one of the most prominent ministers in the denomination in his day, and a great orator. He died in his prime.

<u>James Potter (1782—1872)</u>

The subject of our present sketch was born in Orange County, N.Y., and was brought up in New York City, where he learned a trade. Early in life, he joined the Methodist Church, and became a minister in that connection. But not agreeing with the church in doctrinal views, he was tried for heresy and disowned. As he found that his views harmonized with those of the Christians, he joined that body in 1819, and continued a faithful member and minister among them till his death. He was a member of the New York Central Conference. He died at Jerusalem, N.Y., February 2, 1872, of paralysis, at the age of ninety years.

<u>Reuben Potter (?—?)</u>

Reuben Potter was born and raised in Rhode Island, was converted in his youth, and soon after, began to preach. He was an accomplished young man, of good education, a fine writer, and an able and pleasant speaker. His prospect for future usefulness was bright. While thus growing in usefulness, and, to all appearances, one of the most exemplary of men, it was found by his most intimate friends that he began to indulge in the use of spirituous liquors. At one time, this habit became so notorious that he was tried by his own conference and was expelled from the ministry. After this, he reformed, and in 1823, published the "Gospel Palladium," an able periodical, in his own state—Rhode Island. In 1825, he paid a visit to the churches in Virginia. His preaching was highly acceptable to the people everywhere. During this visit, he delivered a fine eulogy, on the death of a young minister—Nelson Millar. This was pronounced, at the time, by good judges, to be one of the ablest productions of the kind.

There is no doubt of his great ability, and few doubt his sincerity of purpose; but the habit referred to crippled his usefulness. He continued the most of his life fighting against the great temptation, sometimes reforming and sometimes falling.

WILLIAM POTTER (?—?)

William Potter was a minister in the State of Kentucky. He died there many years ago.

HENRY POTTLE (?—1834)

Henry began to preach about 1804, and was very successful in his ministry. He died at Stratham, N.H., January 11, 1834, of heart disease. Sermon on the occasion by Elijah Shaw.

SAMUEL POTTS (1811—1877)

Samuel was born in December, 1811, died in Montgomery County, Ind., February 9, 1877, was converted, joined the church in 1837, commenced preaching in 1857, and was ordained in 1860, in the Western Indiana Conference. He was a good man, and did a good work as a church member; and his great zeal and firmness in the work caused the brethren to call for his ordination, though late in life.

HIRAM PRATT (1814—1856)

This brother died while young. He was born m 1814, was converted about 1832 near Lansingville, and was baptized by James Wescott in 1834. In 1840, he united with the Eastern New York Conference, and a year later, was ordained. In 1841, he became pastor of the churches at Covington and Smithfield, Tioga County, Penn., where he remained three years. He went to Houndsdale, where, by the assistance of Elder W. Cummings, he organized a church, remaining one year. His next field of labor was in Fulton County, N.Y., then in South Franklin, Delaware County, the same state, where he remained some four or five years. In 1850, he was married to Miss Marietta Rice, of South Valley, and the same year, became pastor of the churches at Lansingville and South Franklin, where he continued his labors till 1856, in May of which year, he died of inflammation of the lungs.

He was a prompt man and his entire energies were engaged in his great work. While on his death bed, he exhorted the friends that came to his room, and especially the Elders of the church of which he was pastor, to faithfulness. His loss was greatly felt by his many friends.

JEDIDIAH PRESCOTT (1784—1861)

The Elder wrote an autobiography of his life a short time before his death, which was published in a neat volume, by one of his sons, from which we glean the following:

He was born in Raymond, N.H., in 1784, was a son of Ebenezer and Phoebe (Eastman) Prescott, who were devoted members of the Congregational Church. His father was killed by an accident in 1800, which effected the mind of Jedidiah seriously for some time, but finally he lost his seriousness until the death of his mother soon after, when it was renewed again. From the latter event until 1804, he was very miserable under his conviction. At the latter date, he joined the Freewill Baptist Church, and enjoyed a great peace of mind. In 1807, he was married to Mary Graves, who was a faithful Christian. His impression that it was his duty to preach began to trouble him, which he resisted for many years, but finally yielded, after being severely afflicted in many ways.

In January, 1811, he moved his family to Monmouth, in the State of Maine, and about 1814, began to preach, and soon gath-ered around him a large number of worshipers. Hitherto he had been a member of the Freewill Baptist Church, but cooperating with the Methodists, but after forming an acquaintance with the Christians, he was ordained, November 2, 1817, together with El-der Simon Clough, having joined the Christian Church prior to this time. Sermon on the occasion by Elder Ward Lock. He became a very active and zealous worker in the church, and many were con-verted under his preaching. During his early labors in Monmouth,

Me., he met with opposition, and was subject to many privations incidental to a pioneer life.

His first wife died June 12, 1828. He was married again in 1829. His field of labor, for almost fifty years, was in Monmouth, Me. He had been a professor of religion fifty-seven years, and a minister for forty-seven years. He died June 19, 1861, at the age of seventy-seven years.

? PROSSER (?—1850)

Brother Prosser was a Christian minister who died in 1850, at the age of fifty years.

ZACHARIAH BUCKET (1806—1867)

This minister was born in North Carolina, in 1806, of Quaker parentage, and moved with his parents to Ohio in 1818. He studied law and was successful at the bar. He united with the Christian Church in Randolph County, Ind., in 1860, and began to preach the same year. In 1861, be became a member of the Antioch Christian Conference, in the State of Indiana, and labored faithfully until struck down with paralysis. He died April 1, 1867. He had been married twice and had ten children.

ROBERT PUNCHEON (1778—?)

Of the early life of Elder Puncheon, we have no account, but from his own letters and that of his friends, we learn that he was born in England, in 1778, and was married there to his wife, Elizabeth, in 1800. They emigrated from the old country before 1807, for in that year he and his wife became members of the Christian Church in Philadelphia, at its organization. Elder Puncheon became the officiating pastor of the church and was ordained there in 1808. From this to the year 1844, we have but little account of his labor, but at the latter date he was living in Cincinnati, O., an active minister in the denomination. His wife died in 1846, and at the time, he was confined to his room with paralysis, and had been in that condition for the two years preceding. It is probable he died soon after that date.

DAVID PURVIANCE (1766—1847)

In some respects, this father of the church stands as the father of the denomination in the West. At the time of the separation from the Presbyterians in Kentucky, at the close of the Cane Ridge revival, he was a licensed minister in the Presbyterian Church, and a candidate for ordination. Soon after the separation, he was ordained by the Dissenters, and became one of the six leading men that drew up and signed the Remonstrance and articles of dissent, issued in that day, but he alone, of the six, continued in the same unwavering course during a long life. As such, together with his talent, he became the standard bearer of the Christians in the West. It is mentioned in the proper places in this work, that McNemar and Dunlevy joined the Shakers, Marshal and Thompson returned to the Presbyterians, and some years later, Stone became partially united with the party of Alexander Campbell, who embraced a different system of theology from that held by the Christians at first, leaving Purviance alone, of all its original leaders, to guide the new body to the position it now occupies among sister denominations.

Elder David Purviance was the son of Colonel John and Jane (Wasson) Purviance, and was born in Iredell County, N.C., November 14, 1766. His parents had moved from Pennsylvania in 1764, to the place of his birth. 'In the boyhood of David, his father served in the Revolutionary War, and was promoted to the office of a colonel. After the close of the war, he moved to Sumner County, Tenn. This was, at that time, a wilderness country, full or hostile Indians, by whom his second son, John, was killed, not far from the house. On account of which, and for the protection of the rest of the family, his father moved to Bourbon County, Ky., and in 1800, to Wilson County, Tenn. His mother died in 1810, and his father in 1823, both having left the Presbyterians, and joined the new church, at the time of the separation.

Young David was brought up in the strictest sense, a Presbyterian, and had memorized the larger and smaller catechism when very young. At the age of twelve years, he was sent to a seminary under the care of Dr. Hall, for the purpose of studying the Greek and Latin languages, with a view to the ministry of his church. He made a speedy progress in these studies, and was afterward engaged in teaching the same branches to others. In 1789, he was married to Miss Ireland, a lady of Irish parentage, in North Carolina. Two years later, he moved, in company with his father's family, to Tennessee, and on account of the Indian trouble, mentioned above, he moved to Bourbon County, Ky., where he remained until 1807, when he moved to Preble County, O. During his stay in Kentucky, beside his religious labors, he was, for several years, a representative from Bourbon County in the State Legislature. In this relation, he showed the same good sense and ability, as in the other labors of his life, for although an unpretentious farmer, he was well informed upon every subject and an active worker in the body. In that slave holding community, he was conscientiously an anti-slavery man. He also represented the farming community of his district and gave full satisfaction to the majority of his constituents. He had several sharp contests with some of the leading members of the bar, but he maintained his own ground, to the surprise of many. Indeed, his ability as a debater, and the entire confidence of the people in his honesty, made him more than a match to the brilliant men that represented a class legislation in the body. Elder Purviance was a very plain looking man, and wore such clothing as common country farmers in moderate circumstances wore, soon his entrance to the legislature his fellow-members considered him as one poorly suited for the position he occupied. Mr. Garrard and Purviance were elected to represent Bourbon County in the legislature on a certain issue—an opposition to the establishment of a court of Oyer and Terminer, and other costly measures, bearing hard on the small farmers, as to their title in land. The legal profession was in favor, the small farmer opposed the measure. John Breckinridge, one of the leading lawyers of the day, was the advocate of the bill. After a two days' speech by the latter, there was none of the farmer party that were willing to answer. At the urgent request of his colleague, Mr. Garrard, Elder Purviance undertook the difficult task. He rose to his feet slowly, with his homespun garments, and his timid, embarrassed looks. The house was full, and many strangers had come to hear the able speech of the great Breckinridge. All eyes were riveted on Purviance. and for a while he was greatly confused—it was his first effort. Soon he warmed up to his subject, and delivered one of the ablest speeches of the session, to the astonishment of himself and all others. The bill was lost by an overwhelming majority against it, and Purviance rose at once, from one of the most obscure of the country members to a leader of the farmer party in the legislature. Having served for many years in the legislature as an anti-slavery man in a slave- holding community, and the issue becoming more and more definite, he was defeated upon that issue. From this time, he devoted his entire energy to the cause of religious reformation.

Little did Elder Purviance and his comrades know where they were led during that great awakening about 1800. Their first idea was to form a Presbyterian Church upon a more liberal basis than the one with which they had been connected, and hence the Springfield Presbytery was organized. In about a year, this body was dissolved by a solemn declaration of the six leaders. From this time the Dissenting brethren took the position occupied at this time by the Christian Church, and Elder Purviance continued an acknowledged leader till death. From 1804 to 1807, he did his greatest work in Kentucky. He traveled far and near, holding meetings of days, meeting the brethren in council in the interest of the infant cause, answering objections to the new theology, as it was called, ordaining ministers, organizing churches, and to add to the great labors mentioned, four of his comrades, whom he considered as leaders in the reformation, deserted their post. Such was the strain on his mind and body during this time, that his health became impaired, from which it never fully recovered, during life.

In 1807, he moved, with his family, to the State of Ohio, but not to rest, for beside preaching in various places in the new country where he settled, clearing the timber to make a farm, he was elected to represent the county in the Ohio Legislature in 1808, without any solicitation on his part. He served one year in the House and two in the Senate. From the period of leaving the legislature, his time was entirely devoted to preaching the gospel. At the time of the division between the original Christian Church and the Reformation, as it was called, under the preaching of Alexander Campbell and others, David Purviance became the leading representative man in the former body, as his comrade, Barton W. Stone, took a halfway ground. He made long trips, studied hard, and wrote many articles on the issues of the day. He was a leading member of the Miami Christian Conference in Ohio, as well as one of its first members. He was also a pastor for many years of the Shiloh and New Paris churches, in his own neighborhood.

The attachment that existed between him and Elder B.W. Stone continued through life. Although in the latter part of their lives they became, in a measure, leaders and representative men of two distinct denominations, yet their personal friendship never failed. In 1843, Elder Stone paid him a visit at his home in Ohio. The latter was then broken down with paralysis. Both were old and near their journey's end. They met at the meeting house at New Paris, before a large congregation. They embraced, and on the neck of each other, they sobbed, they wept, and continued in tears for some time. Those that were present spoke of the scene as most affecting. The memories of a whole life, of stirring events came up in this one hour. The congregation was melted to tears. They knew that this would be the last meeting in life. Elder Stone's home was in Jacksonville, Ill., and Elder Purviance's in New Paris, O. The former died the next year, while on a journey in the State of Missouri, and the latter, in four years more passed away at the home of his son, near the place of greeting. His wife died in 1835, at the age of seventy-three, and his death occurred in August 19, 1847, aged eighty-one years.

The goodness, honesty, and sincerity of Elder Purviance was acknowledged by all. His education was more than ordinary for his day, having studied and taught the classic languages in early life, together with such scientific and mathematical branches as were taught in respectable academies in those early days. To this, also, may be added a stirring, studious life, associated with men of culture. As a thinker and speaker, he was not the most brilliant, yet he was respectable in both, but his great recommendation was his firmness and devotion to the cause of truth. His life of over eighty years was an eventful one. Born in the wilds of North Carolina, he continued a frontiersman the most of his life, first in his native state, then in Tennessee, Kentucky, and Ohio. His earliest recollections were of events in the Revolutionary War, where his father performed a prominent part, and not less exciting to the mind was the religious revolution that gave rise to three religious bodies— the Cumberland Presbyterians, the Christians, and the Disciples, and in which he himself was a prominent actor. With sadness, but firmness, he saw five of his early comrades leaving their original positions in the ranks. He served fifteen sessions in the Legislature of Kentucky and Ohio. His death was as calm as his life had been stirring. Not a cloud obscured the horizon of his closing day. Many were the notices and eulogies given at his death, but he needed them not, for his record was on high.

LEVI PURVIANCE (1790—1873)

Many persons whose memoirs are recorded in this volume were intimate personal acquaintances and fellow-laborers of the writer, but to none did he look up with more veneration and confidence than to him whose name heads this article. It is with a peculiar feeling of sorrow that I pen this short sketch of "Uncle Levi," as we familiarly called Elder Purviance. In the fall of 1849, I formed the acquaintance of the Elder in the city of Dayton, O. Ever since that time, we often met, and I always found him a spiritual father and a wise counselor. About ten years ago, when I began to gather materials for this volume, 1 consulted him, and was encouraged to proceed with the work. He promised to render all the assistance he could, observing at the same time that he had contemplated such a work himself. During these years, we met several times; he always made wise suggestions and imparted valuable information. With the accumulation of labor and the weight of four score years pressing upon him, with no hint or murmur of the hardships of the work performed by him, he wrote long and laborious letters for this work, without money and without price.

The above may not be, in the strict sense of the term, a biography of Elder Purviance, but it shows the spirit of the man more clearly than many sentences of eulogy. Hundreds of brethren bear witness to the kindness and self-sacrifice of "Uncle Levi." The following concise account, which is taken from the "Eaton Register," was published soon after the Elder's death. It is mostly taken from an address delivered by our subject at a meeting of the "Old Folks" a short time before his death—being taken down by the editor of the above paper at the time.

"Elder Levi Purviance was the oldest son of Elder David Purviance. He was born in Iredell County, N.C., September 7, 1790, and was consequently eighty-two years six months and two days old at the time of his death, April 9, 1873. When an infant, he was taken by his parents to Wilson County, Tenn., where one of his uncles was killed by the Indians while plowing in a field. In consequence of this, and other hostile demonstrations of the aborigines, his father and mother went on horseback to Bourbon County, Ky., leaving the subject of this sketch with his grandfather. After selecting a home, they returned, and shortly thereafter, moved to Kentucky, where they remained some fifteen years. During- this time, the great revival of religion occurred at Cane Ridge. Elders David Purviance, Barton W. Stone, and others took an active part in the revival, dissenting from the Presbyterian Church on account of its church government and confession of faith. The dissenters assumed the name "Christians," and agreed to stand on the Bible as their rule of faith and practice. They were a devout body of worshipers, evangelical in their faith and practice, and took with them many able ministers who were zealous and energetic in their labors. The deceased cordially espoused the cause of his father and the other dissenters, became a minister early in life, and consistently labored in the cause to within a few days of his death.

In the year 1806, the deceased, then a lad of sixteen years, came with other pioneers to the White Water Country, and commenced clearing land in the wilderness, for a prospective home, one-and-a-half miles west of where New Paris is now located. During the year, he cleared six acres and put it in corn. The next year, his father's family moved from Kentucky, and settled in this small opening in the wilderness, subsisting almost entirely on the corn and vegetables raised on the spot of ground cleared by Levi.

In the year 1811, the deceased was married to Sophia Woods, of Wayne County, Ind., with whom he lived happily for some nineteen years. He obtained his marriage license from George Hunt, then the Clerk of the Circuit Court, who, in the absence of county seat and court-house, lived and performed the duties of his office at his residence on Elk Horn Creek, between where Richmond and Liberty, both in Indiana, now stand. The deceased was at the first court organized in Wayne County, Ind. It was held at a private house.

In 1812, soon after his marriage, our brother volunteered as a soldier, and served in the army at Fort Nisbet, under the command of Capt. Silas Fleming. In 1820, he entered the ministry, and in 1823, .was ordained. Since that time, he spent his manhood and declining years in the service of the Savior. All this time, except ten years spent in Illinois, was spent in Ohio; five years in Miami County, five in Warren, and the remainder in Darke and Preble counties. In his ministry, he was very practical and highly devotional. He passed through life without spot or blemish, beloved and respected by the community.

The deceased married, for his second wife, Mrs. Eliza Adams, of Darke County, O., with whom he lived happily for twenty-two years. After her death, in 1865, he married Mrs. Elizabeth Cox, of

Covington, Miami County, O., with whom he lived in peace and comfort till the time of his death, and who survived him."

The above excellent sketch was written by Brother Morris, a prominent member of the Methodist Episcopal Church, who was well acquainted with Elder Purviance for many years. The article also shows in what estimation he was held by other denominations.

In early life, the Elder became the companion of his honored father, and for many years, till the death of the latter, they lived in the same community, labored in the same churches and conferences, and were more like brothers than father and son. At the death of his father, "Uncle Levi" was an aged man of fifty-five years. In 1849, he had a stroke of paralysis or apoplexy, from which he suffered for some time, and many thought he could not recover; but his strong constitution, his contented mind, and temperate habits, under the blessing of heaven, gave him twenty-four years more of a useful and active life in the cause of Christ. About 1852, when about sixty years of age, he moved to Morristown, Ill. He labored long and faithfully in that bleak prairie country, where he buried his second wife. Alter ten years exposure and hard labor, he returned to his beloved Ohio, and took charge of some of our most important churches; and although he was well advanced in years, he sustained himself well, sometimes preaching as often as three times a day, when near eighty years old. He thus continued in his active pastoral duties until within a week or two of his death. We all became so used to his old age and active labors that we were shocked with surprise when we heard of his death, as if he were a man still in the prime of life.

After preaching for some time in Covington and Franklin, O., he accepted a call to Eaton, the county seat of Preble County, in the same state, and died there April 9, 1873, in his eighty-third year, after a few days' illness, so quietly that the watchers in the room could not decide the precise moment he breathed his last. A sermon was preached on the occasion by Elder H.Y. Rush, editor of the *Herald of Gospel Liberty,* Dayton, O., assisted in the service by two or three other Christian ministers, as well as ministers of other churches.

Elder Purviance was not only a pious, good man and a sound, practical preacher, but an able and easy writer as well. Beside many articles written by him for the denominational and other periodicals, he published a neat volume of the biography of his father and nine other Christian ministers, together with a graphic history of the great revival in Kentucky.

As a man, he was mild, sociable, and full of kindness. As a minister, while he was firm in his convictions of truth, he was so evangelical and practical in his sermons that different denominations claimed him as theirs; and well they might, if they were Christians, for he claimed all the disciples of Christ as brothers and sisters.

? PUTNAM (?—?)

All we know of this brother is, that about the beginning of the present century he was a prominent minister among the Christians of Vermont.

DANIEL QUINBY (?—?)

This brother was a minister in the State of Vermont. For many years, he was a good and faithful preacher, but about 1821, he was carried away into a short-lived fanaticism, originated by a woman called Betsy Niles, and hence called the "Niles Fanaticism." He returned in a short time, and was subsequently a faithful man; but for the want of confidence on the part of his co-laborers, he did not accomplish much after that time.

BOWMAN RABB (1812—1872)

This minister was born in Knox County, O., in 1812, his parents, who were members of the Methodist Episcopal Church, having moved from Virginia sometime previous. His father was a prominent man in that denomination, but joined the Christian Church when Bowman was young. The son was converted, and joined the Christian Church at Hanger school-house, in Knox County, under the labors of Elders Harry Ashley and Samuel B. Marvin, about 1830. Being a devoted young man, he soon became an active lay member. In 1838, he was married to Miss Sarah Squires, began his labors in the ministry in 1840, and was ordained soon after. His labors in Ohio were mostly confined to Licking, Knox, Coshocton, and Columbiana counties. Though his education was limited, and though he labored with his hands to supply a part of his living, yet his godly life and fervent zeal made him useful as a pastor and preacher.

In the latter part of his life, he moved to the State of Illinois, where he continued his labors very faithfully, and was useful to the churches and conferences. He died in the latter state May 28, 1872, aged sixty years.

Benjamin Rainey (?—?)

About the year 1800, this brother was one of the leading ministers in the Christian Church in the South. He was a companion of Elder James O'Kelly, from the time of the separation from the Methodist Church, in 1793. He was an able exponent of the Christian doctrine. He published several pamphlets, showing the peculiar views held by the Christians. One of these pamphlets was published in 1809, in connection with Elder Stringer. He was considered by his co temporaries an able and good man, a safe counselor, and reliable in all his intercourse. Although spoken of frequently by our early writers, I have not been able to find his age or the time of his death.

William Ramsey (1786—1852)

This brother was born in Vincennes, Ind., in 1786, in the midst of an Indian War, his parents having moved to that place from the State of Pennsylvania a short time before. When William was young, his father moved to White River, where the boy was raised among the rough white settlers and Indians that remained in that part of the country. His physical powers were well developed but his educational advantages were few; and as for religious privileges, he had heard but two or three sermons when twenty-one years old. In 1809, he was married to Miss Laura Winship, with whom he lived happily for many years, and raised a large family of children. In 1810, he was converted in the Methodist Church, and received a license to preach in that body. His preaching was powerful and many were converted under his labors.

In 1820, he moved to the State of Illinois, where he met Elder William Kinkade and other Christian Ministers, through whose preaching he changed his views of some church doctrines, and joined the Christian Church, in which connection he continued till death. He was a very zealous, self-sacrificing Christian, and was very useful as a preacher. He was, for a long while, pastor of the Spring Hill Christian Church. His talent as a preacher was of the revival kind, in which he was very 'successful. He died in Illinois, January 8, 1852, aged sixty-six years.

JOHN RAND (1781—1855)

Brother Rand was born in Lunenburg, Mass., in 1781, and moved to Beverly, with the family, when young. In 1795, when fourteen years old, he went to sea. His parents died about this time. He served an apprenticeship of seven years in Boston, Mass., at the carriage-making business. In 1800, he was converted, and joined the Baptist Church, under the care of Dr. Stillman, in the above city. In 1809, he was married to Miss Betsy Babcock, of whom he had thirteen children.

Elders Jones and Smith held meetings in Boston in 1803, and the next year, Elder Rand joined the new church, and soon began to preach. In 1806, he was ordained, in Boston, by Elders Jones, Smith, and Boody. After itinerating for a while, he settled with the church at Exeter, where he continued his labors for eight years. In 1814, he moved to Wood- stock, Vt., where, in connection with El- der Jasper Hazen, he assisted in the publication of a hymn-book, which met an extensive circulation, and, for a while, came into general use in the denomination. After this, he moved to, and labored in, Danville and Bradford, the same state. In 1822, he moved to Milton, Mass., where he remained the rest of his life. From this time till within a few years of his death, he partially retired from active labors in the ministry, but was steadfast in the faith and useful as a member to the end.

In 1837, his wife died. It was a great shock to the husband, as she had been a faithful companion to him through many years, and the family had been one of the most happy. In 1853, he received a stroke of paralysis. He recovered, in a measure, but died May 31, 1855.

<u>SAMUEL RAND (1784—1830)</u>

In his day, Elder Rand was one of the most useful ministers in the Christian Church, and at his death, there was a general mourning throughout the denomination. He was born in Chester, N.H., September 17, 1784, joined the Christian Church in Guilford, in the same state, in 1805, and began to preach in North Carolina in 1807. He soon extended his labors to Portsmouth and other places in New Hampshire, where many were converted under his preaching. In 1809, he was ordained in Portsmouth, preaching his own ordination sermon from I. Corinthians 9:16, "Woe is me if I preach not the gospel." After traveling a few months in different places, in 1810, he settled as pastor with the church at Portland, Me., where he continued the remainder of his life, for the term of twenty years. He was married in 1812, to Miss Lefever, of Salem, Mass., a lady of exemplary life, and a devoted Christian, of whom he had four children. He died in Portland, of a fever, September 10, 1830, aged forty-six years.

Elder Rand was a natural orator, as well as a successful pastor. While his education was limited, and his habits were not of the most studious kind, yet such was his readiness as a speaker, that he sustained himself in the city of Portland for twenty years, with no stipulated salary from the church, and lived well, besides having a large congregation to attend on his ministry. By his habits as a pastor of visiting his entire congregation, he exerted a great influence on the whole parish, and by this, also, he became acquainted with the habits of his people. From the knowledge, attention, and study of the Bible, he adapted his sermons to the wants of his people. His theme during life was practical goodness. He dealt but little in speculative doctrines, having settled in his mind that the Word of God was sufficient as a guide to the believer, he preached it to his congregation, and the result was most glorious. He continued through life to maintain the most friendly relation with ministers of other denominations. In prayer, Elder Rand was particularly gifted. This power consisted in the unshaken faith he cherished that God would answer, and the weaving in of the surrounding circumstances in his petitions to the great and loving Father. It is said that he never failed to carry his congregations with him in his petitions, till they all felt as poor suppliants at the throne of mercy where there was abundance for all.

Few ministers, as local as he, received as many members into the church. In his own church in Portland, he witnessed three extensive revivals. In 1811, he baptized about sixty, and in 1814, about the same number, and again in 1826, 160 were baptized by him. In Salem, Mass., and other places, he baptized many converts at different times. His death, in the prime of life, was considered as a public calamity in the denomination, where he was so highly valued.

DAVID RAWLS (?—?)

David Rawls lived in the South, and was an able and excellent minister, laboring in Virginia and North Carolina.

URIAH RAWLS (?—?)

Uriah Rawls was a Christian minister who lived the most of his life at Holy Neck, Nansemond County, Va. He was converted at the Holy Neck Christian Church, and began to preach there about 1825. Soon after, he became the pastor of the church, which then had but eight members. He continued his pastoral relation with it for many years. In 1846, it numbered over one hundred members, as we learn in a letter of Elder Rawls at the time. He also gave the cheering account that his brother, John Rawls, a member of the same church, had, at his death, which occurred a short time previous, liberated fifty-one slaves. In 1834, Elder Rawls became afflicted with what the doctors called leprosy, from which he suffered much. He was considered one of the good and prominent ministers in the Virginia and North Carolina Conference. He was also a correspondent of our northern papers the most of his ministerial life. He died several years ago.

L.S. RAY (?—1873)

L.S. Ray was a minister of the Eastern Indiana Conference. He lived and labored in Delaware and adjoining counties, and died in 1873.

H. REA (1804—1876)

This Elder was born in Virginia, May 20, 1804, moved with his parents to Ross County, O., and in 1821,' settled near De Graff, Logan County, where he continued to live the remainder of his life —a period of fifty- five years. In 1820, he was married to Miss Anna Elwood, of whom he had thirteen children, all living at the time of the father's death, but one, who fell in the War of the Rebellion. He joined the Christian Church in 1833, began to preach in 1834, and was ordained in 1840, being a member of the Auglaize Ohio Conference. He was a zealous, devoted man, and in an early day had regular preaching at his own house frequently. He died at De Graff, O., November 12, 1876.

REUBEN READING (1795—1870)

This brother was for many years a member of the Deer Creek Ohio Christian Conference, and lived the latter part of his life in Pickaway and Madison counties. He was born in Kentucky in 1795, moved with his mother to where Williamsport, O., now stands, in 1800. His education was limited in his boyhood, but by energy he gained considerable knowledge, especially of the Scriptures. In 1812, he was enrolled in the militia, became a sergeant in the company, and served during the war against England. In a few years after the close of the war, he was married to Miss Rebecca Scott, of whom he had seven children. His first wife having died, he married Nancy Lingo, of whom he had eleven children. In 1837, he was converted under the preaching of Elder I.N. Walter, was baptized by Elder Enoch Harvey, and soon after was ordained. For many years, he labored with great success in the bounds of the Deer Creek Conference, being an able revivalist. He died January 21, 1870.

JOSEPH REDMAN (?—?)

Joseph Redman was a Christian minister that labored in Central Ohio about 1820, moved to Illinois, and preached in that state as late as 1840.

JACOB REEDER (1800—1871)

This brother was born February 7, 1800, lived in Clark County, O., the most of his life, attended church at Knob Prairie for more than forty years, was married about 1820, joined the church in 1835, commenced preaching in 1840, was ordained in the Miami Conference, O., in 1841, and died at his home in Clark County, O., May 22, 1871. During his entire ministerial life, he lived on a farm and accumulated a handsome competency, but being a man of strong constitution, he labored extensively in the ministry. He was, for some time, a pastor of the Enon and .Ebenezer churches, in his own neighborhood. He also had charge of churches farther away. During most of his ministerial life, he was engaged as a pastor. He was very prompt in his attendance, and succeeded well in his pastoral relations. His preaching was of the expository kind, in which he was a strong man. But the most prominent feature in Elder Reeder's life was in connection with the general measures of the denomination. In this, he had few equals. He was cool and deliberate in his calculations, generous with his means, and was naturally a safe business man, and as such was highly esteemed. He served for many years as a trustee of the Western Publishing Association, and the educational interests of the church. He was often called to serve as chairman of conferences, a work to which he was well adapted. For several years before his death, he was not able to travel, but to the last, he felt a great interest in the cause that he served so faithfully for thirty-seven years of his life.

<u>Benjamin Reeves (?—?)</u>

Of this brother we have no further knowledge than that he was an aged minister of the Christian Church in North Carolina, about the beginning of this century.

<u>Thomas Reeves (?—?)</u>

Thomas Reeves lived for many years in the western part of Orange County, N.C. For some time; he was a senior companion of Joseph Thomas (the White Pilgrim) itinerating in the South. The latter speaks in the highest terms of his kindness to him when a boy, and his faithfulness as a minister. In 1807, be lived in Surry County, Va. In 1808, he left the latter state for Tennessee, but returned again in a short time, and from this time until 1820, he was in the habit of visiting at the home of Elder John Hays, of Wake County, N.C. In his old age, he moved to Clay County, Mo., and died many years ago. He was considered a model Christian man.

<u>Willis Reeves (?—?)</u>

Willis Reeves was one of the early ministers of North Carolina and Virginia. It is probable that he and the two preceding were family relations.

<u>James Reid (?—?)</u>

All we know of this brother is that he died in the work before 1826.

<u>Edson J. Reynold (1807—1857)</u>

The subject of this sketch was the second son of Clark and Mary Reynold, of North Lansing, Tomkins County, N.Y. He was born in the above place April 30, 1807. In July, 1831, he professed religion, and was baptized by Elder Ezra Marvin February 27, 1828. He preached his first sermon in the church at North Lansing; where he was a strong member. In August, 1834, he joined the Central New York Conference, and the next year, was ordained at Scipio. He became the pastor of some churches in the neighborhood of his home, and continued his labors with them until 1838, when he took charge of the Henrietta and neighboring churches, till 1841. At this time he moved to Plainville, where he continued till 1847, when he moved to Union Springs, and there continued his labors till forced to desist on account of pulmonary disease. He died at the letter place September 24, 1857, aged fifty years.

During the time of the above pastorates, Elder Reynold traveled quite extensively, and was successful in many revivals. He was also a writer of some note, and wrote much for the periodicals of the church. His views of church polity were very clear and he expressed them freely. Elder 0. E. Morrill, who wrote his biography, speaks of him as excelling in pastoral work; but as he was a consumptive, his voice was weak for the delivery of sermons, though the arrangement of his subjects was systematic and logical. He buried an only son shortly before his death, and the only members of his family that survived him was a wife and an only daughter, the latter in feeble health.

PAUL REYNOLD (1790—1842)

This brother lived in Maine, and for eighteen years was engaged in the work of the ministry. He was born in 1790, entered the ministry in 1824, and was ordained at Solomon, Me., in June, 1829. He was a member of the Stafford Christian Conference. He died in Acton, Me., August 30, 1842, aged fifty-two years, leaving a wife and eight children.

SNOW RICHARDSON (?—1860)

Elder Snow Richardson, at the time of his death, was a resident of Yellow Springs, O., and a member of the Miami Christian Conference. In early life he lived in Butler County, where he joined the Christian Church, and became an acceptable preacher. During his early ministry, he embraced the speculative doctrine held by Elder William Kinkade and others, that the words "begotten" and "created," as applied to Christ, meant the same thing. Whether he made a hobby of this theory in his preaching is unknown to the compiler. Be that as it may, there was an investigation of the matter in conference, and the result of it was, that Elder Richardson was suspended by the body. Being a good man, however, he never ceased his labors as a faithful preacher, likely forgetting all about the subject that caused the separation. He continued to labor in this independent way, doing much good in the cause, until 1853 or '54, when he was received in the same body, and continued faithful until death.

During a considerable portion of his ministry, he lived in Shelby County, O., but the latter years of his life were spent in Yellow Springs, where he died about 1860, leaving a record behind him of an honest, good man. At the time of his death he was not far from sixty years of age.

G.W. RICHMOND (?—?)

G.W. Richmond was for many years a prominent minister of the Christian Church, in the states of New York and Pennsylvania. In April, 1837, he was laboring with great success in the Wyoming Valley, Penn., as he had baptized 115 persons in a little over one month. The revival was spreading throughout the neighborhood, but mostly in Plymouth. The same year, July 2, he had what he considered a Providential escape from the effects of a fearful tornado that demolished every building in the village of Centreville, Penn., where he and brethren Gaylord, Wadham, Benedict, and Farnham intended to remain all night, but by a singular mental impression of the Elder's, they were induced to stay a mile or two out of the path of the tornado. He was a good, earnest and efficient minister. I am not informed of the dates of his birth or death.

JOEL RICHWINE (1805—1870)

Joel was born in the State of Virginia in 1805, moved in early life to Wayne County, Ind., and from there to Madison County, the same state, where he continued through life. About 1833, he joined the United Brethren Church, and soon after received license as an exhorter. In 1836, becoming acquainted with the Christian Church, he fell in with the views held by the latter body, and united with the church. He was ordained soon after, and continued a faithful member and minister in the body for thirty-four years. He was very zealous and ardent in the work. He was not what might be called an able preacher, as he followed some other occupation for a living, but he was gifted in singing and prayer, and was useful in his sphere. He died near Frankton, Ind., May 21, 1870, aged sixty-five years.

LAZARUS RIFFORD (1796—1870)

Lazarus was born in Vermont, in 1796, and was ordained in Randolph, in the same state, in 1841, though he was a preacher for many years before. He was a good man, and had the name of being awake when others were asleep. He died of paralysis, at North Chester, Vt., April 28, 1870, aged seventy-four years.

JOHN ROBBINS (1819—1877)

John was born in Shelby County, O., August 8, 1819, and died near Des Moines, Iowa, May 7, 1877. He was converted, soon after began to preach, and was ordained. In 1847, he moved to Iowa, and was married the same year to Miss Mary E. Clark, a faithful Christian lady, who survived him. Elder W.C. Smith speaks highly of his faithfulness as a minister, and that he (Smith) was brought to the Christian Church through the influence of Elder Robbins.

ABIGAIL ROBERTS (1791—1841)

Few women, in a humble station in life, exerted a greater influence in the church than did Sister Roberts in her own denomination for about sixteen years, from 1814 to 1830. She was the daughter of William and Esther Hoag, of Greenbush., Rensellaer County, N.Y., and was born February 17, 1791. Her parents were members of the Quaker Church, and she was brought up in the same faith. In 1803, her parents moved to Saratoga County, where, in 1809, she was married to Nathan Roberts. In 1814, she was converted under the preaching of Mrs. Nancy Cram, and soon after began to speak in public. At the time of her conversion she was the mother of three children. The husband was converted and joined the Christian Church soon after his wife, and when she began to speak in public, he left his work and traveled in company with her, and was an efficient worker in the cause.

The first labors of Sister Roberts were in connection with her spiritual mother, Sister Nancy Cram, but the latter dying, Sister Roberts carried on the meeting in company with others. From Saratoga County, where she began to preach, she traveled on through the adjoining counties in Eastern New York, where hundreds were converted through her ministrations. About 1824, Sisters Abigail Roberts and Anne Rexford labored together in many places. At that time they held meetings in the State of New Jersey, and in 1826, the church at Johnsonburg was organized mainly through the labors of Mrs. Roberts. In 1827, she extended her visits as far as Milford, N.J., and such was the interest awakened through her preaching, and the opposition of the other churches to her doctrine, that the people, irrespective of denominational lines, built her a fine stone meeting house, that has stood there ever since. The same people also donated a house and some ground, to which the Roberts family moved, and lived there for several years. The crowds that came to hear her during this time were very large, and many were the numbers converted under her preaching. Soon after their removal to Milford, her health began to fail, and although she labored at home and in other places after that, to good success, yet her health never entirely recovered. In 1830, Elder William Lane took charge of the church in Milford, but Sister Roberts, who lived in the place some years after, rendered valuable service in the work. In 1834, the family of Mr. Roberts moved to Putnam

County, N.Y., and one year after to Union Vale, in the adjoining county of Orange. In 1838, Mr. Roberts bought a farm near Hyde Park, Luzerne County, Penn., to which the family moved the same year. During all these years, our sister, though cheerful, and laboring occasionally in the ministry, was clearly failing in health and was sensible of her approaching separation from earthly scenes. She died in her new home, near Hyde Park, Penn., July 7, 1841, in her fiftieth year. Three years later, the faithful husband died and was buried by the side of his companion. In 1856, the bodies of both were removed and deposited in the grave-yard adjoining the meeting house in Milford, N.J., their old home, where a monument was raised by the church to their memory. A son of hers, Philetus Roberts, has been a useful minister in the same church for many years.

Cotton Roberts (1800—1847)

This brother moved from the State of New York to Illinois, and died in the latter state. He was born about 1800, professed religion about 1822, moved to Illinois in 1833, entered the ministry in the latter state, and died of quick consumption, in 1847, aged forty-seven years.

William Roberts (1811—1845)

This was a brother of the preceding, who commenced his religious life in Binghamton, N.Y., and ended his days in DeKalb County, Ill. He was converted in the former place, and for convenience, joined the Methodist Church.

He was born in 1811, commenced preaching in 1835, labored in the bounds of the New York Eastern Christian Conference, for about seven years, but his voice failed him while laboring in Hampden, Delaware County, N.Y., in 1842. He moved to Illinois, where his voice was partially restored, and he labored about one year at Belvedere. His voice failing him again, he resorted to his trade for a living. He died in the neighborhood of the Fairfield

Church. DeKalb County, Ill, October 6, 1845, aged thirty-four years. The church raised a monument to his memory.

John B. Robertson (1800—1878)

John was born in Greene County, O., in 1800, began to preach about 1833, became- a traveling companion of Elder Hallet Barber, and continued on his long circuit in Eastern Indiana and Western Ohio for eight years. He labored in the bounds of the Bluffton Conference, Ind., until about 1846, when he was married to Miss Ruth J. Campbell, and soon after moved to the southern part of Indiana, in Rush County, and united with the Central Indiana Conference. About 1860, he moved to Merom, the location of Union Christian College, for the purpose of educating his children. He continued in that place, preaching what he could in the neighboring churches to the last. He died at his home in Merom, January 12, 1878.

Elder Robertson never occupied a high position in the denomination. He was not a great scholar, nor was he noted for any great gift as a minister, though his talent was quite respectable in knowledge, in sermonizing, and in delivery. But the peculiarity in the life of our brother was his zeal—his entire devotion to the work, his firmness, and his thorough sincerity and conscientiousness in all that he did. When he was converted, he was converted all over. When he began to preach, he gave himself entirely to the Lord. When he read the Bible, he studied its contents for his rule of conduct, and never swerved one iota from what he understood it to teach. He would have made a first class martyr. In early life he became a stem abolitionist, when it cost something to be an anti-slavery man. But it mattered not to him what sacrifice it required, it was ready. He was equally zealous in the principles of peace between nations, and the introduction of arbitration, instead of the sword, to settle misunderstandings; so was he on temperance—total abstinence in all things injurious, like whisky and tobacco, and strict moderation in the use of all articles necessary for use. He once used tobacco, but the moment he was convinced that the use of it was contrary to the teaching of God's word, he used it no more. He was equally firm in his opposition to all secret societies, and it made no difference who of his dearest and best friends belonged to any of these, he would tell them of his convictions, and his reasons for them, kindly but firmly. Doubtless Elder Robertson would .have been far more popular with the masses had he been less rigid, and more of a time server. Many thought him curious, fanatical, and standing in his own light, but those that knew him best, knew that he was one of God's noblemen, and that his frankness in opposing what he considered evil did not grow out from any bitterness or narrowness, but from a large, pure conscience, that would not swerve. He had a large heart, and was full of charity. No man would do more than he for the drunkard, the warriors, and members of secret societies, though he bitterly opposed their practice.

He became a trustee of Union Christian College at its organization, and continued in the same office until death. For many years he was one of the Executive Committee. His whole soul was enlisted in its welfare.

His first wife having died, he married for his second, Mrs. Sarah Cason, in 1870. Although an industrious and economical man, he continued through life in limited circumstances. He died as stated, full of labor, well stricken in years, with not a cloud to obscure his clear sky of faith and hope.

<u>WILLIAM S. ROBINSON (1803—1876)</u>

William was born at Cadiz, Harrison County, O., in 1803, moved, in an early day, with his parents to the neighborhood of Danville, Knox County, of the same state, was married to an estimable lady, and converted, becoming a member of the Christian Church at Danville about 1835. He continued a member of the same church until death. He began to preach soon after his conversion, and continued to labor, more or less, through life. His education was limited, and he followed secular work for his support. He was a member of the Mt. Vernon Conference, O. Elder James W. Marvin, a neighbor of our subject for many years, speaks in the highest terms of his firmness, zeal, and generosity in the cause. He died at his home, near Mt. Vernon, in 1876.

? RODERICK (?—1852)

I am informed that this old Christian minister died about 1852, not far from eighty years old. He lived for many years in the southern part of the State of New York and labored in Steuben and Chemung counties, N.Y., and adjoining counties in Pennsylvania. He was limited in worldly possession.

DANIEL ROGERS (1796—1867)

Daniel was born in 1796, was ordained at Stewartstown, N.H., in 1837, and died in the same place October 30, 1867, aged seventy-one years.

MASON ROGERS (1837—1869)

This young preacher was the grandson of Elder Joshua Howard, of New York State. He himself was born in that state in 1837. In youth, he joined the Christian Church, and in 1855, moved to Wisconsin, where he began to preach. He moved to Canada in 1862 or '63, and was a very useful minister in the province till death. He died January 2, 1869, in Castleton, Ontario, Canada, aged thirty-two years. He left a wife and three children, and many friends, to mourn their loss. His career was short, but from his great zeal and energy in the acquisition of knowledge his prospect for future usefulness was bright.

E.B. ROLLINS (1793—1876)

Elder Rollins was one of those men whose long lives are filled with events worthy of record. His mind was active, his health the very best, his ambition large, and his zeal pushing him to the front of the battle. This stirring, active man was born in Andover, N.H., in 1793, was converted in youth, began to preach in 1815, and entered fully into the work at once. His education must have been respectable, for he wrote a great deal for the press, and was engaged, more or less, all his life in the publishing business. He published, at different times, two religious newspapers, one of which, the "Bethlehem Star," was published at Bethel, Vt., in 1824. His principal field of labor was Vermont, though he traveled extensively through other states. He was pastor of many churches, in laboring with which he succeeded well. But his great fort in the work was as an evangelist, and in conducting general meetings. In his younger days, he could be heard distinctly one mile, so clear and penetrating was his voice.

He retained his vigor to the last. It seems that his excessive labor, constant traveling, and two or three sermons or lectures a day agreed with his constitution. His general weight was 180 pounds. He was strongly built. In 1857, he published a book on the Prophesies, comparing their teaching to that of science and history. In this work, he called himself the "White Mountain Pilgrim." In the latter part of his life, he delivered many lectures on the same subject— the Prophesies. He seems to have made the Old Testament Prophesies a specialty in his studies of the Scriptures. Those that heard him say that his lectures were very clear. He wrote to friends, when on the eve of eighty years, that his health and vigor continued unabated.

He died at East Braintree, Vt., February 1, 1876, of pneumonia, which he contracted on a long journey, being thinly clad. His last words were, "O that men would praise the Lord for his goodness and wonderful work to the children of men." It was a glorious death, at the close of an active, stirring life, to have but a few days sickness, and that caused by his ministerial work in his eighty-third year—the fifty-ninth of his ministry.

FREDERICK ROLLINS (?—1843)
This brother died in Chatham County, N.C. October 17, 1843. He had been a faithful minister for many years.

WILLIAM ROLLINS (?—?)

William Rollins was a minister that lived many years in Moore County, N.C. In his latter years, he preached for the Shallo well Christian Church.

JOSEPH W. ROOK (1830—1875)

Brother Rook was born September 22, 1830, was converted in 1852, continued an active private member in the church until 1870, when he began to preach, joined the Northern Missouri Conference, and was ordained by that body. Elder Killen speaks highly of his kindness and zeal. He died in Sullivan County, Mo., January 17, 1875.

Benjamin Rose was a native of N.C. lifter preaching for some years, he died at his home in Johnston County, N.C., about 1827.

THE ROSSES. Glass Ross was a plain, practical, farmer preacher, and a member of the Bluffton Conference, Ind. Although of limited education, and not of the highest talent as a speaker, and being compelled to work for a living, yet the Elder was counted by his brethren a useful man in the ministry. His whole heart was enlisted in the work, and many were led to the Savior through his instrumentality. In the latter part of his life, he lived near Granville, Delaware County, Ind. He died in that place about 1856, not far from sixty years of age.

JOHN ROSS (1794—1879)

Elder John Ross, one of the leading ministers in Eastern New York for more than threescore years, had but few removals in his long life. He was born October 7, 1794, was converted in 1813, under the labors of Nancy Cram, was baptized by Jabez King the same year, received a common school education, and united with the Christian Church at Burnt Hill at its organization. He enlisted in the war of 1812 against England, was ordained in March, 1819, and was married to Miss Lavina Ames, September 16, the same year. He continued preaching in different parts of the state till September, 1822, when he moved to Charleston Four Corners, N.Y., remaining pastor of the church in that place till 1872, when; on account of failing health, he offered his resignation. It was reluctantly accepted by the church at the time, to satisfy Father Ross, and other ministers filled the place the remaining seven years. But, virtually, he was senior pastor till death, and would doubtless have continued the relation had he lived longer, making one of the longest pastorates in the Christian Church—uninterruptedly for fifty years, virtually for fitty-seven. He died at his home, among his people, December 29, 1879, full of labor and usefulness.

Such is an outline of the life of Father Ross; but the biography of such a man is not contained in these few events. As we look upon the history of the Christians in the great State of New York, we find many ministers of great prominence in the field during the more than sixty years of Elder Ross' ministerial life. In the midst of this large galaxy of names, humble, unpretending John Ross stands with a few others at the head as leaders—among others we may mention King, Thompson, Shaw, Millard, Badger, Morrill, and Hazen (still living-1880), and a few others; but none stand higher in the ranks than our subject. That woman of God, Nancy Cram, through great affliction, became the messenger, under the guidance of the great Spirit, to awake the sleeping communities of Saratoga and Charleston, N.Y., to a sense of their duty. Thompson, King, and Martin followed the good sister to confirm and strengthen the work, Hazen, Shaw, Badger, and John Peavy followed soon after, and Millard, Ross, Hollister, and Sister Abigail Roberts were called to the work through Sister Cram. Shaw and Martin soon returned to New England, Thompson went to other fields, Peavy died early, Badger was broken by paralysis, Millard moved to the State of Michigan to rest and die, but Ross was so fortunate as to stand at his post of duty to the last. But during the last few weeks of his life, both mind and body were broken down by paralysis and old age. The old pastor was there, however, as a central figure for his flock to gather around, if but to receive a word and a kiss from the old lips, now palsied, but in other years had delivered unto them the sweet message of peace. It was a glorious death, after a noble and successful life. The wife of his youth yet (1880) lingers on the shore, the son on whom they both doted having passed over the river in 1848; but the gospel that sustained the patriarch so long was precious to the last.

I have often wondered whether the contemplations of Elder Ross, in his last years, were sad or joyful. In 1869, I met him for the last time in his own conference at Lawrence, N.Y. He was then an old man, broken down with age and labor; but his conversation was interesting, and he was the central figure of the great and strong men composing that large conference—he was the patriarch of the tribe. Few of the comrades of his youth remained then, and as years passed on they went one by one, till at the time of his death, as far as known to the writer, there was none left but Jasper Hazen, in the distant State of Vermont. Doubtless his feelings during these years were a mixture of joy and sadness—of joy because he was so soon to pass over and reunite with the faithful ones •on the other side; of sadness because the dark river had to be crossed, and that he should never meet the companion of his youth on this side, as in other days:

Judging from his life's work—his preaching, his pastoral work, and his writings,—we would infer that the following were prominent traits in the character of our subject.

1st. Quietness and moderation. When he was converted, he quietly went to work to exhort and preach, in a small way. And so he continued to grow more and more efficient till old age and disease interfered with his progress. His remaining so long in one place also shows these characteristics.

2nd. Studiousness. We have no knowledge of his early education; but Brother Francis Hoag, one of the members of his church, and one that knew him thoroughly for many years, says that he had only a common school education in his youth. Neither do we know of his habits of study; but all must know that no man, however talented, could write such letters as he wrote, and sustain himself for so many years so successfully as he did with his large church without being studious.

3rd. Comprehensiveness in thought. As has been said, his education was not extensive, but his thoughts, as expressed in all his writings, are clear, terse, logical, and graphic. Many have expressed wonder at his ability as a writer. Whatever subject he took up, he seemed to have looked all through the points involved. Then starting out slowly, he took the divisions of his subject one by one as if by instinct; and when he came to the end, it seemed that he had said all that was to be said at that time, and that in the very best of order, with, nothing left out.

4th. Kindness of disposition. This was shown by the strong attachment that the members of his church retained for him years after leaving his parish. In his long pastorate, many hundreds attached themselves to his church at Charleston; but moved by the spirit of emigration, many of these settled in the various states of the Union, and in Canada; still, many retained their membership at Charleston, apparently for the sake of the kind pastor, and reported themselves yearly at a meeting appointed for that purpose by the pastor and his church.

5th. Firmness in what he believed to be true. Many changes took place in his conference in the more than half a century of his connection with it; and many a brilliant minister was carried away from his moorings by Adventism, Universalism and other fascinating ideas that pleased for the hour. Elder Ross had a kind word and heart for all these, but he never swerved, not because he was sectarian and bigoted, but because his mind had been fixed upon the liberal principles of the Bible alone as a foundation of faith, and his firmness was unshaken.

6th. Consecration of heart to the work, and a full trust in God. In his early ministry, his salary was small—very small. It is not likely that there was any stipulation between him and his congregations for some time after he began to preach for in those days, ministers had to gather their congregations. Yet, from the beginning, he never turned to the right or to the left from the great work before him. He labored with his hands, and doubtless added to his small income by that means. But this was, to him, always, secondary.

The first and chief work of his life was the ministry of Jesus Christ. His heart was consecrated to his vocation. His trust in God was so firm that he relied upon Him for his daily bread, as well as for his soul's salvation—and he was not disappointed. By economy and industry, he laid up a little for old age.

His life was an even, quiet, and pleasant one. The one sad event that clouded the future of Brother and Sister Ross was the death of their only son, their hope for the future, who died among strangers in a distant state. This cup was so bitter that nothing but the Grace of God and the hope of a reunion in a better land could make it tolerable to the bereaved parents. Peace to his ashes and rest to his soul.

GEORGE NELSON ROSS (1822—1848)

This brother was the only son of Elder John Ross,' of Charleston Four Corners, N.Y., was born in 1822, and was a young man of much promise, at the time of his death. He professed religion in 1836, and united with the church under the care of his father. In 1841, he commenced preaching, and was received into the New York Eastern Conference the year following. In 1843, he traveled in the West, preaching in various places with good success. He extended his travels as far west as Illinois, but in 1864, settled at Hamilton, Butler County, O., where he died February 5, 1848, aged twenty-six years. He had a fine mind, good education, and his prospect for the future was bright, but such is life; with all his advantages, he died far away from home—from doting parents and warm friends, a stranger in a strange land, but the gospel which he received from pious parents, and which he himself had begun to preach, was sufficient for him, and to his aged parents in their sore bereavement.

SETH ROSS, JR (?—1863)

The brother whose name heads this sketch, was for many years an active worker in the Christian cause in New York and some of the Eastern States. Without a regular obituary, we gather the following from the letters of friends, and his own published letters in our papers:

He was born, probably, in Vermont or New Hampshire He began to preach before December 7, 1837, for he was ordained at that date at Readsborough, Vt., by Elders Jabez King and David Ford. From this time he writes frequently to the "Christian Palladium." In 1839, he was laboring in the State of Massachusetts, and in 1840, he settled at Walpole, N.H. In 1842, he labored in Saratoga County, N.Y., and the same year, he settled as pastor oi the Burnt Hill Church in the same county. He was married to a sister of Elders Abijah and Moses Kidder, and in 1815, he buried two little children, a son and daughter. From 1849 to 1853, he was pastor of the church at Washington, N.H. After which he remained two years at Boscawen and Columbia, together with neighboring churches. October 24, 1859, his wife Elvira was buried, while the Elder was so sick he could not attend the funeral. He afterward married a Mrs. Hubbard, a sister of his former wife. In the latter part of his life, also, he labored some in Marlow and Walpole, N.H. He finally moved to Sharon, Vt., where he died in 1863.

Elder Ross was a firm, reliable and conscientious man. Some of his sermons were able productions, but ordinarily his discourses were plain, practicable, and unpretentious. He was not so much of a revivalist, as he was a good, substantial and faithful pastor. Such is the judgement of those who knew him well.

<u>THOMAS ROSS (1754—?)</u>

Thomas Ross was born in Maryland, about 1754. In early life he joined the Methodist Church, and was a minister in that body for many years. He finally joined the Christians, and preached extensively in Brown and Clermont counties, O. He died in Brown County. He was the grandfather of Elder Naaman Dawson. He was considered an able man.

Daniel Rote (1790—1864)

This brother was born in Eastern Pennsylvania in 1790, joined the Methodist Church at an early age, but for an honest difference in views, he left them in 1831 or 32, joined the Christian Church, and was baptized by Elder John Case, in 1832. He soon after began to exhort, and was ordained at Fairfield, Lycoming County, Penn., March 9, 1833, by Milliard, Marvin, and others. In one year after, he had organized four churches in his own neighborhood, of 143 members in the aggregate. He continued his labors in Pennsylvania for many years, and was one of the leading men in the organization of the Pennsylvania Christian Conference, of which he became a member. In 1846, he left his home and work in Pennsylvania, and moved to De Kalb County, Ill. In his new home in the West, he entered heartily to the work of the ministry, and was very useful in the cause.

About 1860, disease and old age came upon him, so that he was not able to labor much, but his heart was in the work to the last. In 1862, he received a stroke of paralysis, from which he never entirely recovered. He died May 24, 1864, aged seventy-four years, leaving an aged companion in a dying state, from the same disease. He had been a successful man in his day.

Alexander Rowing (?—1831)

Alexander Rowing was an old minister in limited circumstances, living near Williamsport, Pickaway County, O., and died there about 1831. He was counted an able preacher.

Caleb Royce (1812—1850)

Caleb was a young minister at the time of his death, residing at Starkey, N.Y. Having started to cross Seneca Lake from Starkey to Hector, in company with two young lady friends, Misses Lanning and Bellows, while far out in the lake, the boat was capsized by a gust of wind. Having secured the two young ladies so far as to have a hold on the boat, he undertook to swim to shore for another boat. Though an expert swimmer, he never reached the land. The ladies were rescued and his body was found soon alter.

He was born in 1812, and entered the ministry in 1840. He made quite a proficiency in the work, having had the charge of several churches. At the time of his death, he was pastor of the churches of Milo and Hector. His death occurred August 15, 1850, at the age of thirty-eight years.

W.D. RUTHERFORD (1818—1867)

This brother was born in Bath, N.Y., in 1818. He was of English parentage, and was brought up in the Presbyterian Church, but joined the Christians in 1834. In 1841, he united with the New York Central Conference, and was ordained in 1843. In 1845, on account of changing his location, he united with the Tioga River Christian Conference, and died in Corning, Steuben County, N.Y., July 18, 1867, aged forty-nine years.

MOSES SAFFORD (1771—1816)

Elder Safford was born in 1771, began his labors in the ministry at Kittery, Me., in 1802, and died in the same place, April 28, 1816, at the age of forty-five years.

ALEXANDER SAGE (1792—1853)

Alexander was born in 1792, was converted when quite young, and became a faithful minister. He is spoken of as a useful man. He died near Terre Haute, Vigo County, Ind., December 23, 1853.

LEVI SANDERS (1816—1863)

This brother was brought up in the Quaker Church. He was born August 17, 1816. His early efforts to acquire an education were commendable, and in which he succeeded well. He attended school for some time at Ann Arbor University, in the State of Michigan, and was converted during that time. At the first California excitement, he started with a company to the land of gold, and spent some time in that country. About 1852, he joined the Christian

Church, began to preach, and soon after joined the Central Illinois Conference. Being of a timid and modest disposition, he advanced slowly, but surely, in the work. He was married August 30, 1855, to Miss Mary E. Outten, and was ordained September, 1858. He labored mostly with the churches in Vermillion and adjoining counties in Illinois, extending his work, also, to the western part of Indiana. His exemplary life and his education and ability soon gave him a high position among his .brethren.

September 4, 1862, he was appointed Chaplain of the 125th Regiment Ill. *V.I.*, to serve in the War of the Rebellion. During the siege of Knoxville, Tenn., in 1863, while sitting at the door of his tent, he was struck by a piece of a shell from the enemy, and was killed instantly, leaving a wife and several children, and many brethren, to mourn their loss. Brother Sanders was highly respected, both as a preacher and scholar. He was, for a time before his death, the school examiner of his county, and spent considerable time in this work. His education would have given him wealth and position in society, had he desired it, but he preferred the humble position and small salary of a minister more than all the honor the world would give.

PHILIP SANFORD (1788—1869)

Philip was born in Westport, Mass., in 1788, converted in 1807, began to preach in 1808, moved to the State of New York in 1812, and was ordained at Galway, in the latter state, by Elder Elijah Shaw, and others, in 1816. During his stay in New York, he was very successful as a minister. We are not informed at what time he returned to Massachusetts, but it is probable that he spent the greatest part of his ministerial life there. He died at Westport, Mass., April 18, 1869, aged eighty-one years.

ELIJAH SCARBOROUGH (?—1864)

Elijah Scarborough lived, the latter part of his life, within a few miles of Columbus, Bartholomew County, Ind., on a farm. He was in good circumstances, and was a member of the Central Conference, Ind. He was a zealous, energetic preacher, of the old-fashioned type. When he spoke, it was done with much earnestness. It is probable that he was originally from one of the Southern States, as he frequently made long visits to the South, especially to Arkansas and Tennessee. He would stay for months at a time, holding meetings almost every day. He was a little lame in one foot, otherwise, hardy and tough—a regular pioneer. He died at his home in Indiana, not far from 1864, about seventy years old. He was highly respected for his goodness, by his co-laborers in the conference.

<u>DORSEY SCOTT (?—?)</u>

Dorsey Scott was a young minister that died in the State of Illinois, at the age of thirty-six years.

<u>JOHN SCOTT (1788—1847)</u>

This bro-her was a pioneer minister, and was willing to suffer any privation for the sake of the good cause of Christ. He was born in Virginia in 1788, moved to Kentucky when young, was married to Polly Crystal in 1812, was converted and commenced preaching about 1815. In 1818, he moved to Jennings County, Ind., where he remained for some time, but moved, the same year, to Laurence County, Ill. He was active in the ministry m both places. In the latter place, he organized a church in his own house. In 1824, he moved to Fountain County, Ind., and organized the first Christian Church in that county, the same year. Through his labors there, the Cole Creek Conference, Ind., was organized. He was ordained by this conference in 1825. In 1827, he moved to Illinois, to Fulton County, where he continued very active. When the Spoon River Conference was organized, he became one of its most prominent members. While he had the charge of some churches near his home, his travels in breaking new grounds, knew no bounds. Being appointed a delegate to the Cole Creek Conference Ind., (now the Western Conference) in 1847, while on his way there, he was taken sick with a fever. He stopped at the house of Mr. Peters, in

Champaign County, Ill., 160 miles from his home, where, after sixteen days' suffering, he died at the age of fifty-nine.

He had two sons in the Christian ministry when he died. He raised an excellent family, who became useful citizens. One of his daughters married Brother Thomas Harlass, who died in Merom, Ind., a few years ago. Elder Lucas, of Waverly, Iowa, speaks of him as a natural orator, with limited education, but extraordinary power as a speaker. At the beginning of his sermons, he was pale and trembling, but when warmed up and during the closing exhortation, the congregation would often be standing on their feet forgetting all about time and the surrounding circumstances. He had a tall and commanding form.

George Seager (1833—1865)

George was born in Phelps, Ontario County, N.Y., December 18, 1833, began to preach in 1851, and was ordained in the Northern Wisconsin Conference. In 1864, he was drafted into the United States" service, in the War of the Rebellion, and became a member of Company F. Wisconsin Cavalry. He died of erysipelas at Jeffersonville, Ind., April 10, 1865, aged thirty-two years.

Robert Seeper (?—1854)

Robert Seeper was a member of the Auglaize Conference, O. He died about 1854.

Joshua Selby (1783—1871)

Joshua was born in the State of Maryland, February 10, 1783, moved to Bourbon County, Ky., in 1804 or '5, and was married to Miss McCalla, October 22, 1807. She died in 1824, and in 1826, he was married to Elizabeth McCormick. The next year, he moved to Rush County, Ind., where he remained till death. In 1808, he joined the Christian Church, in Harrison County, Ky., and soon after, began to preach. He never made preaching his life work, but he continued a faithful local preacher for more than sixty years. He was a quiet, peaceable man, a good counselor, a member of the

Hurricane Christian Church, in Rush County, Ind., and of the Central Conference, the same state. He died at his home in Rush County, October 26, 1871, aged eighty-nine years.

ELIAS SEWARD (?—1868)

Elias Seward was born not far from the year 1800, and lived the most of his life in Hamilton and Butler counties, O. He was ordained in 1847, and labored in the neighboring churches for about twenty years. For the want of sufficient support to maintain an expensive family and the approach of old age, he did not labor much in the latter part of his life. He died in Hamilton, Butler County, O., in 1867 or '68. In person, the Elder was a tall, fine-looking man, of a mild and pleasant disposition.

? SHAKLE (?—?)

Brother Shakle was an aged man and a faithful minister in the State of Kentucky. He died many years ago.

JOHN SHANNON (1783—1852)

This Elder was born in 1783, was converted at the Cane Ridge Revival, in Kentucky, in 1802, and became a preacher soon after. He died in Licking County, O., September, 1852, aged sixty-nine years. He was a member of the Central Conference, O.

JAMES W. SHARRARD (1780—1860)

James W. Sharrard was born not far from 1780, was converted among the Baptists, and labored in that connection for some time, as a public speaker. He afterward joined the Christians and continued a licentiate minister for many years, but in 1838, he was ordained in Canada, Elder O.E. Morrill officiating. He spent the most of his- ministerial life in Canada. Although at the age of twenty-one, he could hardly read, yet such was the grasp of his mind and ambition, that he became not only a good English scholar, but also versed in the Greek language. He was a talented man, and acquired a good property. He died in Canada, not far from 1860, at the age of about eighty years.

ELIJAH H. SHARRARD (1811—1848)

Elijah, a son of the preceding, was born in Pickering, Canada West, in 1811, was converted in 1824, and joined the Christian Church at the above place, in 1832, the very day he was twenty-one years old. He left home on a preaching tour, and joined the New York Central Conference. From 1836 to 1845, he lived and labored, chiefly, in Onondaga and adjoining counties in New York. He devoted the most of his time to preaching. At the latter date, he went to Green County, Wis., where he preached considerable, while making a farm preparatory to removing his family, a wife and two children, to his new home. In 1848, he returned to his home for his family, but while making preparation for the journey, he was taken sick with typhus fever, of which he died January 9, 1848. The Elder had more than ordinary talent as a preacher, and was entirely devoted to the work.

CALVIN SHAW (?—1851)

Calvin was originally from the State of Vermont, but died in the bounds of the Northern New York Conference. In 1823, he was ordained at Williston, Vt., and labored faithfully in that state until 1843, when he moved to the neighborhood where he died. He had many afflictions in the latter part of his life. In 1848, he buried his wife and some other near relations about the same time. He died suddenly at his home, July 23, 1851. Elder Ira Allen speaks highly of his virtues.

ELIJAH SHAW (1793—1851)

This was one of the most devoted, active, and talented ministers in the ranks of the Christians, not only in one department of labor, but in all. It seemed all the same to him, whether as a pioneer, a missionary, in the hut of the peasant, as pastor of a fashionable church in a proud city,, as editor, evangelist, traveling agent, or what not, he was the plain, devoted Elijah Shaw.

He was born in Kensington, N.H., December 19, 1793. He was from a decidedly pious family. He professed religion at the age of sixteen, and was baptized by Elder Douglas Farnum. Two years after, in 1811, he entered the ministry, and was successful at once. Many were converted under his preaching the first years of his ministry. He was ordained March 31, 1814. For two years after his ordination, he labored in New England as an evangelist. In 1816, he went as a missionary to the State of New York, then a comparatively new country, and entirely new as to his own denomination, except a small portion in the eastern part of the state. During this time, he was often a companion of Elders Millard and Badger. On one occasion, when his garments were much the worse for wear, Elder Millard asked him: "Brother Shaw, don't you feel like going home?" His answer was, "I hardly dare to think of home. Home has no comparison with this place."

On his first visit to New York, he was absent thirteen months. After a short visit, and constant preaching among his old friends, he returned the second time to his field of labor in the then far West, where his work was blessed in the conversion of hundreds. In June, 1818, he returned again to his home in New England, and July 16, he was married at Andover, N.H., to Miss Julia True, a sister of Elder William True, a companion of the Elder in a part of his journeys in New England and New York. She was a kindred spirit with her husband. Immediately after their marriage, they started to their distant western home in the State of New York, where they continued to live until 1827. There is no calculating the amount of good accomplished by Elder Shaw, during these years. At the latter date, he returned to New England, after spending eleven years of his early life in the states of New York, Pennsylvania, Ohio, and in Upper Canada, countries then on the frontier.

Many were the hardships endured by the early ministers in those times, and Elder Shaw endured his full share of them, but it mattered not to him, as long as he saw souls converted. From 1827 to

1835, he labored mostly in New England, sometimes as pastor, and sometimes as an evangelist. Part of this time he was pastor of the Christian Church in Portland, Me. He traveled extensively through every state in New England, attending general meetings and conferences, everywhere bearing the brunt of the labor. The wonder is, that a man of so delicate a constitution could hold up under such constant work. While laboring with all his might in the conversion of sinners, he never lost sight of general measures that would add to the better organization of the denomination.

In 1835, he became editor of the "Christian Journal", a new periodical, started in Exeter, N.H. He continued his labor as resident editor of the "Journal" (and finally "Herald and Journal") for five years. Then in 1848, he moved his family to Lowell, Mass., where he became pastor of the church in that place, still continuing his contribution to the paper as one of its editors. In 1841, he traveled as missionary in the service of the New England Missionary Society, and in 1842, he became connected with the New Durham Academy as agent to raise funds. We next find him in Franklin, N.H., then in New Bedford, Mass. It is almost impossible, in a small space, to mention his various labors. From 1842 to 1850, were, perhaps, the most active years of his life, not excepting the eleven years of his early life in the West. In 1850, he made another journey to the West, accompanied by his wife. He passed over the field of his early labors, and met hundreds of his spiritual children and friends of other years. While on this trip, he went as far as the State of Michigan, and attended a session of the New York Central Christian Conference, at Honeoye Falls, where he met the venerable Badger, struck down with paralysis, very near the end of his journey, and David Millard, with many other co-workers of his early life. His journey was a perfect ovation, and thousands of the younger generation gazed with veneration upon him who had been the spiritual guide of their fathers and mothers. The writer of these notes had the privilege, at that time, of witnessing some of these reunions, and of grasping the hands of these old patriarchs, Shaw, Badger, and Millard, at the Central Conference, N.Y., at Honeoye

Falls; the two former passed away soon, but Father Millard remained with us twenty-three years longer. This journey, while it lasted, stimulated both mind and body of the old veteran, but after his return, it was found there was more loss than gain to his health and strength. According to his custom, however, he entered upon his duties as usual. He finally moved to Fall River, Mass., with the purpose of resting for awhile, but he had been so accustomed to labor, that inactivity did not agree with him. He took charge of the church at Portsmouth, R.I., intending to preach on Sundays, and rest through the week. His wife was taken sick and lingered for weeks upon the brink of the grave. The loving husband watched unremittingly by the sick bed of his companion. The labor and the anxiety were too much for his overworked constitution. Before the full recovery of his wife, Elder Shaw was taken sick, and after waiting for two weeks as patient as a child, he died May 5, 1851, in his fifty-eighth year.

The writings of Elder Shaw would make a valuable volume if collected and published together, as he always wrote on practical subjects. His "Memoirs," compiled by his daughter, is an interesting volume. It is a clear index of the character of our subject.

ABRAM SHEPHERD (?—1828)

Abram Shepherd died near Mechanicsburg, Champaign County, O., about 1828. He was then a very old man, having been born about 1750. He moved from Kentucky to Ohio. He is said to have been a very good man. He preached constantly to the last.

MARK H. SHEPHERD (1810—1839)

This young man had a short but brilliant career in the ministry. He was born in 1810, and was raised in Deerfield, N.H. He professed religion in 1827, and commenced preaching the year following. In 1830, he moved to the State of Maine, and for five years continued his pastoral relation with churches in that state,, where he was very successful in the conversion of sinners and the strengthening of the denomination. In 1835, he moved to Athens, and labored one year, with fair prospects of future usefulness, when he was taken with bleeding at the lungs, from the effect of which he lost his voice. He was an excellent man and an able preacher. He died May 5, 1839, at the age of twenty-nine years.

<u>George Shidler (1776—1828)</u>

This faithful and energetic preacher was born in Washington County, Penn., on May 12, 1776, and was brought up in the same community. He was married to Abigail Wolverton when young, and soon after, moved to Athens County. O., where he continued to reside till 1806, when he moved to Preble County, the same state. The first year of his residence in Preble County, he raised a crop of corn in the midst of the forest trees, with no fence around the patch, and had a tolerable crop.

Hitherto, he had never made a profession of religion; but in 1808, under the preaching of Elder David Purviance and others, he gave his heart to the Lord. With a man of the temper of our subject to be converted meant to be a worker in the cause. He was baptized the same day that he professed religion, and from that time became an active worker in the church, both publicly and privately. In 1810, he was ordained by Elders David Purviance and Abraham Vorhees. He at once entered into the active work of a traveling preacher. He made long trips to Indiana, Kentucky, and Pennsylvania, and his labors were blessed in the conversion of many. His principal work was in his own state, in Preble and adjoining counties. At the time of his death he was pastor of Seven Mile Church, near his home, and of Bank Spring, further away. He had charge of these two churches for many years, and they had prospered well under his fostering care. His talent was of the exhortation kind, though he was a plain, practical, and efficient preacher as well. He was very popular among his neighbors as a straightforward and upright man, and to this day, more than fifty years after his death, his name is a popular one among the older residents of the community in which he lived.

He died suddenly. Having been in Hamilton, Butler County, on business, he was taken sick on his way home. He stopped at the house of Brother Pottinger, where every attention was given him; but he grew worse and worse every day. His family was with him, and so were many of the neighbors; but all remedies and nursing failed. He died August 27, 1828, aged fifty-two years.

JOHN SHIELD

John Shield was, by birth, an Irishman. But whatever faith he professed in his youth, at an early day he became an active minister in the Christian Church, in the State of Ohio. About 1816, he lived in Columbus and preached much in that neighborhood. He was highly respected for his firmness and ability as a Christian and minister. He had some of the Irish brogue in his speech to the last. He was a large man, and a fluent and positive speaker. He taught school in Columbus. He was a man of culture and great self-control, and was Justice of the Peace in Franklin County before Columbus was laid but. He moved to New Orleans, where he and all his family died of yellow fever, his wife dying first. A piece of poetry was composed by the husband, on her death, called "Shield's Lamentations."

JACOB SHIVELY

This was a minister laboring in the State of Kentucky, about 1825. I find, by the periodicals of that day, that a minister of that name preached in Columbia County, Penn., in 1833, likely the same person. He has been dead many years.

EPHRAIM SHOCKLEY (1794—1842)

Ephraim was born about 1794, and was a resident of Fair Haven, Mass., for a time. He moved from the latter place to Honeoye Falls, N.Y., and united with the New York Central Christian Conference about 1830. He was a man of great moral and Christian worth. He died at Honeoye Falls, N.Y., June 25, 1842, aged forty-eight years.

<u>Leonard Shoemaker (1812—1874)</u>

This brother was born December 12, 1812, was converted, and began to preach in 1837. He was married to Maragret McKinney, a daughter of Elder James McKinney, of Pleasant Hill, Montgomery County, Ind. In his early ministry, he labored in the bounds of the Western Indiana Conference, then moved to the Miami Reserve, in Howard County, and connected himself with the Tippecanoe Conference. Later in life, he moved again to the bounds of the- former conference, and became connected with that body. In 1857, he moved to Merom, Sullivan County, in order to avail himself of the advantages of education in the Merom Bluff Academy, an institution of learning that preceded Union Christian College in that village. He was very active in the work of bringing the above college to Merom. He continued to live in the village; preaching in the surrounding churches until within a few years of his death, and until his five children, four daughters and one son, were educated, when he moved to Waynetown, in the same state, and where he died September 21, 1874, in consequence of a fall from his carriage, while acting as an agent of the Church Extension Society.

The Elder was not an educated man, but he had advanced ideas, and was a great lover of education. He was a large, heavy man, full of earnestness in his pulpit work. He was also a self-sacrificing man, as were most of his comrades in the pew West. All through life he was in limited circumstances, yet such was his estimate of education that he moved to Merom, as he expressed it, for no other purpose than to give the children, that God had given him, the advantages of education, which he could not give them in the place he lived before moving. He succeeded well. He brought up five well-educated children; the son graduated with honor in Union Christian College, and became a prominent minister in the same church. The four daughters became good scholars, and two of them married ministers. The Elder himself was a successful preacher, an able revivalist, and was very useful to the end of his days. He was also a believer in order and system in church matters. He was a good man, and though he died in his strength, yet he had, for thirty-seven years, performed a good work in the church and in society.

W. SHOW (1792—1869)

This Elder was born September 1, 1792, and began to preach in 1822. He moved from Laurel Hill, Penn., to Hardin County, O., in 1837. He carried the same spirit of activity that be had exercised so much to the interest of the cause in Pennsylvania with him to the State of Ohio. He helped to organize the Auglaize Christian Conference in 1838, of which he continued an active member until death. He was the means of gathering scattered members in Hardin and Marion counties, O., and to organize them into Christian Churches, and assisted largely in building for them houses of worship. For many years before his death, he was so afflicted with rheumatism, that all his preaching was done in a sitting posture. His wife died two years before her husband. They never had any children of their own, but they brought up four or five children that were given them, and did a good part by them.

The Elder was a benevolent man. Beside assisting many churches in building meeting houses, and ministers who were engaged in preaching, and the poor of his own community, be donated, a few years before his death, tor religious, educational, and benevolent purposes, the sum of $4,500 at one time, and willed $1,000 more at his death. The rest of his property, he donated for destitute churches near his own home. He died September 12, 1869, in Hardin County, O., aged seventy- seven years. He was a tall, well-formed man, with energetic utterance. As a minister, his usefulness consisted more in assisting others than in what he did personally. His preaching was deliberate, more in a conversational tone than in the impassioned declamation of public speakers, generally.

<u>JOHN SHOWERS (?—1872)</u>

This brother was a minister in the eastern part of the State of New York. He labored for some time in Fulton and Saratoga counties, in that state, where he was quite successful. He was received a member of the New York Eastern Conference in 1812, and died in 1872.

<u>JAMES SHURTLIFF (?—?)</u>

We find the first account of this brother in Lewis County, Va., in 1827, in the same neighborhood as his brother Oliver. From 1830 to 1835, we see an account of his laboring in Meigs and adjoining counties, as co-laborer with Barzillai Miles and others.

<u>OLIVER SHURTLIFF (?—?)</u>

Oliver Shurtliff, a brother of the above, lived in Frederick, Lewis County, Va., where he buried his wife in 1827.

<u>WILLIAM SIBLEY (1813—1873)</u>

This Elder was born in 1813, was converted in June, 1831, commenced preaching in North Rush, N.Y., in April, 1843, and was ordained November 11, the same year. After thirty years of faithful labor in the ministry, he died in North Rush, the place where he began his ministry, March 28, 1873.

<u>SAMUEL SILSBY (?—?)</u>

Samuel Silsby was converted under the labors of Elder Joseph Badger, in 1818. He labored with success at Chili, N.Y., in 1824. In 1839, he was living in Rochester, Mich., and occasionally writing for our periodicals. From Michigan he moved to the State of Iowa, and the last account we have of him, he was living with one of his daughters in that state. It is reported that he is dead, though we have no particulars of the event.

<u>Richard Simonton (1787—1849)</u>

This minister of Christ filled a wide sphere in the Christian Church, in the State of Ohio, for many years, and though not a learned man, nor in any way noted as a great orator, yet his good, sound sense and exemplary deportment gave him a power that few others possessed. He was born in North Carolina in 1787, of poor but respectable parentage. His parents moved to Warren County, O., about 1801, where Richard grew up, a lively boy, full of fun and innocent mischief. About that time, the Christians held meetings in the house of Jedediah Tingle, near the village of Lebanon, the county seat of Warren County. Great crowds attended these meetings, and scores were converted. Among the converts was Richard Simonton, who gave his heart to God, and soon became as active in religion as he had before been in fun and frolic. He at once became a zealous worker in these meetings, and took public part in the exercises.

About this time, he was married to Mary Hatfield, a lady of great moral worth, who became a valuable help to her husband during his active ministry. Soon after their marriage, they moved to the adjoining county of Preble, where he continued to sing and exhort, to the edification of the congregations. Not long after, he moved back to Warren County, where he continued to live the balance of his life. After his return to Warren County, he was ordained in the Bethany Christian Church, of which he became pastor, and continued in the same relation till near the close of his earthly pilgrimage. The Fellowship Church, in the same neighborhood, together with the Sycamore and Burlington churches, in Hamilton County, were the societies that received the principal part of the Elder's life labors, and well did he serve them. All were strong churches during his life. Soon after the commencement of his ministry, he became one of the most prominent members of the Miami Conference, O., and, doubtless, his influence as a member had much to do with the growth of the churches within its territory.

The Elder lived near the village of Lebanon during his entire married life, except the short time he spent in Preble County. He had a small farm, but never suffered his labor on the place to interfere with his religious duties. His education was limited, but his strong and active mind overcame, in a great degree, his early deficiency in this respect. While he did not pretend to master abstract subjects of Theology, his masterly manner of speaking, and his strong common sense, together with his thorough knowledge of human nature, made him an opponent not to be easily vanquished. His faith in God was unshaken. He believed in the efficacy of prayer, and while engaged in this, his whole soul was drawn out in his petitions. While he was an earnest believer in heart-felt religion and a thorough conversion of the whole man, he was not of a gloomy or morbid disposition; on the other hand, he was full of wit and cheerfulness, sometimes bordering on eccentricity. This made his discourses lively, and drew many to hear him that might otherwise have stayed away from meeting.

His first wife died in 1834, of cancer, and some years later, he married a widow lady, by the name of Smith, with whom he lived happily to the end of his days, and who survived him. He raised a large family of children, one of whom, Elder Hiram Simonton, is yet (1880) a prominent minister of the same church. For about thirty years, he was esteemed one of the strong and reliable ministers of the church in the south-western part of Ohio, the field of his labors. He died September 24, 1849, aged sixty-three years.

<u>CHRISTY SINE (1800—1859)</u>

This brother, for many years, was a leading Christian minister in the Shenandoah Valley, Va. He was the pastor of several churches, taught a select school on Timber Ridge, held many debates with ministers of other churches, and wrote a great deal for the periodicals of the denomination. In a word, he was a stirring, live man in the cause.

He was born not far from the year 1800, and began to preach about 1827, in Hampshire County, Va., having been married some years previous. About 1830, he moved to the vicinity of the Timber Ridge Christian Church. Here he taught a school of some seventy or eighty pupils for seven or eight years, preached in the surrounding communities, where many revivals followed, and several new churches were organized through his instrumentality. He continued his pastoral relations with the Timber Ridge Church for about twenty-two years.

In his personal appearance, the Elder was a tall, heavy-built man, with a dark complexion. He had a very commanding appearance in the pulpit. Although his voice was somewhat harsh, yet his utterance was fluent and clear, and he generally seemed to be master of his subject. In his intercourse, he was sociable, and his conversation was usually oh religious subjects. His greatest forte, aside from religion, was history, of which he was very fond, and of which he made use largely in his sermons. He was, by trade, a saddler, an occupation he followed part of the time for many years. After the death of his first wife, in 1845, he married again. The name of his second wife was Nancy Murphy. He died of dyspepsia, which turned into dropsy, about the year 1859.

JAMES SISK (1809—1867)

James was born in 1809, commenced preaching about 1842, and continued a faithful minister till death. He lived for many years in Randolph and Jay counties, Ind., and was an acceptable member of the Bluffton Conference. He was a delicate looking man, unassuming in his appearance, but his success and perseverance in the work were wonderful. He generally carried on a small farm, as his salary was not sufficient for the support of his family; yet he would suffer nothing to interfere with his appointments. He was very successful in the conversion of sinners, as his trust was entirely in the Lord. He died April 27, 1867.

PELEG SISSON (?—1826)

In the "Christian Register" of 1836, I find that this minster died October 25, 1826.

Thomas Sliter (?—1863)

Thomas Sliter was a licentiate or unordained preacher in the Miami Reserve Conference, Ind. He died about 1863.

Daniel Smith (1784—1827)

The subject of this sketch was born in New Hampshire in 1784, and was one of our early ministers. He had been in the ministry several years at the time of his death. He died at Portsmouth, N.H., March 13, 1827, in the forty-third year of his age.

David Smith (?—1840)

David Smith was a member of the New York Central Conference. He died about 1840.

F. Smith (?—?)

F. Smith died at West Campton, N.H., before the year 1875.

Elias Smith (1769—1846)

This indefatigable worker in the cause of the Reformation that gave rise to the Christian Church in New England was of Baptist and Congregational parentage. He tells us his father was a Baptist and his mother a firm Congregationalist. He was born at Lynn, in the State of Connecticut, June 17, 1769. Through the influence of his mother and her brother, and only by the mere consent of his father, Elias was christened early in life, though much against his own will. He always looked back upon the act with detestation and abhorrence.

In 1782, his father moved to Woodstock, in the State of Vermont, when Elias was thirteen years old. At this time, and even before he left the State of Connecticut, his mind was much exercised on religious subjects. In the beginning of the Revolutionary War, when he was only five years old, the peculiar Northern Lights that appeared about that time, and was regarded by many as a token of something terrible, had a great influence on his young mind. At the age of sixteen, he was converted, though, as it was common then in

New England, he had great doubt of the reality of the work. In 1789, he was baptized in Woodstock, by Elder Grow, of the Baptist Church, and at the same time joined that people. Soon after, his mind became much exercised on the subject of preaching, and after much resistance on his part, he yielded to the divine call, as he regarded it, and preached his first sermon in July, 1790. At that time he was teaching school, an occupation which he followed for several years. Doubts of his call to the work returned after this, and he finally decided to preach no more. It is useless to describe all the perplexity of his mind during this period. He was finally satisfied of the reality of the "call to preach" by a singular dream, which he says was verified in almost every particular. From this time, he never doubted his mission. When convinced that God had called him to this great work, regardless of all other considerations, he gave up his school, bid his parents, kindred, and friends farewell, and proceeded upon his mission in the name of the Lord. His success as a preacher was great from the beginning. His first field of labor was Piermont, Vt., then Haverhill, Mass., Lee and New Market, N.H., and Salsbury and Woburn, Mass. Indeed, he held meetings all around, but those mentioned above were the central places of his labor during that period. He soon extended his labors as far as Boston. In the latter city, he received much encouragement from Dr. Stillman and Elder Tillman, two prominent Baptist ministers of the town. His mind was much exercised on the doctrine of election, and kindred subjects, but on the whole, he passed a sound orthodox examination in the Baptist Church, In 1792, he was ordained at Lee, N.H. The principal ministers engaged in the exercises were Dr. Shepherd, Elder Baldwin, and others, all prominent preachers in the Baptist Church.

January 7, 1793, he was married to Miss Mary Burleigh, of Lee, N.H. He was now in good circumstances for a young minister. The churches were well pleased with his labor, his income was sufficient for his maintenance, and all things seemed to promise him a bright future. In the midst of all his prosperity, however, the Elder was unhappy. He felt that he was bound, that the people of his congregation had bought him. He was longing for freedom. He resigned his charge of the churches, to the regret of his people. After his release in 1794, he traveled through many parts of Massachusetts and Connecticut, and in company with his father, he paid a visit to his birth place in Lynn, in the latter state. He next took charge of the Baptist Church in Woburn, Mass., and was installed as pastor there in 1798. These ceremonies were not to his taste, but the reasoning of Dr. Stillman, in whom he had great confidence, prevailed. Now we see plain Elias Smith a regular clergyman of an aristocratic church, with broadcloth garments, three cornered hat, and all the paraphernalia of a fashionable minister. It was not in the nature of the man, however, to bear this torment long. He left Woburn in 1801, not knowing where to go or what to do, only that he was determined to preach a free gospel in his own way, accountable to none but God alone. From this time until his entrance upon the practice of medicine, in 1817, a period of sixteen years, his life vas such a constant scene of labor, persecution, and hardship, that it is a wonder his iron constitution did not break down under the burden. In 1802, in connection with others,' he stood upon the platform of a free gospel and the right of private judgment to all in matters of religion. Besides constant preaching, pamphlet after pamphlet proceeded from his busy pen. These pamphlets generally bore hard on the ministers of the day. One of his first printed productions was a comparison of the apostles of Christ with the clergymen of his time. Another was the "Ministers Looking-glass." These subjects, with many similar ones, were handled in the Elder's peculiar racy style. As might be expected, these brought on rejoinders from the persons assailed, and many bitter invectives were pronounced against him. Many friends turned from him. Bad reports were circulated against him, especially his financial affairs at Woburn. He was sued, and at one time there was fair prospect of his being imprisoned for debt. These financial troubles were caused by his having, sometime before, entered into mercantile relation with others, and come out sadly embarrassed. It is true he came out honorably, but the reports continued. Mobs were raised against him in Portsmouth, N.H., and his life was really in danger at times, but the more he was persecuted the harder he labored, and the more friends came out on his side; so while he had many bitter enemies, he had also many intense friends.

The church organized by him in Portsmouth, N.H., in 1803, of only four or five members, soon grew to a membership of one hundred and fifty, and the probability is, that more than half of these would have died, if necessary, with their pastor. There was no halfway work in this movement. In 1804, the Baptist Church at Woburn, disowned him, Elias claiming that he had withdrawn from that church two years before. In 1805, Elder Abner Jones, who had proclaimed the Bible alone as the perfect creed of Christians, seven years previous, visited him at Portsmouth, and continued his labor for several weeks. From this time the two men became hearty co-workers in the Reformation. While in this place, owing to the publication of an anonymous pamphlet, supposed to have been written by Elias Smith, he came very nearly being mobbed several times. At one time, while preaching from the text, "Ye have not yet resisted unto blood/' the mob surrounded the church and but for the prompt action of the congregation, serious consequences would have followed; his friends gathered around him twenty deep, and conducted him to his home, which they watched through the night.

In the same year, he commenced a publication of a religious periodical, issued quarterly, which, in 1808, was converted into the *Herald of Gospel Liberty,* the publication of which is continued to this day (1880). This enterprise was suggested by Hon. Isaac Wilber, of Compton, R.I., a member of Congress at the time, and a plan was decided upon, but after reflecting on this, the Elder decided to take the responsibility upon himself and discard the arrangements with Wilber and others. The subscription list numbered 274 at first, but soon increased to 1,500. In 1810, he was induced to move the paper and his family from Portsmouth, N.H., to Portland, Me., a step that he always regretted. The next year, he again moved, this time to Philadelphia, Penn., and in 1812, he prepared and published his "Bible Dictionary." During his stay in that city, he not only published this book, the *Herald,* and other productions of his pen, but had charge of the church and made extensive journeys to Virginia, North Carolina, and other states. But while here, his expenses were greater than his income, from sickness in his family and the outlays made to publish the works that he wrote. His debts were pressing heavily upon him, and for the purpose of decreasing his expenses, he determined to return to Portsmouth, N.H., and took his wife with him, that they might make arrangements to move back. She finished her visit before he did, an<J returned to Philadelphia under the care of Elder Plummer. Elder Smith was taken sick soon after with the typhoid fever, and before his recovery, his faithful wife died, and one of his daughters was seriously ill, although she afterward recovered. He was now surrounded with trouble and sorrow on every hand. A short time before his wife's death, he had written to her to be ready to return to Portsmouth by a certain day. His debts were large and the money due him for papers and other things not easy to be obtained. As soon as he recovered, he began to preach and write with his former energy, and the thousands who heard his sermons or read his productions at this time had no conception of the sore anxiety and trouble by which he was weighed down. In the latter part of 1814, he was married again to Rachel Thurber, of Providence, R.I.

From the foregoing we may judge as to what were some of the reasons why he took the course he did in 1816. At this time, he was forty-seven years old, his family was large, and his debts were of great magnitude to one in his circumstances. He was then in the zenith of his physical powers, but his labors for the last fourteen years had been immense enough, indeed, to break down a person of less fortitude, and the wonder is that both mind and body had not become a wreck. Moreover, the system of church finances, which he and his co-laborers had encouraged, believing that God would provide means of support, was now very much against him, although, had his family been smaller, or had he not been embarrassed by the debts incurred in the publication of his books and paper, he might have done differently. As it was, we, at the present day, can hardly conceive of any plan for supporting his family different from the one he adopted. It is well known that, with all his talent and energy, he lacked sufficient stability to succeed, or as Elder Moses How says, "If Elias Smith had the stability of Abner Jones, he would certainly be considered one of the greatest men of his time."

From 1816 to 1840, he practiced medicine, preaching very seldom, although he wrote a great deal on the subject of medicine. For twenty-three years of this time he was not connected with any denomination whatever, although he advocated Universalism a part of this time. In 1840, he again united with the Christian Church, and it was his intention then, at seventy-one years of age, to enter the work he had left twenty-four years before, and with the same zeal. He was in good health, a hale, hearty old man, but the habits of the preceding years, the absence of old associates, and the lack of confidence on the part of the brotherhood prevented the accomplishment of much good in the last years. He died at Lynn, Mass., June 29, 1846, aged seventy-seven years.

Much of the character of Elder Smith, as a man, writer, and minister, may be seen in the preceding pages; but his true greatness, originality, and boldness are to be witnessed in the results of what was a mighty work, accomplished in an age of sectarian bigotry, and under most unfavorable circumstances. Everyone has defective qualities, and the Elder was no exception to the rule.

Gordon Smith (1802—1848)

Gordon was born in Meredith, N.H., October 28, 1802. At the age of twenty- four, he was converted, and began to preach soon after. He labored for twelve years in New England and Canada, with great success. In 1838, he moved to Ohio, where he labored zealously until 1845, his field of labor being, for the greater part of the time, in the northern part of the state. His last place of residence was in York, Sandusky County, O. In September, 1845, in company with his wife, he started on a journey through the East, intending to spend a year or so among the scenes of his former labors. While on the way, he was taken 'sick. He traveled for some days, until he arrived at the house of a friend, Josiah Lane, where he died, four weeks later, October 17, 1848, at the age of forty-three years.

HOSEA SMITH, JR (1792—1854)

This brother was the son of Hosea and Abigail (Hersey) Smith, both natives of Massachusetts. Our subject was born in Pembroke, Me., whither his parents had moved some time before, in May, 1792. His educational advantages were few, but he could read and write quite well, and was used to all manual labor.

In 1811, he was married to Miss Mary Damon, and soon settled in Washington County, Me., on some new land he had purchased, where they labored hard to secure for themselves a comfortable home. They were the parents of thirteen children, eleven of whom joined the Christian Church during their father's life time, and one (Elder E.P. Smith) has been a minister tor a number of years. In 1819, Mr. Smith and his wife were converted under the labors of Elders Ne wall and Nutt, were baptized by the latter, and at once became active and working members of the church. It was the great desire of Elder Nutt and others that Brother Smith should enter the ministry, and he was strongly urged to do this, but would not consent for some time, feeling his unfitness. In a few months he began his ministry as a licentiate, but was not ordained till 1831. His principal fields of labor were at Charleston, Lubec, and Eastport, Me., the Province of New Brunswick, and he was especially successful at Deer Island, where he labored for twenty years. He died in Charlotte, Washington County, Me., March 7, 1854.

He was peculiarly mild in his manners and disposition, and his great influence was due not so much to eloquence and brilliancy as a speaker as to a pious, consistent life and the sympathy which he had for all in sorrow and trouble. His best gifts were shown in his pastoral relations.

JACOB SMITH (?—?)

Jacob Smith was a minister in the Central Indiana Chris tian Conference.

JAMES SMITH (?—1841)

James was a native of Virginia, and was of Methodist parentage. He was a member of that church, and commenced preaching in 1801. In 1807, he moved to Mt. Vernon, O., where he remained until 1840. For twenty years of his 'Stay in this place, he served as clerk of the county court, and was, for a time, the president of a bank, and although engaged in secular labors, he did not neglect the work of the ministry, but preached whenever opportunity offered. In 1811, he became convinced of the fallacy of the doctrines of the trinity, and infant sprinkling, and the next year, he, with many others, left the Methodist Church, and in 1813, were organized into a Christian Church by Elder George Alkire. Elder Smith still continued his labors as pastor with the same success as had characterized his past efforts.

He practiced medicine for ten years before his death, at Mt. Sterling, O. He died in that place, having been thrown from a horse a few hours before, June 13, 1841. He was a man of more than ordinary talent, and his writings show much culture and power. His secular pursuits were a serious hindrance to a very active ministry, but for all his other interests he seemed to consider religion as the chief thing.

JOHN SMITH (1798—1841)

John was a native of Vermont, was born in 1798, was converted in that state in 1812, commenced preaching before he was twenty years of age, and had nearly completed his forty-third year when he died. The first years of his ministry he spent in traveling from place to place, and generally on foot, as he was very poor. In 1825, he was married to Miss Lucy Whitney, and in the same year, moved to Bangor, N.Y., where he labored faithfully for ten years, but in 1834, he was severely afflicted and for six years was unable to walk or stand. He bore his suffering with great fortitude, and was very happy to think that he could attend family prayers, and once in a great while could visit the house of God, and communicate so easily with his friends. He was greatly beloved by his flock, and many date their new birth to his prayers in their behalf. He died at his home in Bangor, N.Y., March 24, 1841.

JOHN SMITH (1803—1865)

This brother was born in Pennsylvania in 1803. He embraced religion early in life, soon began to improve his gift, and was ordained in 1840. He spoke with a great deal of energy, and was more powerful in exhortations than in sermons requiring deep thought and logical reasoning. He was, in the beginning of his ministry, a member of the Valley Virginia Christian Conference, but in 1846, he joined the Rays Hill Pennsylvania Conference, and continued a member until his death in 1865.

JOSEPH SMITH (1811—1850)

Joseph was born in New Hampshire, in 1811. The last ten years of his life were spent in New Bedford, Mass., preaching, and a part of the time, editing the "New Bedford Reporter," but becoming embarrassed in his business affairs, he went to California in 1849 or '50, for the purpose of improving his finances. He settled at Stockton, where he still labored in the cause of the Master. He died in the beginning of his usefulness in the above place, in June, 1850, in his thirty-ninth year.

JOSEPH SMITH (1790—1843)

Joseph was born in 1790, and brought up under the influence of the Methodist Church. He began his ministerial labors in that church, but in 1835, in consequence of a greater affinity of feeling and harmony of belief, he united with the Christian Church. He was baptized by Elder Benjamin Taylor soon after, and from that time until his death, his interests and labors were wholly for the latter church. He died at Lyons, Mich., December 16, 1843. He practiced medicine during a few of the best years of his life. He stood high in the estimation of his neighbors as a benevolent and upright man.

JOSEPH SMITH (?—1834)

Joseph Smith is spoken of in a letter from Elder Shaw, in 1834, as a good and devoted man, and had been in the ministry for thirty years, or since 1804, and that he was well advanced in years at the time of his death in 1834, at Kennebunk, Me.

ROBERTSON SMITH (?—1828)

Robertson Smith died August 26, 1828, as we learn from the "Christian Almanac" of 1836.

ROBINSON SMITH (?—1826)

Robinson Smith was a co-laborer of Elder Badger, in New York, and is mentioned in a letter of Elder Joseph Badger as having died about 1826, in Genesee County, N.Y.

SARAH SMITH (1845—1872)

Sarah was born in Ohio in 1845, was converted under the preaching of Elder Marts, of the Auglaize Conference, when fifteen years of age, and con tinned a humble follower of the Master until her death at Greenville, Mich., April 27, 1872, in her twenty-seventh year. She left, at her death, a volume of sermons, some prose writings, and also some poetry. It is said by those who knew her, that she was an, able speaker and expounder of the truths of the Bible. Dying so young, her usefulness was cut short.

URIAH SMITH (?—?)

Uriah Smith was a brother of Elias Smith and was first a Baptist minister, but became a Christian preacher during the time of the Reformation. There are no dates either of his birth or death.

W.D. SMITH (1836—1878)

This brother was born in 1836, was converted under the labors of Elder Hayes, preached in Clay County, Ind., through the influence of his spiritual father, in 1867, and was ordained at Merom in 1868. The boy was left an orphan in early life, and his educational privileges were not good. He spent three years in a cavalry company in the War of the Rebellion. He was a distant relation of the celebrated Daniel Boone, the mighty hunter and warrior. In the war he had many narrow escapes. When he began to preach, he entered into the work with all his might. In Clay and Owen counties, Ind., he had great success in winning souls to Christ. Revivals followed his labors everywhere. In 1876, he moved to Eastern Illinois, and labored with several churches in that part of the country with much success. He labored two years with the Jack Oak and other churches, and then moved to Arthur, McVille, and Mansfield. He organized churches in the two latter places, and the work of the Lord was prospering in his hands. In the midst of his usefulness, he was struck down with disease. He died of pneumonia, November 10, 1878, after a few days illness, leaving a wife and four children, with many friends, to mourn his departure.

ABRAHAM SNETHEN (1794—1877)

In many respects, Abraham Snethen is the most noted man in the list of ministers in this volume. The compiler has had, at several times, an opportunity to hear from our subject a detailed history of the events of his peculiar early life, from his own lips. His career began in the wild woods of Kentucky, and he continued a pioneer man during his long life. The life of our brother reads much like a novel, yet it is very instructive as showing what a man of the least advantages of education, wealth, and culture can accomplish by following the true path. Many events in the life of our brother will appear strange, if not incredible, to those that never knew but one phase of society. Few can realize the influence of superstition on the lower classes in many rural districts, such as the native place of Snethen; such as signs, witches, ghosts, lucky and unlucky days, and many other kinds of fetishism, together with the pride they take in personal bravery, so that every community has its bully or best man in a fight, second best and so down to the lowest grade—the coward. Brother Snethen had a full experience of all these, and such was the philosophic power of his mind that he turned them all to good account, both in conversation and preaching; like a man rising out of a mist and, from an elevated position, looking calmly upon the medium whence he came, thus making his life-work in the service of God, strong upon the misfortunes of the past.

Our subject was born in Bourbon County, Ky., January 15, 1794. His father was from New Jersey, and his mother, whose maiden name was Castro, was born in Virginia. His parents moved to Bryant Station, Ky., about the time it was besieged by the Indians. They settled, finally, in the mountain part of Bourbon, on Goose and Grapevine creeks. The land was poor, the neighbors were poor and ignorant, and their principal means of support was hunting, and boiling saltpeter, from the different caves around. William Snethen, Abraham's father, was somewhat of a horse jockey, and our subject was brought up to that occupation. An event connected with horses, occurred when Abraham was a boy of fifteen. A fine young filly was taken sick, and as was the custom, the family concluded that the animal was bewitched. As the parents had to go away that day, Abraham was left in charge of the sick filly, and was strictly commanded to allow no person to have any fire or water on that day, as the witch herself (generally a woman) might be the one to ask for these, and if obtained, the colt must die. In a short time old Mother Cornega, a fast friend of the family and a good woman, came from a long distance on foot, to visit the Snethens. About the first thing she asked of the boy, was for fire to light her pipe, then water to quench her thirst; both were granted. The good woman went home, not suspecting the reputation she was gaining, the parents returned, found what had been done in their absence, and as they thought, who the witch was. The filly died, the boy got a whipping, and the warm friendship between Mother Cornega and the Snethens was blasted for life.

Hitherto the boy had never been to meeting, for none was held within reach. In 1811, he went to a place on the south fork of the Kentucky River to gather corn, some forty miles from home. While at this place he quarreled with Ned Bowman; Ned's grandfather, old Cornelius Bowman, a Methodist preacher, held a meeting in the neighborhood. Abraham went to the meeting, not to hear preaching but to fight j\ed. During the sermon he was deeply convicted, gave up fighting Ned, threw away his cards and became a much better man, generally. Before this he had been a good fighter, though a small man, was an expert in dancing and card playing, and other games of chance; and although a believer in witches, ghosts, signs, lucky and unlucky days, yet his pride led him to defy all these, especially the witches, ever since he was whipped by his father for letting Mother Cornega have fire and water, and so lose the valuable filly. Indeed, he boasted of being a witch himself, and by some ingenious manipulation, such as shooting blood from the sun, he led some of his ignorant neighbors to believe that he was versed in the black art.

In 1812, there was a meeting held in his father's neighborhood, or, as it was called, the "diggins." It came around as follows: James, or, as he was generally called, "Danger" Smith had married a wife who had been a member of a Methodist Church in her Virginia home. Samuel Brown, a traveling Methodist preacher, while on his rounds, heard of this ex-sister, came to "Danger's" house and asked permission to preach in his dwelling. Smith consented— not that he cared anything about the meeting, but out of respect for his good wife. The meeting was announced many weeks ahead, but unfortunately before the time for holding it came, old "Danger" died. The minister came to time and the whole "diggins" were out; not so much to hear the preacher, as to see the show. Abraham was among the number, and to him it was his second meeting in life. The preacher began the service as usual, by reading and singing from his pocket Bible and hymn-book. Being a poor singer, and none of the congregation able to assist in that kind of singing, that part of the service was a failure. When the prayer came and the good man was kneeling on the rough and dirty floor, the performance was so odd that it produced a general titter in the congregation. To add to the cousternation.at this time, Dan Sibers, a half-drunken ruffian, to show his smartness, moved forward taking hold of the preacher's hair with both hands, spoke in a deep guttural voice, "Ain't I a roarer?" This was too much even for the pioneer minister; he soon rose to his feet and closed the meeting with very few remarks. Off went the preacher over the hills. The congregation dispersed to talk of the oddity of the service. Jim, a son of "Danger" Smith's, was at work boding saltpeter, as he did not care about the meeting, although he did not wish to oppose it, as it was held by consent of his dead father. When Sibers and others told him what had occurred, Jim said it was wrong and that he must whip Sibers for his mean act. They fought; Sibers was badly worsted and for a time lay as a dead man. All these confirmed the people, generally, that religious meetings were bad things—something in the nature of witchcraft, and for the sake of peace, a decree was passed that no meetings should be allowed in the "diggins" in the future. In 1827, when Snethen had become an earnest and successful minister, he returned to that place, and by reluctant consent, had permission to hold one meeting, the first held in the place since the Smith and Sibers fight. He told his experience. Had consent to preach again. The result was, he had great success, thirty-six of the simple mountaineers were soundly converted, and many more came to the conclusion that preaching the gospel was not the bad thing they had thought it to be. As Snethen could not stay, he gave up the church to old Billy Strong, a pioneer Baptist minister of the neighborhood.

Abraham having heard in his mountain home of the great Ohio River, and a state of the same name on the other side, in 1814, concluded, by way of an adventure, to go and see both. He went to Cincinnati; it looked to him like a new world. He attended meeting. The old conviction of the Bowman meeting of 1811, came back. He was converted, and began to preach, but was a member of no church. In this state of mind he went back to Kentucky, but in

1815, settled at the mouth of the Big Miami River, in Ohio. May 3, 1815, he was married to Lydia Richard, in Butler County, O., but moved to Preble County, on Twin Creek, the next day. His wife was of New England parentage, was a moderate scholar, and became the teacher of her husband. In 1820, he was baptized by Elder George Shidler, the same year joined the Miami Ohio Conference, and soon was ordained by Elders G. Shidler and D. Purviance. He continued his residence in Preble until 1835, when he moved to White County, Ind., and later in life, to Crooked Creek, near Logansport, where his wife died in 1870. In 1871, he moved to Kansas, where he labored for some time, but before his death, returned to Indiana. For awhile he was pastor of the Christian Church in Merom, the seat of Union Christian College. He died January 1, 1877, in his eighty- third year.

Elder Snethen was a small man, blind in one eye, compactly built, and capable of great endurance. He had a philosophical mind, a cheerful disposition, a clear and poetical imagination, a musical voice, and a smooth and easy delivery. He was a natural orator, but as simple as a child. Wherever he labored, he was respected and loved by his congregations. For many years he was considered the father of the Tippecanoe Conference. As a pioneer preacher, he had few equals. Like most men of his class, no obstruction was too great for him to overcome that he might reach his appointments. One reason he gave for being thus valiant in his course was, that when a young man, at one time, he and an another young man and two ladies, went to a dance across the Kentucky River, in the days of his folly. When they came to the stream, they found it full up to the banks, with a very strong current, the mush ice covering the entire surface and the canoe on the other side. After consulting awhile, Snethen proposed that the ladies should turn aside from sight and he would get the canoe. He stripped himself, swam across the angry stream, brought the canoe back in safety, took his companions over, and enjoyed the dance. Years after that, when he came to the Wabash or other streams in similar condition, on his way to an appointment, if, for a moment, he thought of turning back, the remembrance of his energy to serve the devil, as he expressed it, came up, and the question arose: "Did I swim the Kentucky River to go to a dance, and shall I turn back when I have an appointment to preach Christ to perishing sinners?"

Since 1832, he often went by the name of the "bare footed preacher." During this year, he attended a camp meeting at Honey Creek Church, in Miami County, O. He was very poorly clad, and had no shoes on his feet. The meeting, for some time, continued lifeless, and preachers that officiated could not get the attention of the congregation. It was proposed by several that "little Abe Snethen," as he was familiarly called, should be invited to the stand. Others objected, saying that such a minister would be a disgrace to the denomination. But finally, bad as he appeared, he was invited to preach. His success was far beyond his own expectation. Christians wept and shouted, the stragglers gathered up close to the stand, and in the midst of the excitement, the venerable Elder Samuel Kyle cried out with a loud, stentorian voice: "Lord, send us more bare-footed preachers to convert the people."

One peculiarity of Brother Snethen was, that he frequently disappointed his congregations in this way; his looks were against him but his ability as a speaker was so superior that his congregations were taken by surprise. No one that knew him doubted his sincerity. Like many other pioneers, his generosity knew no bounds. His house was a free tavern to the traveler. He fed all that came, both man and beast. His wife was like himself in her liberality. He always carried on a farm. He lost three or four that he had cleared, by his indiscriminate liberality. Both he and his companion and children worked very hard. He had twelve children. They were a happy family. At the time of meetings of days, generally near his own house, he fed all that came, and was happy in doing so. At one of these meetings, there was no meat in the house to feed the crowd, and for a time they did not know what to do, but the Elder took his gun to try what the Lord had in store for him. He did not go far until two fat deer came up close to him, as much as to say, "We will become the sacrifice this time; take us." He had them both and was strongly impressed that it was of the Lord. He continued thus in limited circumstances through life, but few men enjoyed what he had more than he. He brought up a fine family of children. His hope of the future was the brightest, and thus he died in peace with all, full of labor, usefulness, and hope.

WILLIAM SNETHEN (?—1856)

William Snethen was a brother of the above, and was born in Kentucky. He lived and labored within the bounds of the Tippecanoe Conference, Ind., and was a member of that body at the time of his death in 1856.

ROBERT SNODGRASS (?—?)

Robert Snodgrass labored in Ohio and .Kentucky. At one time he was a member of the Kentucky Conference, and at another time labored in the bounds of the Deer Creek Conference, O. He was an able preacher, and died before 1826, about fifty years of age.

CALVIN SOUTHWICK (1823—1869)

Calvin was killed at the battle of Fredericksburg, Va., in the War of the Rebellion. He was converted in the Methodist Church, but soon after joined the Christian Church, and in 1842, was ordained to the work of the ministry in the New York Eastern Conference. His ordination took place at South Valley, N.Y., where, united with East Worcester, he labored for three years or more, going from there to Summit and North Harpersfield, where he remained for about seven years. He was preaching at Reidsfield and Gilboa when he entered the army. Just before he was struck down, he observed to a friend that he could see nothing, and laid down his gun as if to fall back, but stepped forward and immediately fell, pierced with many bullets. He was about forty years old at the time of .his death.

Thomas Soyan (1785—1850)

This Elder was born in 1785, moved from Kentucky to Indiana, was a member of the Tippecanoe Conference, and was ordained about 1838. He died near Argos, Ind.

Josiah Spaulding (1803—1843)

Josiah was born in the State of Vermont, in 1803. He received as good an education as the common schools afforded in those days, and by his energy, Was able to add greatly to his knowledge in after years. In 1823, he went to Ohio, and in the next year, confessed the Savior, was baptized by Elder A.C. Morrison, and united with the Christian Church at Monroe, Ashtabula County, O. Although actively engaged in the work of farming, he was not remiss in church duties, nor did he grow lukewarm in his profession, but his zeal increased and he soon devoted his whole time to the cause of the Master. He was ordained at Pembroke, N.Y., in 1831, and took charge of the church at Royalton, in the same year. In this place he was married to Miss Laurinda Sawyer, by whom he had four children, all of whom survived him. In 1835, he organized a church at Parma, O., and was preaching there and at Richfield, ten miles distant, while his family resided in the neighborhood.

His health was very poor after his return to Ohio, although he continued to preach in several places, and moved to Jack- son, Mich., some two years before his death. He returned to Ohio in September, 1843, but lived only a few weeks after his return, and died at the residence of his brother, in Monroe, O., October 19, 1843, aged forty years. He was a man of pure heart, deep piety, and earnestness, but his poor health had impaired, to a great degree, his usefulness in the ministry.

James Spencer (?—?)

James Spencer was, for many years, a mild, pleasant, devoted, and useful minister in the Vermont Conference; but about 1823, he became a believer in one of the wildest fanaticisms of modern times, called the "Niles Fanaticism," from the woman who pretended to a new revelation, began to call for converts, and to the wonder of all, James Spencer became one of them. How long he remained among them we have no means of knowing; but after a time, he came to his right mind, and began to preach among the Christians, wherever there was an opening. But it is likely that he was never fully restored to the confidence of his brethren.

JAMES SPENCER (1808—1853)

This minister was an active lay brother, laboring earnestly for the advancement of the cause, both by his personal influence and by his writings. His home was near Broom, Schoharie County, N.Y., and his membership was in the church at that place. In 1851, he joined the New York Eastern Conference, and for the last two years of his life, he labored untiringly as a minister. He died February 28, 1853, of inflammation of the lungs, in the forty-fifth year of his age.

JOSEPH SPENCER (?—?)

Joseph Spencer labored for. many years in the Eel River Conference, Ind.; but about 1856, he moved to Iowa, where he died.

JAMES S. SPOONER (1806—1842)

This Elder was born in Lyndon, Vt., in 1806. When quite small, he moved with his parents to New Hampshire, where he was converted in 1823. While in this state, he began to preach, and soon after, moved to Moira, N.Y., where he was ordained by Elders Smith and Newland, in 1827. While in New York, he labored chiefly at Orleans, in Jefferson, and at De Kalb, in St. Lawrence County. He moved from this state to East Gwillimbury, Canada, and became pastor of the church in that place in 1830. He remained pastor of this church till his health failed. He died June 15, 1842, aged forty-eight years.

John Spoor (1795—1864)

This brother was one of the most prominent ministers of the Christian Church for many years. He was born in Charleston, N.Y., September 11, 1795. He was the third child in a family of six children. His educational advantages were limited, and whatever proficiency he attained in letters was the result of study after leaving home, and was gained under great disadvantages. He made a public profession of religion in 1813, and was baptized the same year by Jonathan Thompson. He was one of the first members of the church at Charleston, and that at a time when there were not over sixty persons members of the Christian connection in that state.

He began to preach in August, 1815, and was ordained in June, 1818, by Elders Ross, Thompson, and King, in his native place, where he labored nearly a year, when he went to Freehold. His first meetings were held at the house of Philip Vosbury, in Coxsackie. A revival began at once, and the powerful work continued in the country around for four years, until the church at Freehold and its branches numbered 500 members. He aided in the organization of the first Christian Church in Dutchess County, labored with great success in Rensellaer County, gathering, while there, churches in the towns of Berlin and Petersburg, and also in South Adams, Mass. He resided, for a time, at Steventown as an honored and successful pastor. His ministry of eighteen months in New York City was attended with much good; but his health failing, he returned to Freehold.

His last public ministry was at Medusa, N.Y., where he had preached often when in the prime of life. The church was greatly revived, and the people heard him gladly, although he was then enfeebled with age. He possessed a commanding presence, a noble form, and a musical voice; he was easy in manner and gestures, and made a free use of appropriate language, thereby easily commanding the attention and awakening the interest of his hearers.. In Freehold, he baptized 470 persons. During his entire ministry, he baptized between 1,400 and 1,500 persons, solemnized about 1,000 marriages, and attended not far from 1,500 funerals—an unusual amount for one whose labors were confined principally to a rural district.

For nearly fifty years, the Elder was one of the most active and successful ministers of the Christian Church. He did not travel like Badger, Millar, Walters, and some others, but he occupied a very important position in the eastern part of New York and the western part of Massachusetts, and his influence is felt to this day in every place he visited. One particular trait is noticeable in his writings— he always speaks well of his co-laborers in the work, and of the kindness shown him even by the most bitter sectarian or most obstinate unbeliever. From this it may be inferred that none could resist his cheery disposition, his unassuming manner, and, above all, his unaffected piety. He died in April, 1864, at his home in Freehold, N.Y., in the sixty-ninth year of his age. An able sermon was preached, on his death, by Elder Warren Hathaway, and was printed in pamphlet form.

ENOCH SPRINGER (?—?)

Enoch Springer was a native of New York, and was a minister of the Methodist Church until his removal to Indiana in 1841, when he joined the Cole Creek Conference, and soon became a prominent minister in the Christian Church. He labored faithfully in this church for a year, when he was killed by the limb of a tree falling upon him while he was on his way to an appointment. He was not far from forty-two years old at the time of his death.

JAMES STACKHOUSE (1783—1854)

This brother was one of the early pioneers of the Christian Church in Ohio. His labors were confined chiefly to Miami and Logan counties. In the time when it was not customary for ministers to receive much salary, he spent twenty-two years laboring to support his family, preaching when he could. After his removal to Marion County, Ind., he organized several churches, and was an able and efficient pastor among them for many years. He did not preach for some time before his death, owing to a disease of the throat. He died at his residence near Marion, Ind., June 2, 1854, in his seventy-first year.

MARTIN STALEY (1785—1859)

Martin was born in 1785, and died July 19, 1859, aged seventy-four years. He was a prominent Christian minister in North Carolina. The "Christian Sun" says that he spoke for hours while the whole congregation was bathed in tears.

AMASA STANTON (1812—1879)

Amasa was born in Charleston Four Corners, N.Y., July 16, 1812, and died in Wayne County, the same state, March 20, 1879. He attended meeting under the pastorate of Elder John Ross, was converted April 12, 1831, and was baptized by Elder Ross the 15th of June following. He was impressed with the duty of preaching soon after his conversion. He had sufficient education to make a successful school teacher. July 16, 1834, he preached his first sermon at Root, N.Y., and was ordained the following year. For four years he labored successfully as an evangelist, after which he became pastor of the church at Berne. September 10, 1839, he was married to Miss Maria Sterling, a sister of Elder Badger's wife, at Honeoye Falls. About this time, he labored extensively in Monroe, Livingston, and adjoining counties; but in the midst of his labor, he had a violent attack of sore throat, which interrupted his ministerial work for a time, and of which he never fully recovered. He became pastor of the churches at Lakeville, North Rush, Naples, Bristol, Honeoye Falls, and Marion. He continued in the latter place till death, although, on account of the throat disease mentioned, he did not labor as pastor for the last few years of his life.

The Elder was an able man in the ministry. He served the Marion Church for eighteen successive years, changed the place of worship from the country to the village, and had a fine church building erected. On account of failing health, he opened a grocery store for his son and daughter, but he continued preaching, when he could, to the last. During this time, he labored with the churches at Rush, Sodus, and Alton. In 1872, he had a fine house of worship erected at North Rush. He was one of the first trustees of Antioch College. In 1876, he met the Tioga River Conference, of which he was a member, for the last time, and presided over the session. His health being poor, his brethren gathered around him with affection, fearing that they should see his friendly face among them no more.

AMOS STARK (1776—?)

Amos was born in 1776, and began to preach in 1803. He was a brother-in-law of Elder David Ford— both had been in the ministry for nearly half a century when Elder Walter visited them at their homes in New York, in 1854. Elder Stark bought a meeting house and presented it to the members of the Christian Church at South Berlin about this time. We have no definite account either of his various experiences in the ministry or of his latter days.

JOSEPH STARKEY (1805—1878)

Joseph was born in Derbyshire, England, in 1805, of poor but respectable parents. When a young man, he enlisted in the British Army, came to Canada as a soldier, took leave of his regiment, came to the States, made his home with Thomas Farnsworth, and married his daughter Mary, who survived him. He moved to Hermon, St. Lawrence County, N.Y., was converted, and was baptized in July, 1835, by Elder Alpheus Field. He soon began to exhort, became an active worker, and was ordained in 1838, Elders Allen and Banister officiating. He died at his home in Hermon, August 31, 1878.

Elder Starkey was a firm, faithful, and devoted minister, with considerable ability. He filled a wide field of usefulness in the bounds of the Northern New York Conference for many years, and his departure from labor, when in a ripe old age, was sincerely mourned by his brethren.

ELIZABETH STILES (?—1862)

This female laborer is said to have been a talented, faithful, and devoted minister for several years. She was a sister of Elder Osborne, of the State of Maine. She was married to Martin Stiles in 1815, and died in 1862.

AMOS STEVENS (1806—1843)

The following is from the pen of Elder Josiah Knight, an intimate friend of the deceased:

"Amos Stevens was born in Strafford, Vt., of respectable parents, December 30, 1806. In early life, he was deeply impressed with a sense of his sinful condition, and fled for refuge to Jesus, the sinner's friend, and soon found peace in believing in him. He united with the Christian Church in his native town, and soon felt his mind drawn out to call sinners to repentance. On May 18, 1827, he joined the Vermont- Conference, and received a license to preach. In May, 1829, he was married to Miss Lucinda Lampson, a member of a respectable family, and also a worthy member of the Christian Church in West Randolph, Vt. He found in her a faithful and confiding companion, and one who shared with him all his joys and sorrows till the ties that united them were broken by the ruthless hand of death.

He continued faithful in the discharge of his ministerial duties until full proof was made of his usefulness and ability to do the work of the ministry, and on June 23, 1831, he was publicly set apart for the work by ordination. Sermon by Elder Edward B. Rollins. After his ordination, he devoted the most of his time, for seven years, to traveling and preaching the good news of salvation. In connection with the writer of this sketch, he traveled in many parts of New England; nor were his labors in vain, especially in Pomfret, Stowe, Morristown, Randolph, and Braintree, Vt., and Piermont, N.H. In 1832, a committee was appointed by the Vermont Conference of "Christian Brethren" to compile and publish the "Union Hymn Book." The members of the committee were Elders A. Stevens, J.L. Green, and J. Knight. The compilation of the book was mainly attended to at the residence of Elder Stevens, at Stowe, Vt. The volume was stereotyped, contained 432 pages, and was in general use in Vermont for several years.

In the winter of 1831-32, in company with the writer, Elder Stevens traveled in Lower Canada, and organized eight churches; as follows, at Sutten, Broome, Shefford, Stukeby, Farnam, Stanstead, Hattey, and Bolton. These were organized under the name of Christian Brethren churches, some years before the union of that body with the present Christian Church; and it may be that these churches were somewhat neglected after that union—at least, some of them became low and probably extinct. Elder Stevens was, at this time, a member of the Vermont Conference of Christian Brethren, and took a very active part in bringing about the union of this body and the Christian Connection. June 13, 1836, he and Elder B. Allen were appointed delegates to the Mass Conference for the purpose of laying before that body the subject of the contemplated union. The results of this meeting were favorable and the union was afterward consummated.

In the spring of 1838, he left his native state and emigrated west, settling in Woodstock, Champaign County, O., where he soon organized a Christian Church. He was not extensively known in Ohio till he joined the Central Conference, which he did at Appleton, Licking County, in August, 1839. His preaching, at that time, made a favorable impression on the minds of the people, and all believed that a valuable acquisition had been made to the ministry of Ohio —and much more so when, in the next session, he proved himself to be an able debater and a safe and able counselor.

In 1841, he labored hard, in connection with others, to found a college, to be called the La Fayette University, to be located at New Carlisle, Clark County, O., but failed in the attempt; yet good was done by calling attention to the subject. In 1842, he was elected President of the conference; and such was the worthiness with which he filled that position that he was unanimously chosen to fill the same place the following year—and never was the chair filled with more satisfaction. He had a good knowledge of parlia-

mentary usages, and always treated all classes kindly and respect-
fully, yet was firm and unwavering in his purpose. He remained at
Wood- stock, as pastor of the church there, some five years, during
which time he labored considerably in other places. In 1843, he left
Woodstock and took the pastoral charge of the church in Dayton.
But he had been there only two months when the hand of disease
was laid upon him. He spoke of his departure with great composure of mind, and said that the nearer he approached his end the
more he was convinced of the truth of the principles we advocate.
He died December 27, and his funeral took place three days later—
on his thirty-seventh birthday.

Elder Stevens was about five feet nine inches in height, well pro-
portioned, of light complexion, full face, and his open, frank, and
manly appearance would not fail to attract the attention of any congregation of strangers. His social qualities were more than ordinarily developed. His manner of preaching was not so exciting as it
was convincing. His arguments were strong and his reasoning irresistible."

JAMES STEVENS (1825—1867)

James was born in 1825. He was converted when quite young,
and soon felt that it was his duty to preach. For the purpose of fitting himself more carefully for this profession, he entered Oberlin
College, O., and there graduated with honor. He soon entered upon
the work of the ministry, but his health would not permit him to
engage in it as actively as he desired. For the purpose of recruiting
his strength, he went to Vineland, N.J., where he remained till
about four weeks before his death, when he returned to his former
home in Freehold, N.Y. He died at that place September 6, 1867, at
the age of forty-two years.

LEVI STICKNEY (1801—1858)

Levi was born in Canada, in 1801, and there grew up to manhood. He was converted under the preaching of Elders Morrison
and Blodget, soon after began to preach, and was ordained in

Canada, where he traveled extensively, and also in New York and Ohio. He joined one of the conferences of Ohio, but in 1847, moved to Michigan, where, in 1855, he was married for the first time, being fifty-four years old. He settled in the wilds of Michigan, preparing for himself a home, but preaching regularly. He died at Lapeer, Mich., September 3, 1858, of jaundice, in the fifty-eighth year of his age. Elder Cannon speaks of him as a very good man.

WILLET STILLMAN (1776—1826)

Elder Stillman was born in 1776. He was pastor of the church at Plainfield, N.Y., tor some time, and died there, of lung disease, November 16, 1826. Sermon by Elder J. Hayward, his intimate friend and fellow-laborer.

EPHRAIM STINCHFIELD (?—?)

Ephraim Stinchfield was, for more than forty years, a prominent preacher in Maine, New Hampshire, and Vermont, his home being at Gloucester, Me. In 1806, he held a great revival in Woodstock, Vt., in company with John Rand and Elias Smith. In 1819, he did much in putting down the "fanaticism of Jacob Cochrane" near York, Me. We learn, in the life of Mark Fernald, that in 1836, he was very ill, being stricken with paralysis, but know nothing more concerning his last days.

PETER STIFF (1793—1848)

This brother was born in the State of Virginia, but removed to Ohio when quite young. While living in Logan County, O., he was married to Miss Harrison, and after her death to Miss Beard, who, with four children, survived him. In 1840, he joined the Auglaize Christian Conference as a licentiate. He became an active minister and continued his labors in that conference until 1846, when he removed to Fulton County, ill. He then joined the Spoon River Conference, and remained a highly esteemed member of that body until his death, November 16, 1848, in his fifty-fifth year. His death was caused by the running away of his horses while hauling rails. He fell under the load and died instantly.

MICHAEL STOCKWELL (?—?)

Michael Stockwell was a minister in Kentucky and Indiana about 1810 and 1825.

ELIJAH STODDARD (1815—1867)

Elijah was a native of New York, but a member of the Michigan Central Conference at the time of his death, which was occasioned by the fall of a tree, at Vermontville, Mich., January 1, 1867, aged fifty-two years.

BARTON W. STONE (1772—1844)

This noted man was the son of John and Mary (Wasson) Stone, and was born near Port Tobacco, Md., December 25, 1772. His father died when he was quite young, and in 1779, his mother moved with a large family of children and servants to Pittsylvania County, Va., on the Dan River, then the wildest part of the state. His earliest recollections were of the events of the Revolutionary War, and the rudeness and low morality of the people about them.

He was sent to school early, and here his love for books was fostered and strengthened with his growth in years. His early religious impressions were received from both the Baptists and Methodists, as there were many persons of both denominations in the country, and great good was done by them, both by example and precept. In 1790, he attended the Guilford Academy, under the instruction of Dr. David Caldwell. During his stay at this school, after a great struggle of mind, he was converted, and in 1793, in company with others, became a candidate for the ministry in the Presbyterian Church. His difficulty in satisfying himself in regard to the Trinity was so great that, after several examinations, he gave up the task, and started to Georgia, for a visit to his brother, where he was sick for several weeks with a fever. After his recovery, he obtained a position as teacher of languages at a Methodist Academy, near

Washington, Ga., and remained there until 1796, to the full satisfaction of the trustees, and with great improvement to himself, especially in the French language.

This same year we find him with a license to preach, from the Orange Presbytery, N.C., and an appointment to travel in company with Robert Foster, who soon gave up the work as too difficult to perform. This was very discouraging to young Stone, and he had made up his mind to go to the wilds of Florida, to be rid of the ministry, when he was dissuaded by a good old mother in Israel. He then started on a long journey to Tennessee, accompanied a part of the way by his friend Foster. From Tennessee Stone traveled to Kentucky, and from there again to the Carolinas and Georgia. During this trip, he had many hairbreadth escapes from hostile Indians and the robbers that infested the country at that time. He preached a great many sermons while out this time, and was now fully committed to the ministry. From seeing the great cruelty with which slaves were treated, while in South Carolina, he had become a decided anti-slavery advocate; and when, some years after, he had his principles practically put to the test by the possession of human beings, he never faltered but liberated them all immediately.

In 1798, he received a call from the Cane Ridge and Concord churches, in Kentucky. As he was about to be examined before the Transylvania Presbytery for ordination, the old trouble of the Trinity came up again; but through the assistance of Robert Marshall and James Blythe D.D., he was enabled to pass by accepting the Confession of Faith, as far aa consistent with the Bible in his mind. He now entered with great enthusiasm and energy upon the work of saving souls, and with the hearty co-operation of the churches in the task.

In 1801, in the midst of a great revival, he was married to Miss Elizabeth Campbell, of Muhlenburg, Ky. This revival spread through all the country around, and Elder Stone was one of the most prominent actors in the work. From long and severe labor, he had an attack of hemorrhage of the lungs; but he was cured of this

in one night by a "profuse pulpit sweat." From the time of his settlement with the churches at Cane Ridge and Concord until 1804,
when the separation from the Presbyterians took place, he assisted
in carrying on revivals constantly.

And now, in 1804, came the great trial as the Presbyterians began to re-examine their Theology from the basis. The first man
tried for heresy was Richard McNemar, who was soon disowned.
Then came Stone, Marshall, Thompson, Dunlevy, and David Purviance, who was a candidate for the ministry, and they all shared a
like fate. But there was a greater trouble still for Stone. No sooner
had they decided their course of adopting the Bible as their only
creed, and while yet in the midst of the reformation, than a body of
Shakers, from New York, visited the place, and two of the leading
men, Dunlevy and McNemar, joined that body. To add to the dis-
couragement of Stone, Marshall and Thompson returned to the
Presbyterians, leaving Stone alone of all the ordained ministers that
had assisted in the organization of the new body; but Elder David
Purviance, who was a licentiate at the time, though ordained soon
after by the new church, and many others were added, making up,
in a great measure, the delinquency of those mentioned.

In 1809, Eider Stone lost his only son, and the year following
found him mourning the death of a faithful wife. He traveled, after
this, for a year and a half, generally in company with Elder Reuben
Dooly, through Tennessee, Kentucky, Ohio, and other states. In
1811, he was married to Miss Celia Bowen, a cousin of his former
wife, from Nashville, Tenn. After his marriage, he lived for some
time in his old home, in Bourbon County, Ky.; but he finally
moved to Tennessee, and from there to Lexington, Ky., where he
taught a High School, with great success. During this time, he studied Hebrew, with a Prussian doctor, which he said was of great use
to him in his farther researches after truth. He afterwards took
charge of the school in the Rittenhouse Academy, at Georgetown,
Ky., where he soon organized a large church of some 200 members. He gave up the school that he might devote his whole time to
the pastoral work; in return for this, the brethren were to discharge

the debt that he had incurred in purchasing a small farm situated near that place. As they failed to keep their promises, he started a private school, and thus paid the debt, although he was nearly broken down by such constant labor.

From this time till 1826, Elder Stone's life was like that of thousands of other ministers in early times—traveling from one place to another, preaching and exhorting the people to repentance. His labors, during this time, were attended with great success. In 1826, he commenced the publication of the *Christian Messenger,* a periodical of great ability, which he published alone until 1832, when Elder Johnson became a partner in the concern. The publication of this paper continued, with short intervals, until 1843. After 1834, it was published in Jacksonville, Ill. In 1830 or '31, Alexander Campbell visited him in Kentucky, and after some discussion, they agreed to unite their labors. In 1834, Stone left Kentucky and moved to Jacksonville, Ill., where he remained the rest of his life.

In 1841, at the age of sixty-nine, he was struck with paralysis, which disabled him from active labor for the rest of his life. In 1843, his health improved so much that, in company with some of his children, he visited his old friends in Indiana, Ohio, and Kentucky, and returned in better health. In 1844, he started on a visit to his children and friends in Missouri; while there he was seized with another stroke of paralysis, and died in Hannibal, Mo., November 9, 1844, in his seventy-second year. .

ABRAHAM STOUT (?—1874)

Abraham Stout was a member of the North-western Ohio Conference. He died in 1874.

JOHN STRAIT (1758—1861)

John was born in 1758, and grew to manhood in the State of R.I., and there preached among the Freewill Baptists. In 1776, he entered the Revolutionary War, and was in the battle of Plymouth, and several others. He served all through the war, but he never regretted having entered the ministry. In 1785, he was fully ordained to the work. He continued his work in New England until 1818, when he moved to Gallia County, O., where he joined the Christian Church, and lived a long life in that body as an able and devoted minister, a co-laborer, but senior in age, of Joseph Baker, George Alkire, and others.

On his hundredth birthday, August 31, 1858, a meeting was appointed at his house, in Gallia County, and a great crowd assembled to do honor to the old patriarch. Elder J.W. Brown preached a sermon, assisted in the exercises by Elder A. Drake, of the Christian Church, and ministers of other denominations. At the close, Elder Strait preached a sermon of more than half an hour in length. It was a scene seldom witnessed, and one of great interest to the visitors. He lived nearly three years longer, and died in 1861, in his 103rd year. His life was one of great usefulness, and his example was the admiration of all that knew him. His ministerial work was confined, mostly, to the south-eastern part of Ohio.

? STRINGER (?—?)

Brother Stringer was a minister that labored in some of the Southern States. About 1809, in connection with Elder Rainy, he published a pamphlet in vindication of the Christian doctrine.

CYRUS STRONG (?—1849)

Cyrus was a minister in Champaign County, Ill., for many years. In the "Palladium" of April, 1841, he says that for the last nine years he has labored almost alone as a minister with two churches in his neighborhood. He commenced his ministerial career in 1821, and closed it by death in 1849, not far from seventy-five years of age. The brethren of the different churches where he labored speak highly of him as a good man and an able minister.

JOSEPH STURDYVANT (?—?)

Joseph Sturdyvant was a minister who was active in the work about 1808.

<u>Henry Sullings (?—1860)</u>

Harvey Sullings was, for a long time, a noted man among the New England ministers. Not only was he an able pastor, but also a shrewd business man. He had earned quite a large property, and did a great deal towards organizing churches by giving freely from his abundance. He had charge of the church at Bristol, R.I., for some time, but during his later years he did not hold any regular pastorate, although he preached occasionally. He died about 1860, between sixty and sixty-five years of age.

In early life, Elder Sullings had been in the whaling business, and made many voyages to distant seas in pursuit of his avocation. In this calling he made money. He was also engaged as a hardware merchant. In all such occupations he was a successful man in business. In the midst of all his success, however, he turned his attention to the ministry, and was equally zealous in promoting the cause of Christ, as he had been in his other occupations. Being in good circumstances, it is probable that he did not receive the remuneration for his labors in the ministry that men with more limited means did, nor is it probable that he could so entirely disentangle his mind from his business, as if he was a poorer man. Be that as it may, while he did not hold as high a position in the denomination as his talent would indicate, yet he was useful in assisting weak churches, and especially in rearing houses of worship.

<u>James Sullivan (1791—1856)</u>

James was born in Lincoln County, N.C., in 1791, was married about 1810, moved to Clark County, O., in an early day, served in the war of 1812, was converted under the preaching of Nathan Worley, and began to labor in public soon after. It is not likely that he was ever ordained, but he labored almost constantly in the latter part of his life. He lost his property and was in limited circumstances, but brought up an excellent family of children —eight in number. Having seen the evils of slavery in his young days, he became an intense opposer of the institution, and made three trips on foot to his native state, to speak against the cruelty of it, preaching constantly on these journeys He was well versed in the Scriptures. He died in 1856, near Dayton, O.

? SURBER (?—?)

Brother Surber was a minister of some prominence, who lived, for awhile, in Des Moines, Iowa, but moved to Kansas, and died there several years ago.

EMILY B. SWANK (1825—1876)

This sister, whose maiden name was Hunt, was born in the State of Kentucky, February 25, 1825, was married to M.D. Swank, M.D., April 18, 1850, and died in Indianapolis, Ind., September 13, 1876. When quite young, she was left an orphan in the care of a kind brother. She received academic education in. her youth, and became a successful school teacher. She had an active mind, and high aspirations to make herself useful. She studied medicine and delivered many lectures on that subject. She also took an active part in the reforms of the day; such as temperance, freedom of the slaves, rights of women, and for the purpose of more successfully agitating these subjects, she edited a temperance and anti-slavery paper for fifteen years, and at the same time lectured successfully on the same subjects. During these years, her mind took a skeptical turn as to church influence in the promotion of these reforms. For the purpose of further mental development, she attended eight successive terms at Antioch College, Yellow Springs, O., during which time she became acquainted with the liberal sentiments of the Christian Church. She joined the church at the above place, and soon the Miami Conference, O., where she was ordained and continued a faithful member until death. She labored faithfully, as far as health would permit, and was an able expounder of Christian ethics to the last.

ABRAM SWART (1823—1863)

This brother was born in North Hampden, N.Y., in 1823, and was converted in the same place under the labors of Elder H.A.

Pratt. In 1853, he entered the school at Starkey Seminary and remained there four years, two of which were spent as an assistant teacher. In 1855, he married Miss Maria Jamison, also an assistant teacher. He commenced preaching while at Starkey, and was ordained in 1858. He then became the pastor of the church at Kirkwood, N.Y., and after he left that place, he went to Smithfield, Penn. He entered the army, in 1862, and was made Captain of Co. C., 141st Penn. Regiment. He was killed at the battle of Fredericksburg, Va., May 3, 1863.

CALEB SWEET (1799—1861)

This brother was born in 1799, was ordained at Otsego, N.Y., in 1824, began to preach in 1845, and was ordained in 1849, in Jackson, Penn. He preached twelve years for the churches at Jackson and Laurence, Tioga County, Penn., and died at Caton, Steuben County, N.Y., March 13, 1861. Elders C.D. Kinney and C. Newall speak highly of Elder Sweet as a good, faithful, and useful minister.

PENTECOST SWEET (1787—1870)

This Elder was born in Rhode Island, in 1787, but when a child moved with his parents to Sterling, Conn. He was married to Eliza Farnum in 1813, and in the same year, embraced religion under the labors of Elder Douglas Farnum. At that time, he could neither read nor write. In 1815, he moved with his family to Smithfield, Penn., and in 1821, after having held a successful meeting for some time, the result of which was a great revival, they organized a church with no regular pastor, although Elder Sweet acted as leader in the services. This arrangement continued till 1826, when he was regularly ordained, took the pastorate of the church, and held that position until his death, July 25, 1870, at the age of eighty-four years.

<u>Ezra B. Swem (1815—1871)</u>

Ezra was a native of New Jersey, but removed with his parents, when small, to Pennsylvania. In 1835, at the age of twenty, he left home and moved to Ohio, where he remained for two years, then went to Indiana, where he was married to Miss Phoebe Gregg. Here he remained for two years when he returned to Montgomery County, O., and was converted under the labors of Elder Nathan Worley, in 1839. He entered the ministry in the same year, but never devoted his whole time to the work, as he carried on the business of wagon making during a greater part of the time. In 1853, he moved to Iowa, where he remained engaged both in preaching and secular pursuits until his death, November 17, 1871, at the age of fifty-seven. He was a man of more than ordinary natural talent, and was very useful. While in the State of Indiana, Elder Swem lived and labored in Wayne and Henry counties, and was a member of the Bluffton Conference. He exerted a good influence in the churches in his field of labor. In Iowa, where he died, he was considered by the brethren a valuable acquisition to the infant cause in that state, and was greatly mourned when called away.

<u>William Swem (1825—1855)</u>

This brother was born in 1825. He received a license to preach when twenty-five years of age, and in 1851, a year later, was ordained. He was a good, faithful minister, but somewhat local in his labors. He died September 25, 1855. His field of labor was in Kentucky.

<u>Nathaniel Tatem (?—1835)</u>

This brother was pastor of the church at Providence, Va., for many years. He died in New York City in 1835. while there on business. Elder I.N. Walter speaks of him as an accomplished gentleman, an able physician, and a talented minister of the gospel.

William Tatem (?—1853)

This Elder was a son of the preceding. He was converted in 1835, soon after entered upon the work of the ministry, and became pastor of the church at Providence, Va., where his father had been an honored pastor for many years. He was also an able physician, and, at one time, a representative from the city of Norfolk in the Virginia Legislature. He was an able debater and a powerful defender of the principles of the Christian denomination. He died in Norfolk, Va., in 1853.

John B. Taets (1791—1876)

This aged veteran was born September 30, 1791, in Dutchess County, N.Y., and moved, about 1803, to South Westerloo, where he remained until his death. November 7, 1814, he was married to Miss Mary Boardman, with whom he lived happily for more than sixty years, and who survived him. He was converted in 1815, under the preaching of Elder Jasper Hazen. After an urgent persuasion, he joined the Baptist Church, and was baptized in that connection. But his union with that church lasted only three days, he joining the Christians at the expiration of that time on account of his views being more in harmony with the doctrine of the latter body. He soon began to preach, and became an active and successful minister. He was quite powerful in revivals, often baptizing more than sixty converts at one time. He organized many churches, among which were those of Medusa and Medway. He was pastor of the church at Westerloo until 1844. Part of the time, Elder John Spoor labored there in connection with him. Like many others, he was carried away from his moorings by the Miller excitement in regard to the speedy coming of Christ; and although he never joined the Advent denomination, it is probable that the effect of that excitement injured his influence in his own church. He was a plain, earnest man, well respected by all who knew him. In his latter years, his mind and body failed together; but on the subject of religion, his thoughts were wonderfully clear to the last. He died May 10, 1876, in his eighty-fifth year.

JESSE TATTON (1825—1875)

Jesse' was born in the Province of New Brunswick in 1825, and for three years, followed the seas as a sailor. He moved to Ontario, Canada, in 1844, and settled in the township of King. He joined the Christian Church, began to preach, and in 1852, was ordained. He soon became an efficient minister, and filled a wide sphere of usefulness for more than twenty years of an active, stirring life in the church. He was not only a zealous man, but he was studious, liberal, and systematic as well. He wrote for our papers, was active in conference, and was a powerful advocate of the general measures of the denomination. His labors were mostly confined to Canada, where he lived; but he was interested in the welfare of the church everywhere. As a pastor, he labored for six years at West Gwillimsbury, then four years at Browham, and after that, at Markham. He had a meeting-house built at Ringhood. At White Vale, he continued three and a halt years, and at Oshawa, three years. This last was the fifth church he had charge of—and he succeeded well in all of them. He was married twice. At his death, he left five sons. He died September 26, 1875, deeply lamented by his church, the community, and the entire denomination, of which he had been a useful member.

BENJAMIN TAYLOR (1786—1848)

Benjamin was born in Beverly, Mass., July 22, 1786. He was one of fourteen children—five daughters and nine sons; four of the latter became ministers of the gospel, three in the Christian and one in the Baptist Church. One of the daughters married a minister. His parents were members of good standing in the Baptist Church, but united with the Christian Church in their latter years. When Benjamin was quite young, his parents removed to New Hampshire, where he was converted and baptized by Elder Webster, of the Baptist Church, but did not join that church on account of the doctrine of election; but he was, from this time forward, very attentive to religious duties.

In 1804, he went to sea, was imprisoned in France for some time, and on his return, was nearly shipwrecked. During all this time his mind was very much exercised as to whether it was his duty to preach or not. After his return from his sea voyage, he found his father living at Salem, Mass., and here he became acquainted with the principles of the Christian Church, from the small body organized there by Elder Abner Jones, and in 1809, united with this church. He soon began to speak and pray in public with great earnestness, and was urged to devote his time and talent to the work of the ministry. He finally consented to accompany Elder John Rand to New Bedford, and some of the adjoining churches, exercising his gift for the benefit of many and pleasure of all, although he was still timid and doubtful to a great degree. After spending two years in this way, in June, 1811, he vas prayerfully set apart to the work by Elders Jones, Hix, Hathaway, Farnum, Phillips, Easty, and Crossman, in the presence of nearly two thousand people, at Assonet, Mass. His first charge as a pastor was at New Bedford, and during his stay there he was married to Mrs. Mary Rodman, of Newport, R.I., with whom he lived very happily until death separated them. While in New England, he labored chiefly with the churches of New Bedford, Taunton, and Swansea, although he preached occasionally at other places. He had had wonderful success in all these places and especially at Swansea, where there was a revival of two years duration, and great numbers were added to the church. While at this place, he was chosen a member of the Legislature, a place that he filled with great credit to himself and satisfaction to others.

He labored in New England from 1809 to 1831, in which year he moved to the State of Michigan with his family. This state was, at the time, a wild country, and his neighbors were chiefly Indians of the Pottawattamie tribe. With many of these he formed pleasant and friendly relations, as with the two chiefs, Sagamaw and Shornoble. He remained in the West nine years, doing a great deal towards straightening the infant cause in Michigan, but as his health was not good and the brethren in the East were calling for him to return, he decided to do so, and accepted the pastorate of the church at Providence, R.I., for one year. In 1841, he was appointed pastor of the Bethel Chapel, and for the next eight years, he did much for the cause of Christ among the seamen. At the end of this time, his health had become so poor that he felt it was necessary to give up his position, and decided to return to Michigan, hoping that rest and change of air would be beneficial. In July, 1848, he, with great suffering, accompanied by his faithful companion, returned to their old home in Michigan, where, after suffering with dropsy for eight weeks, he died, September 24, 1848, aged sixty-four years, to the sorrow of the whole denomination.

Elder Taylor stood very high in the estimation of his brethren, during nearly forty years of his ministerial life. He was a man of firmness and reliability, and though not a great scholar, yet he was well informed upon all subjects. A neat volume of biography of his life and labors was published by Elder E. Edmund, of Boston, which had quite a circulation, throwing much light, not only on the work of Elder Taylor, but on those of his co-laborers also.

JAMES TAYLOR (?—?)

James Taylor was a brother of the preceding. He was second in age, Benjamin being the eldest and John the youngest. He was ordained in Assonet, Mass., in 1828, at the same place where his brother Benjamin had been ordained seventeen years before—his brother Benjamin preaching the ordination sermon. He was pastor of the Middle Street Christian Church at New Bedford, Mass., for a number of years, where he was very successful as pastor and speaker. He had charge of the church at Middleton, R.I., where he baptized. 104 persons during the months between April, 1836, and February, 1837. He died at Washington, D.C., in 1862 or '63.

JOHN TAYLOR (1805—1872)

John was a younger brother of the subject of the preceding sketch, and was born in Sutton, N.H., in 1805.' He was converted in 1817, and entered the ministry in 1830, at the age of twenty-five. As an evangelist in New Hampshire, Vermont, and other places, he did efficient work and gathered many into the fold of Jesus. Shortly after, he was ordained pastor of the Christian Church at Wareham, Mass. His pastorates were at Wareham, Mass., Portsmouth and Providence, R.I., (he was in the latter place eleven years) Plymouth and New Bedford, Mass., and Westerly, R.I. In 1847, he went to Westerly, and found a small church of thirty persons, and a small Sabbath-school. He soon brought the church to a more prosperous condition, and the Sabbath-school, where he labored so untiringly, to a flourishing state. He took this school on an annual excursion down the river, for twenty years, without a storm or anything to prevent on the appointed day. His interest in the young, as such,, was peculiar and showed itself in all his labor and plans for good. He was pastor of the church at Westerly for twenty- five years, with the exception of six months service at the Mariner's Bethel, in Providence, of which his brother Benjamin was the founder. He had charge of the River Bend Cemetery from its commencement, till the failure of his health compelled him to relinquish it, after seventeen years of faithful studious care. His eminent adaptation to this peculiar trust, his faithfulness, trust, and befitting tenderness in interring and guarding the sepulcher of the precious dead, justly endeared him to many hearts and homes.

As a minister, he was very successful, as much from his sympathy and earnest desire for the salvation of all, as from the stirring appeals to such, to return from the error of their ways. He was stricken with paralysis some time before his death, which occurred October 12, 1872, in the sixty-eighth year of his age, lamented by all in the village where he had lived and served as a pastor for so many years, and by the entire denomination.

WILLIAM TEGARDEN (?—1857)

This Elder was converted under the labors of Robert Hawkins in 1826 or '27, and, like that brother, became a zealous local minister. He did a great deal of good for the cause in the section of the country where he lived, but he never devoted himself wholly to the work of the ministry, as a great deal of his time was spent on his farm. He lived a consistent life, and was well respected by all who knew him. He was a member of the Mt. Vernon Conference for many years before his death. He died in 1857, at an advanced age.

The following incident shows the firmness of Elder Tegarden: In 1840, Elder A.C. Hanger, then a young minister, visited Father Tegarden at his home in Columbiana County, O. By some means, the latter had failed to secure the periodicals of the church and keep himself posted; so there he labored faithfully with a small church of about thirty members, having been informed that that and one or two other churches were all that was left of the entire Christian denomination. So glad was he, when the young man informed him differently, that he could hardly sleep that night for joy. After that, Elder Tegarden kept better posted.

E.D. TERRY (?—?)

E.D. Terry was a native of New York, and in 1834, was pastor of the church at Stanfordville, the same state. He has been dead many years.

Y. TERRY (?—1866)

This brother grew up in Charleston Four Corners, N.Y., under the teaching of Elder J. Ross and pious parents, who carefully developed his mild disposition. He was converted when quite young, and already manifested a great desire for knowledge. He attended school at Union College, N.Y., at Antioch College, O., and likely studied Theology at Andover, Mass. After spending some years in teaching and studying, he showed that his mind had been greatly developed, with no loss of fervency and devotion in the cause of religion.

His last charge was at Fall River, Mass., where his prospects of future usefulness were bright. He was very happy in his relations here—the church cheerfully co-operating in all the plans of their talented young pastor, and a loving wife was with him to aid by her presence and counsel; but the fell destroyer entered this happy home and community, December 18, 1866, and took the brightest ornament. The neighboring ministers were so much enlisted in behalf of the young widow that they voluntarily filled the pulpit of the deceased for the remainder of the year that she might receive the full salary.

MOSES TEWKSBURY (1777—1852)

Moses was born in 1777. He lived in Hartland, Vt., after 1795, and was converted in that place in 1810. Seven years later, he began to preach. He was a zealous and faithful member of the conference in his native state, and was well respected by all his co-laborers. He wrote frequently to our periodicals, and his letters are evidently the productions of a person well acquainted with the leading subjects of the day, and one with a good command of words. He died about 1852.

DANIEL THARP (?—?)

Daniel Tharp was a member of the Eastern Ohio Conference. He died several years ago.

ADAM THOMAS (1782—1859)

This aged minister spent the last years of his life in Montgomery County, Ind. He was born in Kentucky, in 1782, where he lived until his father moved to Ohio, in 1805, where, a year later, he was married to Miss Jane McJimsy. His father died in Miami County, where he had settled on coming to Ohio, in 1843, at the age of eighty-eight years. About 1811, Elder Thomas united with the church at Rocky Springs, and soon after, began to speak and pray in public. He served for a short time in the war of 1812, and was not ordained until 1815. It is probable that he would have been set apart to the full work of the ministry much sooner but for his limited means of support—for in those days preaching was almost entirely a gratuitous work. After his ordination, Elder Thomas took charge of the church at Lost Creek and at Lower Stillwater, which he held until his removal to Indiana, in 1831. Here, he was a co-laborer of James McKinney, Dudley, and others of the Cole Creek Conference. With these, he traveled through a greater part of Western Indiana and Eastern Illinois, enduring the many privations and great toil of a pioneer minister without a murmur.

One of his sons, Elder Joel Thomas, became a co-laborer with him, and a prominent minister in the conference of which his father had been a faithful member for so many years. Although Father Thomas lived to the advanced age of seventy-seven years, he was a great sufferer for many years; but he bore all with meekness and patience. He died August 11, 1859. The Elder's great power was shown more forcibly in revivals and in gatherings where warm appeals and rousing exhortations were required than in the pastorate, or in sermons requiring argument and deep research.

ELIAS THOMAS (?—1830)

Elias was a member of the Conference of Christian Brethren in Vermont, and was a well-respected and faithful member of that body till his death, in 1830. His wife was a minister also, and traveled with Rachel Hosmer for some time. Elder Thomas was very local in his labors. He was very diffident and retiring in his manners, although a very useful man. He died in the house in which Reuben Dodge had died two years before, and in which Seth Allen died four years later.

FREDERICK THOMAS (1804—1858)

Thomas was born near Philadelphia, Penn., in 1804, was converted when quite young, and soon began an active ministry with such companions in the work as F. Plummer and W. Lauer, both of whom speak highly of him as a young man of great zeal and energy. He labored for some time with the church at Fairview, N. j., and in 1854, removed, with his family, to South Bend, Laport County, Ind., where he labored in the ministry until the close of life, April 25, 1858, at the age of fifty-four years.

<u>Hazael Thomas (1811—?)</u>

Hazael was born in Chester County, Penn., moved with his. parents to Ohio in 1815, and from there to Brookville, Ind., in 1818. In 1827, he attended meeting in Franklin County, Ind., and under the preaching of Elder William Hubbard, of the Christian Church, was deeply convicted. Three years later, he joined the United Brethren Church in Montgomery County, O., and in 1831, joined the Christian Church under the preaching of Elder John O'Kane, at Lebanon, in the same state. Soon after, he was licensed to preach in the Miami Conference, and was ordained by Elders James Maple and Isaac Dearth. The latter part of his life was spent near Prince William, Carroll County, Ind. He was a zealous man, and devoted much of his time to the work of the ministry. He died several years ago.

<u>Joseph Thomas (1791—1845)</u>

Joseph was one of the most noted men of his age. He commenced his life in North Carolina, and had traveled as missionary through nearly all the old states in the Union, and finally died of the small-pox, in Johnsonburg, N.J., far away from family and relatives. He was somewhat eccentric in his manners and speech, and one of his peculiarities was the wearing of white garments, from which practice, arose the name by which he was best known— "The White Pilgrim."

He was born in Orange County, N.C., March 17, 1791, his parents having moved from Pennsylvania soon after their marriage. At seven years of age, owing to the-loss of property and the intemperate habits of his father, he was adopted by a. family that treated him very cruelly; but after two years of suffering, he was taken to the home of a married brother, in Virginia. While there, he was confined to his bed for two years with white swelling. In 1803, he was taken to the home of another brother in the same state, but although moved from one place to another, and afflicted as he was, he had been able- to obtain a moderate education by the time he was of age. In 1806, at a camp-meeting, he was deeply convicted, began to pray in private, and in a year after, at the age of sixteen, he received the evidence of a full pardon. He was much exercised at the time as to what church or denomination he should unite with, as he did not believe thoroughly in any of the doctrines of the people around him; but a few months later, he- heard of a body of people called Christians, who had dispensed with creeds, bishops, discipline, etc., and he determined to- know more of them. For this purpose, he visited one of the ministers, Elder Rainy, and was so well satisfied with the views and manners of government of that body that, in a few weeks, he united with the church and was baptized by pourings at Raleigh, N.C., by Elder O'Kelly, at the same time receiving a license to preach. This was in 1807, before he was seventeen. He now began to travel and preach in company with Elder J. Warren, and was, in a short time, several hundred- miles from home and friends, in the southern part of Virginia but the relations between Elder Warren and himself were not pleasant, and he left him and began to labor with Elder Thomas- Reeves, in the western part of Virginia, in whom he found a genial companion and faithful guide. In 1808, Elder Reeves- left him and returned to Tennessee, but Elder Thomas still remained in that part of the country, traveling, as he had done- for some months, when he, too, left the place and returned to his native state.

From this time forward, there was no cessation in his labors and as he says in his journal: "I now found that persecution and popularity had united to toss my name abroad, and they were balanced to my advantage, so that by the one I was not abjectly depressed, nor by the other elevated in my own estimation, beyond the moderation of Christian character." His co-laborers while in that part of the country, were, O'Kelly, Rainy, Haggard, Halloway, Guirey, Barrett, Reeves, Dooly, and others. After traveling extensively through the wild uncivilized regions of Virginia and the Carolinas, sometimes on horseback, sometimes on foot, in all kinds of weather, often fording or swimming rough and dangerous streams, frequently without money or sufficient food and clothing, meeting persecution and ridicule from both the ungodly and the sectarian, after enduring suffering that few are called on to endure, he arrived, May 24, 1811, in the city of Philadelphia, passing through Tennessee, Kentucky, Ohio, and Pennsylvania, to reach it. At this time, he was baptized by immersion, not being satisfied with the pouring that he had received at Raleigh, N.C., by Elder O'Kelly.

April 5, 1812, he was married to Miss Christiana Rittenour, of Frederick County, Va., who was a faithful and devoted companion. With her he lived happily until his death, but his marriage made no change in his career; he labored and traveled as he always had done. Sometimes his wife accompanied him, but not often, and as the family increased, she was content to remain at home with a double care and responsibility, thus assisting him in the work to which he had devoted his life.

Elder Thomas' biography closed in 1817. With no dates to guide for the eighteen years of his life which followed, we will state this: Soon after 1817, he removed with his family to Madison County, O., and soon organized a church, near his home, of which he assumed the pastorate, although he still continued his itinerant labors, chiefly in Ohio. He wrote frequently for the different periodicals of the denomination, on different subjects, of Theology and his travels. He also composed several pieces of poetry, which were published in his autobiography. In 1835, he took a long journey through the Eastern States, and during the whole journey, thousands of people were called together to hear the wonderful western preacher. While on his return home, at Johnsonburg, N.J., he was stricken with that fatal malady, the smallpox, and his eventful life was terminated April 9, 1835, in his forty-fourth year.

Of the character and talents of Elder Thomas, we may say that he was a man of real ability. He had some eccentricities —the wearing his white garments at all times, to the exclusion of all others, may be counted one of them. His constant traveling, in all weathers, on foot, as well as on horseback, exposed to so many dangers and persecutions, with no pay, would be counted very odd in other places and times. In his case, it was perfectly natural. When he gave himself to the Lord as a minister, there was no halfway work. He vowed, and his vow was sacred, in his mind. When these oddities are Considered, he appears as a person of shallow mind; but as we see the man in all his character, we see, under all, a mind and heart, calm, clear, and powerful, a sincere seeker after truth, and boldness enough to follow it without regarding the customs of society. His poetical productions were admired by many; but being composed in a hurry, with no deliberate revision, they show us only that the man had in him a poetical gift. Brother Thomas was a good man, and his death was a great loss to the church.

JOSEPH THOMAS (?—?)

Joseph Thomas was a nephew of Joseph Thomas, the "White Pilgrim." For many years, he was a member of the Deer Creek Conference, O., and labored in the bounds of that conference with great success. Later in life, he moved to Illinois and settled at Pontiac, in that state. A short time before his death, he spent a year or more in Greene County, O., and preached for the Ebenezer and other churches in that neighborhood. He returned to his home in Illinois, and died soon after. Elder Thomas was a zealous, faithful man in the ministry, and his labor was attended with much success.

P.M. THOMAS (1808—1877)

Elder Thomas was born in Sweden, Genesee County, N.Y., December 12, 1808, was converted in 1826, entered the ministry in 1829, and was ordained in 1841, at the Parma church, N.Y. In 1831, he was married to Miss Lucy Chapman, of whom he had two sons. In 1844, he moved to Ogle County, Ill., where he exerted a good influence in the ministry. In 1862, his companion died, and two years later, he moved to the State of Iowa, where he labored with success to the end. After serving in the ministry for more than fifty years, he died at Waterloo, March 2, 1877.

Alexander Thompson (1792— 1864)

This brother was born in the State of Maine, June 1, 1792. He was converted under the labors of Elder Burnham, baptized by the same in 1812, in his native place. Two years later, he was married to Miss Betsey Clark, and soon after, moved to Clermont County, O. He commenced his ministerial life in 1813, and continued a licentiate for many years, as he was not ordained until 1831. In 1848, he moved to Brown County, where he remained until his death, April 12, 1864, in his seventy-second year. He was an excellent man, and a good pastor, but confined his labors to one or two churches, which were always in a prosperous condition.

Hubbard Thompson (?—?)

Hubbard Thompson was a native of New York, and there he labored, lived, and died.

Jesse Thompson (1795—1858)

Jesse was converted in 1818, and was ordained to the full work of the ministry three years later, at Andover, N.H. He died at Ballston, Saratoga County, N.Y., in July, 1858, at the age of sixty-three. He was an able, plain-spoken, and effective speaker, tall and slim in person.

John Thompson (?—?)

John Thompson was a Presbyterian minister during the greater part of his public life, but was one of the founders of the Christian Church. He was one of the leaders of the revival at Cane Ridge, and was one to encourage and assist in the organization of a church without creeds, and with the Bible alone for the rule of faith and practice; yet when McNemar and Dunlevy joined the Shakers, he and Robert Marshall made haste to return to the Presbyterians. He died in Crawfordsville, Ind., a few years ago, quite aged.

JOHN T. THOMPSON (1799—1878)

Brother Thompson was born near Chester, Delaware County, Penn., in 1799, was converted in 1815, soon after was baptized by Elder Frederick Plummer, and at once began to speak in public, in company with Elder Plummer. In 1822, he was married, and in 1844, was ordained by Elders Plummer and Flemming. His labors were mostly confined to Delaware, Buck, Montgomery,, and Philadelphia counties, Penn., and to Salem, Gloucester, and Burlington, N.J. He was pastor, at different times, of the Mt. Zion Church, in the city of Philadelphia, and at Adalusha, Carversville, and Ridley. He was a very zealous, self-sacrificing man, but his being opposed in his ministerial work, for a time, by his companion crippled his success, in a measure. He was taken sick at Carversville, N.J., and died there, May 2, 1878.

JONATHAN S. THOMPSON (1794—1866)

Elder Thompson wrote an excellent autobiography of his life and labors, which should have been published in book form; being too voluminous for this work, extracts are taken from it for the following sketch:

He was born in Weathersfield, Vt., in 1794. When fifteen years old, December, 1809, he was converted, and in June following, he began to preach, and was ordained before reaching his seventeenth year. After laboring faithfully in his native state for three years, he went to Charleston, N.Y., to assist in a great revival carried on by Sister Nancy Cram. He was prevailed on to remain in this place as pastor of the church. He remained there for four years and then went to Oneida County, an entire new field of labor. Here he remained nine years, bringing order out of disorder and organizing many strong and self-supporting churches. After three years in Vermont and thirteen in New York, he removed to New Jersey, where, in July, 1826, he commenced his labors in Johnsonburg, and with the assistance of Elder Clough, he organized a church of which he remained a pastor for nine years. In 1835, he removed to Milford, where he remained until 1838, when his wife died, and he concluded to travel, but received a call from the church at Fall River, Mass. At the expiration of a successful, pastorate of two years, he became the pastor of the Christian Church in Boston. He remained there two years, when he took charge of the church at Swansea, Mass., where he continued five years. In 1848, he removed to Providence, R.I., and took the pastorate of the Bethel Chapel, and in 1851, he took charge of the church at Parma, N.Y., where he remained five years. In 1856, he went to Oshawa, Canada West, where belabored until 1860, when his failing health induced him to return to his old home in Parma, where he preached occasionally, as his health would permit, until his death, December 10, 1866, at the age of seventy-two, and fifty-six in the ministry.

The above is an outline of the work and removals of Elder Thompson. Beside his pastoral world, he was always connected with the general enterprises of the denomination. He was a live man. Having commenced his ministerial career early, and at a time when it cost something to be a Christian minister, he entered the work with all his energy. His great heart and brains were fully enlisted, and from the time of putting on the harness, it never was taken off until removed by death. As for his talent, whether the most brilliant or not, the fact of his sustaining himself so long and so well in such places as Boston, Fall River, and Providence, is a proof sufficient that he was not lacking in ability as pastor and preacher.

MOSES THOMPSON (?—?)

Moses Thompson was a member of the Kentucky Christian Conference in 1826. He was a zealous, faithful man, and died at the age of thirty-eight years.

SAMUEL THOMPSON (?—1845)

Samuel Thompson was a brother who lived and labored in the ministry in the vicinity of the church on Ludlow Creek, Miami County, O., and died in that neighborhood about 1845.

Elijah Tillman (1819—1879)

Elijah was born in Preble County, O., April 14, 1819, and died in Cass County, Ind., in 1879. He was converted in 1840, began to preach at once, and the same year was married to Miss Mary Anne Rhinehart. He moved to Darke County, O., where he lived seven years, and then moved to Pulaski County, Ind., and was ordained by the Tippecanoe Conference in 1849. During his stay in Pulaski, he labored in that and in adjoining counties with great success, but in 1869, his health being poor, he moved to Cass County, near Logansport, where he remained until death. He was true, zealous, and firm in his profession, and stood high with his brethren in the Tippecanoe Conference.

Samuel Tingle (1795—1861)

Elder Tingle was born in 1795, in Warren County, O., was a member of the Methodist Church for some years, and had begun to preach among them, when he removed to Allen County, near Lima. Here he united with the Auglaize Christian Conference, and commenced a long and useful ministry in the Christian Church. He died July 4, 1861, in Hardin County, in the sixty-sixth year of his age. One of his sons, Elder j. F. Tingle, became an able minister in the church of his father, so that the dead father is still speaking through the living son.

? Townsend (1755—1846)

This minister was born in 1855, and spent the latter part of his life in Wolfe- borough, N.H., where he died in 1846, at the advanced age of ninety-one years.

Daniel Travis (?—1826)

Daniel Travis was a native of Tennessee, and died there July 6, 1826.

DAVID TREECE (?—1874)

David Treece was a member of the Southern Illinois Conference, and was a faithful minister at the time of his death in in 1873 or '74.

GEDEON W. TRIP (?—1879)

Elder Trip lived in South Wesport, R.I., on a farm owned by himself, for many years. He was an able preacher, and had charge of many churches in his time. He died December 13, 1879, suddenly, while feeding his stock.

MARTIN TRIP (?—?)

Martin Trip was a native of New England, and died before the year 1826, in some part of the West.

THOMAS TRIP (1803—1859)

Thomas was born in 1803, joined the Christian Church in 1851, was ordained to the full work of the ministry in 1854, and labored faithfully until his death, March 20, 1859, in the fifty-sixth year of his age.

D. TROUT (?—1854)

D. Trout was a member of the Kentucky Christian Conference. He died the year preceding the session of 1855.

OLIVER TRUE (1788—1870)

Oliver was born in Connecticut, in 1788, was converted in 1806, commenced preaching about 1819, and a year later, became pastor of the church at West Mendon, N.Y. In 1846, he lived at Norwalk, O., preaching occasionally, and working at his trade— carpentering. From this time, we have no special account of his labors, except that he traveled extensively through Ohio, Pennsylvania, and New York, and wrote for the papers, more or less, all through his ministry. He was an able theologian, and was very familiar with every part of the Bible. He died at Brockport, N.Y., April 13, 1870, of pulmonary disease, after a ministry of over fifty years, in the eighty-second year of his age. He was very poor at the time of his death.

WILLIAM TRUE (1783—1844)

This Elder was born in Vermont in 1783, commenced preaching in 1815, at the age of thirty-two, in the State of Vermont, but in 1816, he moved to Perry, N.Y., near Silver Lake. About a year later, he moved to Covington, Penn., where he remained until his death. He organized many churches, among others one at Castile, N.Y., which he served as pastor for many years. He died in 1844, in the sixty-first year of his age. He was always spoken of as an excellent man and an able pastor.

WILLIAM TRUE, JR (1793—1818)

This brother was born in Andover, N.H., in 1793, began to preach in 1813, and was ordained a year later, at Andover. He took his family to Brutus, N.Y., in 1816, where he labored with great success until 1818, when his health failed. In company with Elder Elijah Shaw, he returned to his father's house, in Andover, where he died October 11, 1818, in the twenty-sixth year of his age.

THOMAS TRUETT (1816—1875)

This minister was born in 1816, in Alamance County, N.C., and died in 1875. He spent thirty years in the ministry. He was pastor of the Shallow-Ford Christian Church, and a member of the North Carolina and Virginia Conference. His peculiar forte was in exhortation.

OLIVER TUCKERMAN (1817—1868)

The subject of this sketch, for many years, held a prominent position in the Christian Church, in New England. Commencing his religious life in Portsmouth, N.H., he labored extensively through the greater part of New England, and several provinces of the British dominion, but the great work of his life was done in the city of Portland, Me. Those who remember the destructive fire that destroyed the greater part of that beautiful city, will also remember the subject of our sketch, for he was then one of the most prominent and active men in that town to assist the destitute families that suffered so severely in that great catastrophe.

He was born in Portsmouth, N.H., March 1, 1817. was baptized, and received into the church at Portsmouth, April 6, 1834, by Elder Moses How, and commenced preaching in New Hampton, N.H., in November, 1839. He was ordained, a year later, by Elders Fernald, Blodget, Burnham, and Barry, at Newton, N.H. He then returned to the northern part of New Hampshire, and traveled there and in Canada until 1841, when he took charge of the church at Newton, N.H. From 1842 to 1850, he labored in different places in New Hampshire, Rhode Island, and Massachusetts, organizing churches and strengthening those that were weak.

In 1850, he went to Maine, where he labored four years in much the same way, visiting some of the churches in the British Provinces in the meantime. In the winter of 1854-55, he supplied the Bonney Street Church in New Bedford. Afterwards, he took charge of the church at Salisbury Point, and remained there until 1857, when he moved to Portland, Me., where he spent the remainder of his life. Under the encouragement of the First Parish Unitarian Church and others, he accepted the position of minister at large, and with the co-operation of his wife, gathered the poor children of the city into a Sabbath-school, held at the chapel erected for the purpose, and supplied them with clothing etc. from funds donated for that purpose. He was also connected with the Bible Society, as another branch of his duty in this position. A Christian Church was re-organized, of which he was elected pastor; and although few in number, they were well united, and assisted him cordially in his charity and missionary labors.

After the great fire in Portland, in 1866, many were left destitute, and great suffering resulted. Elder Tuckerman was one of the most active laborers in the work of alleviating this distress, as he was a member of the committee appointed by the city for this work.

These duties were very pressing, and by his great exertions at this time, it is likely that he hastened the disease that terminated his life. His health had been very poor for some time, but no serious apprehensions were aroused until he had served for some time on this committee, when he was compelled to resign. His death followed, January 24, 1868.

His death was a source of much sorrow, especially to those whom -he had assisted while in their great distress. The ministry was his principal work for many years, and he often subjected himself to much toil and sacrifice in order to meet his appointments. He bestowed much thought upon his sermons, which were well arranged and logical—not eloquent, perhaps, but generally delivered free from notes, and at times with an inspiration that gave large freedom of speech. He impressed his hearers with his earnestness and sincerity, which, with a somewhat pathetic voice and manner, won the hearts and attention of all. He stood high in the denomination as a prominent worker in the field, and passing away in his prime, caused great sadness in the church.

JAMES TURNER (?—1842)

James Turner labored in Tuscarawas and adjoining counties in Ohio. When the Disciples first came around, he labored with them, through the influence of Barton W. Stone, but returned to the Christians. He died about 1842.

S. TURNER (?—?)

S. Turner was born in Warren County, N.C. He was an excellent man and did good work. He died at a ripe age, in full faith of a blessed immortality.

JAMES TUTTLE (?—?)

James Tuttle is mentioned chiefly in the life of Mark Fernald, who speaks of him in 1816 as one of the oldest ministers in the conference at that time.

<u>LITTLEJOHN UTLEY (1775—1859)</u>

The following is from the pen of J.D. Gunter:

"Elder Littlejohn Utley was born in Wake County, N.C., fourteen miles south-west of Raleigh, February 7, 1775. His education was limited. He was not converted till after his marriage, which took place in 1797, to Sarah Walton. They brought up ten children, who became active and useful members of society. Two sons moved to Utah, and one is a Baptist minister The others, some now dead, filled their part well in society. Shortly after his marriage, he went to a dance, and on the way home he determined to pursue a different course, which he did. He soon entered the ministry of the Christian Church, and was ordained April 28, 1822, by Mills Barrett and John Hayes. He labored in Chatham, Wake, and Orange counties. He preached after he was eighty years old. He baptized] Mr. Bryant Stroud when he was unable to hold him up, and took a colored man to perform the manual part. His last pastorate was at Damascus, five miles from the University of North Carolina. He did much good for his Master, and was very much loved by all who knew him. He would take no salary, but would accept a gift. He was noted for his liberality, lively disposition, and fondness for children. He died of dropsy, May 13, 1859, in the eighty-fifth year of his age. A grand-daughter furnishes the following account of her grandfather's death:

'Grandfather's holy life and triumphant death was a beautiful proof of the reality of the religion that sustains the Christian in the dying hour. When near his end a friend asked if he knew him, and he replied, "I know one thing—I know that the gift of God is eternal life through Jesus Christ our Lord." His last words to his physician were: "Prepare to meet thy God." On the morning of his death he became delirious, his mind seemed lost to all else but the sweet prospect of a happy entrance into the brighter world. He asked for his Bible that he might hold family prayer, and while a friend read a favorite psalm, he became as composed as an infant, but ere the oft-repeated duty was performed, he fell asleep in Jesus—died as he had lived, a child of God.' The funeral was preached from a text of his own selection, found in II Timothy 4:6th, 7th, and 8th verses. 'For I am now ready to be offered etc.'"

After a stormy and laborious voyage, his rest was sweet.

Zerah S. Vail (1818—1878)

This brother was born in Camillus, Onondaga County, N. Y., August 18, 1818. He was of Welsh extraction. He became affected about religion in August, 1830, and was converted December 20, the same year. He first united with the Methodist Church, although he continued with them but a few months, when he left them, and through the neglect of duty, relapsed into coldness. He remained in this condition about five years. He then renewed his religious profession, returned to his first love, and united with the Ripley Christian Church, in Huron County, O. He was impressed with the duty of preaching, from the time of his conversion, but was reluctant to enter the sacred work. He commenced his ministry, and preached his first sermon in a school house in Branson, Huron County. O., to a crowded congregation. He was ordained October 9, 1842, by Elders N.E. Loren. J.B. Sacket, Patrick Mallory, and Gordon F. Smith, the last named being a Freewill Baptist. His field of labor was first in Huron County, then extended to Sandusky, Seneca, and Erie counties. He also made journeys to the State of Michigan and other places.

In addition to his regular preaching, he lectured on temperance, and during the war, extensively on the subject of government. He was an ardent Union man, and did much to muster men into the service in the darkest days. Such was his feelings of patriotism that he requested to be buried, wrapped in the flag of his country— which was done. Another request of his was carried out. It was, that the Bible that he carried in his ministry should be laid on his breast.

The substance of the following is from a paper published in the neighborhood of our brother's home: Elder Vail was a man widely known as a minister, a controversialist, and an able speaker on temperance and civil government. His health had been failing for some time, and a severe attack of flux on an already weakened constitution terminated his life August 23, 1878. He was married three times—to Miss Sallie M. Robinson in 1838, to Eliza Elliott in 1847, and to Permelia Ford in 1851. One of his sons died in the service of his country, after passing through fifty battles and skirmishes. His funeral occurred on the twenty-fifth. Sermon by Elder Stamp. Six ministers acted as pall-bearers. The Bible was placed on his breast and the flag of his country around his body, as he requested.

For many years, Elder Vail occupied a high position in the Huron Conference, O. For some years, he was almost alone as a pastor, connected with the body. He continued to labor with great activity, writing much for our papers, attending the general meetings of the church, holding long debates with champions of contrary views, publishing pamphlets and tracts on various subjects, and doing all, apparently, that any man could do in spreading the views that he held so dearly as the truth of God. His education was not extensive when he began to preach, but by diligence and hard study, he became a well-informed man. He had written a full autobiography of his life and labors to within a few years of his death. This may be published in a volume by itself by his faithful widow.

CORNELIUS VAN AUSDAL (?—1868)

This aged brother died in 1868, in the bounds of the Bluffton Conference, Ind. He was retired from the active ministry for many years, although he preached occasionally. He was past eighty years of age when he died. There are no accounts of his early life and labors.

JOHN VAN BUSKIRK (1795—1874)

John was born in Alleghany County, Va., November .19, 1795, moved with his parents to Pickaway County, O., in 1797, was converted in 1822, under the labors of Elder George Alkire, was baptized by Elder James Burbridge, and began to preach in public the same year. His father being a member of the Catholic Church, strenuously opposed the son in this Protestant work. But the young man continued fast in his course, and was ordained by Elders Gardner and Burbridge. He continued preaching very earnestly for about twenty years, when his health failed, in a measure, and the remainder of his life was less active. Still, he continued a useful minister to the last. He died on his farm in Pickaway County, O., September 18, 1874, at the ripe age of seventy-nine years, respected by all that knew him.

<u>Peter Van Buskirk (1826—1873)</u>

Peter was the son of the preceding brother. He was born in Pickaway County, O., May 3, 1826. Being raised under the influence of religious parents, he was converted early, in 1840, at the age of sixteen, and was baptized by Elder Enoch Harvey. He soon joined the Deer Creek Conference, O., as a licentiate. He was never ordained, as he never felt like entering fully into the work. Yet he was a useful minister, in a local way, and was greatly lamented when taken away in his prime, October 13, 1873.

<u>B.F. Van Doozer (?—1846)</u>

Our present subject began his ministerial career in New York. He was an active minister of the Erie Conference for many years. He afterwards traveled extensively through Illinois, writing frequently for the "Palladium," and manifesting great zeal in the cause. He was a member of the Illinois and Wisconsin Conference for some time; but for some irregularities of conduct, the conference withdrew its fellowship from him. He afterwards enlisted in the Mexican War, and died while in the service, August 10, 1846.

<u>Charles Van Loon (?—1846)</u>

This minister was a native of N.Y. He died in Poughkeepsie, N.Y., very suddenly, November 22, 1846, in his twenty-eighth year, leaving a wife and one child. Although young, he was well known as a fearless advocate in the cause of human freedom and temperance. He was an able minister and one that had already proved himself very energetic in the cause of Christ. He had preached in the morning, and was preparing to preach at night when he took a spasm and died in a few hours.

ABRAHAM VOORHEES (1771— 1860)

This Elder was born in 1771, united with the Christian Church in Kentucky, in 1802 or '3, and was ordained in Preble County, O., by Elders Reuben Dooley and Josiah Conger, in 1812. He moved to Marshall County, Ind., where he remained until his death. He commenced preaching in the Presbyterian Church, but when the Christian Church was organized, he was one among the first to embrace its doctrines, and he continued a steadfast believer in them to the last. He did not travel as much as some, but the churches near him were his care, and were in a prosperous condition at the time of his death; for, although old and feeble, he still preached until a few weeks before his death. He died July 31, 1860, in the ninetieth year of his age, after a ministry of more than sixty years. He was not talented as a speaker, but his pastoral capacities were remarkable. His singleness of purpose and consistent life were greatly respected by all.

JOHN VOORHEES (?—1850)

John Voorhees was at one time a member of the Miami Christian Conference, but he left that body and the church for a time. He was on the eve of returning, when he died, in 1850.

JOHN VORHEES (?—1862)

John Voorhees was a member of the Tippecanoe Conference, Ind., and died the year preceding the session of 1863.

CALEB WADE (?—1853)

Caleb Wade was a brother of Elders Ebenezer and David Wade, both Christian ministers. He preached many years in his native state, Massachusetts, and was well respected by all with whom he was associated. He died in Otsego, N.Y., November 11, 1853, at the age of seventy years.

DAVID WADE (?—?)

David Wade is the second brother in the Wade family who were ministers in the Christian Church. He was a member of the New York Central Christian Conference for many years, but we have no definite account of his death.

EBENEZER WADE (1785—1864)

Ebenezer was born at Middlebury, Mass., April 20, 1785. He moved to Cuyahoga County, N.Y., in 1816, where he united with the Methodist Church and was licensed to preach by that body, which he did until 1821, when he met Elder Shaw, of the Christian Church. From him he learned the views of that body and as they met his approval, he united with the church and was ordained for the work of the ministry in the New York Central Christian Conference, of which he remained a faithful member until his death at West Nile, N.Y., August 8, 1864, at the age of seventy-nine years. He was the brother of Elders David and Caleb Wade, and father of Elders Joseph F. and Edwin R. Wade, and Mrs. Molancy Parker— all ministers in the Christian Church.

J.C. WAGONER (1814—1852)

This Elder was born in Hunterdon County, N.J., September, 1814, of Presbyterian parentage. His father died when he was very small, and he was soon compelled to depend upon himself for subsistence and means of getting an education, which was quite limited. He was converted under the labors of Elder William Lane, and joined the Christian Church at Milford, N.J. In 1841, he became a member of the New Jersey Christian Conference, and at once began his labors in the ministry. In 1843, he was ordained, having taken charge of the church at Milford, N.J., the year previous. In this place, he remained for three years; at the end of that time he removed his family to Columbia County, N.Y., laboring successfully among the churches at Canaan, Chatham, and Lebanon for three years. He returned to Westbury, where he remained three years, then moved to Plainville, where he died, after a year's labor in that place, July 27, 1852, in his thirty-eighth year. He was highly spoken of as possessing more than ordinary energy and talent. He was sincere and conscientious in his work, and efficient as a pastor. He commenced his ministerial career in his native place, and continued a successful pastorate for three years in a place that had had some of the most talented men in the Christian Church to precede him.

JOHN WALKER (?—?)

John Walker was brought up in Orange County, N.Y. He preached for many years in that state, then moved to Missouri, where he died. He was quite successful in the work.

DAVID WALLACE (?—1832)

Elder Wallace was educated for a Presbyterian minister in his native state, Pennsylvania, but taught school for several years. About 1801, he joined the Christians at Spring Dale, Hamilton County, O., under the labors of Elder Thompson, who soon after returned to the Presbyterians. Elder Wallace then took charge of the churches left vacant by their old pastor. His field of labor was very extensive, and he was quite successful in his efforts. After ministering to different churches in Warren and Hamilton counties for many years, be returned to Pennsylvania, where he died in 1832, being an earnest worker to the last.

WILLIAM WALLEY (1822—1869)

William was born in 1822, and died November 12, 1869. He was a member of the Central Ohio Conference, and was ordained September 2, 1858. He traveled some in the West, and was a faithful, zealous preacher. He died in Union County, O.

<u>Isaac N. Walter (1805—1856)</u>

Very few men in the present century have performed such continued labor, in the same length of time, as Elder Walter. Commencing his career in the backwoods of Ohio, in an early day, his father dying when he was eleven years old, he received but seventeen and a half months of common school education, and had access to but few books in his early life; yet his sphere became one of the most conspicuous in its usefulness, not only as a preacher but as an editor and writer of note. It is true, he made no pretentions to learning, but in history and the practical branches of education, he had acquired an extensive knowledge. But the peculiar success of Elder Walter was manifested in his pulpit labors, and his incessant activity in his ministerial work. As a pulpit orator, judging from the results, it would be difficult to find his superior; for it must be remembered that in those days, a champion of the doctrines of the Christian Church was compelled to contend with the bitter persecution of sectarianism and many thought, indeed, that they were doing God a service when they put obstacles in the way of ministers of this unorthodox church, as it was considered. In the midst of all this opposition, we find this uneducated young man battling with the college bred giants of the popular churches, and not only coming out of the contest victor, with thousands testifying to the truth of the cause which he was defending, but many more came forward with the purpose of devoting themselves to the advocacy of this cause.

When he left the city of New York in 1840, on account of ill health, in his thirty-fifth year, he had not only brought the church, organized with seventeen members in 1834, to a membership of five hundred, but had then baptized 2,343 persons, crossed the Alleghany Mountains thirty-one times, preached, on an average, one sermon a day for the preceding seven years, had baptized, in the city of New York, 517 persons, attended over 300 funerals, married 891 couples, and visited 1,117 sick persons—all this in six years. The above will give an outline of his labor. In this sketch we can give but a glance at his fruitful life of over fifty-one years, and a ministerial life of about thirty.

Elder I.N. Walter, the son of John Walter, Jr., and Mary his wife, was born in Highland County, O., January 27, 1805. His parents moved from Grayson County, Va., to Lees Creek, in Highland County, O., in 1797, having for their nearest neighbors on the east, the inhabitants of Chillicothe, thirty-three miles away, and those of Cincinnati on the west, sixty miles away. They were connected with the society of Friends, although his mother afterward united with the Christians. When Isaac was a babe, a Scotch gentleman stopped at the cabin, and while there, predicted that the child would one day be a noted minister. When he was eleven years old, his father died, and from this time forward he was compelled to contend with all the disadvantages of poverty, and he did it man-fully. During his youth, he greatly enjoyed the privileges of attending debating societies, in which he took an active part and was excelled by none. His social qualities were well developed even then: and by common consent of his companions, Isaac was the leader in all the sports of youth.

In 1823, he was converted in a Methodist meeting, and joined that church on probation. From this time forward he was very conscientious in the performance of all church duties. As an instance of this, he spoke to his mother at breakfast, in the presence of others, saying, "Mother, shall we not thank God for his mercies?" She answered quietly, "Yes, my son," and from that time forward there arose in that home, an altar of prayer where, as is the custom of the Quakers, there had been nothing to indicate the profession of religion, but the plain dress and speech and quiet way of living. Elder Walter, from the time of his conversion, had been trying to avoid an intellectual, or soulless religion, as well as a fiery, emotional one, and the conversations he held soon after, with Elder Long and Dr. Aldrich, were the means by which he became acquainted with the Christian Church and its views. These were very congenial to his mind, as the great arguments and discourses on creeds, doctrines, etc., of which he had heard so much heretofore, were very distasteful to him. Soon after meeting these ministers, he united with the Christian Church, and a year later, began to preach, and at once entered fully into the work, and such was his success, that a call was soon made for his ordination. Yet his first sermon was a complete failure. It is said by the residents of Plattsburg, in Clark Co., that his first sermon was delivered there, and that the boy was so mortified with his poor success that he ran away from his congregation, and hurried home, many miles away, without food or rest. In the days of his great success, friends were fond of telling this anecdote. August 14, 1825, he was ordained by Elders Britton, Long, Aldrich, and Zimmerman, near Charleston, Clark County, O. His field of labor was, at this time, very extensive, occupying some half a dozen counties. Great numbers were converted under his preaching in these places. July 26, 1826, he removed to Dublin, Franklin County, O., where he remained until his removal to New York City in 1834. He held the pastorate of the church in Dublin during this time, but traveled extensively, holding protracted and camp meetings, which were very common in those days. He was, by this time, one of the leading ministers of the denomination in the West.

His first trip to the East was in company with Elder Long, starting from Ohio in the spring of 1827. These journeys were not accomplished so easily then as now, but they, nothing daunted at the prospect, started from Central Ohio, crossing the Ohio River at Wheeling, passing through South-western Pennsylvania to Maryland, turning sometimes to Virginia and North Carolina, at other times back to Pennsylvania, and thence to New York through New Jersey. From there, they went to New England, everywhere holding meetings of some kind, and sometimes preaching every day for months. Hundreds were converted and baptized during journeys of this kind. In 1833, he held a meeting of five or six weeks in New York City, and the year following, removed his family to that city and took the pastoral charge of the church organized by himself some time before. In 1840, he returned to his beloved Ohio, and as soon as he recovered somewhat from the illness brought on by his incessant and arduous labors during his stay in New York, he urged the proposition of building a college in the West, and in connection with others, labored to establish a religious periodical in Ohio. From this effort the *Gospel Herald* was published at the town of New Carlisle, Clark County, O., with Elder Walter as editor, in 1844. A western Christian hymn book was published about the same time. His connection with the *Herald,* as editor, continued for three years, to the general satisfaction of the brotherhood. At the expiration of that time, he resigned the editorial chair, but contributed to it regularly to the end of his life. From New Carlisle he moved to Springfield, where his family remained until after his death, although he would often be gone from home for more than a year at one time. From 1846 until the close of his career in 1856, with a shattered constitution and ill health, he labored constantly, spending most of the time in Ohio. He visited different parts of the South and East and spent ten months in New York City as pastor of the church again. In the month of March, 1855, while on his way to attend a meeting at Merom, Ind., he took a severe cold, and from the effects of, this he never recovered. He was not able to preach until the following September, when he preached twice in Cincinnati, and baptized one person. This was his last effort. On the last day of June, 1856, he left home for a trip to the South and East, if health would permit, but that night, while in Columbus, O., he had a hemorrhage of the lungs, and after a repeated attack, he died triumphantly on July 9, 1856, in his fifty-second year.

The life of Elder I.N. Walter, prepared with great care by Elder A.L. McKinney, was published two years after his death, and from this is taken the following, as showing the great success and arduous labor of this servant of God: "On January 27, 1855, he numbered his fiftieth year, over thirty of which he had been an active, efficient minister, having traveled a sufficient number of miles to girdle the earth a little over six times, had crossed the Alleghany Mountains fifty times, preached 8,243 sermons, attended 1,829 funerals, baptized 3,392 converts, received 8,971 into church membership, prayed with 1,907 sick persons, and had married 1,052 couples."

The death of Elder Walter was most triumphant. He remarked to one of the ministers who came to see him, "I have not preached thirty years for naught; I am now going to my reward." To others he said, "See in what peace a Christian can die." About five minutes before he ceased to breathe, he said to his wife, "Is there a light in the room?" and on being answered in the affirmative, he said: "The room is as dark as midnight to me, but I shall soon meet our children, James Henry, and Amanda, and friends gone before." He then said to his wife and children who were present, "Now kiss me;" to his friends, "Now straighten my limbs." Then folding his arms across his breast, it was all over instantly. Thus ended the active, stirring life of our brother in the meridian of his days; his strong constitution broke down at that period, the fire of his zeal in the good cause burned out his strength, and he passed away in triumph. He was fortunate in the selection of a companion as the following will show:

He was married April 15, 1824, to Miss Lydia Anderson, daughter of Major Anderson, an amiable, excellent lady, who was a worthy partner of his joys and sorrows, and who, by her unremitting and uncomplaining efforts, was an invaluable assistant to her husband in his labors. In early life, when the pay for ministers labors was next to nothing, she -worked as few women work, to keep the family. In later years, when, through incessant toil, her husband's health had failed him in a measure, Sister Walter was constant in her attention. Whether in aristocratic New York, or in the backwoods of Ohio, she was the same faithful companion, filling the station of wife, and mother in whatever position she might be placed. Her faithfulness as a wife, doubtless, made his ministry far more efficient than it would otherwise have been. After the death of her husband, Sister Walter manifested the same untiring interest in all the movements of the denomination as before. After sixteen years of widowhood, she died at her daughter's, Sarah Cathcart, in

Springfield, O., in 1872. Thus after a short separation, the loving pair are united again.

JOSEPH WARBINGTON

Joseph Warbington was an Ohio minister. He was brought up in Hamilton County, and was, for many years, a member of the Sycamore Christian Church. Moving to Shelby County, in the same state, where ministerial labor was scarce, and Brother Warbington being a zealous lay brother, as was often the custom in that day, he began to hold meetings near his, home, a few miles front Sidney, the county seat. Soon after, he was ordained to the full work and became a member of the Auglaize Conference, where he continued until death. He died several years, ago at his home in Shelby County, greatly lamented by his brethren. He was a farmer by occupation, but did much to build up the cause in his own and adjoining counties.

C.G. WARD (?—?)

Although a fellow-student for a year or more with the subject of this sketch, in the Meadville Theological School, yet I have been able to find but few dates of his various changes. Before 1844, he was a minister laboring in the bounds of the Erie Conference, Penn. Feeling the want of more education, he was induced to attend a few sessions at the above school, although he was a married man and had a small family. He, continued in Meadville for two years, and, graduated in the two years course, in 1846. He then labored for some years in Chautauqua and adjoining counties in the states of New York and Pennsylvania. Afterward, he became a minister at large under the patronage of the Unitarian Church, under the care of Dr. Elliott, in the city of St. Louis, Mo. In this field, it is said he was quite successful. From Missouri he returned again to Pennsylvania, and during the coal oil excitement in Western Pennsylvania, he took the coal oil fever and for some time was engaged in that work. Failing of success, he moved to the State of Indiana, and finally died, some years ago, in the city of Indianapolis.

In the latter part of his life he was not engaged in the regular ministry, yet he preached occasionally, and was always warm and zealous on the subject of religion, and died in the faith that he preached so early in life.

SIMON WARD (?—1875)

Simon Ward was a minister in the Christian Church who lived on Timber Ridge, Hampshire County, Va., for a number of years. He was a member of the Timber Ridge Church and of the Valley Conference, Va. He was somewhat local in his labors, but an earnest and zealous advocate of the Christian doctrine, and very firm in his conviction. He was a neighbor of Elders Alamong and Sine, and a co-laborer with these and others in that part of Virginia. He died at his home about 1875, not far from seventy-three years of age.

J. WARREN (?—?)

J. Warren was a minister of North Carolina, and the first traveling companion of the "White Pilgrim" in 1807, and was then advanced in years.

JOSEPH WASSON (1782—1854)

Joseph was a pure- hearted, conscientious man, devoting his entire energy to the spread of the gospel, and receiving but little or no remuneration for his services. He was a man of fine constitution, but the privations and hardships that he endured without complaint were very great indeed. He was a lover of peace, and at the time of the division between the Christians and Disciples, he, although firm in his conviction, was very anxious to heal the breach, and though he failed in his object, yet it is said that he was the principal agent in the preservation of the Christian Church in South-western Indiana.

He was born in North Carolina, August 13, 1782, and was the son of James and Catherine Wasson, members of the Presbyterian Church, in which church he grew up, but was converted at the

Cane Ridge revival, and united with the new body called "Christians." He began to preach in 1810, moved to Indiana in 1812, and was ordained soon after by Eiders Kinkade, Aldridge, Miller, and Moutry. As a pastor, he was well liked, and the churches of his charge were generally in a very prosperous condition. He had few enemies, and was acknowledged by his most bitter opponents to be a good, although mistaken, man. He died July 13, 1854, in the seventy-second year of his age.

HOWARD WATKINS (1812—?)

This Elder was a Vermont minister. He was born in 1812, was converted in 1833, and commenced preaching in 1837. We have no account of the time of his death.

EDWARD WEBBER (1794—1842)

Our present subject was born in New Hampshire in 1794, was converted in 1812, and began to preach soon after. He traveled and preached through different parts of New Hampshire and New York, and was ordained at the town of Kortright, N.Y., December 2, 1816. During his stay in this state, he was very successful, and indicated, in some degree, by his labor what his future might have been had he devoted himself wholly to the ministry. But on his return to New Hampshire, his aged parents demanded his care. He soon received some public office, and his time and attention were so fully occupied that he gave up his active ministry for several years before his death, although preaching occasionally. He died at his home in Rumney, N.H., April 6, 1842, when in his fiftieth year.

WILLIAM BROCK WELLONS (1821—1877)

Elder Wellons rose from comparative obscurity to be, decidedly, the leading man in the Christian Church in the Southern States. Commencing his religious career in 1834, at the age of thirteen, and being called away in 1877, in his fifty-sixth year, the intervening forty two years make as active a period of labor as is rarely found in the life of one man. The substance of the following sketch is taken from an address delivered at the time of his burial:

He was the son of Hartwell and Mary W. Wellons, a religious couple that lived, at the time of his birth, on a farm near Littleton, Sussex County, Va. His father was a substantial farmer and a prominent, active member of the Christian Church at the Barrett's meeting-house in the adjoining county of Southampton. His mother was a woman of mild disposition and deep piety. The boy's early life was spent on a farm. His education was such as could be acquired by winter schooling, and the care of wise and prudent parents, together with the boy's industry during that early period of life. At a camp meeting, held at Mar's Hill, he was converted, October 21, 1834. In the next month, November, he united with the church at Barrett's. This act became a stimulant to him, not only in his religious progress, but in his intellectual pursuits as well. In 1840, he began to teach school and at the same time held social and prayer meetings with great success. Many were converted during these meetings. He continued teaching at Airfield, Southampton County, for two years. In 1845, he joined the Eastern Conference, Va., as a licentiate, and the next year was ordained by the same body. Soon he became a successful pastor and very efficient as a revivalist. At this period, he devoted the most of his time to the work of an evangelist, traveling as an itinerant minister among the churches. His labor in this work was peculiarly successful, and many were converted under his preaching, but in the latter part of the year 1848, he settled as pastor of the Christian Church in Newberne, N.C. While in this field, he formed the acquaintance of an excellent widow lady, near his own age, Mrs. Sarah L. Beasley, to whom he was married April 12, 1850. Immediately after his marriage, he moved to Suffolk, Va., where he continued to reside the remainder of his life, and where he died, of pulmonary consumption, February 16, 1877, in his fifty-sixth year.

Before this time, Elder Wellons had been a regular contributor of the "Christian Sun," the denominational organ of the Christians in the South, founded by Elder Kerr in 1844, and carried on, afterward, at Raleigh, N.C., by Elder H.B. Hayes and others, and with which he had been connected as associate editor since 1849. In 1855, he became editor-in-chief, and the paper was moved to his home in Suffolk. This paper he continued to publish and edit until the War of the Rebellion, and at the close of the war, it was renewed by him on his own expense, thus becoming proprietor as well as manager. This he continued to conduct until 1876, when, on account of failing health, it was transferred to other hands and finally sold by him before his Heath. Thus we see that for more than a quarter of a century he was an active agent in the publishing interest of the church. In every department of labor he was very successful. For many years, while editing and publishing the "Sun," he was one of the most successful pastors of four or more churches in his neighborhood. Under his appointment of only once a month, these churches became very strong, numbering several bundled members. At the Antioch church, in 1859, sixty-five candidates were baptized by him in just thirty four minutes, although indisposed at the time. One year before, the same number were baptized. The church numbered 450 members in 1859. The other churches of his care were also prosperous. Beside his editorial work and the management of the finances of the publishing department and his arduous work as a preacher and pastor, he was very active in the temperance work, being an officer in many of the organizations for the promotion of that reform. Indeed, in 1876, he was pastor of Suffolk and Bethlehem churches, editor of the "Sun," President of the Suffolk Collegiate Institute, President of the General Christian Convention of the South, President of the Eastern Virginia Conference, Secretary of the Supreme Council of Friends of Temperance, Secretary of the Virginia Friends of Temperance, and Corresponding Secretary of the Association of "Union Christian Churches of America." In all these, his offices were by no means nominal, but he himself was one of the leading spirits in them all.

By marriage, Elder Wellons became the owner of slaves, at a time v hen it cost something to be, not only an Abolitionist in the

North, but to be a slaveholder in one -of the border states like Virginia. It is too early in the day, yet, to judge fairly the slave issue in the United States in the last forty years. The Elder, like those of his co-religionists in all the churches in the slave states believed that slavery was right. This had been taught him from his infancy, not less by ministers of the gospel than by politicians; nevertheless, it became the greatest sorrow of his life. Northern ministers that visited his home and his churches speak of him as very kind to his servants. He himself was, also, for many years, very friendly to the northern ministers and the northern branch of the church, in spite of their anti-slavery proclivities. In this spirit, Elder Wellons attended the general Quadrennial Convention of the church held in Cincinnati, in 1854. The anti-slavery element ran high in that body, he himself being on the committee to report on the subject. He introduced a minority report, partly justifying the institution, but the discussion became so warm that, with many tears, he left the body, never uniting heartily with the northern branch of the church again, but doubling his energy to make the southern branch as prosperous as possible.

When the war cloud of the Rebellion hovered over his beloved native state, he was a staunch Union man, and did what he could to stay the tide of secession, but when his state seceded, in keeping with the general southern sentiment of State Rights, he followed it and became as active a secessionist as he had been a Union man before. Through the first year of the war, he continued his work in Suffolk, as editor and minister, but when Suffolk was evacuated by the Confederates and the Union army was about to take possession, he left his home and much of his property and moved to Petersburg. Here he was as active as ever, doing all he could for the failing cause, but mostly in his sphere of a religious man and minister.

At this time, he became editor and manager of the "Army and Navy Messenger," a religious periodical published by the Evangelic Tract Society for distribution among the Confederate soldiers and sailors. He also continued his ministerial labors, preaching frequently, especially in hospitals and among the sick and wounded, and often visiting battle-fields to administer to the wants of the sick, wounded, and dying. When Lee surrendered at Appomattox, he hurried to Greensborough, N.C., to assist Johnson's forces; but before he reached that place, Johnson, too, had given up the unequal contest. Our subject then turned to his home in Suffolk to abide the result of the war. His home was desolate. The house was dismantled, type and presses were cast into the river, and desolation and dismay ruled supreme.

Thus, in 1865, he found himself poor, homeless, disloyal to his government, the church of his choice scattered, thousands of his brethren killed, and the faithful work of twenty years blasted. But he was not the man to stand still and repine. He began to preach, re-organized the churches, called the scattered members together, urged submission and good behavior on his fellow-confederates, borrowed money to start the "Sun" afresh, and in a short time, in connection with his faithful coworkers, the Christian Church in the South assumed form and symmetry.

In 1866, he was appointed President of the general convention of the church in the South, held at Mt. Auburn, N.C. This body drew up and published a volume containing its "Declaration of Principles," together with forms and rituals to be used by the body. Some of the churches and members opposed this measure, as an innovation in the church; but by the strong influence of Elder Wellons and others, it was carried, and it remains in use at this time. The views expressed in this "Declaration of Principles" are about the same as those held by the denomination generally. Some years before his death, he became very active in a "Christian Union" movement, an organization started for the purpose of uniting the various denominations of Christians in one body.

He died before reaching the period of old age, greatly lamented by his co-laborers in the work. His career was not long, but it was so active that he lived a long life in a few years. In 1874, the honorary title of Doctor of Divinity was conferred upon him by the Trustees of Rutherford College, N.C., in consideration of his eminent ability as a theologian.

WALTER WELLS (?—?)

Walter Wells was a minister in Switzerland County, Ind., at the time of his death.

ZACHEUS WELLS (1778—1845)

This Elder was a member of the Indiana Central Conference at the time of his death, although he had spent the greater part of his life in Vermont, in which state he commenced preaching, in 1818. He died in Allensville, Ind., September 22, 1845, from apoplexy, in the sixty-seventh year of his age.

JAMES WELTON (1786—1871)

James was born in Bradford, Vt., May 4, 1786. He was converted under the labors of Elder Abner Jones, in 1802, and united with the first Christian Church in New England. He began to preach soon after, through the encouragement of Elder Jones and others. He labored for some time with good success, but became discouraged, and ceased preaching for several years. In 1822, he re-commenced his work in the ministry, joining the Vermont Conference. In 1832, he moved to New York, in 1833, joined the New York Central Conference, and a year later, was ordained. In 1836, he moved to Covington, Penn., in which state he remained until death. He died April 10, 1871, aged eighty-five years.

He was married in 1813, to Miss Susana Chase, with whom he lived happily until her death. She died in 1853, leaving a son, Rev. A.J. Welton, and three daughters. From the many letters written to our periodicals by this earnest brother, we judge that he was an energetic person, doing whatever he did with all his might. His field of labor, in the latter part of his life, was in Northern Pennsylvania and Southern New York, embracing Tioga County, Penn., and Steuben, Chemung, Tioga, and Broom counties, N.Y. He was buried at Covington, Penn., by the side of his companion, who had preceded him eighteen years.

<h2 style="text-align:center">JOHN WEST (?—?)</h2>

John West was a minister in Virginia in an early day. Elder James Burlingame speaks of him as a man of talent. He died many years ago.

<h2 style="text-align:center">JAMES WESTON (1770—1841)</h2>

James was born in New Hampshire. He moved into Rockingham, Vt., when quite young, and while there, embraced religion among the Methodists. He afterward became a preacher in that denomination. After preaching in Vermont for some time, he moved to Schuyler, N.Y., still continuing an active ministry. In the year 1812, he moved with his family to Mentz, Cayuga County, at that time a howling wilderness. Some fifteen years before his death, he gave a large sum of money toward the erection of a chapel that was to be opened to ministers of all denominations. But when he heard the minister in the dedication sermon advise that the doors should be closed to all except the Methodists, and that the Christians should be excluded, he meekly took up his hat and walked out, observing to a friend that he had been striving to live a Christian life for twenty years, and if they were driven out, he would go with them. He did so, and in 1827, he joined the Western Christian Conference, of which he continued a useful member until his death. He died May 30, 1841, aged seventy-one years, with a full belief in the gospel that he had preached for thirty-five years.

<h2 style="text-align:center">SIMON WHETSTONE, SR (1807—1859)</h2>

This Elder was born in Fayette County, **O., in** 1807, and was converted in that place in 1829. In 1850, he was ordained in the Auglaize Christian Conference, having labored as a licentiate for many years before. His greatest power was witnessed in revivals, as he was an earnest and enthusiastic speaker when he saw before him the penitent and humble seeker, and realized hat a loss they would sustain if they went away without the blessing. He died from the effects of cold, contracted in a damp bed after the exhaus-

458

tion of severe pulpit labor, February 16, 1859, in his fifty-second year.

SIMON WHETSTONE, JR (?—1880)

This young minister, a son of the preceding, was brought up under the care of a zealous Christian father. He embraced religion early, and began to preach when young. He was married to a daughter of Elder D. Richardson, and was a zealous member of the Ohio North-western Conference. He died February 13, 1880, praising God with his last breath.

SAMUEL WHISLER (1811—1876)

This brother was born in Bucks County, Penn., May 24, 1811, and moved with his parents to Columbiana County, O., in 1821. In this place, he was married to Elizabeth R. Pike in 1837, was converted in 1849, commenced preaching soon after, and in 1851, moved to Whitley County, Ind. From the latter place, in 1855, he moved to Edna, Cass County, Iowa, and was ordained by the Iowa South-western Conference in 1860. He died November 18, 1876.

STEVEN WHITAKER (1772—1857)

This aged brother died at his home in Sheridan, Chautauqua County, N.Y., April 1, 1857, in the eighty-fifth year of his age. He was converted in Hopkinton, N.H., in 1815, under the labors of Elder Abner Jones. A year later, he moved to Schuyler, N.Y., where, soon after, a prosperous church was organized, principally through his own labors, although he was not ordained until 1829, thirteen years later. In 1834, he moved to Sheridan, Chautauqua County, N.Y., ' where he ministered faithfully to the wants of the brethren until old age came on him, and he retired from the active ministry. He was more useful as an evangelist than in the more confining duties of a pastor.

? WHITAKER (?—?)

Brother Whitaker was a minister of Carrol County, O., and was quite local in his labors. He died several years ago.

AMOS WHITCOMB (1788—1840)

Our present subject was a native of the State of New York. He moved to Michigan in 1835. He was a live and active worker in the church and conference, and was deeply lamented by his friends and parishioners in Kalamazoo, Mich., where he died August 13, 1840, aged fifty-two years.

AARON WHITE (?—?)

Aaron White was a minister in Indiana. He died there some years ago.

HENRY WHITE (1807—1864)

The subject of this sketch had been a minister of the gospel for nearly thirty years at the time of his death, having spent the greater part of this time in the bounds of the Indiana Central Conference. Although a man of limited education and poor health, he wielded a powerful influence over his different congregations, and accomplished much good, both as a successful pastor and as a trustworthy counsellor. He died suddenly, of heart disease, in Taylorsville, Ind., February 16, 1864, in the fifty-seventh year of his age. In his ministerial work, he deceived his appearance greatly. Generally poorly clad, and otherwise obscure looking, his tact and skill as a speaker were wonderful.

HENRY WHITE (1815—1838)

This Elder was very young, and although of short career, was greatly lamented by his co-laborers. He was born in 1815, and learned the trade of tailor, which he followed for some time. He commenced preaching soon after his conversion, some two or three years before his ordination, in 1838, as pastor of the church of Mattapoisett, Mass., by Elders Jones, Morgridge, and others. He had attended school during the time between his conversion and ordination, and had given signs of great worth. In 1838, his health failed and he resigned the pastorate he had held for two years, and went to Havana, Cuba, where he died soon after, in the twenty-fourth year of his age.

Thomas White (1806—1858)

Thomas was born on the Welsh Hills, in Licking County, O., in 1806, being of Welsh descent. After receiving a somewhat better education than was commonly given in those days, he commenced teaching, and was very successful in that profession. He was converted when quite young, and united with the Christian Church near Granville, O. He did not commence his ministry until 1840, when he became a member of the Ohio Central Conference; and after its division into two conferences, by locality, he became a member of the Mt. Vernon Conference. His labors in Ohio were confined chiefly to Licking and Knox counties, where he was quite successful in his pastoral relations. He was considered by his brethren as a man of strong mind, but not an eloquent speaker or a strong revivalist, although a very successful pastor. About 1851, the care of a large family, and limited circumstances, induced him to move to the West, and he settled in Green County, Wis., where he still labored in the ministry, as health would permit, until his death. He died in 1858, at Jordan, Wis., in his fifty-second year.

Elder White was the first Christian minister the compiler conversed with, and under his administration, he was received into the church in 1843, and was baptized by him some time after. The White family, though in limited circumstances, became quite noted in Licking County, O. Samuel, a brother of Thomas, became a very prominent lawyer, a leading antislavery man, and a member of the legislature. He died in 1844, while standing as a candidate for Congress. Our subject, also, as well as other members of the same family, was quite talented.

WILLIAM WHITE (1806—1875)

This brother was born in 1806, and was killed November 5, 1875. He was riding in a buggy, by the side of his wife, near Ithaca, N.Y., and, when about to cross the railroad track, the train came, he was thrown from his buggy and instantly killed.

JAMES WHITEHEAD (?—1841)

This aged veteran, after leaving his friends in New York and Pennsylvania, where he had labored for many years, died at Vermillionville, Ill., August 4, 1841. His age is not given, but he was quite old as he had been a minister in the Christian Church since 1803.

FREDERICK WHITFIELD (?—1864)

Frederick was a native of England and received his education in that country. He was a nephew of the celebrated Methodist divine, George Whitfield, and after emigrating to New Brunswick, he began to preach the Methodist doctrine, but from a diligent study of the Bible, he came to the conclusion that many un- scriptural things were taught in the discipline, and consequently abandoned it, together with his sectarian name, and took the New Testament as his rule claiming no name but Christian. At this time, he had no knowledge of a body claiming such views and name, but after emigrating to Canada West, he became acquainted with some of our ministers, soon united with them, was ordained at Saltfleet, June 11, 1832, by Elder J. Badger and others, and became one of the most influential and zealous of our ministers in the Province, laboring there for many years with great success. In 1848, he removed to Iona County, Mich., where he labored until 1860, when he returned to Canada and settled at Burford, where he died about 1864. He had preached very successfully in Canada, Michigan, and New York, and at one time published a religious periodical in Canada.

DANIEL WHITLEY (1776—1841)

This brother was born about 1776, in early life he became a member of the Methodist Church, and continued in that body for many years. In 1821, he began to preach in the Christian Church, having become a member a few months before, and was a faithful worker in the vineyard for nearly twenty years. He died at his home in Smithfield, Va., January 3, 1841, in his sixty-fifth year.

ISAAC WHITLOW (?—1860)

Isaac was a native of Indiana, was a member of the Tippecanoe Christian Conference, and died in 1860.

DAVID WHITMAN (?—1852)

David Whitman was a brother of Elder Thomas Whitman. He was converted under the labors of Elder Hallet Barber when young, and soon after began to preach. He was faithful and zealous, and his prospects for future usefulness were bright. He became a member of the Tippecanoe Conference, Ind., and died in the work in 1852.

WILLIAM WHITTEN (?—?)

William Whitten was a native of England, and from 1810 until 1819, was a prominent minister in New Bedford and other places in Massachusetts. He returned to England in 1819, after a stay in America of about seventeen years. He was an intimate friend of Elder Levi Hathaway, and is often spoken of in the autobiography of the latter.

SAMUEL WILDE (1805—1875)

Samuel was born in 1805, embraced religion early, began to preach, and was so successful, that he was ordained soon after. His health failed soon, so that his labors were cut short. He died in New Bedford, Mass., December 26, 1875. His lot was to suffer more than to labor.

Francis A. Wilkins (1811—1874)

Francis was born in Highland County, O., September 25, 1811, moved to Indiana with his parents, and was married to Miss Hester Bates, who died in 1848. In 1850, he was married to Miss Jane Van Ausdal, who died June 11, 1864. He then moved to Minnesota, where he died May 8, 1874. He was a good man and an able preacher.

Abraham Williams (1806—1845)

Abraham was in the ministry but a short time before his death. He was born in 1806, and died near Williamsport, O., September 13, 1845, aged thirty-nine years. He was pastor of the Hay Run Church for some time before his death, and exerted a good influence over his parishioners.

George A Williams (?—?)

George A. Williams lived in Johnston, R.I., for many years, and was a minister of the gospel about fifteen years. He died near Worcester, .Mass.

Jeduthun Williams (1799—1879)

Elder B.A. Cooper sends the following items of his intimate friend and co-laborer for many years: Elder Williams was born April 27, 1799, was converted under the labors of Elder William Caldfield, and was married September 7, 1824, to Miss Mary Calhoun. Both were then members of the Christian Church, she having joined the first Christian Church in the neighborhood, the Clear Ridge, now Clearfield Church. This church was organized by Elder William Caldwell, and out of it grew Rockfield and Mt. Union. Through the recommendation of Elder Caldwell, Brother Williams was ordained December 11, 1836, and was left with the care of the churches in the vicinity, when the former moved to the West. He labored faithfully until others came to his assistance. His voice was weak, and his delivery was not the best, but his pure life, fatherly counsel, and his great zeal made him a successful pastor. Though his education was limited, his knowledge of the Scripture was quite good. He was firm in his conviction of what he considered the truth. His house was often used for a place of worship, as well as the preacher's home, while his devoted wife was equally hospitable and generous in the good cause. His ministerial labors were local, confined mostly to the Ray's Hill Conference, of which he was an honored member until his death, August 6, 1879, in his eighty-first year.

JOHN WILLIAMS (1786—1847)

John was born m 1786, was converted in 1808, began to preach in 1817, but never devoted his time wholly to the ministry. He lived on his farm in Miami County, O., for over forty years, and died there from dropsy, December 20, 1847. His education was limited, but he was a very energetic man, a successful preacher, and, in a local way, did a great amount of good in his day.

S.J. WILLIAMS (?—1863)

This brother was a minister of the Southern Indiana and Illinois Conference, and died in 1863.

ZACHARIAH WILLIAMS (?—1850)

Zachariah Williams lived in Lewis County, Ky., and died there about 1850. He labored through Ohio and Kentucky in an early day, with wonderful success. He had a strong voice, and was a loud and earnest speaker. There is an anecdote told of this brother that shows his confidence in the efficacy of prayer. When his wife opposed his preaching, he prayed that the Lord would either convert or kill her. She being taken sick about that time, he became fearful that his prayer was about to be answered. He prayed earnestly that she should not die, and she recovered.

FRANCIS WILLIAMSON (1773—1833)

This Elder was born in Southampton County, Va., November 19, 1773. His parents were in good circumstances, for his father's greatest ambition was the accumulation of property, but his mother, a talented and noble-minded woman, sought for higher attainments, and so instructed her children, although she had not made a profession of religion while Francis was young. His only chance for religious enjoyment during his youth was in the cabins of his father's slaves. Although the son of a rich planter, his educational facilities were greatly neglected, but with a great longing and thirst for education, he was enabled to acquire some knowledge of the common branches and history, before leaving his father's house. September 17, 1801, he married Miss Elizabeth Warrell, of whom he had eight children, four of whom were brought up to maturity. After his marriage, he moved to Hertford County, N.C., where he lived in affluent circumstances, devoting much of his time and energy to the acquirement of useful knowledge. In this place, he and his wife united with the Methodist Church, and he soon began to preach, and was ordained to the work of the ministry in that denomination. But while a zealous and faithful minister, he maintained that independence of mind which could brook no interference from human creeds, and as he did not work in harmony, with the rules of the church, he was disowned by that body, although he continued the ministry alone, as regards ministerial relations, with the same ardor and zeal that had characterized his labors heretofore, and was very successful in leading souls to Christ. This was his condition at the time of the division in the conference from the introduction of Episcopacy by Dr. Coke and Bishop Asbury, and he soon joined the O'Kelly party, as it was called, and became one of the leading advocates of a free gospel. The movement was new and different views were held by the different ministers who withdrew with O'Kelly, but they decided upon these points: the name "Christian," "Bible alone for a creed," and the "right of private judgment" to each individual member: The Elder built a convenient frame meeting-house on his plantation, and organized a thriving church on these views. The party that had withdrawn from the Methodists now organized themselves into two conferences, one in Central North Carolina, and the other in Northern North Carolina and Virginia, and our brother was connected with the latter body. He and his wife were baptized by immersion by Nelson Millar, and immersion soon became the prevailing mode of baptism, though bitterly opposed by James O'Kelly, who insisted on effusion or sprinkling, while Elder Williamson and the majority insisted only that the candidate should be free to choose for himself. While in one of these discussions, as O'Kelly was trying to fasten his peculiar mode on the churches, the noted answer of William Guirey was given as to the leader of the movement. "Neither you nor I; Christ is the leader of his own church."

In 1822, in company with his eldest son, Elijah, he made a journey to Ohio as far as Columbus, and was surprised, as well as pleased, to find so many brethren of the same faith, converts from the great reformation in Kentucky. With these he had heavenly meetings, and great success attended his labors, especially in Columbiana County, where scores were brought to "a means of saving grace." At the session of 1822, of the conference of which the Elder was a member, while he was absent, the body adopted a constitution which was construed by Elder Lindsay and others into a creed, and in the session of 1823, he was among those who opposed the constitution with all his power, but the majority voted against him, and for this reason he left the conference and refused to unite with the body again, although he continued an active minister until his death, at Murfreesborough, Tenn., September 11, 1833, at the age of sixty years.

He had, from conscience, liberated all his slaves in spite of the great opposition of his slave-holding brethren, choosing to live in comparative poverty rather than to enjoy riches in what he considered wrong doing. He was a very conscientious man, and in all his movements, he never consulted expediency in matters of religion. For him to believe that a certain course was right, was sufficient, and he followed it with no regard to consequences. This is apparent in his withdrawal from the Methodists in the independent manner he did, at a time, too, when persecution ran high in all the country, and also his disconnection with the Virginia Conference. It is probable that the constitution adopted by that body, was nothing more than a declaration, in writing, of the liberal principles of the Christian Church, but to his mind it savored of creed—man-made creed, and with these impressions he withdrew. But more particularly do we see the workings of conscience, in the liberation of all his slaves, by this act, not only bringing upon himself great loss of property, but the distrust and unfriendliness of his slave-holding neighbors; but regardless of all this, as soon as he felt this act to be a duty, he did it.

In the preparation of his sermons, his sons say that he spent two or three hours a day in a room by himself, in prayer and study, where he also wrote his sermons, although the written sermons were never taken to the pulpit with him, nor even the notes. In his delivery he began with a moderate voice, but as he grew interested in his subject, Le spoke with greater force, and even became quite excited towards the close.

H. WILSON (?—?)

H. Wilson lived in Drayton, Canada, and organized a Christian Church there about 1849. He was an excellent man, and died many years ago.

JAMES WILSON (?—?)

James Wilson came with Jabez King and Jonathan Thompson to New York from Vermont, in 1813, and was advanced in years at that time. He assisted in the ordination of Elder Samuel P. Allen.

LEONARD WILSON (?—1863)

This minister was a member of the Tippecanoe Indiana Conference, and died in 1863.

MATTHEW, WILLIAM, AND ZACHARIAH WILSON.

These three ministers labored in Kentucky in an early day. We are informed that all three have been dead some years.

Samuel Wilson (?—1840)

Samuel Wilson began to preach near Williamsport, **O.,** and after preaching in that vicinity for several years, moved to Southern Illinois, where he died about 1840.

Lewis Winans (1789—1865)

Lewis was born in 1789, was converted.in 1825, and was ordained in the New York Eastern Conference in 1832. He was pastor of the churches of Gilboa, Schoharie, Roxbury, and Olive Bridge, in the counties of Schoharie, Delaware, and Ulster. He died at Shokan, Ulster County, N.Y., June 14, 1865, in the seventy-fifth year of his age.

Moses Winchester (1798—1868)

Moses was born in Westmoreland, N.H., in March, 1798, where he commenced preaching, and where he spent his life, with the exception of a few years. These were spent in Shrewsbury, Vt., where he died March 7/1868, aged seventy years. He was a quiet, unassuming man, very fortunate in his pastoral relations, and quite a good preacher.

John Winkly (?—1869)

This minister was a resident of Stafford, N.H., some years, and died there in 1869.

James Winters (1797—1867)

James was a native of New York, but moved to Ohio at an early age. He was converted, united with the United Brethren Church, and was a minister of that denomination until 1863, when he united with the Christian Church, and was baptized by his brother, Elder John Winters. He was a member of the Tippecanoe Christian Conference, Ind., at the time of his death, March 23, 1867, in the seventy-first year of his age.

ISRAEL WOOD (?—1866)

This brother was an aged minister at the time of his death at Fall River, Mass., September 20, 1866. He was a member of the Rhode Island and Massachusetts Christian Conference in 1840.

JOHN WOOD (1799—1863)

John was a minister in the regular Baptist Church until 1859, four years before his death, when he joined the Indiana Union Christian Conference. He died in Gibson County, Ind., December 7, 1863, at the age of sixty-four.

SQUIRE WOOD (1819—1856)

This Elder was born in 1819. He was pastor of the Salimony Church, Huntington County, Ind., at the time of his death, February 15, 1856.

PONTIUS WOOLEY (?—1828)

This minister died in Sandusky, O., August 16, 1828. He is mentioned in the letters of the early ministers, as a prominent and useful man in the denomination.

SAMUEL WORKMAN (?—?)

Samuel Workman traveled and preached in Southern Indiana and Kentucky, in an early day, and has been dead some years.

CALEB WORLEY (1795—1870)

Caleb was the eldest son of Elder Nathan Worley. He was born in Kentucky in 1795, was converted, and began to preach early in life. Although he never possessed the peculiar gifts of his father, as a speaker, yet he became an able and useful minister. He became somewhat deaf when young, and it became worse as he grew older, till, in old age, it was very difficult to converse with him. This crippled his usefulness, to a great extent, although he continued to labor with great zeal until quite old. He lived in Covington, Miami

County, O., for many years, and there raised an excellent family. He died in that place in 1870, at the age of seventy-five.

MALCOLM WORLEY (?—?)

Malcolm Worley was an older brother of the following, Elder Nathan Worley, and was educated for a Presbyterian clergyman, but at the time of the Cane Ridge revival he united with the Christians and preached among them until the Shakers came from New York, when he joined them, giving them all his property. He is mentioned here with McNemar, Dunlevy, Marshall, and Thompson, as one of the founders of the Christian denomination in the West. He was a man of talent, but somewhat eccentric in his manner. He has been dead many years.

NATHAN WORLEY (1773—1847)

Nathan was born January 7, 1773, on the James River, in Botetourt County, Va. His parents were members of the Presbyterian Church, and his father was a ruling elder in that body for many years. When Nathan was fourteen years of age, his parents moved to Kentucky and settled at Lexington. His father was not able to give all his children a finished education, and as was the custom with some Presbyterian parents in that day, he chose one who should receive a classical education to fit him for a ministerial career. The choice fell on Malcolm, an older son, and the rest received such as they could get in those early days. His father died in 1788, when Nathan was fifteen years of age, and three years later, March 2, 1791, he was married to Miss Rachel Greer, of Fayette County, Ky., and in the same year, he and his wife joined the Presbyterian Church, but after the separation in 1804, he left that body and joined the Dissenters.

In 1805, he moved his family to Ohio on his own land, near the, at that time, village of Dayton, and although he toiled early and late for the support of his family in this new country, he did not lose the spirit of reformation of which he had taken so largely while in Kentucky. Here he called the people together for prayer meetings, and prayed and exhorted them to repent of their ways. He had the entire confidence of his neighbors, and by the influence of his example, many were converted. He met, at this time, many severe trials and discouragements, and his faith was greatly shaken when he found that the leaders in the reformation were so unstable. After McNemar, Dunlevy, his own brother Malcolm, and others went to the Shakers, and a few years later, Marshall and Thompson returned to the Presbyterians, the good man's faith was well-nigh shaken, and for a time, to use his own expression, he hung on the fence. But he had not taken the stand he did without due deliberation, and now he trusted to the Lord, and was brought safely through these difficulties. He continued to minister to the different churches as a licentiate until 1815, when he was regularly set apart to the work, by fasting, prayer, and laying on of hands, by Elder Reuben Dooly and Hugh Andrews. From this time until his death, he gave himself almost entirely to the ministry. He was pastor of several churches constantly, and also traveled, whenever his charge would permit, through Western Ohio, Eastern Indiana, and also in Kentucky.

He lived on his farm near Dayton until after the death of his wife in 1835. She had proven herself a true helpmate, and had assisted him much by her encouragement, advice, and by her economical life at home. After her death, he sold out and bought property in Preble County, and moved to it but spent, as usual, the greater part of the time in the ministry. He soon sold his property, gave up the cares of this world, and devoted his whole time to the work of an evangelist, visiting from church to church, and none were more welcome than he. He preached in Cincinnati for some time, and while there, married a widow lady, a worthy member of that church, with whom he lived happily, at Germantown, Montgomery County, O., until his death, April 29, 1847, in the seventy-fifth year of his age.

In person, Elder Worley was tall and slim, with a swarthy complexion, and with keen, black eyes that could hardly fail to send terror to the heart of the evil doer.- He was a reformation preacher, and his great success was owing, in some degree, to a spiritual and forcible representation of truth. His power over an audience was remarkable, and there were but few who could equal him in this respect, although it would be difficult to explain the cause. Elder Worley was, in every respect, a man of peaceful habits, and was so well liked by all that no one would think of making him the subject of a jest. There is an anecdote related of him, illustrative of his popularity with the world, and of his entire confidence in the teachings of the Scriptures: Knowing how well he was thought of by irreligious as well as religious classes, and reading in Luke 6:26, "Woe unto you when all men shall speak well of you," it impressed him at once that something was the matter with himself—that he was a time server, perhaps. The subject grieved him greatly for several days. Two young men, though not religious, yet the warmest friends of good Father Worley, determined to relieve his mind by a stratagem. One night, as he was returning from the village after dark, they placed themselves within hearing, and talked loudly on the subject, whether there were any good people or not. Just as the old gentleman came within hearing, one of the young men said, with an oath: "There is that black old Worley; some people think he is good, but he only deceives them. He is the biggest hypocrite of them all." The Elder, not understanding the trick, went home, the happiest of mortals, clapping his hands as he went, and thanking God that the "woe" was removed— hat some, at least, did not speak well of him.

Another peculiarity of Elder Worley was his non-sectarianism; for, although he firmly believed in the principles of his own church, he was ready to fraternize with any denomination, often doing as much to build up other churches as his own. If he could bring sinners to a knowledge of the truth, it made no difference to him what church they joined, nor did he make any special effort to have them unite with his own church. He was firm in his convictions, and was among the last of those, who came out of the Reformation, to be immersed; for, during that time, sprinkling or immersing was practiced according to the candidate's desire. In 1832, he became convinced that immersion only was baptism, and was baptized by Elder Levi Purviance. After this, he would perform the rite of baptism in no other manner.

As a husband, father, and neighbor, he was one of the kindest of men. The following is an instance of his power as peacemaker: At one time, he was appointed one of a committee to settle a difficulty of long standing between two prominent ministers. On [retiring with the committee to consult upon- the subject, he immediately said, "Let us pray." He did so, with such power and fervency, that, at the close of the prayer, the opponents clasped hands, and the strife was at an end, never to be renewed. His field of labor, as a pastor, was mostly confined to Montgomery, Preble, Warren, and Butler counties, but his travels covered a much larger territory. He filled a wide field of labor in his day, and left a great vacancy at his death.

In analyzing the elements of Nathan Worley's character, we find that he possessed full faith in the truth of Christianity. Every Bible utterance came to him with authority as from God, and he had un-bounded confidence that God would answer his petitions; hence, when he addressed a throne of grace, there was no formality in his utterance. He also felt that sinners must be saved through Christ, and through Him alone. Add to these, a tall form, solemn counte-nance, earnest, firm, and fluent delivery, dark, piercing, eye, with a soul on fire, and we have the irresistible speaker, Nathan Worley. It is no wonder that every feature of the man is remembered to this day as a minister of force and power in the pulpit.

R.C. WORTEN (?—1867)

R.C. Worten was a member of the Bluffton Conference, Ind. He died about 1867.

VANDOVER WRAY (?—1865)

Vandover Wray was ordained in the Indiana Central Conference in 1840, and continued a member of that Conference for many years. He lived on a farm, in one of the southern counties of Indiana, was an industrious man, and was highly respected as a neighbor. As a minister, he was much esteemed as zealous, firm, and reliable in all his relations. He died at his home in Indiana about 1865.

JAMES WRIGHT (?—1874)

James Wright was a member of the Indiana Western Conference. He died about 1874.

LEMUEL WRIGHT (1793—1864)

Lemuel was born in Bloomingburgh, N.Y., October 20, 1793, was converted in the same state, under the labors of Elder Benjamin Howard, in the spring of 1833, commenced preaching about 1838, moved to Ohio two years later, thence to Iowa in 1843, and was ordained at Moscow, Iowa, in 1844. He traveled extensively through Iowa, but his health was poor, and while on one of these journeys, he was taken seriously ill at the house of Elder W.H. Phillips. He died there November 27$ 1864.

W.H. WYATT (1798—1874)

Brother Wyatt was born in Montgomery County, Ky., January 28, 1798, and died in Henry County, Ind., December 15, 1874. He was converted when young, and commenced preaching in Kentucky about the year 1815. From Kentucky, he moved to Indiana, and ' was ordained by Elders Martindale and Hendricks. From Indiana, he moved to Illinois, thence back to the former state, where he died, as stated. The Elder was not an able preacher, but was very faithful and zealous in the work, and thus occupied a useful position in the vineyard. His knowledge of the doings of the denomination was wonderful. Many of the sketches of minister's lives in this volume were obtained through him.

ANDREW WYLIE (1838—1872)

Andrew was born in Putnam County, W. Va., in 1838. He moved to Madison County, Ind., in 1858, and was converted while there in 1860. He was received into the Miami Reserve Conference in 1869, and died March 14, 1872, aged thirty-four years. He had already shown signs of future usefulness.

PETER YOUNG (1784—1836)

Elder Young was one of the first of the Christian ministers in New England. He was born in York, Me., April 29, 1784, was converted in that place, under the labors of Elder Elias Smith, in 1803, was baptized a year later by the same, and immediately began to preach, although he was not ordained until 1808. He was ordained by Elders Smith, Rand, and Safford. The same year, he had one leg amputated within six inches of his body. Notwithstanding the inconveniences arising from his unfortunate condition, he labored faithfully for about thirty-three years, and was very successful in bringing souls to Christ. As a writer, he was interesting and instructive, with a very pleasing style of composition. He wrote frequently for our periodicals. He died in Farmington, Me., May 23, 1836, aged fifty- three years.

GEORGE ZIMMERMAN (?—?)

George Zimmerman was brought up near Williamsport, O., and united with the church near that place early in life. His ministerial labors were confined principally to the central part of the state. He has been dead several years. He has a son of the same name, still a minister in the Christian Church.